A Romantic in Spain

Lost and Found Series

New editions of the best in travel writing—old and modern—from around the world

Old Provence by Theodore Andrea Cook
Two Years in the French West Indies by Lafcadio Hearn
The Pilgrimage to Santiago by Edwin Mullins
The Silent Traveller in London by Chiang Yee

*Classic Travel
Writing*

A Romantic in Spain

Théophile Gautier

*Translated by Catherine Alison Phillips
Foreword by Robert Snell*

An i

This edition first published in 2001 by

INTERLINK BOOKS
An imprint of Interlink Publishing Group, Inc.
46 Crosby Street, Northampton, Massachusetts 01060 and
99 Seventh Avenue, Brooklyn, New York 11215
www.interlinkbooks.com

First published 1926
Foreword copyright © Robert Snell 2001
All rights reserved.

Library of Congress Cataloging-in-Publication Data
Gautier, Théophile 1811–1872.
  [Voyage en Espagne. English]
  A romantic in Spain / Théophile Gautier.
    p. cm.
  ISBN 1-56656-392-5
  1. Spain--Description and travel. 2. Spain--Social life and customs--19th
century. 3. Gautier, Théophile, 1811–1872--Journeys--Spain. I. Title
  DP41 .G2713 2001
  914.604'7--dc21
                                     2001000997

Cover image: The Metropolitan Museum of Art, H.O.
Havemeyer Collection, Bequest of Mrs. H.O. Havemeyer,
1929 (29.100.10)

Printed and bound in Canada

To request a free copy of our 48-page full-color catalog,
please call us at **1-800-238-LINK**, write to us at
Interlink Publishing, 46 Crosby Street, Northampton, MA 01060
or visit our website: **www.interlinkbooks.com**
e-mail: sales@interlinkbooks.com

Contents

Foreword

For those who only know Théophile Gautier as the luxuriantly maned poet of "art for art's sake", or as a flamboyant (or superannuated) Romantic, this vivid travelogue will come as a surprise and a revelation. Gautier was a professional writer *par excellence*, and a highly prolific one. As well as poetry, he produced novels (*Mademoiselle de Maupin, Le Capitaine Fracasse*), short stories and nouvelles, memoirs and ballets (*Giselle, La Péri*). He spent most of his career at the heart of Parisian literary, *salon* and studio life, and he knew everybody who was anybody, from Victor Hugo (his hero and mentor) to Delacroix, Nerval, Balzac, Flaubert, Berlioz (who set his lyrics to haunting music) and Baudelaire (who dedicated *Les fleurs du mal* to him).

For nearly forty years, as probably the first important European writer to make a living from a mass medium, he also turned out regular journalism, in an almost weekly *feuilleton*: he wrote theater, dance and, above all, art criticism. For Gautier was "a poet steeped in painting", "a man for whom the visible world exists" (as he described himself to those unsparing chroniclers of the age, the Goncourt brothers). His travel writing—his journeys took him to Belgium, England, Italy, Russia and Constantinople—is part of this immense and, as he discovered, increasingly wearisome journalistic toil; in it, as everywhere else in his work, the visual image dominates. His account of his journey to Spain in 1840 was mostly published in instalments in Emile de Girardin's *La Presse*, before it appeared in book form. It was written at a time in Gautier's life when he was feeling both securely established, and still full of the hopefulness of youth; it is among the freshest and most alive things he ever wrote.

The book rattles along like a stagecoach. It is driven, in part, by the tension between Gautier's depiction of himself as a quintessential Parisian—worldly, skeptical and just a little blasé—and his obvious eagerness for new sensations; between his self-conscious and gently self-satirized Romantic quest for "local colour", and the actual texture and tenor of his experiences. This, as his excellent translator Catherine Alison Phillips points out, acts as a corrective to any tendency on his part to find the picturesque at all costs; when he does find it, which is frequently, he is able to persuade us of its palpable existence. The theme of the Parisian adrift—the "feuilletoniste errant", nostalgic for the asphalt and even for that lowest form of sophisticated entertainment, the vaudeville—recurs and intertwines with another theme: the lamentable encroachment of "civilized" uniformity (a theme with a particularly modern resonance, in the age of globalization and corporate capital). Thus in Madrid, for example, we hear him deploring the triumph of Paris fashion, and the displacement of traditional women's dress by the omnipresent and odious shawl.

The English—world leaders, in their day, in the appropriation of foreign cultures and the export of northern European mores—come in for special opprobrium. In Andalusia, by now thoroughly acclimatized to the land of his dreams, Théophile is much taken with a *majo*'s costume and orders one for himself. The tailor, whose hatred of frock coats equals only his own, recalls with regret "the happy days when a stranger dressed like a Frenchman would have been hooted in the streets and pelted with orange peel." But how things have changed. "'Alas, sir, it is only the English who buy Spanish costumes now,' he said, as he finished taking my measurements."

Gautier contrasts English snobbism with the "spirit of egalitarianism" he finds in Spain. At the sight of an Englishwoman in Gibraltar, with her "dead expression... angular gestures and a methodical bearing, a savour of cant and an absence of anything natural", he feels he is "face to face with the spectre of civilisation, my mortal enemy..."

Gautier's readiness to call a spade a spade, and his extraordinary ability to convey the immediacy of his sensual experience, are done full justice by his English translator—from his accounts of the succession of bad, minimal or simply bizarre meals which, too irregularly for his liking, punctuate his narrative, to his word paintings of art and architecture, landscapes and streets, public spectacles and days and nights on the road. It is often his eye for the telling detail, as much as his facility as an orchestrator of set-piece descriptions, which enables him to elicit a spark of recognition in the reader. He describes, for example, the heat of the arid country south of Madrid in July. He and his travelling companion Eugène Piot are cooped up in an unusually grand, mule-drawn coach, "decked with curtains and green Venetian blinds... a travelling Turkish bath." Gautier notes, with penetrating observation, that "the sky at noon is the colour of melted lead; the ground a dusky grey with specks of glittering mica, and the faintest tinge of blue in the far distance", but it is the remark which follows, that to find shelter "one must keep to the narrow band of scant blue shadow cast by the wall", that (to use one of Gautier's own favorite expressions) can really transport the reader into the intensity of the experience with him.

There is an unbearably unblinking account of a bullfight; Gautier has done his homework and informed himself thoroughly about the finer points of the ritual, just as, later, he is able to introduce us to the expressive repertoire of the fan, and to take us off on a tour of the cafés of Madrid to sample the varieties of refreshment on offer: *agraz, chufas, sorbetes, quesitos, spumas, barquillos...* He clearly relishes such enumeration, and there are plenty of passages of description which catch the reader up in his manifest delight in his own verbal energy and inventiveness. Here he is in the choir of Burgos cathedral: "On raising one's head, one perceives a sort of dome formed by the inside of the tower... it is a giddy abyss of sculptures, arabesques, statues, miniature columns, ribs, lancets and pendentives. One might look at it for two years without seeing everything. It clusters as thickly as a cabbage, and is open-worked like a fish-slice [*touffu comme un chou, fenestré comme une truelle à poissons*]; gigantic as a pyramid, yet delicate as a woman's ear-ring, one cannot imagine how such filigree-work can remain suspended in the air throughout the centuries!" Gautier's encounters with the prodigies of the visible world induce in him a sense of wonder that can border on the delirious (informed, in this instance, by his preoccupation with the culinary. What, though, later on his journey, are we to make of the women of Seville whose teeth remind him of Newfoundland puppies?).

The book as a whole has this plethoric, almost junk-shop-like quality, as much through the shifting variety of its moods and ironies as the heterogeneity of its subject matter. Gautier can be opinionated, evocative and funny all at the same time. He finds the Escorial "an architectural nightmare", and is chilled by its atmosphere of death. "I advise those persons who have the idiocy to maintain that they are bored to go and pass three or four days at the Escorial; there they will discover what real tedium means, and will find amusement for the rest of their lives in the thought that they might be in the Escorial, but are not" (he means it). The book is rich in anecdote: the story, for example, of the bandits of La Mancha, who, most unlike the colorful brigands of Romantic mythology, spell out the miserable reality of their lives to some travellers they have kidnapped—and obtain an amnesty. There are surreal, Buñuelesque images which, like some of Gautier's more arresting and excessive similes, seem to come out of nowhere. They can startle with a sense of the sinister, bleak or tragi-comic: the priest's hat, "at least three feet long; the brim rolled upwards, forming a sort of horizontal roof before and behind the head", or the "poor wretch whose profession was to have no nose and to imitate a dog."

Into all this Gautier weaves accounts of his own states of mind, and these lend depth and a note of gravity—albeit an abbreviated and muted note (this is not the Romantic confessional)—to his perceptions and musings. In Toledo he is seized with "an immeasurable sadness", and doubts his very identity: "I felt so absent from myself, so far removed from my sphere, that it all seemed an hallucination..." (One suspects that Gautier was not the first or the last on whom Toledo had this effect of *dépaysement*). In Granada he spends four days and nights encamped in the Alhambra; they are, he writes, "the most delicious moments of my life" (he was still recalling them in his final years). If the book has an emotional keynote, it is probably the "serene melancholy" he describes in Granada: a fully conscious surrender to the present, sensual moment, together with an incipient, gnawing awareness of the passing of time.

The 1845 edition of the book contains a lengthy appreciation of Goya, who had died in 1828 (it was the first sustained account of

Goya's work to be published outside Spain, and it played a major part in establishing the painter's towering modern reputation). Goya, Gautier writes, appeared just in time to record the old Spain, and this, of course, is what he himself is doing in his own fluent and idiosyncratic portrait, made from his own personal and cultural perspective. By 1845 the railway was extending its tentacles right across Europe, and reaching out to the Iberian Peninsula; transported by "fantastic carriages" of a more archaic kind, Gautier journeys through a world for which he feels nostalgic even as he savors it. In the process—such is his ability to savor—he gives us a classic of travel literature which no serious voyager to Spain should dream of being without.

Robert Snell
Brighton, July 2001

Robert Snell is the author of *Théophile Gautier: A Romantic Critic of the Visual Arts* (Oxford: Clarendon Press, 1982).

Introduction

"IN 1840," wrote Théophile Gautier, "I set out for Spain on May 5th. The Carlist war was hardly over, and bands of soldiers, transformed into robbers, made travelling dangerous. For seven or eight years past, the Peninsula had been almost closed, and I was the first traveller to venture into it. I stayed there for five or six months, and returned at the beginning of winter."

To the young men of Gautier's generation—he was then in his twenty-ninth year—Spain was indeed an unknown and fabulous land. Their fathers, led by Napoleon, had imposed upon Spain a hated alien domination, only to be driven forth in the end after the grim struggle of the Peninsular War. In 1823 the French armies had once more intervened to restore the absolute power of that most contemptible of monarchs, Ferdinand VII. But since then, Spain had been in a constant state of smouldering discontent, ending in seven years of cruel civil war.

Democrats of all shades of opinion, from advanced Jacobins on the French model to moderate Liberals demanding no more than a constitution and some voice in the government, had been revolted by Ferdinand's bigoted and oppressive rule; while his brother Don Carlos found more favour in the eyes of the clericals and reactionaries, of whom he was the willing instrument.

Popular discontent came to a head in 1833, when Ferdinand, who left no son to succeed him, bequeathed his crown to his baby daughter Isabella, with his strong-minded wife, Queen Maria Cristina, as regent. The Carlists at once rose in revolt, and for seven years guerrilla warfare raged, with its accompaniment of atrocities, in the famished mountain regions, already impoverished by a generation of fighting. The treasury was empty, and large parts of the country were ravaged and destitute; so it was not unnatural that the clerical sympathies of the rebel Carlists should have marked out the Church for attack by the other parties: in 1835 the property of the religious orders was confiscated, and the convents pillaged and robbed of their treasures.

For eight years the Queen Regent Cristina managed to carry on the government, but in 1841 she was forced to resign in favour of her most famous general, Espartero, called the *Pacificador*, who in 1839, by the Convention of Vergara, had received the submission of the principal Carlist leaders. But by the time Gautier's book appeared, Espartero had fallen in his turn, as the result of another military revolt, leaving Spain with her civil discords still unresolved.

But to the young band of Romantics in Paris, all that happened beyond the Pyrenees was transfigured by the poetic imagination. The real Spain might be closed to them; but had not Abel Hugo, the poet's brother, translated some of the old epic *romances* of the Cid (1821); and had not Emile Deschamps published his *Poème de Rodrigue* (1828), drawn from the same source? Moreover, since the days of Napoleon's all-embracing dreams of empire, men were, as Gautier says, "full of nostalgias", and drawn towards distant, strange, exotic lands. Chateaubriand had long since given to the world his *Itinéraire de Paris à Jerusalem* (1811); Stendhal had rediscovered antique Rome (*Promenades en Rome*, 1829); Lamartine had published a *Voyage en Orient* (1835); Mérimée a *Voyage en Corse* (1840). And poetry and the stage had done their work: the sparkling dialogue and dramatic situations of Mérimée's *Théâtre de Clara Gazul* (1825); the voluptuous charm of Musset's *Contes d'Espagne et d'Italie* (1830), the vast prestige of Victor Hugo's *Les Orientales* (1829): all these had worked upon Gautier's sensibilities, so that "on setting foot in Spain"—to quote Sainte-Beuve—"he at once recognized in it his true clime and his true country." Was it not his poetic fatherland? He had never ceased to hear the summoning note of Hernani's horn, which had cast its spell over him as a young man, when, clad in the famous rose-coloured waistcoat, he had fought on the Romantic side at the stormy first performances of Hugo's epoch-making drama. The "fine, heroic, Castilian exaggeration" of

Hernani, its "stately Spanish magniloquence", its "language, so proud
and haughty in its familiarity", imbued him with the spirit of the old,
heroic Spain, the land of hidalgos and paladins, of the cloak and sword
and the *Pundonor*.

But the Ernani through which he drove on his first night in Spain
seemed no more than a mass of tumbledown hovels; and when he awoke
to the light of day, he found another Spain than that of his dreams. It was
Gautier's great merit that he could cast aside all literary preconceptions,
and, looking upon Spain as it was, paint it with a mastery which can
never be surpassed. Enchanted palaces, gardens and fountains, chilly
cloisters and arid sierras: he brings them all before us in a superb series of
pictures, so vivid that it seems as though we had seen them ourselves.

For, as all critics are agreed, and as he himself explained to the
Goncourts, Gautier's essential gift was that of *vision*. Starting life in a
painter's *atelier*, "I was," he says, "the painter of our band… I set upon
the palette of style all the tones of the dawn and all the tints of sunset."
This was the novel element in Gautier's travel-notes. Lamartine might
indeed claim that the descriptions in his *Voyage en Orient* were
"transcribed vision" (*le regard écrit*); he certainly describes picturesque
groupings and compositions, much in the style of the romantic
engravings of the period. Mérimée, again, sometimes varies his sober
archaeological descriptions with a pictorial touch:

> "*Over the valley,*" he says in the Voyage dans le Midi, "*there still reigned
> a thick fog, pierced here and there by the tops of trees. Above it appeared
> the town, like a pyramid resplendent with light. At intervals, the wind tore
> long openings through the mist, giving rise to a thousand accidental effects
> of light, such as English landscape-painters so happily invent.*"

Or let us see how Chateaubriand describes the ruins of Carthage:

> "*Fig-trees, olive trees and carob trees were already putting forth their first
> leaves; great angelicas and acanthuses formed tufts of verdure among frag-
> ments of marble of every colour. My eyes wandered afar over the Isthmus,
> over two seas, distant islands, a smiling land, blue-tinged lakes and azure
> mountains. I descried forests, vessels, aqueducts, Moorish villages,
> Mahomedan hermitages, minarets and the white houses of Tunis.*"

Compare this with Gautier's picture of the Straits of Gibraltar and the difference both of vision and of method is at once clear. In the word-pictures of Chateaubriand and Mérimée, colour and composition are only indicated in the most summary way. A landscape may be compared with a picture, but it is not seen with the painter's eye. If we now turn to any of Gautier's landscapes, for example, the view over Andalusia from the Sierra Morena or of the Sierra Nevada from the Alameda of Granada, we shall see the truth of Sainte-Beuve's remark that in his descriptions "it is not ink that he uses, but colours and lines; he has a palette, he has crayons."

But how does he contrive to convey his impressions with such uncanny vividness? The reason may best be expressed in the words of Baudelaire:

> It is the consequence, he says, of "a knowledge of language which is never at fault, of that magnificent dictionary whose leaves, stirred by a divine breath, open so aptly that there springs forth the right word, the one and only word; lastly, of that sense of order which sets every stroke, every touch in its natural place, and omits no shade of colour. When we consider that Gautier combines with this marvellous faculty an unlimited understanding of the mystic correspondences between all things, and the symbolism which is everywhere—that treasury of all metaphor—we understand why he is able, without respite or fatigue, and with never a mistake, to define the mysterious attitude which the objects of creation assume before the eyes of man... To handle a language with skill and science is to conjure up images by a species of magic evocation. It is then that colour speaks, like a deep-toned, thrilling voice; that monuments arise and stand out in relief against the depths of space; that animals and plants, the representatives of ugliness and evil, contort themselves into unequivocal grimaces."

The secret of Gautier's descriptive power could not be better divined or expressed.

The space devoted to landscape, architecture and art was, indeed, so preponderant in Gautier's articles, that the inhabitants of the country were almost relegated to the position of comic or picturesque adjuncts to the scene. Such, at least, was the impression of his friends. "Why, Théo," said his editor's wife, Delphine de Girardin, on his return to Paris, "are there no Spaniards in Spain?" It was perhaps in response to this question that he wrote his charming story *Militona*

(1847) which should certainly be read in conjunction with the present work. The idyllic loves of the young Spanish girl, whose charm and beauty are described with such loving care (for, though Gautier held that "man is ugly, everywhere and always," this was far from being his attitude towards woman), find a foil in a series of clever character-studies drawn from Spanish life, and placed in the setting described in these *Travels*.

But Gautier was more than a "colourist writer" and an able story-teller. He was above all a poet. "I have worn out my life," he says, "in pursuing the Beautiful, under all its Protean forms, in order to depict it; and I have only found it in nature and the arts." And so it was that, unlike Victor Hugo in his journey to the Rhine (*Le Rhin*, 1840), he has no eyes for the philosophy of history, the deep social and political currents bearing humanity to its mysterious and unknown bourne; unlike Mérimée, he uses the vocabulary of architecture and archaeology with an eye to picturesqueness rather than to accuracy. He sees and he describes only what appeals to his sense of beauty or the comic, or what stirs his deep sense of poetic symbolism. His dazzling atmospheric descriptions,—for if Hugo was, to use Gautier's words, the "poet of fluids", Gautier is the poet of light—often end, like his early sonnets, in a mood of meditative melancholy and reflexion. Others,—for instance, the famous word-picture of the oleander in the Generalife gardens—are so instinct with his passionate worship of beauty that his emotion is transferred to us almost more directly than by the verses of *España*. While his description of the Escorial, evoking as it does a sensation of numbing chill, both moral and physical, by a series of low-toned colour harmonies and words with the weight of granite or the cold glitter of ice, produces a direct and irresistible impression: the dead hand of bigotry and despotism seems to hold us, cold and helpless, in its icy grasp.

With such powers of vision and expression, Gautier was an art critic of a very high order. He does not, as a rule, describe pictures in terms of technique, like the brothers Goncourt, who paint a picture before us, stroke by stroke and wash by wash—witness their wonderful essay on Chardin—but he shows us the artist's characteristic devices of colour and composition as surely as if we were standing before the canvas;

while, by transposing the picture, as it were, into terms of words, he produces in us the emotion which it was intended to arouse. His contrast between the earlier and later manners of El Greco and his descriptions of Ribera or Zurbaran are happy examples of his peculiar descriptive skill. As Sainte-Beuve says, if all the pictures he describes were destroyed tomorrow, we could still see them in his descriptions.

It has been the fashion to decry the Romantics, whose provocative and challenging attitude blinded many of their critics to the value of their achievement. The present age, which has assimilated and profited by the treasures with which they enriched both thought and language, can afford to ignore the extravagances which marked their early struggles. These *Travels*, in spite of some defects due to hurried composition, will suffice to reveal a great artist in words—in more than a metaphorical sense—whose sharp, immediate reaction to beauty is here expressed in pages of high poetic merit; and a poet with a deep sense of the sadness of human destiny, and a horror of death and dissolution, which carry us back to the Middle Ages, to the days of François Villon.

Tomb of Ferdinand and Isabelle

PART I

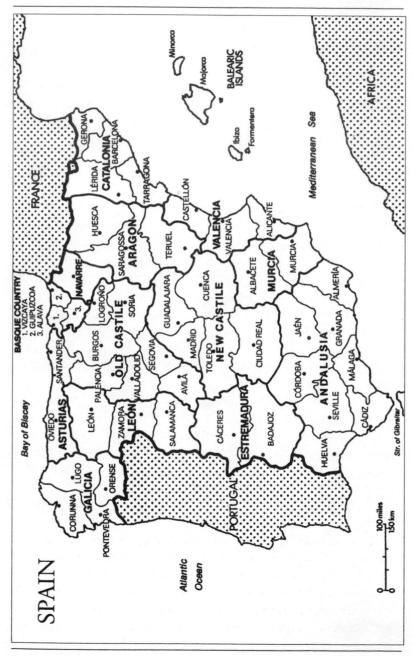

I. Paris to Bordeaux

A FEW weeks ago, I carelessly let fall the remark: "I should be glad to go to Spain!" By the end of five or six days, my friends had removed the prudent conditional with which I had qualified my wish, and were telling all and sundry that I was going on a journey in Spain. This positive assertion was followed by questions of: "When are you starting?"

Little knowing what an obligation I was laying upon myself, I answered: "In a week's time."

At the end of a week, people began to show surprise at seeing me still in Paris.

One would say: "I thought you were in Madrid!" "Are you back again?" would ask another.

I now understood that I owed it to my friends to be away for three months, and that I must discharge this debt with all possible speed, under pain of being ceaselessly harassed by officious creditors. The greenrooms of the theatres, the bitumen and asphalt of the boulevards, with their varying degrees of elasticity, were forbidden ground till further orders. All I could obtain was three or four days' grace; and on the fifth of May I prepared to rid my country of my unwanted presence by climbing into the stage-coach for Bordeaux.

I will pass very lightly over the first few stages, which have nothing of interest to offer. To right and left stretch out all kinds of cultivated lands in stripes like those of a tiger or zebra, just like those tailors' cards on which are stuck patterns of trousers and waistcoats. Such a prospect is a joy to agricultural experts, landowners and other middle-class persons, but meagre fare for the enthusiastic traveller with a turn for description, who sets off field-glass in hand, to note down particulars of the universe. I started by night, so that my first memories, from Versailles onwards, are but faint outlines blurred by the darkness. I regret having passed through Chartres without being able to see the cathedral.

Between Vendôme and Châteaurenault—pronounced *Chtrno* in the postillions' language, so cleverly imitated by Henri Monnier in his admirable character-sketch of travelling by stage-coach—rise wooded hills in which the inhabitants hollow out dwelling-places in the living rock, and dwell underground like the ancient Troglodytes. They sell the stone obtained by their excavations, so that each house which they hollow out produces another in relief, like a plaster cast taken out of a mould, or a tower drawn out from the lining of a well. The chimney, a long tube hammered through the thickness of the rock, comes out level with the ground, so that the smoke rises in blue spirals from the very surface of the earth, without visible cause, as from a *solfatara* or volcanic soil. It would be quite easy for the facetious traveller to throw stones into the omelettes of this hidden population, and absent-minded or short-sighted rabbits must often tumble all alive into the stew-pot. This mode of construction saves one the trouble of going down to the cellar to fetch wine.

Châteaurenault is a little town with steep streets winding in spirals, and edged by unsteady, toppling houses, which only seem able to stand upright by dint of leaning against each other: a great round tower, standing on some mounds of the old fortifications, draped here and there with a mantle of green ivy, adds a little character to its appearance. Between Châteaurenault and Tours there is nothing worthy of note. In the middle, the ground: on each side, trees: long yellow bands stretching out as far as the eye can reach, and known in the jargon of the road as "tail-ribbons" (*rubans de queue*); that is all; then the road takes a sudden plunge down between two steepish slopes, and in a few minutes we see the city of Tours, famous for its prunes, Rabelais and M. de Balzac.

The much-vaunted bridge of Tours is not very extraordinary in itself; but the appearance of the town is charming. When I arrived, the sky was tinged with a blue of extreme delicacy, across which lazily trailed a few wisps of cloud; the limpid surface of the Loire was broken by a line of white, like a streak scratched on glass with the point of a diamond; this curve was formed by a little waterfall pouring down from one of the sand-banks which are so frequent in the bed of this river. The dark mass of Saint-Gatien was drawn upon the limpid air, its Gothic spires adorned with balls and swelling curves like the towers of the Kremlin, which gave the town a most picturesquely Russian appearance against the sky; the picture was completed by a few towers and steeples belonging to churches whose names I do not know; white-sailed boats floated on the azure mirror of the stream with the gliding motion of a sleeping swan. I would fain have visited the house of Tristan l'Hermite, the dread confidant of Louis XI, which has remained in a state of wonderful preservation, with its terribly significant ornaments of loops of cord mingled with other instruments of torture; but I had not the time. I had to content myself with walking along the Grande-Rue, which must be the pride of the inhabitants of Tours, and attempts to vie with the Rue de Rivoli.

Châtellerault, which has a great reputation for its cutlery, has nothing remarkable save a bridge with ancient towers at each end, producing the most feudal and romantic impression imaginable. As to its arms factory, it is a great white mass with a multitude of windows. I can say nothing of Poitiers except that its cobblestones are simply execrable, for I passed through it in driving rain on the blackest of black nights.

When day returned, the coach was travelling through a wooded country, with apple-green trees planted in soil of the most brilliant red. This produced a most singular effect: the roofs of the houses were covered with grooved Italian pantiles; these tiles were also of a vivid red, a strange colour to eyes accustomed to the swart and sooty hues of the roofs of Paris. By a vagary of which the motive escapes me, the builders in these parts begin their houses with the roof; the walls and foundations come afterwards. The timber frame is laid on four stout planks, and the tilers do their work before the masons.

It is about here that the long orgy of hewn stone begins, which will not stop till we reach Bordeaux; the tiniest doorless, windowless hovel is of hewn stone; the garden walls are made up of great blocks laid one on top of the other without mortar; along the road-side, by the doors, you see enormous heaps of magnificent stone, with which it would be easy to build a Chenonceaux or an Alhambra at small cost; but the inhabitants are content just to pile it up, covering the whole with a roof of red or yellow tiles, of which the rounded edges are arranged first one way and then the other, the wavy border forming quite a graceful effect.

Angoulême, a city perched fantastically upon a very steep hill, at the foot of which the Charente sends up a prattling noise from two mills, is built on this plan; it has a sort of spurious Italian appearance, further increased by the masses of trees crowning its steep rocks, and a great, spreading, parasol-pine like those of Roman villas. An old tower which, if I can trust my memory, has a telegraph on top of it (the telegraph has saved many an old tower), adds severity to its general appearance, and enables the city to make quite a good show on the horizon. As we climbed the rising road, I noticed a house daubed outside with rough frescoes, representing something in the nature of Neptune, Bacchus or perhaps Napoleon. The painter having neglected to put the name beside it, all suppositions are permissible, and may be defended.

So far, I admit that an excursion to Romainville or Pantin would have been quite as picturesque; nothing could have been duller, more insignificant and insipid than these interminable strips of country, like those continuous ornaments by the aid of which lithographers manage to include all the Paris boulevards on the same sheet of paper. Hawthorn hedges and rickety elms, rickety elms and hawthorn hedges, and beyond that, perhaps, a row of poplars, like tufts of feathers stuck in the flat earth, or a willow with its distorted trunk and hoary wig—so much for the landscape; for figures, an occasional stone-breaker or road-mender, as tanned as an African Moor, who rests his hand on the shaft of his hammer to watch you pass; or some poor soldier on his way to rejoin his corps, sweating and stumbling under his load. But beyond Angoulême the aspect of the country changes, and we begin to grasp the fact that we are some way from the suburbs.

On leaving the department of Charente, we come upon the first of the *landes:* these are vast sheets of grey, violet or bluish earth, with more or less pronounced undulations. Rare patches of close-growing moss, russet-toned heather, and stunted broom form the sole vegetation. It has the desolation of the Egyptian Thebaid, and at any moment one might expect to see a train of camels or dromedaries go by; one might almost believe that no man had ever passed this way.

Having crossed the *landes,* we enter rather a picturesque region. Here and there, along the edge of the road, are grouped houses, buried like nests in groves of trees, like pictures by Hobbema, with their great roofs, their wells fringed with wild vines, their great oxen with astonished eyes, and their fowls pecking about on the dunghill; all these houses are, of course, of hewn stone, and so are the garden walls. On every side one may see buildings begun, then left for some whim, and begun again a few steps away; the natives are very much like children who have been given for a New Year's present a box of bricks, with which one can build any sort of building by means of a certain number of rectangular pieces of wood; they take off the roof, remove the stones of their houses, and build an altogether different one out of the same stones; along the edge of the road bloom gardens surrounded with the cool, damp shade of fine trees, and diapered with flowering peas, marguerites and roses; and one looks far down into meadows where the cows stand breast-deep in grass; a cross-road, all fragrant with hawthorn and wild roses, a group of trees beneath which one can see an uncoupled wagon, a few peasant women with their bell-shaped caps, like the turban of an *ulema*, and a tight red skirt: a thousand unexpected details rejoice the eyes and beguile the journey. As one goes past scarlet roofs washed over with bitumen, one might think oneself in Normandy. Flers and Cabat would find pictures there ready-made. It is about this latitude that *bérets* begin to appear; they are all blue, and their shape is smarter and more elegant than that of the hats.

It is about here, too, that one meets the first ox-wagons; these carts have quite a Homeric and primitive appearance; the oxen are harnessed by the head to the same yoke, adorned with a little sheepskin frontlet; they have an air of mildness, gravity and resignation, which is quite sculptural, and worthy of the Aeginetan bas-reliefs. Most of them wear housings of white linen to protect them from the flies and gad-flies; there is no more curious sight than these sheeted oxen, slowly lifting towards you their damp, sheeny muzzles and their great dark-blue eyes, which the Greeks, those discriminating judges of beauty, found so striking that they made them the regular attribute of Juno: *Boôpis Hērē*

A wedding that was going on at an inn gave me an opportunity of seeing a few of the natives of the place, for I had not seen ten people during a journey of more than a hundred leagues. These natives are very ugly, especially the women; there is no difference between the old and the young ones: a peasant woman is equally withered and wrinkled whether she be twenty-five or sixty years of age. The little girls have caps as big as their grandmothers, which make them look like the Turkish street-boys, with huge heads and frail bodies, in Decamps' sketches. In the stables at this inn I saw a monstrous black goat, with immense spiral twisting horns and yellow flaming eyes, and a more than diabolical appearance, which would have made him a fit president for a witches' Sabbath in the Middle Ages.

Night was falling as we arrived at Cubzac. There used to be a ferry across the Dordogne, and the breadth and swiftness of the stream made the crossing dangerous. The ferry is now replaced by a suspension bridge of the boldest design. Everybody knows that I am not a very great admirer of modern inventions, but this is a construction really worthy of Egypt or Rome, owing to its colossal dimensions and imposing appearance. Spans formed by a series of arches of progressively increasing height lead to the hanging platform. Ships in full sail can pass beneath it, as beneath the legs of the Colossus of Rhodes. A pair of cast-iron towers, made lighter by their open-work construction, serve as supports for the wire ropes, which cross one another with a symmetry cleverly calculated to distribute the resistance; these cables are drawn upon the sky with the tenuous delicacy of a spider's web, adding still more to the wonder of its construction. Two cast-iron obelisks stand at each end, like the peristyle of a Theban monument, and this adornment is not out of place, for the mighty architectural genius of the Pharaohs would not disown the bridge of Cubzac. It takes thirteen minutes to cross it, watch in hand.

One or two hours afterwards, the lights on the bridge of Bordeaux—another wonder, though of less striking appearance—glittered at a distance which my appetite would fain have had shortened, for speed in travelling is always achieved at the expense of the traveller's stomach. After exhausting our stocks of chocolate, biscuits and other provisions for the journey, our ideas began to become cannibalistic. My companions looked at me with avid eyes, and if we had had yet another stage to travel, we should have renewed the horrors of the raft *Medusa*, eating our braces, the soles of our boots, our opera hats and other such food for the shipwrecked, who digest them perfectly well.

On alighting from the coach, one is assailed by a swarm of touts, who distribute one's belongings among them, twenty of them being needed to carry a pair of boots. This is nothing out of the ordinary; but, funnier still, there are, as it were, spies posted by the hotel-keepers, on the look-out to snap up passing travellers. All these ruffians shout themselves hoarse, pouring out in their peculiar jargon a string of eulogies and abuse: one will seize you by the arm, another by the leg, another by your overcoat-button. "Monsieur, come to the Hôtel de Nantes, it is so comfortable there!" "Don't go there, Monsieur; it is the hotel for bugs: Hôtel des Punaises, that is its right name," hastens to add the representative of a rival inn. "Hôtel de Rouen! Hôtel de France!" vociferates the band as it follows you.

"Monsieur, they never clean their saucepans; they cook with lard; the rain pours into the bedrooms; you will be fleeced, robbed, murdered."

Each one tries to put you out of conceit with the rival establishments, and this procession will not leave you until you have definitely entered a hotel of some sort. Then they fall to quarrelling, exchanging blows and calling one another brigands and robbers, and other highly likely epithets; then they hurry off as fast as they can, in pursuit of fresh prey.

In the style of its buildings Bordeaux bears a strong resemblance to Versailles: one can see that the idea which they had in their heads was to outdo Paris in size; the streets are wider, the houses more spacious, the rooms higher. The theatre is of vast proportions; it is like the Odéon run into the Bourse. But the inhabitants find it hard to fill their city; they do all they can to appear numerous, but not all their Southern turbulence suffices to people these disproportionate buildings; the lofty windows seldom have curtains, and the grass grows desolately in these great court-yards. What lends animation to the town are the *grisettes* and the women of the people; they are really very pretty: almost all of them have straight noses, cheeks without pronounced cheekbones, and great black eyes in a pale oval face, producing a charming effect. Their head-dress is most original; it is composed of a brilliantly coloured Madras kerchief, put on in the Creole fashion, very much on the back of the head, so as to confine the hair, which is drawn low down on the nape of the neck; the rest of their attire consists in a great shawl falling straight down to the heels, and a print dress with long folds. These women have a brisk and sprightly walk, and supple, rounded, naturally slender figures. They carry on their heads their baskets, parcels and jugs of water, which, it may be said in passing, are of a very elegant shape: with their amphoras on their heads, and the straight folds of their costume, they might be taken for Greek maidens, Princess Nausicaas on their way to the fountain.

The cathedral was built by the English, and is rather fine; the doorway contains some life-sized figures of bishops, executed with more care and fidelity to nature than the ordinary run of Gothic statues, which are treated as arabesques, and entirely sacrificed to the exigencies of the architecture. On visiting the church, I saw leaning up against the wall Riessner's magnificent copy of the *Scourging of Christ*, after Titian; it was waiting for a frame. From the cathedral my companion and I betook ourselves to the Tour St. Michel, where there is a vault that has the property of mummifying the bodies placed in it.

The lowest story of the tower is occupied by the custodian and his family, who do their cooking at the mouth of the vault, and live there on terms of the most intimate familiarity with their gruesome neighbours; the man took a lantern, and we went down a spiral staircase with worn steps into the gloomy hall. The dead, numbering about forty, are stood upright all around the vault with their backs to the wall; this erect attitude, contrasting with the usual recumbent posture of the dead, lends them a phantom-like appearance of life which is most alarming, especially by the flickering light of the lantern as it oscillates in the guide's hand and makes the shadows shift with it.

The imagination of poets and painters has never produced a more horrible nightmare; the most monstrous of Goya's *Caprichos*, the delirious visions of Louis Boulanger, the *diableries* of Callot or Teniers are nothing to this, and it outdoes all the composers of fantastical ballads. No more abominable spectres have ever come forth from the night of Germany; they are worthy to take part with the witches in *Faust* at the Sabbath on the Brocken.

Here are to be seen distorted, grimacing faces, half-hairless skulls, gaping sides, showing through the ribs, as through a grate, lungs like dried and withered sponges; here the flesh is reduced to dust, and the bones are coming through: there the skin, no longer sustained by the fibres of the cell-tissue, but turned to the consistency of parchment, floats about the skeleton like a second shroud. None of these heads has the impassive calm set by death as its supreme seal upon all that it touches; their mouths open in a horrid yawn, as if convulsed by the immeasurable weariness of eternity, or wear the sardonic sneer of nothingness mocking at life; their jaws are out of joint, the muscles of their necks are swollen; their fists are clenched in fury, their backbones are bent in the contortions of despair. One would think that they were angry at being drawn from their tombs, and disturbed in their slumbers by the curiosity of the profane.

The custodian showed us a general who had been killed in a duel. The wound could clearly be seen, like a wide, blue-lipped mouth grinning in his side. A porter who suddenly expired while lifting a huge weight, a Negress, hardly any blacker than the white people placed at her side, a woman who has still all her teeth and an almost fresh tongue, a family poisoned by mushrooms, and, as the last touch of horror, a little boy who bears all the marks of having been buried alive.

His face is sublime in its suffering and despair; never has the expression of human agony been carried further; the nails are buried in the palms of the hands; the nerves are stretched like strings on the bridge of a violin; the knees are drawn up convulsively to form an angle; the head is thrown violently backwards; the poor little body, by an unheard-of effort, has turned right over in his coffin.

The place in which these dead bodies are collected is a vast cellar with flattened vaulting; the ground is suspiciously springy, and consists of human remains fifteen feet deep; in the middle rises a pyramid of debris in a more or less well-preserved condition; these mummies exhale a sickly, dusty smell, more unpleasant than the bitter odour of bitumen and natron in Egypt; there are some which have been there for two or three hundred years, others for only sixty: the stuff of their garments or shrouds is still quite well preserved.

On leaving this place, we went to see the bell-tower, made up of towers connected at the top by a balcony of an original and picturesque design; then the Church of St. Cross, beside the alms-houses, a building with round arches and twisted columns, ornamented quite in the Byzantine style, with a running design carved in the Greek key-pattern. The doorway is enriched with a number of groups, which are carrying into effect, with considerable effrontery, the precept: "Be fruitful and multiply"; fortunately the arabesques of leaves and flowers disguise the strangeness of this mode of interpreting Holy Writ.

The Museum is housed in the splendid mansion occupied by the *Mairie*, and contains a fine collection of casts and a great number of remarkable pictures, among others two little canvases by Bega which are pearls of great price; they have the warmth and freedom of Adrien Brauwer with the delicacy and elaboration of Teniers; there are also some Ostades of great delicacy, some Tiepolos in the most baroque and fantastic manner, some Jordaens, some Van Dycks and a Gothic picture which must be by Ghirlandajo or Fiesole; the Paris gallery possesses nothing to equal this picture so far as mediaeval art is concerned; but the pictures could hardly have been hung with less taste or discrimination: the best places are occupied by great daubs of the modern school, of the time of Guérin and Léthiers.

The harbour is crowded with vessels of every nation and varying tonnage; in the misty twilight they might be taken for a multitude of drifting cathedrals; for nothing so much resembles a church as a ship, with its masts soaring aloft like spires; and the intricate open-work of its rigging. To end up our day, we went into the great theatre. Conscience forces us to say that it was full; and yet they were playing *La Dame Blanche*, which is anything but a novelty. The house is almost the same size as the Paris Opera, but much less ornate. The actors sang as much out of tune as at the real Opéra-Comique.

At Bordeaux, Spanish influence begins to make itself felt. Almost all the shop-signs are in two languages; the booksellers have at least as many Spanish as French books. A great many people can *hablar* in the language of Don Quixote and Guzman d'Alfarache; this influence increases as one approaches the frontier; and, if the truth be told, in this frontier land where the two national colourings shade into each other, the Spanish tinge prevails over the French; the dialect spoken by the natives bears a closer relation to Spanish than to the language of their mother country.

II. Bordeaux to the Frontier

WHEN we leave Bordeaux, the *landes* once again begin, more melancholy, and, if possible, gaunter and more desolate than ever; heather, broom and *pinadas* (pine forests); from time to time, perhaps, the crouching figure of some wild-looking shepherd keeping his flock of black sheep; an occasional hut in the style of an Indian wigwam. It is a most dismal scene, little calculated to refresh the spirit; no trees are to be seen save pines, with incisions in them from which the resin flows. This great salmon-pink gash forms a strong contrast with the grey tones of the bark, and makes these sickly trees, drained of most of their sap, look absolutely miserable. It is like a forest unjustly murdered, raising its arms heavenwards to cry out for justice.

We went through Dax in the middle of the night, and crossed the Adour in frightful weather, through driving rain and a north wind that would have torn the horns off an ox. The nearer we drew to sunny lands, the keener and more cutting grew the cold; had we not had our coats with us, we should have got our noses and feet frost-bitten, like the soldiers of the Grand Army during the Russian campaign. When day broke, we were still among the *landes*; but the pines were mingled with cork-trees: I had always imagined them to be shaped like corks, but in reality they are enormous trees whose curious habit of growth, and rugged, contorted branches, give them something of the character at once of the oak and the carob-tree; a variety of pools of brackish leaden-coloured water extended along both sides of the road: a salt breeze met us in gusts; the air was full of a vague, mysterious sound booming upon the horizon; at last a bluish outline appeared upon the background of pale sky: it was the range of the Pyrenees. A few moments later a scarcely visible blue line—as it were, the sign manual of the Ocean—heralded our arrival. It was not long before Bayonne appeared in the shape of a mass of closely packed tiles, with a squat, awkward church-tower; we do not want to speak ill of Bayonne, for a town seen through the rain is naturally hideous. The harbour was not very full. Along the deserted quays a handful of decked boats loitered with an air of delightfully desultory idleness. The trees forming the promenade are very fine, and somewhat mitigate the austerity of all the straight lines traced by the parapets and fortifications. As for the church, it is colour-washed in canary-yellow and brownish tones; it contains nothing worthy of note, save a sort of canopy of red damask, with a few pictures by Lépicié and other painters in the style of Van Loo.

In its language and customs Bayonne is almost a Spanish town; the hotel where we stayed was called the Fonda San Esteban. Knowing that we were to make a long journey in the Peninsula, they gave us every sort of advice: buy yourselves red sashes to bind tight round the body; provide yourselves with blunderbusses, combs and phials of insecticide solution; take biscuits and provisions with you; the Spaniards lunch off a spoonful of chocolate, dine off a clove of garlic washed down with a glass of water and sup off a paper cigarette; moreover, you had better provide yourselves with a mattress and a stew-pot, to make your bed and dinner. The French-Spanish phrase-books for the use of travellers were not calculated to reassure us. In the chapter on "The Traveller at the Inn" one reads the following alarming remarks:

> "I should like to partake of something."
> "Take a chair," replies the innkeeper.
> "Excellent; but I would rather take something a little more nourishing."
> "What have you brought?" continues the proprietor of the inn.
> "Nothing," sadly replies the traveller.
> "Well, then, how do you expect me to prepare you any food? The butcher's is over there, and the baker's beyond: go and get some bread and meat, and, if there is any coal, my wife, who knows a little about cooking, will prepare your provisions."

The traveller, in a rage, makes an appalling uproar; but the innkeeper, quite unmoved, enters "Six reals for the row" to his account.

The Madrid coach starts from Bayonne. The driver is a *mayoral*, wearing a pointed hat trimmed with velvet and silk pompons, a brown jacket adorned with coloured embroidery, leather gaiters and a red girdle: this is a first instalment of local colour. From Bayonne onwards, the country is extremely picturesque; the chain of the Pyrenees is more clearly outlined, and mountains with lovely, curving lines form an ever-changing horizon; the sea makes frequent appearances to the right of the road; at every turn one has a sudden glimpse, between two mountains, of a dark blue, soft and deep, broken here and there by scrolls of foam, whiter than snow, of which no painter has ever been able to give any idea. And I here make my public apology to the sea, for speaking lightly of it; but this was when I had only seen it at Ostende, which is no more nor less than the canalized Scheldt, as my dear friend Fritz used so wittily to maintain.

The clock on the church of Urrugne, as we passed by, bore the following dismal inscription in black letters: *Vulnerant omnes, ultima necat* (All wound, the last one kills). Yes, you are right, sad dial, each hour wounds us with the steely point of your hands, and every turn of the wheels bears us away to the unknown.

The houses of Urrugne and Saint-Jean-de-Luz, not far away, have a bloody and barbarous appearance, due to the odd custom of painting the shutters, the doors and the beams enclosing the masonry compartments *rouge antique* or blood-red. After Saint-Jean-de-Luz we come to Béhobie, which is the last French village. The war has given rise to a frontier trade in two commodities: firstly, in bullets found on the battle-field, and secondly, in human contraband. They export Carlists like bales of goods; there is even a tariff: so much for a colonel, so much for an officer; the bargain is made, the smuggler arrives, carries off his man, takes him over the frontier and delivers him at his destination like a dozen handkerchiefs or a hundred cigars. On the other side of the Bidassoa one sees Irun, the first Spanish village; half the bridge belongs to France and the other half to Spain. Quite near this bridge is the famous Isle of Pheasants, where the marriage of Louis XIV was celebrated by proxy. It would be difficult to celebrate anything there today for it is no bigger than a medium-sized fried sole.

A few more turns of the wheels, and perhaps I shall lose one of my illusions, and see the disappearance of the Spain of my dreams—the Spain of the *Romancero*, of the Victor Hugo ballads, of Mérimée's tales and the stories of Alfred de Musset. As I cross the frontier-line, I recall what Heinrich Heine, the kind and the witty, said to me at Liszt's concert, in his German accent full of sly humour:

"How will you manage to talk about Spain when you have been there?"

III. Irun to Vergara

HALF the bridge across the Bidassoa belongs to France, the other half to Spain; you may have a foot in each country, which is highly majestic: on the one hand the gendarme, grave, worthy and serious, beaming at his rehabilitation by Edouard Ourliac in Curmer's *Français*, on the other hand, the Spanish soldier, dressed in green, enjoying the soft indolence of repose with a beatific nonchalance on the green grass. At the end of the bridge you run straight into Spanish life and local colour: Irun has no sort of likeness to a French village; the roofs of the houses project in a fan shape; their tiles, alternately convex and concave, form a kind of crenellation of an odd, Moorish appearance. The balconies project very far over the street, and are made of ancient ironwork, wrought with a care which surprises one in an out-of-the-way village like Irun, and suggests a great and vanished opulence. The women pass their lives on these balconies, shaded by awnings with coloured stripes, like so many airy habitations attached to the body of the building; two sides are left open, giving passage to cool breezes and ardent glances; but do not look here for those tawny hues, as of a meerschaum (forgive the comparison), those sooty tones, as of an old pipe, which a painter might expect to find; everything is whitewashed, after the Arab fashion; but the contrast of this chalky tone with the dark brown of the beams, the roofs and the balconies, produces, none the less, a good effect.

At Irun the horses left us, and they harnessed to the coach two mules, shaved half-way up their bodies. Half skin, half hair, like those mediaeval costumes resembling portions of two different costumes sewn together by chance, these beasts, when so shaven, look very curious, and seem alarmingly thin; for, thus laid bare, their anatomy can be studied in its minutest details—their bones, their muscles, down to their smallest veins; with their hairless tails and pointed ears they look like enormous mice. Beside the ten mules our numbers were swelled by a *zagal* and two *escopeteros* adorned with their blunderbusses (*trabucos*). The *zagal* is a sort of foot-boy, a deputy-*mayoral,* who puts the brake on the wheels during the perilous descents, looks after the harness and the springs, hurries up the relays, and dances attendance on the coach like a fly on the wheel, but much more efficaciously. The costume of the *zagal* is charming, most light and elegant; he wears a pointed hat embellished with velvet ribbons and pompons of silk, a chestnut or snuff-coloured jacket with cuffs and collar made of pieces of different colours—usually blue, white and red— and a great arabesque blooming in the middle of his back, breeches trimmed with constellations of filigree buttons, and on his feet *alpargatas,* or sandals laced with cords; add a red sash and a gaily coloured cravat, and you have a most characteristic figure. The *escopeteros* are guards, or *miqueletes,* whose function is to escort the coach and frighten away *rateros* (as they call petty thieves), who could not resist the temptation to rifle an isolated traveller, but are held in awe by the edifying appearance of the blunderbuss alone, and greet you, as they go by, with the inevitable *Vaya usted con Dios*: "Go, and God be with you." The costume of the *esccopeteros* is almost the same as that of the *zagal,* but less smart and ornate. They take up their position on the outside, at the back of coach, thus commanding a view of the country-side. In describing our caravan, we have forgotten to mention a little postillion who rides a horse at the head of the train and sets the pace for the whole file.

Before starting, we had also to have a visa for our passports, which were already fairly well bedizened with them. During this important operation, we had time to take a look at the population of Irun, which has nothing remarkable about it, except that the women wear their hair, which is unusually long, braided into a single plait, which hangs down below the waist; shoes are rare, and stockings still more so.

For some time past, my ears had been puzzled by a strange, husky, inexplicable noise, both alarming and comical; one might have taken it for a host of jays being plucked alive, of children being whipped, of amorous cats, of saws grating against a hard stone, of scraping cauldrons, of rusty prison hinges swinging open and forced to give up their prisoner; I thought at least that it was a princess being murdered by a savage wizard; it was nothing but an ox-cart coming up the street of Irun, the wheels of which were whining like the caterwaulings of a cat for lack of grease, which the driver no doubt preferred to put into his soup. This wagon was certainly of a most primitive type; the wheels were solid and turned in one piece with the axle, like the little carts which children make out of the rind of pumpkins. This noise can be heard half a league away, and is not unpleasing to the natives of the region. By this means they have a musical instrument which costs nothing, and plays all by itself so long as the journey lasts. It seems as musical to them as a violinist playing exercises on the E string does to us. A peasant would have no use for a wagon which did not creak: this antediluvian vehicle is called a *caroso*.

Upon an ancient palace, transformed into an ordinary house, we saw for the first time that plaster placard which degrades so many other palaces, with the inscription: *Plaza de la Constitución*; the true nature of things is bound to come out somehow or another: no better symbol could be chosen to represent the present state of the country. A constitution for Spain is like a handful of plaster dabbed on to granite.

As the road was a steep one, I walked as far as the city gate, where I turned round and cast a farewell glance at France; it was indeed a magnificent sight: the range of the Pyrenees descends in harmonious curves towards the blue expanse of the sea, which was cut here and there by a streak of silver; and thanks to the extreme limpidity of the air, one could see very, very far away, a line of faint salmon-pink, advancing into the blue infinity and hollowing out a vast curve in the edge of the coast. Bayonne and its advanced outpost, Biarritz, occupy the tip of this point, and the Gulf of Gascony is traced as clearly as on a map; from this point onwards we shall see the sea no more until we reach Cadiz. Farewell, old Ocean!

The coach galloped at full speed up and down slopes of extreme steepness; on that precipitous road it was like tight-rope walking without a balance-pole, and could only be managed thanks to the prodigious skill of the drivers and the extraordinary sure-footedness of the mules; in spite of our pace, from time to time there fell on to our knees a laurel branch, a little bunch of wild flowers, or a string of wild strawberries, like rosy pearls threaded on a blade of grass. These bouquets were thrown by the little beggar boys and girls, who ran barefoot after the coach over the sharp stones: this fashion of begging alms by first bestowing a present has a touch of nobility and poetry.

The landscape was charming, a little Swiss perhaps, with a great variety of scenery. Rounded hills, between which could be seen still higher ranges, curved up on each side of our way: their slopes, patterned with various crops and wooded with evergreen oaks, formed a strong contrast with the misty mountain-tops in the distance; villages with red-tiled roofs bloomed at the foot of the mountains among masses of trees, and every moment I expected to see some Kätli or Gretli come forth from these newfangled chalets. Fortunately, Spain does not carry musical comedy to these lengths.

Torrents advance and retire like capricious women, forming little waterfalls, dividing and meeting again among the rocks and pebbles in the most diverting fashion, and serving as a pretext for a host of bridges as picturesque as could be seen. These bridges, which are infinite in number, are of a singular character; their arches are hollowed out almost as high as the balustrade, in such a way that the road along which the coach passes seems to be no more than six inches thick; a sort of triangular pier generally stands in the middle, forming a bastion; the functions of a bridge in Spain are not very tiring; there could be no more perfect sinecure; for three-quarters of the year one can stroll about underneath it; it stands there, imperturbably calm, with a patience worthy of a better fate, waiting for a river, for a trickle of water, or even for a little moisture; for it knows that its arches are nothing but arcades, and that their title of bridge is a piece of pure flattery. The torrents I mentioned just now are at the outside four or five inches deep, but that is enough to make a deal of noise, and serves to give life to the solitudes through which they pass. At long intervals, they perhaps turn a mill or a factory, by means of weirs built as if on purpose for landscape-painters; the houses which are scattered about the country-side in little groups are a strange colour: they are neither black, white nor yellow: they are the colour of a roast turkey, like the houses of MM. Feuchères, Sechan, Dieterle and Desplechin in the staging of *La Tarentule*; groups of trees and patches of evergreen oaks set off to advantage the great lines of the mountains and the misty austerity of their tones. We lay great stress upon these trees, for nothing is so rare in Spain, and from this point onwards we shall hardly have occasion to describe any.

We changed mules at Oyarzun, and arrived at nightfall at the village of Astigarraga, where we were to sleep; we had not yet come in contact with the Spanish inn; the picaresque and creepy-crawly descriptions in *Don Quixote* and *Lazarillo de Tormes* returned to our minds, and the very thought made our whole bodies itch. We expected to find omelettes adorned with hairs dating from Merovingian days, mixed with feathers and claws, gammons of rancid bacon with all the bristles on them, equally suitable for making soup or for cleaning shoes; wine in goatskins, like the one which the good knight of La Mancha slashed so furiously; or, what is worse, we even expected to find nothing at all, and trembled lest we might have nothing to partake of save the cool of the evening, and have to sup, like the valiant Don Sancho, off a tune on the mandolin, with nothing to wash it down.

Profiting by what little daylight was left, we went and looked at the church, which, to tell the truth, was more like a fortress than a place of worship: the tiny windows pierced in it like loop-holes, the thickness of the walls, the solid buttresses, gave it a robust, four-square attitude which was rather warlike than pensive. This style was often repeated in the churches of Spain. All round it extended a kind of open cloister, in which was hanging a bell of sturdy dimensions, which is rung by moving the tongue with a rope, instead of pealing this enormous mass of metal.

When they took us to our rooms, we were dazzled by the whiteness of the bed and window-curtains, the Dutch cleanliness of the floors, and the care taken over every detail. Big, handsome, well-set-up girls, with magnificent braids falling over their shoulders, perfectly dressed, and bearing no resemblance to the slatterns we had expected, were coming and going with an activity auguring well for our supper, which was not long in coming; it was excellent and very well served. At the risk of appearing over-minute, we shall give a description of it; for the difference between one people and another consists precisely in these thousands of tiny details, neglected by travellers for the sake of high considerations of poetry and politics, which one can very well write about without going to the country.

First they serve a meat soup, differing from ours by its tinge of red, due to the saffron with which it is powdered in order to give it a colour. Here is local colour for you at once—red soup! The bread is very white and very close, with a smooth, light, slightly golden crust; to a Parisian palate, it is decidedly salt. The forks have turned-back handles and flat prongs, cut like the teeth of a comb; the spoons, too, have a spatulate shape unlike our plate. Their linen is a sort of coarse damask. As for the wine, we are bound to admit that it was of the finest possible bishop's violet, so thick that it could be cut with a knife, and the decanters which held it lent it no transparency.

After the soup, they brought the *puchero*, an eminently Spanish dish, or rather the only Spanish dish, for it is eaten every day from Irun to Cadiz, and *vice versa*. The following ingredients go to make up a good, comfortable *puchero*: the haunch of a cow, a piece of mutton, a fowl, a few ends of sausage of the kind known as *chorizo*, stuffed with pepper, *pimiento* and other spices, slices of fat bacon and ham, and over all a strongly flavoured sauce of tomatoes and saffron: so much for the animal part. The vegetable part, known as *verdura*, varies according to the season; but cabbage and *garbanzos* are always the basis of it; the *garbanzo* is almost unknown in Paris, and we cannot define it better than by saying that it is a pea with an only too successful ambition to be a bean. All these ingredients are served up in different dishes, but one mixes them on one's plate in such a way as to produce a most complicated mayonnaise, which tastes very good; this mixture will appear somewhat uncivilized to those gourmets who read Carême, Brillat-Savarin, Grimod de la Reynière and M. de Cussy; yet none the less it has its charm, and pantheists and eclectics ought to like it. Next come chickens fried in oil, for butter is unknown in Spain, fried fish— trout or haddock—roast lamb, asparagus and salad; and for dessert, little macaroons, almonds roasted in the pan and exquisitely flavoured goat's-milk cheese—*queso de Burgos*, which has a great, and sometimes deserved, reputation. At the end, they bring on a tray with wine of Malaga, sherry and a brandy, or *aguardiente*, which is like French *anisette*; and a little bowl (*fuego*), full of glowing charcoal, to light the cigarettes. This meal, with a few unimportant differences, is to be found invariably in every part of Spain...

We left Astigarraga in the middle of the night; as there was no moon, there is naturally a gap in our narrative; we passed through Ernani, a village whose name calls up the most romantic memories; but we saw there nothing but heaps of hovels and ruins vaguely outlined in the darkness. We passed Tolosa without stopping, but noticed houses adorned with frescoes, and gigantic escutcheons carved in stone: it was market-day, and the market-place was covered with asses and mules in their picturesque harness, and peasants with strange, wild faces.

After much driving up hill and down dale, crossing torrents by stone bridges without mortar, we at last arrived at Vergara, the place where we were to dine, with great satisfaction, for we had lost all memory of the *jicara de chocolate* swallowed at the inn at Astigarraga while we were still half asleep.

A Country Inn

IV. Vergara to Burgos

AT Vergara, which is the place where the treaty between Espartero and Maroto was concluded, I first caught sight of a Spanish priest. His appearance struck me as rather grotesque, though, thank God, I have no Voltairian ideas with regard to the clergy; but in spite of myself Beaumarchais' travesty of Basile came into my mind. Imagine a black cassock, a cloak of the same colour, and, to crown all, an immense, prodigious, phenomenal, hyperbolic and titanic hat, of which no epithet, however swelling and gigantic, can give even a slight approximation to an idea. This hat was at least three feet long; the brim rolled upwards, forming a sort of horizontal roof before and behind the head. It would be difficult to invent a stranger and more fantastic shape; but, on the whole, it did not prevent the worthy priest's costume from being most venerable, and he walked with the air of one whose conscience is perfectly at rest as to the shape of his head-gear; instead of bands, he wore a little blue and white collar (*alzacuello*) like the priests in Belgium.

After Mondragón, which is the last small village—or, as they say in Spain, the last *pueblo*—in the province of Guipúzcoa, we entered the province of Alava, and it was not long before we found ourselves at the foot of the mountain of Salinas. A switchback is nothing by comparison; and when you are first faced with it, the idea that a carriage can drive up seems just as absurd as that of walking about head downwards on the ceiling, like a fly. But the miracle was effected, thanks to six oxen which were harnessed to the coach in front of the ten mules. Never in my life have I heard such an uproar: the *mayoral*, the *zagal*, the *escopeteros*, the postillion and the driver of the oxen vied with one another in shouting, in abusing one another, in cracking whips and in goading on the team; they pushed at the rims of the wheels, supported the body of the coach from behind, tugged at the mules' halters and the horns of the oxen with incredible fire and fury. The coach produced the most astonishing effect imaginable at the end of this interminable string of animals and men. There were at least fifty feet between the first and last beasts of the team. We should not forget to mention, in passing, the church-tower of Salinas, which is of rather a taking Saracenic shape.

If one looks backwards from the top of this mountain, one sees the different ranges of the Pyrenees rising above each other in endless vistas; one might compare them to immense draperies of striped velvet, thrown down at random and crumpled into fantastic folds by the whim of some Titan. At Royave, a little farther on, I observed a magnificent effect of light. Standing out against a sky of lapis lazuli, so dark as to be almost black, there suddenly appeared a snow-covered crest (*sierra nevada*) which we had been unable to see before, owing to the proximity of the mountains there. Soon, every time we crossed the edge of a plateau, fresh mountains inquiringly raised their snow-laden heads, bathed in cloud. This snow was not compact, but divided into narrow veins, like the silver threads in a tinsel gauze, and the contrast with the azure and lilac tints of the precipices made it seem even whiter. The cold was piercing enough, and became more and more intense as we went on. The wind had not gained much warmth by caressing the pale cheeks of these fair but chilly virgins, and came to us as icy as if it were blowing straight off the Arctic or the Antarctic. We wrapped ourselves in our cloaks as impenetrably as possible, for it is most humiliating to have one's nose frost-bitten in a torrid country; grilling is more admissible.

The sun was sinking as we entered Vittoria: the coach drove through all sorts of streets of poorly built houses in a gloomy style, and stopped at the *parador viejo*, where our luggage was thoroughly examined. It was our daguerreotype camera which caused the worthy Customs officials the greatest uneasiness; they would not go near it without taking infinite precautions, like people who were afraid of being blown up; I believe they took it for an electric machine; we took care not to undo this salutary idea.

As soon as our belongings had been examined, and our passports stamped, we were free to disperse ourselves about the cobble-stones of the town. We at once took advantage of our liberty, and, crossing a rather fine square surrounded by arcades, we went straight to the church; it was already filling with shadow, which accumulated in a mysterious, threatening way in dark corners, where one could vaguely distinguish a few phantom forms. The yellow flames of a few small lamps flickered in a sinister way and gleamed through the smoke like stars in a fog. A chill as of the tomb crept over my skin, and I was seized by a slight sensation of fear, when I heard a lamentable voice quite close to me murmur the consecrated formula: *Caballero, una limosna, por amor de Dios* (For the love of God, Sir, an alms); it was a poor devil of a wounded soldier begging for charity. For the soldiers do beg here, a fact excused by their abject poverty, for they are most irregularly paid. It was in the church at Vittoria that I made the acquaintance of those dreadful coloured wood-carvings which the Spaniards use to such strange excess.

After a supper (*cena*) which caused us to regret the one we had had at Astigarraga, the idea of going to the theatre came into our heads; as we drove up, our interest had been whetted by a high-flown notice announcing an extraordinary performance by some French Herculeses, ending with a certain *baile nacional* (national dance), which seemed to us big with promise of cachuchas, boleros, fandangos and other frenzied dances.

The theatres in Spain have as a rule no distinctive front, and are only differentiated from the other houses by two or three smoky lamps hanging up over the door. We took two orchestra stalls, called *asientos de luneta*, and plunged bravely into a passage of which the floor had neither planks nor tiles, but was made of plain, natural earth. They are scarcely more particular about the walls of passages than they are about those of public buildings bearing the notice: "Commit no nuisance, under pain of a fine." But by holding our noses tightly, we arrived at our places only half stifled. Add to this that smoking goes on incessantly between the acts, and your idea of a Spanish theatre will not be a very fragrant one.

However, the inside is more comfortable than the approach would lead one to expect; the boxes are fairly well-placed, and though the decorations are very simple, they are fresh and clean. The *asientos de luneta* are numbered arm-chairs standing in a row; there is no attendant at the door to take your tickets, but a little boy comes and asks you for them before the end of the performance; all they take from you at the outer door is a check giving you the right of entrance.

We hoped to find here the Spanish feminine type, of which we had so far met with but few examples; but the women who filled the boxes and galleries had nothing Spanish about them but their fans and mantillas; this was a good deal, it is true, but it was hardly enough. The audience was chiefly composed of soldiers, as in all towns where there is a garrison. They stand up in the pit, as in quite primitive theatres. If it had had a row of candles and a snuffer, the resemblance to the Hôtel de Bourgogne would have been complete; but the lamp-glasses were made of strips of glass arranged like the sections of a melon, and held together at the top by a ring of tin, which does not point to a very advanced state of industrial development. The orchestra was composed of a single row of musicians, almost all playing brass instruments; they kept lustily blaring out the same refrain from their cornets, reminding us of Franconi's fanfare.

Our Herculean compatriots lifted heavy weights and twisted a number of iron bars, to the great satisfaction of the assembly, and the lighter of them mounted on the tight rope, with other feats which are, alas, too well known in Paris, but were probably new to the population of Vittoria. We were fuming with impatience in our stalls, and I polished up the lens of my opera-glass with furious energy so as to lose nothing of the *baile nacional*. At last they took down the trestles, and the Turkish attendants carried off the weights and all the apparatus of the Herculeses. You can well imagine, friendly reader, the impassioned suspense of two enthusiastic and romantic young Frenchmen, about to witness a Spanish dance, in Spain, for the first time.

At last the curtain rose upon a scene which had some ineffectual aspirations towards the fairylike and enchanting; the cornets blared out the above-mentioned flourish more furiously than ever, and the *baile nacional* stepped forward, in the shape of a dancer and his lady, both armed with castanets.

I have never seen anything sadder and more lamentable than these two great ruins who "failed to console each other": never has this twopenny-halfpenny theatre seen upon its worm-eaten boards such a worn-out, broken-down, toothless, blear-eyed, bald and ruinous pair; the poor woman was plastered with a common white cosmetic, giving her a sky-blue tinge suggestive to the imagination of such anacreontic analogies as a corpse which had died of cholera, or a drowned man who was not keeping very well; the two red patches which she had dabbed on to her high, projecting cheek-bones, in order to add radiance to her lustreless, fishy eyes, made a most singular contrast with this blue; in her veined and skinny hands she shook a pair of cracked castanets, which clattered like the teeth of a fever-patient, or the joints of a moving skeleton. From time to time, by a desperate effort, she tightened the flabby muscles of her knees, and managed to lift her poor old leg, proportioned like a baluster, so as to produce a nervous little caper, like a dead frog under the stimulus of the voltaic battery, and make the copper sequins on the dubious rag which served her as a skirt quiver and flash for an instant. As for the man, he frisked about in his corner in a sinister fashion; he raised himself up, then flopped down again like a bat crawling about on the stumps of its wings; his face was that of a gravedigger at his own funeral: his brow, wrinkled like a hussar's boot, his nose like a parrot's beak, his cheeks like a goat's, gave him a most fantastic appearance, and if he had carried a Gothic rebeck in his hands, instead of castanets, he might have posed as the leader in that Dance of Death which we see on the frescoes at Basel.

They did not once look at each other throughout the whole dance; one might have thought that they were mutually afraid of their own ugliness, and feared to burst into tears at the sight of each other, so old they were, so decrepit and funereal. The man, in particular, fled from his partner as if she had been a spider, and a quiver of horror seemed to convulse his aged parchment-like face each time some figure of the dance forced him to go near her. This macabre bolero lasted five or six minutes until the fall of the curtain put an end to our torture and that of these poor wretches.

Such was the first appearance of the bolero to two poor travellers enamoured of local colour. Spanish dances exist only in Paris, like sea-shells, which are only to be found in curiosity shops, and never at the sea-side. O Fanny Elssler! You who are now in America among the savages! Even before our visit to Spain, we were quite sure it was you who invented the cachucha!

We went to bed in some disappointment. In the middle of the night they came and woke us up, and made us resume our journey; it was still bitterly cold, with a temperature like that of Siberia, explained by the altitude of the plateau we were crossing and the snows with which we were surrounded. At Miranda, our luggage was once again examined, and we entered Old Castile, *Castilla la Vieja*, the Kingdom of Castile and Leon, symbolized by a lion holding a shield covered with castles. These lions, which occur so often that one grows tired of them, are usually carved in greyish granite, and have rather an imposing and heraldic air.

Between Ameyugo and Cubo, insignificant little villages at which one changes horses, the scenery is extremely picturesque; the mountains crowd one upon the other, drawing closer and closer together, and immense perpendicular crags, as precipitous as any cliff, rise from the edge of the road; on the left a torrent, crossed by a bridge with a truncated Gothic arch, seethes in the depths of a ravine, turning a mill, and splashing the stones which bar its course with foam; that nothing may be wanting to complete the effect, a Gothic church, crumbling into ruin, rises amid the rocks, with a tumble-down roof and walls covered with an embroidery of parasitic plants; in the background is the vague bluish outline of the Sierra. This view is fine, no doubt, but the pass of Pancorbo surpasses it in strangeness and grandeur. The rocks barely leave room for the road to pass, and one comes to a spot where two great masses of granite, inclined towards each other, form, as it were, an arch of some gigantic bridge, severed in the middle in order to bar the road before some army of Titans; another and smaller arch, hollowed through the rock, adds still further to the illusion. No theatrical decorator has ever imagined a more picturesque or better-planned scene; when one is used to the flat vistas of the plains, the surprising effects which one comes upon in the mountains at every turn strike one as fabulous and impossible.

The inn at which they stop for dinner had a stable as its ante-room. This architectural arrangement recurs invariably in all Spanish inns, and in order to reach one's room one has to go past the hind quarters of the mules. The wine was even blacker than usual, and had, moreover, a certain tang of goatskin which was more or less local. The servant-girls at the inn wore their hair hanging down to the middle of their backs; except for this, their dress was that of Frenchwomen of the lower classes. Generally speaking, the national dress has only survived in Andalusia, and there are now but few ancient costumes in Castile. As for the men, they all wore the pointed hat, edged with velvet and with silk pompons, or else a wolfskin cap with a rather wild-looking outline, with the inevitable snuff- or soot-coloured cloak. For the rest, their faces had nothing characteristic about them.

Between Pancorbo and Burgos, we came upon three or four half-ruined little villages, as dry as pumice-stone, and the colour of toasted bread, such as Briviesca, Castel de Peones and Quitanapalla. I should doubt whether Decamps ever found walls more thoroughly baked, scorched, browned, rough-grained, brittle and scratched than these in the heart of Asia Minor. Along these walls browsed a few donkeys, very much like Turkish asses, which he really ought to go and study. The Turkish ass is a fatalist, and one can see from his humble, contemplative air that he is resigned to all the blows that fate has in store for him and will bear them without complaint. The Castilian ass has a more philosophical and deliberate appearance; he understands that he is indispensable; he is one of the family, he has read *Don Quixote*, he boasts his descent in the direct line from Sancho Panza's famous grey ass. Side by side with the asses were also straying some pure-blooded dogs of a magnificent breed, perfect in the feet, loins and head, among them some tall, beautiful finely-built greyhounds in the style of Paolo Veronese and Velasquez; not to mention a few dozen *muchachos* or ragamuffins who had eyes sparkling like black diamonds, for all their rags.

Old Castile is doubtless so called from the great number of old women whom one meets there: and such old women! The witches in *Macbeth*, crossing the heath of Dunsinane on their way to brew their hell-broth, are charming young girls by comparison: the vile harpies of Goya's *Caprichos*, which I had hitherto taken for nightmare figures and monstrous figments of the imagination, are simply portraits of appalling truthfulness; most of these old women have beards like mouldy cheese and moustaches like grenadiers; and as for their clothes, you should only scc them! One might take a piece of stuff and work for ten years at soiling it, wearing it threadbare, making holes in it, patching it, and fading its original colour, without achieving such a sublimation of rags and tatters! These charms are enhanced by a wild, savage look quite unlike the humble, piteous bearing of the poor in France.

Shortly before we arrived at Burgos, a great building was pointed out to us on a hill in the distance; this was the Cartuja de Miraflores (a Carthusian convent), of which we shall have occasion to speak in more detail later; soon afterwards, the cathedral spires began to outline their fretted edges more and more distinctly against the sky; half an hour later we entered the ancient capital of Old Castile.

The *plaza* of Burgos, in the midst of which rises rather a poor bronze statue of Charles III, is spacious and not lacking in character. It is enclosed on every side by red houses, supported upon pillars of bluish granite. All sorts of little booths are set up under the arcades and in the *plaza*, and through it wander endless numbers of asses, mules and picturesque peasants. The rags of Castile appear here in all their glory. The most humble beggar drapes himself in his cloak as nobly as a Roman emperor in his purple. I can find no better comparison for these cloaks, both in colour and consistency, than that of great ragged-edged pieces of tinder. The cloak of Don Cesar de Bazan, in the play *Ruy Blas*, is nothing to these flaunting, triumphant rags! They are so worn, so dry, and so inflammable, that one feels it to be imprudent for the wearers to smoke, or strike their flint and steel. Even the little children of six and eight have their cloaks, which they wear with ineffable gravity There was one poor little devil, whom I cannot recall without laughing, who had nothing but the collar of a cloak left, which hardly covered his shoulders; but he draped himself in imaginary folds with such a comically piteous air that he would have drawn a smile from the very incarnation of hypochondria. The convicts condemned to the *presidio*, or hard labour, sweep and scavenge the town without taking off the rags in which they drape themselves. These cloaked convicts are quite the most amazing ruffians one could see. Each time they ply their brooms, they go and sit or lie on some door-step. It would be perfectly easy for them to escape; but when I mentioned this point, the answer was that their natural goodness prevented it.

The inn at which we alighted was a real Spanish *fonda* in which nobody understood a word of French; we were forced to bring forward our Castilian, and make our throats raw with choking over the abominable *jota* (j), a guttural, Arabic sound which does not exist in our language; and I am bound to say that, thanks to the extreme intelligence which distinguishes this people, they understood us fairly well; they did, indeed, sometimes bring us candles when we asked for water, or chocolate when we wanted ink; but apart from these perfectly venial blunders, it all went off as well as possible; the servants at the inn were a troop of dishevelled slatterns with the loveliest names imaginable: Casilda, Matilde, Balbina; names are always charming in Spain: Lola, Bibiana, Pepa, Hilaria, Carmen, Cipriana serve as labels to the most unpoetical creatures one could possibly see; one of these girls had hair of the most violent red, a colour very frequent in Spain, where, in spite of the general ideas to the contrary, there are many fair women, and, above all, many with auburn hair.

They do not put a twig of blessed box in the bedrooms here, but great palm-shaped branches, plaited, interlaced and twisted with great elegance and care. The beds have no bolster, but two flat pillows placed one upon the other; they are usually very hard, though made of good wool; but they are not in the habit of carding their mattresses, they only turn the wool over and over with the ends of two sticks.

Opposite our windows we had rather a curious shop-sign belonging to a master of surgery, who had had himself painted with one of his pupils, sawing the arm off a poor devil sitting on a chair; and we could see the shop of a barber, who, I vow, bore no resemblance whatever to Figaro. Through the glass windows we could see the gleam of quite a well-polished brass shaving-bowl, which Don Quixote, if he were in this world, might easily have taken for the helmet of Mambrin. Though Spanish barbers have lost their costume, they have retained their skill, and shave you with great dexterity.

For a town which has been for so long past the first city in Castile, Burgos has not preserved a very Gothic appearance; with the exception of one street, in which one finds a few windows and porticoes of the period of the Renaissance, with escutcheons and supporters, the houses hardly go back beyond the beginning of the seventeenth century, and have only the most common appearance; they are antiquated without being antique. But Burgos has its cathedral, which is one of the finest in the world: unfortunately, like all Gothic cathedrals, it is wedged in a mass of mean buildings, which prevent one from appreciating it as a whole and obtaining an impression of its size. The principal entrance opens on a *plaza* with a pretty fountain rising in the middle of it, on top of which is an exquisite white marble figure of Christ, a target for all the ragamuffins of the city, whose most cherished pastime is throwing stones at sculpture. The doorway is magnificent, with ornaments as rich, as intricate, and as florid as lace-work; but unfortunately it was scraped and planed, up to the level of the first frieze, by some Italian prelates with a taste for simple architecture, sober walls and ornaments in "good taste," who desired to adapt the cathedral to the Roman taste, and had the deepest pity for those poor barbarous architects who were not great exponents of the Corinthian order, and appeared unaware of the charm of the Attic style or the triangular pediment. Many people are still of this opinion in Spain, where the *Messidor* style flourishes in all its purity, and prefer to the most perfect and richly sculptured Gothic churches all kinds of abominable buildings pierced with many windows and adorned with Paestumnian columns, just as they did in France, before the Romantic school restored the Middle Ages to honour, and revealed the meaning and beauty of the cathedrals. Two finely pointed spires with a fretted outline, punched out, as it were, into open-work, scalloped and embroidered, covered with sculptures down to the smallest detail, like the setting of a ring, soar up to God with all the ardour of faith and all the aspiration of an unshakable conviction. Our unbelieving towers would not dare to risk themselves in the heavens with nothing to support them but a lacework of stone and ribs as slender as a cobweb. Another tower, less lofty, but also carved with unimaginable richness, marks the spot at which the arms of the cross meet, and completes the magnificence of the design. An innumerable host of statues of saints, archangels, kings and monks gives animation to the whole structure; and this stone population is so numerous, so crowded and so swarming, that it surely exceeds the population of flesh and blood which occupies the town.

Thanks to the charming courtesy of the political leader Don Henrique de Vedia, we were able to visit the cathedral in the minutest detail. An octavo volume of description, an atlas with two thousand plates, twenty rooms full of plaster casts, would not be enough to give a complete idea of this prodigious flower of Gothic art, more thickly-clustering and intricate than the virgin forests of Brazil. We shall be forgiven a few omissions and negligences, for we have only been able to write a mere letter, hastily scrawled on the corner of a table at the inn.

At the very first step which one takes in the church, one is arrested by an incomparable masterpiece, as if a hand had grasped one by the collar: this is the carved wooden door leading to the cloister; among the bas-reliefs is one representing the entry of Our Lord into Jerusalem; the door-posts and metal-work are loaded with delightful little figures, so gracefully formed, and of such delicacy, that one cannot understand how such a lifeless, opaque material as wood can have lent itself to such a wayward, spiritual fantasy. Surely it is the finest door in the world, after that of the Baptistery at Florence, by Ghiberti, which Michelangelo, who understood such matters, thought worthy to be the gate of Paradise. Such a splendid page should be modelled and cast in bronze, to ensure to it such immortality as man is able to command.

The choir, containing the stalls, which they call *silleria*, is closed by a grille of hammered ironwork, wrought with a skill that passes belief; the stone floor, as is usual in Spain, is covered with immense pieces of esparto-grass matting, besides which, every stall has its carpet of dried grass or rushes. On raising one's head, one perceives a sort of dome formed by the inside of the tower which we have already mentioned; it is a giddy abyss of sculptures, arabesques, statues, miniature columns, ribs, lancets and pendentives. One might look at it for two years without seeing everything. It clusters as thickly as a cabbage, and is open-worked like a fish slice; gigantic as a pyramid, yet delicate as a woman's ear-ring, one cannot imagine how such filigree-work can remain suspended in the air throughout the centuries! What men were these, who achieved such marvellous constructions, unsurpassed by the sumptuous prodigality of a fairy palace? Is their race extinct? And can it be that, with all our boasted civilization, we are in reality nothing but degenerate barbarians? My heart is wrung with a profound melancholy when I examine one of these prodigious edifices of the past: I am seized by a vast discouragement, and my only remaining aspiration is to retire into a corner, lay a stone beneath my head, and wait, in contemplative immobility, for death whose immobility is absolute. What use is it to work or to bestir oneself? Human effort, however intense, will never surpass these men. And yet the names of these divine artists are unknown; and if we would find some trace of them, we must search the dusty archives of the monasteries. When I think that I have spent the best part of my life in making ten or twelve thousand verses, in writing six or seven poor octavo volumes and three or four hundred bad articles in the newspapers, and that this has made me tired, I am ashamed of myself and of my age, in which such efforts are needed to produce so little. What is a flimsy sheet of paper compared with a granite mountain?

If you will join us in making the round of this immense madrepore, built by the prodigious human polypi of the fourteenth and fifteenth centuries, we will begin with the Little Sacristy, a spacious enough hall in spite of its name, which contains an *Ecce Homo*, a *Christ upon the Cross* by Murillo, and a *Nativity* by Jordaens, in a richly carved wooden frame; in the middle of it stands a great brazier for lighting censers, and perhaps cigarettes too, for many Spanish priests smoke, which is no more improper, to our mind, than taking snuff, an enjoyment which the French clergy do not scruple to permit themselves. The brazier is a great brass bowl standing on a tripod, filled with glowing charcoal or burning fruit kernels covered with fine ash, to form a slow fire. In Spain the brazier takes the place of fire-places, which are rare.

In the Great Sacristy, beside the little one, can be noticed a *Christ upon the Cross* by Domenico Theotocopuli, called El Greco, an extravagant and singular painter, whose pictures might be taken for sketches by Titian, if they were not easily recognizable by a certain affectation of angularity and violent negligence. In order to give his paintings the appearance of being executed with great energy of touch, he occasionally throws on to the canvas touches of incredible impetuosity and brutality, with slender, steely lights gleaming through the shadows like sabre-blades: all this does not prevent El Greco from being a great painter; the fine works of his second manner have a great resemblance to the romantic pictures of Eugène Delacroix. You have no doubt seen at the Spanish Museum in Paris the portrait of El Greco's daughter, a magnificent head which no master would disown, and you can judge what an admirable painter Domenico Theotocopuli must have been when he was in his sober senses; it appears that his anxiety to avoid any resemblance with Titian, whose pupil he is alleged to have been, deranged his brain, and forced him into these extravagances and caprices, through which the magnificent faculties with which he was endowed by nature are only able to shine in intermittent flashes; El Greco was also an architect and a sculptor, that sublime trinity and brilliant triangle which is often to be found in the firmament of the highest art. This sacristy is surrounded with cupboards formed in the panelling, having columns adorned with flowers and garlands in the richest of styles; above the panelling runs a row of Venetian mirrors, the use of which I am at a loss to explain, unless they are there purely for ornament, since they are placed too high for one to be able to see oneself in them; above the mirrors, the oldest of which are touching the vaulting, are ranged the portraits of all the bishops of Burgos in chronological order, from the first of them to the one who at present occupies the episcopal throne. Although these portraits are painted in oils, they have the appearance of pastel or tempera; for in Spain pictures are not varnished, and owing to the neglect of this precaution we have to regret the loss of many masterpieces, destroyed by the damp. Though these portraits are for the most part in the grand style, they are not paintings of the highest merit; besides, they are hung too high for one to be able to judge the merit of their execution. The middle of the hall is occupied by an enormous buffet and some immense baskets of woven grass, in which are ranged the church ornaments and the utensils used in celebrating divine service; two branches of coral, far less complicated in their ramifications than the simplest arabesque in the cathedral, are preserved as curiosities in a pair of glass cases; the door is embellished with the arms of Burgos carved in relief, and powdered with little red crosses.

The hall of Juan Cuchiller, through which we next pass, has nothing remarkable about it architecturally, and we were just hurrying out of it, when we were asked to raise our heads and look at a most curious sight. It was a great coffer, held to the wall by iron clamps. A more crumbling, worm-eaten and patched-up chest would be hard to imagine; it must surely be the patriarch of all the trunks in the world. But it has an inscription in black letters, running as follows: *Cofre del Cid*: which, as you can imagine, at once gives a vast importance to these four planks of mouldy wood. If we are to believe the chroniclers, this is the very chest which the famous Ruy Diaz de Vibar, better known under the name of the Cid Campeador, had filled with sand and stones, when, hero though he was, he was as short of money as a mere man of letters; he carried it as surety to an honest Jewish usurer, who lent money on goods left in pawn, but forbade him to open the mysterious chest until he, the Cid Campeador, had returned the sum borrowed. Which proves that the usurers of that time were of a more accommodating nature than those of today. Nowadays one would find few Jews, or even Christians, either simple-minded or kind-hearted enough to accept such a pledge. M. Casimir Delavigne made use of this legend in his play *La Fille du Cid*, but he has replaced the chest by a tiny box, which could contain no more than "the gold of the Cid's word"; and no Jew, not even one of the heroic age, would lend anything on such a little comfit-box: the historic chest is large, broad, heavy and adorned with every kind of lock and padlock; when full of sand, it must have taken at least six horses to move it, and the worthy Israelite might have supposed it to be full of clothing, jewels or plate, and so resigned himself more easily to the Cid's caprice a caprice foreseen by the penal code, like many other heroic imaginings. So, with all deference to M. Anténor Joly, the staging at the Théâtre de la Renaissance is incorrect.

V. Burgos

ON leaving the hall of Juan Cuchiller, one enters another apartment decorated in a very picturesque style; oak panelling, red hangings and a ceiling in a sort of Cordova leather, producing a very good effect; in this apartment are to be seen a finely painted *Nativity* by Murillo, a *Conception*, and a robed picture of Christ.

The cloister is full of tombs, most of them enclosed by very strong, close gratings; they are all tombs of illustrious persons, hollowed out in the thickness of the wall, and embellished with coats of arms and rich carving. On one of them I noticed a most beautiful group of Mary and Jesus holding a book in his hand, and a chimera, half animal, half arabesque, the figment of a most curious and astonishing imagination. On all the tombs lie life-sized statues of knights in armour or robed bishops, which, through the meshes of their gratings, might easily be mistaken for the dead men whom they represent, so lifelike are their attitudes and so minute their detail.

As I passed by, I noticed on a door-post a charming little statue of the Virgin, of exquisite workmanship and extraordinary boldness of conception; instead of the modest, contrite air generally given to the Blessed Virgin, the sculptor has represented her with an expression in which sensuous pleasure is mingled with ecstasy, in the transports of a woman conceiving a God. She stands there with head thrown back, drawing in with her whole soul and body the ray of flame breathed out by the symbolic dove, ardour and purity being blended with a rare originality; it was hard to find a novel treatment of a subject so oft-repeated, but to genius nothing is trite.

A description of this cloister alone would demand a whole letter; but since we are able to dispose of so little space and time, you will pardon us if we say only these few words, and then return to the church, where we shall choose at random, to right or to left, the first masterpieces that present themselves, without selection or preference; for everything is fine, everything is wonderful, and the things we do not speak about are at least as good as the things about which we shall speak.

We will first pause before that Passion of Jesus Christ, carved in stone by Philip of Burgundy, who is unfortunately not a French artist, as his name, or rather his nickname, would lead one to suppose. This is one of the greatest bas-reliefs in the world; according to the custom of Gothic art, it is divided into several compartments, the Garden of Olives, the Bearing of the Cross, the Crucifixion between the two thieves, an immense composition which, in the fineness of its heads and its exquisite detail, is equal to the softest and most delicate works painted by the miniaturist's brush of Albert Dürer, Memling or Holbein; this epic in stone is completed by a magnificent Descent into the Tomb; the groups of sleeping apostles which fill the lower panels of the Garden of Olives are almost as fine and pure in style as the prophets and saints of Fra Bartolommeo; the heads of the holy women at the foot of the Cross have a pathetic and mournful expression of which none but Gothic artists possessed the secret. This expression is here united to a rare beauty of form; the soldiers are remarkable for those strange, savage accoutrements lent by the Middle Ages to Jewish or Eastern personages of antiquity with whose costume they were unacquainted; they have, moreover, a bold, swaggering bearing which is in the happiest contrast with the idealized melancholy of the other figures; the whole is set in an architectural frame of incredible taste and delicacy, wrought with the elaboration of goldsmith's work. This sculpture was completed in 1336.

And since we are talking about carving, let us at once mention the choir-stalls, a wonderful piece of woodwork which is perhaps without its equal in the whole world. The stalls are so many marvels; they represent in bas-relief subjects from the Old Testament, and are separated from one another by fabulous monsters and fantastic beasts forming the arms of the chairs. The flat surfaces are formed of inlaid work enhanced with engraved lines in black, like niello-work on metal: caprice and arabesque have never been carried further. We find in them an inexhaustible vein of inspiration, an unexampled richness, an unflagging invention both in form and idea; it is a new world, a creation in itself, as rich and complete as that of God, in which plants are alive, men blossom into flowers, a branch ends in a hand, or a leg in foliage; where a chimera with cunning eye spreads out its wings armed with claws and a monstrous dolphin spouts water from its nostrils. An inextricable entanglement of floral motives, foliage, acanthus-plants and lotuses, of flowers whose cups are adorned with crests and spirals, of fretted, contorted foliage, of fabulous birds, impossible fish, and extravagant sirens and dragons of which no words can give an idea. The wildest fantasy reigns in all these inlaid ornaments, whose yellow tones, on a background of dark wood, give them the appearance of Etruscan vase paintings, which is borne out by the bold and primitive character of the line. These designs, in which the pagan genius of the Renaissance peeps out, have no relation to the use for which the stalls are destined; at times, even, the choice of subject displays an entire disregard of the sanctity of the spot. Here are children playing with masks, dancing women, gladiators wrestling, peasants at the vintage, young girls teasing or caressing a fantastical monster, animals plucking at the harp, and even little boys imitating in the basin of a fountain the famous Brussels Mannekenpis. With a little more slenderness of proportion, these figures would be equal to the purest Etruscan; unity of the whole, with infinite variety in detail: such is the difficult problem of which the artists of the Middle Ages almost always found a happy solution. From a distance of five or six paces, this woodwork, for all its extravagance of execution, is grave, solemn, architectural, sober-hued and altogether worthy to serve as a frame for the pale, austere faces of the canons.

The Chapel of the Constable, *Capilla del Condestable*, is a complete church in itself; the tomb of Don Pedro Fernandez Velasco, Constable of Castile, and his wife, occupy the middle of it, and are not its least ornament: these tombs are in white marble, and of magnificent workmanship. The male figure lies in his battle armour, enriched with arabesques in the best style, of which the sacristans take rubbings on damped paper which they sell to travellers; the woman has her little dog at her side; her gloves, and the flowered pattern of her brocaded robe, are rendered with unspeakable delicacy. The heads of the pair rest upon marble cushions, adorned with their coronets and armorial bearings: gigantic coats of arms decorate the walls of this chapel, and on the entablature are figures bearing stone staves for holding banners and standards. The retable (for so they call the architectural façades which accompany altars) is carved, gilt, painted, and varied by arabesques and columns, and represents the Circumcision of Jesus Christ, with life-size figures. To the right, on which side is the portrait of Doña Mencia de Mendoza, Countess of Haro, is a little Gothic altar, illuminated, gilt, sculptured and embellished with an infinite number of tiny figures, which might be by Antonin Moine, so light and dainty are their lines; upon this altar is a Christ of jet. The high altar is adorned with sheets of silver and crystal suns, the glittering reflections of which form a play of light of extraordinary brilliance. In the centre of the vault blooms a sculptured rose of incredible delicacy.

In the sacristy beside the chapel, is to be seen, set in the panelling, a Magdalen ascribed to Leonardo da Vinci: the softness of the dusky half-tones, melting into the lights by an imperceptible process of gradation, the light touch with which the hair is painted, and the perfect roundness of the arms, make this supposition quite probable. In this chapel is also preserved the ivory diptych which the Constable used to carry with him on campaign, and before which he used to say his prayers. The *Capilla del Condestable* belongs to the Duque de Frias. As you go by, just glance at the statue of St. Bruno in painted wood, by Pereida, a Portuguese sculptor, and the epitaph, which is that of Villegas, the translator of Dante.

A great staircase of most beautiful design, with magnificent carved chimeras, kept us wondering for a few minutes. I do not know what it led to, nor into what hall the little door opens in which it ends; but it is worthy of the most resplendent palace. The high altar in the chapel of the Duke of Abrantes is one of the strangest inventions that one could see; it represents the genealogical tree of Jesus Christ. This curious idea is carried out in the following manner: the patriarch Abraham is lying at the base of the composition, and into his fruitful breast plunge the branching roots of an immense tree, every branch of which bears an ancestor of Jesus, and is divided up into as many twigs as he has descendants; the summit is occupied by the Blessed Virgin, enthroned on the clouds; the sun, moon and stars, of silver or gold, glint through the blossoms on the boughs. One can hardly think without awe of all the patience required to carve out this leafage, to hollow out these folds, to throw these branches into relief, and make all these figures stand out upon the background. The retable wrought in this fashion is as high as the front of a house, and, with its three tiers, rises to a height of at least thirty feet; the second tier contains a Coronation of the Virgin; and the last a Crucifixion, with St. John and the Virgin. The artist is Rodrigo del Haya, a sculptor who lived in the middle of the sixteenth century.

The Chapel of St. Thecla is the strangest thing imaginable. The architect and the sculptor seem to have made it their object to crowd the greatest number of ornaments into the smallest possible space; they have succeeded perfectly, and I defy the most industrious inventor of adornments to find room in the whole chapel for a single rosette or flower motive. It is bad taste of the richest, most charming and adorable kind: it consists of nothing but twisted columns entwined with vine-stocks, an endless development of volutes and garlands, of cherubim with wings beneath their chins, great foaming clouds, blown flames streaming from vases, rays spread out in a fan, leafy, full-blown rosettes; all gilt and painted in their natural colours with the brush of a miniaturist. The brocaded patterns of the draperies are executed thread by thread, stitch by stitch, with alarming minuteness. The saint, surrounded by the flames of the pyre, which are fed by Saracens in extravagant costumes, raises to heaven her lovely enamelled eyes, holding in her tiny hand, painted the colour of flesh, a large blessed palm curled in the Spanish fashion. The vaulting is wrought in the same fashion. The rest of the chapel is occupied by altars of smaller size, but equal richness: we no longer have the delicacy of the Gothic, nor the charming taste of the Renaissance; purity of line is replaced by elaboration; but is still very lovely, like everything excessive but complete in its kind.

The organ is of formidable proportions, with its batteries of pipes arranged on a horizontal plan, like cannon taking aim, and producing a menacing and bellicose effect. The private chapels have each their organ, but on a smaller scale. In the retable of one of these chapels we saw a painting of such beauty that I am uncertain to what master to ascribe it, unless to Michelangelo; without a doubt, the qualities of the Florentine School at its finest period shine triumphantly in this magnificent picture, which would be the pearl of even the most splendid museum. And yet Michelangelo hardly ever painted in oils, and his pictures are fabulously rare; I should like to believe that it is a composition painted by Sebastiano del Piombo after a cartoon by this sublime artist, and over his outlines. We know that Michelangelo was jealous of Raphael, and sometimes made use of Sebastiano del Piombo so as to unite colour with design and outdo his young rival. However this may be, it is a wonderful picture; the Blessed Virgin, in a seated position and nobly draped, is veiling with a transparent scarf the divine nudity of the little Jesus standing at her side. Two angels absorbed in contemplation float silently in the ultramarine sky; in the background is to be seen an austere landscape, rocks, stretches of country and a few walls. The head of the Virgin has a calm, power and majesty of which words can give no idea. The neck rises from the shoulders in a line of such chaste and noble purity, the figure is instinct with such gentle maternal quietude, the hands are so divinely formed, the feet have such elegance and nobility of style that one cannot take one's eyes from the picture. Add to this marvellous design a simple, vigorous coloration, sustained in tone, with no false chiaroscuro, but with a certain fresco-like character in perfect harmony with the style of the architecture, and you have a masterpiece whose peer will only be found in the schools of Florence or of Rome.

There is also in the Cathedral of Burgos a Holy Family by an unnamed artist, whom I strongly suspect of being Andrea del Sarto, and some Gothic paintings on wood by Cornelis van Eyck, the companions of which are to be found in the Dresden Gallery: pictures of the German school are not rare in Spain, and some of them are of great beauty. We will mention in passing some pictures by Fr. Diego de Leyva, who became a Carthusian monk in the Cartuja of Miraflores at the age of fifty-three: among others the one representing the martyrdom of St. Casilda, whose two breasts have been cut off by the executioner; the blood spurts in great jets from the two red patches left on her bosom by the amputated flesh; the two severed globes lie beside the saint, who is gazing with an expression of feverish, convulsive ecstasy at a great angel with a melancholy, dreaming expression who is bringing her a palm: these terrifying pictures of martyrdom are very numerous in Spain, where love of realism and truthfulness in art is carried to its utmost limits. The painter will not spare you a single drop of blood; one is forced to see the shrinking of the severed muscles, the quivering of the live flesh, with its dark crimson contrasting with the bloodless, blue-tinged white of the skin, the spine cleft by the scimitar of the executioner, the purple weals left by the rods and lashes of the torturers, the gaping wounds vomiting blood and water from their livid mouths: all is rendered with a terrible truthfulness. Ribera has painted subjects of this kind; which would make the very *Verdugo* (executioner) recoil in horror, and all the ghastly beauty and diabolical energy which characterize this great master are required in order to render bearable these savage pictures worthy of the slaughter-house or the knacker's yard, which might have been painted for cannibals by a minion of the torturer. It is indeed enough to take away one's appetite for martyrdom, and the angel with his palm seems but a poor consolation for such agonizing torments. Yet Ribera often refuses even this comfort to his tortured subjects, whom he leaves writhing like the severed portions of a serpent among tawny threatening shadows lit by no divine ray.

A craving for truthfulness, however repellent, is a characteristic feature of Spanish art: the ideal and the conventional form no part of the genius of this race, which is totally devoid of aesthetic sense; sculpture is not enough for them; they must have coloured statues, painted Madonnas dressed in real clothes; material illusion can never be carried far enough for their taste, and this unbridled love of realism often makes them overstep the bounds which separate statuary from Curtius' waxworks.

The famous Christ of Burgos, which is the object of such veneration, and can only be shown when all the tapers are alight, is a striking example of this singular taste: this is no stone or painted wood; it is a human skin (or so they say), stuffed with the greatest care and art. The hair is real, the eyes have lashes, the crown of thorns is a real brier; not a detail is forgotten. There could be no more lugubrious or disturbing spectacle than this tall, spectral figure of the Crucified One, with its deceptive suggestion of life, yet deathly in its immobility; the skin, dark-hued and discoloured, is streaked with long trickles of blood, so skilfully imitated that one might imagine they were really flowing. No great effort of imagination is required to believe in the legend which relates that this miraculous crucifix bleeds every Friday.

Instead of a curving, billowy drapery, the Christ of Burgos wears a white skirt embroidered with gold, which falls from waist to knee; this attire produces a singular effect, especially to us, who are not accustomed to seeing Our Lord in such a costume. In the foot of the Cross are set three ostrich eggs, a symbolic ornament of which the significance escapes me, unless it be an allusion to the Trinity, the germ and principle of all things.

We came out of the Cathedral bewildered, crushed and sated with masterpieces, with our powers of wonderment exhausted, and had barely the strength to glance absent-mindedly at the Arch of Fernando Gonzales, an attempt at classical architecture made by Philip of Burgundy during the early Renaissance. We were also shown the House of the Cid: when I say the House of the Cid I express myself badly; I mean the place where it may have stood: it is a square piece of land enclosed by stone stumps: not the slightest trace remains which might authorize such a belief, but, on the other hand, there is no proof to the contrary, and in that case there can be no objection to relying upon tradition; it is worthwhile to examine the House of the Cords, so called from the twisted loops curling round the doors, framing the windows and playing over the whole structure; it is the dwelling-place of the political head of the province, and we met there a few alcaldes belonging to the neighbourhood, whose faces would have aroused suspicion in a lonely part of a wood, and who would have been well-advised to ask themselves for papers before allowing themselves to go about freely.

The Gate of St. Mary, built in honour of Charles the Fifth, is a remarkable specimen of architecture. The statues standing in its niches are short and squat, but have qualities of strength and power which easily redeem their lack of slenderness; it is a pity that this superb triumphal gateway should be obstructed and degraded by some kind of plaster walls, put up there under the pretext of fortification, which it is urgently necessary to pull down. Near this gate is a promenade along the banks of the Arlenzon, quite a respectable stream at least two feet deep, which is a great deal for Spain. This promenade is adorned with four statues in a tolerably fine style representing four kings or Counts of Castile—namely, Don Fernando Gonzales, Don Alonso, Don Enrique II and Don Fernando I. This is about all there is worth seeing at Burgos. The theatre is even more uncivilized than the one at Vittoria. They were playing that evening a piece in verse: *El Zapatero y el Rey* (*The Shoemaker and the King*), by Zorilla, a distinguished young dramatist who is much in vogue in Madrid, and has already published seven volumes of poetry, the style and music of which are highly praised; all the seats were booked in advance, so we had to deny ourselves this pleasure and wait for the next day's performance of *The Three Sultanas*, which was interspersed with supremely comic songs and Turkish dances. The actors did not know a word of their parts, and the prompter bawled them at the top of his voice, entirely drowning all they said. The prompter, by the way, is protected by a tin shield, rounded like "the top of an oven", against the *patatas, manzanas* and *cascaras de naranja,* the potatoes, apples and pieces of orange peel with which the Spanish public—an impatient audience if there ever was one—never fails to bombard the actors who fail to please it. Everyone takes a supply of missiles in his pockets. If the actors have played well, the vegetables return to the stewpot and go to swell the *puchero.*

For a moment we thought we had found in one of the three sultanas the true Spanish feminine type: great black arched eye-brows, a slender nose, a long oval face and red lips; but an officious neighbour informed us that she was a young Frenchwoman.

Before leaving Burgos, we went to visit the Cartuja de Miraflores, which lies half a league from the town. A few poor infirm monks have been allowed to stay behind in this Carthusian monastery and await their end. Spain has lost much of its picturesque character by the suppression of the monasteries, and I do not see what she has gained in other respects. These wonderful buildings, the loss of which will be irreparable, had been preserved up to that time in a state of the most scrupulous integrity, but will now degenerate, fall in and add their ruins to those which are already so frequent in this hapless country; an unheard of wealth of statues, pictures and works of art of every kind will be lost, and nobody will benefit by it. They might, it seems to me, have imitated some other side of our revolution in preference to its stupid vandalism. Cut one another's throats in the name of the ideas which you think you possess, manure with your corpses the stricken fields ravaged by war: well and good; but the stone, the marble and the bronze touched by the hand of genius are sacred: spare them. In two thousand years your civil discords will have been forgotten, and the future will only learn that you were a great nation from the marvellous fragments unearthed by excavation.

The Cartuja stands on the top of a hill; the outside of it is austere and simple; a grey stone wall, a roof of tiles; all for the idea, nothing for the eye. Inside are long whitewashed cloisters, cool and silent, cell doors, windows with leaded panes in which are set a few pious figures in stained glass, and, in particular, an Ascension, the composition of which is peculiar: the Saviour's body has already disappeared; all that one sees are his feet, the imprint of which is left hollowed out in a rock surrounded by wondering saints.

The prior's garden is enclosed in a little court-yard, in the midst of which rises a fountain from which the glittering water distills drop by drop. A few vine-twigs lend a touch of gaiety to the melancholy walls; a few groups of flowers and flowering bushes grow here and there, rather at random, in picturesque disorder. The prior, an old man with a sad, noble face, attired in garments as much like a monk's frock as possible (they are not allowed to retain their habit), received us with great courtesy, asked us to sit down round the brazier, for it was not very warm, and offered us cigarettes and *azucarillos* (sugar-cones) with cold water. A book was lying open on the table; I took the liberty of glancing at it: it was the *Bibliotheca cartuxiana*, a collection of all the passages, taken from different authors, in praise of the life and order of the Carthusians. The margins were annotated by his hand in that fine old priestly script, firm, upright and rather large, which suggests so much to our thoughts, and could not come from the hand of a man of the world, full of haste and spasmodic emotions. And so this poor old monk, left there for pity's sake in this abandoned convent, whose vaultings will soon crumble over his unknown grave, still dreamed of the glories of his order, inscribing with his trembling hand some forgotten or newly discovered passage on the white pages of his book.

The cemetery is shaded by one or two tall cypresses, like those in Turkish cemeteries: this mournful enclosure contains four hundred and nineteen Carthusians who have died since the building of the convent; thick, rank grass covers the earth, in which one sees neither tombs, crosses nor inscriptions; they lie there pell-mell, humble in death as they were in life; this nameless cemetery has a silent calm which rests the soul; a fountain stands in the midst of it, weeping tears limpid as silver over all the poor forgotten dead: I drank a sip of this water, filtered through the ashes of all these saintly men; it was pure and icy as death.

But if the habitation of man is poor, that of God is rich. In the midst of the nave are placed the tombs of Don John II and his wife, Queen Isabella. One is amazed that human patience should have carried such a work to completion. The base of the tombs is formed by sixteen lions, two at each angle, supporting eight escutcheons with the royal arms. Add to these a corresponding number of virtues, allegorical figures, apostles and evangelists, and let branches, foliage, birds, animals and interlacing arabesques meander through them all; and even then you will have but a faint idea of this prodigious work. The crowned statues of the king and queen lie at full length on top of the tomb. The king holds his sceptre in his hand, and wears a long robe with an incised leafy pattern of inconceivable delicacy.

The tomb of the Infante Alonso is on the Gospel side. The prince is represented on his knees before a *prie-Dieu.* The composition is half sunk in the wall, and framed in a Gothic arch round which twines with inexhaustible and vagrant fancy a vine in high relief, with little children clinging to it while they pluck its grapes; these wonderful monuments are carved in alabaster by the hand of Gil de Siloe, who also carved the sculptures of the high altar; to right and left of this altar, which is of rare beauty, open two doors, through which one can see two Carthusians, motionless in their white shroud-like habit: these two figures, which probably represent Diego de Leyva, produce an illusion at the first glance. Stalls by Berruguete complete the general effect, which one is astonished to find in a desert region.

From the top of the hill they pointed out to us in the distance San Pedro de Cardeña, where are the tombs of the Cid and his wife Doña Ximena. With regard to this tomb, they tell a strange story, which we will relate, though without going bail for its authenticity.

During the French invasion, General Thibaut had the idea of bringing the bones of the Cid from San Pedro de Cardeña to Burgos, intending to place them in a sarcophagus on the public promenade, in order to inspire the population with heroic and chivalrous sentiments by the presence of these noble remains. People add that in a fit of warlike enthusiasm, the honourable general himself slept beside the hero's bones, in order to raise his courage by this glorious contact, a precaution of which he had no need whatever. The plan was not carried out, and the Cid returned to the side of Doña Ximena, at San Pedro de Cardeña, where he has remained for good; but one of his teeth, which had come loose and been locked up in a drawer, has disappeared, and no man knows what has become of it: the one thing lacking to the Cid's glory is that he should be canonized; he would have been if before his death, he had not had the Arab, heretical, and disreputable idea of desiring that his famous horse Babieza should be buried with him, which caused doubt to be cast upon his orthodoxy. With regard to the Cid, may we point out to M. Casimir Delavigne that the hero's sword is called Tisona, not Tizonade, which rhymes too perfectly with *limonade*? In all this no prejudice is intended to the fame of the Cid, who, in addition to his merit as a hero, had that of inspiring to such good purpose the unknown poets of the *Romancero*, Guilhen de Castro, Diamante and Pierre Corneille.

VI. Burgos to Madrid

THE *correo real* (royal mail) by which we left Burgos, merits a special description. Picture to yourself an antediluvian coach, the model of which has been abolished, and could only be found in the Spain of the fossil age; enormous, concave wheels, with very thin spokes, are placed very far to the back of the coach-body, which was painted red in the days of Isabella the Catholic; it is a body of extravagant proportions, in which open all kinds of windows of contorted shapes, and is adorned inside with little satin cushions, which may have been pink at some long-distant date, all picked out with stitchery and trimmings of chenille which, we are at liberty to suppose, used to be of several colours. This venerable coach was suspended in primitive fashion from ropes, and tied together at the critical spots with esparto-grass cords. To this conveyance was added a train of mules of reasonable length, with an assortment of postillions and *mayorals*, with astrakhan jackets and sheepskin trousers of the most Muscovite appearance, and off we went amid a storm of shouts, abuse and cracking whips. We went at a hell of a pace, devouring the miles, while vague outlines of things went fleeting past to right and left of us with the rapidity of an illusion. I have never seen such headstrong, restive and untamed mules; at every relay it took an army of *muchachos* to hitch one to the coach: the diabolical brutes came out of the stable rearing up on their hind legs, and the only means of reducing them to the state of quadrupeds was by means of a bunch of postillions hanging on to the halter. I believe it was the idea of the feed awaiting them at the next *venta* that fired them with the ardour of beasts possessed by the devil, for they were alarmingly skinny. On leaving a little village they would begin to bolt and prance, so that their legs became entangled in the reins: next followed a confusion of kicks and blows passing all imagination; the whole train came down, and a wretched postillion riding at the head of it, on a horse which had probably never been in harness before, was drawn out from under the heap, almost flattened out, with blood pouring from his nose. His mistress, who was watching our start, gave such heart-rending shrieks, that I could hardly have believed they could issue from a human breast. At last they managed to disentangle the ropes and get the mules on their feet again; another postillion took the place of the wounded one, and we started off at a pace which would be hard to equal. The region through which we were driving was of a curiously wild character: it consisted of great arid plains, without a single tree to break their uniformity, ending in mountains and hills of an ochreous yellow, over which distance cast but the faintest tinge of blue. From time to time we passed through dirt-coloured villages built of compressed clay, for the most part in ruins. As it was Sunday, rows of haughty Castilians, draped in their tinder-coloured rags, were standing motionless as mummies along these yellowish walls, lit up by a pale gleam of light, occupied in *tomar el sol* (sunning themselves), a recreation which would cause the most phlegmatic German to die of boredom in an hour.

On that day, however, this peculiarly Spanish enjoyment was quite excusable, for the cold was cruel; a furious wind was sweeping over the plain with a din as of thunder, or like chariots filled with armour rolling across vaults of bronze. I do not think one could meet with anything more savage, more barbarous or more primitive in the kraals of the Hottentots or the encampments of the Kalmucks. I took advantage of a lull to go into one of these huts; it was a windowless hovel with a hearth of rough-hewn stones in the centre, and a hole in the roof to let out the smoke; the soot-stained walls were of a bituminous tone worthy of Rembrandt.

We dined at Torquemada, a *pueblo* on the banks of a little river choked with ancient ruined fortifications. Torquemada is remarkable for a complete absence of window-glass: the only panes of glass are in the *parador* (wayside inn) which, in spite of this unheard-of luxury, has, none the less, a kitchen with a hole in the ceiling. After swallowing a few *garbanzos*, which rattled in our bellies like leaden shot in a tambourine, we got back into our box, and the steeplechase was resumed. That coach, behind those mules, was like a saucepan tied to the tail of a tiger: the noise it made excited them yet the more. A stubble-fire which someone had lighted in the middle of the road almost made them take the bit between their teeth. They were so nervous whenever we met another carriage coming in the opposite direction, that they had to be held by the bridle, and have a hand held over their eyes to shade them. It is a general rule that whenever two carriages drawn by mules meet each other, one of them is bound to upset. Well, what was to happen, happened. I was busy revolving in my mind a fragment of some hemistich or another, when I saw my friend, who was sitting opposite, describe a hasty parabola in my direction; this strange behaviour was followed by a most rude shock and a general smash.

"Are you dead?" asked my friend, as he completed his curve.

"Not at all," I answered. "Are you?"

"Not very," he replied.

And we got out by the shortest way, through the bashed-in roof of the poor coach, which was broken into a thousand pieces; we saw with infinite satisfaction the case of our daguerreotype camera fifteen paces away in a field, as pure and intact as if it had still been in Susse's shop, engaged in taking views of the colonnade of the Bourse. As for the mules, they had bolted, dragging to perdition the front of the coach and the two small wheels; our losses amounted to one button, which flew off with the violence of the shock, and could not be recovered. We really could not have had a spill in better style.

One of the most comical things I have ever seen was the *mayoral* lamenting over the remains of his coach; he tried to fit the pieces together again, like a child who has just broken a glass, and when he saw that the damage was irreparable, he broke out into appalling imprecations, dancing, thumping himself and rolling about on the ground, in emulation of the most violent demonstrations of grief in antiquity; or else he became pathetic, and indulged in the most touching of elegies. The chief cause of his affliction was the fate of the pink cushions, which lay about here and there, torn and dust-stained;

these cushions were the height of magnificence conceivable to his *mayoral's* imagination, and his heart bled at the sight of so much vanished splendour.

Our position was not particularly lively, though we were seized by a somewhat misplaced fit of uncontrollable laughter. Our mules had vanished into thin air, and we had nothing left but a broken-down coach with no wheels. Luckily the *venta* (inn) was not far off. We went there and found two *galeras* which salved us and our baggage. The "galley" thoroughly deserves its name; it is a cart with two or four wheels, but with no bottom or floor; a criss-cross arrangement of twisted reed ropes forms a sort of net in the lower part of it, in which are placed the luggage and parcels. Over this is spread a mattress, a regular Spanish mattress, which does not in the least prevent one from feeling the corners of the boxes piled at random in the net. The victims group themselves as best they can upon this new species of rack, beside which the gridiron of St. Laurence or Guatimozin was a bed of roses; for they could at least turn over. What would those philanthropists say who provide post-chaises for convicts to travel in, if they could see the galleys to which the most innocent people are condemned when they visit Spain?

In this pleasing vehicle, devoid of any sort of springs, we advanced at the rate of four Spanish leagues an hour, that is to say, five French leagues (about 12 miles), a league more than the best-equipped mail-coaches on the finest roads; it would have taken English horses—racehorses or hunters—to make a better pace, yet the road along which we were driving was broken by the steepest ascents and the most abrupt descents, down which we always galloped at the top of our speed; it requires all the skill and confidence of Spanish postillions and conductors to prevent them from getting dashed into fifty thousand pieces at the bottom of a precipice: we ought to have been upset all the time, instead of only once.

We were shaken up like mice which one tosses about in the mouse-trap in order to stun them to death against its walls, and it needed all the austere beauty of the landscape to prevent us from succumbing to depression and stiffness; but these lovely hills, with their severe lines and dark, tranquil hues, gave such character to the ever-changing horizon that they more than made up for the jolting of the galley. An occasional village, or an ancient convent built like a fortress, gave variety to these scenes of an Oriental simplicity, recalling the distant landscape of Decamps' *Joseph Sold by His Brethren*.

Dueñas stands on a hill, looking like a Turkish cemetery; its caves, hollowed out in the living rock, are ventilated by little turrets, broadening out turban-wise in such a way as to produce the impression of a minaret. A church with Moorish outlines completes the illusion. On the left one catches an occasional glimpse of the canal of Castile down in the plain; this canal is not yet completed.

At Venta de Trigueros they harnessed to our galley a rose-pink horse of striking beauty (we had given up mules), fully justifying the much-criticized horse in Eugène Delacroix's *Triumph of Trajan*. Genius is always in the right; what it invents does exist, and nature imitates it even in its most eccentric fancies. After driving along a road with embankments on each side and arcaded buttresses of a somewhat monumental character, we at last entered Valladolid, slightly bruised, but with our noses intact, and our arms still adhering to our shoulders without the aid of black-headed pins, like the arms of a new doll. I say nothing of our legs, which had gone so fast asleep that all the pins in England seemed to be pricking them, while they tingled as with the swarming of a hundred thousand invisible ants.

We alighted at a splendid *parador*, scrupulously clean, where we were given two fine rooms, with a balcony overlooking a *plaza*, carpeted with coloured mats, and with walls distempered in yellow and apple-green. Up to the present we have found no justification for the accusations of dirt and destitution brought by all travellers against Spanish inns; so far we have found no scorpions in our beds, and the promised insects have not made their appearance.

Valladolid is a great city, almost entirely depopulated; it could hold two hundred thousand souls, but has no more than twenty thousand inhabitants. It is a clean, tranquil, elegant town, already showing some traces of the proximity of the Orient. The façade of San Pablo is covered from top to bottom with wonderful early Renaissance sculpture. Before the doorway stands a row of granite pillars, set up like posts, upon which are heraldic lions holding up in every possible position the coat of arms of Castile.

Opposite is a palace of the period of Charles the Fifth, with a court-yard surrounded by graceful arcades and carved medallions of rare beauty.

In this gem of architecture the State monopoly retails its wretched salt and abominable tobacco. By a fortunate accident, the front of San Pablo overlooks an open space, so that one can take a daguerreotype view of it—a difficult matter in the case of mediaeval buildings, which are almost always wedged among masses of miserable houses and shops; but the rain, which fell incessantly during the time we spent at Valladolid, did not allow us to take a single view. Twenty minutes of sunshine, which interrupted the downpour of rain at Burgos, had enabled us to take a very clear and distinct picture of the two cathedral spires and a large portion of the doorway; but at Valladolid we had not even these twenty minutes, which we regretted all the more because the city is full of charming architecture. The building where the library is housed, which they intend to turn into a museum, is in the purest and most delightful style; though some of those ingenious restorers who prefer plain boards to bas-reliefs have shamefully defaced its fine arabesques, enough of it is still left to make it a masterpiece of elegance. We would point out to draughtsmen an inside balcony, forming a round projection at the corner of a palace, on this same Plaza de San Pablo, and making a *mirador* of a very original character. The slender column from which the two arches spring is of a most happy design. It is in this house, we are told, that the terrible Philip II was born. We may also mention a colossal fragment of a granite cathedral begun by Herrera in the style of St. Peter's at Rome, but left unfinished; this building was abandoned in favour of the Escorial, that gloomy caprice of Charles the Fifth's melancholy son.

In a church which had been shut up we were shown a collection of pictures taken from the suppressed monasteries, and collected there by orders from a high quarter; this collection proves that the men who pillaged the churches and convents were excellent artists and connoisseurs, for they left behind them nothing but horrible daubs, the best of which would not fetch fifteen francs in a bric-à-brac shop. There are a few tolerable pictures in the museum, but nothing of a high order; on the other hand, there are a quantity of wood-carvings and ivory

Christs, remarkable rather for their antiquity and large size than for the actual beauty of the workmanship. In any case, those who go to Spain to buy curiosities are bitterly disappointed: there are no arms of value, not a single rare edition, not a manuscript; nothing.

The Plaza de la Constitución in Valladolid is very spacious and fine; it is surrounded by houses supported on great bluish granite columns, hewn all in one piece, and producing a fine effect. The Palace of the Constitution is painted apple-green, and adorned with an inscription in honour of Isabella the Innocent, as they call the little queen here, and a clock-face lit up at night like that of the Hôtel de Ville at Paris, an innovation which seems to cause the inhabitants great delight. Under the pillars a multitude of tailors, hatters and bootmakers—the three most flourishing trades in Spain—have set up shop; the chief cafés are here, and all the movements of the population seem to centre on this spot. In the rest of the town you hardly meet more than an occasional passer-by, a *criada* (servant-girl) going to fetch water or a peasant driving his ass. This impression of loneliness is still further increased by the large area covered by this city, in which there are even more open spaces than streets. The Campo Grande, at the side of the principal gate, is surrounded by fifteen convents, and could hold even more.

At the theatre they were playing that evening a piece by Señor Bretón de los Herreros, a dramatic poet who is thought highly of in Spain. This piece bore the somewhat odd title *El Pelo de la Deso* (Dehesa), which means literally *The Hair of the Pasture* (Like Pasture, like Coat), a proverbial expression that is rather hard to understand, but corresponds to our proverb, "The barrel always smells of herrings." (You cannot make a silk purse out of a sow's ear.) It is about an Aragonese peasant who is to marry a girl of good family, but has the good sense to understand that he can never become a man of the world. The comic element in this play consists in the perfect imitation of the Aragonese dialect and accent—a merit not very perceptible to strangers: the *baile nacional*, though not such a dance of death as the one at Vittoria, was still very poor. On the next day they played *Hernani, or the Honour of Castile*, by Victor Hugo, translated by Don Eugenio de Ochoa; we were careful not to miss such a treat: the piece is translated scrupulously, line by line, except for certain passages and scenes which have had to be cut out in order to satisfy the exigencies of the public. The scene of the portraits is reduced to nothing, for the Spaniards consider themselves insulted by it, and think that it turns them indirectly to ridicule. There are also many things omitted in the fifth act. In general, the Spaniards are annoyed whenever they are spoken of poetically. They maintain that what Hugo, Mérimée and, in general, all those who have written about Spain, have said of them, is a libel. They are libelled indeed, but to their advantage: they reject with all their might the Spain of the *Romancero* and the *Orientales;* and one of their chief pretensions is that they are neither poetical nor picturesque—pretensions which are, alas, only too well justified.

The play was very well acted: the Ruy Gomez of Valladolid was certainly as good as the one of the Rue de Richelieu, and that is saying a good deal. As for Hernani, the *rebelle empoisonné*, he would have been very satisfactory, if he had not had the depressing idea of dressing like those troubadors which one sees as ornaments on clocks. Doña Sol was almost as youthful as Mademoiselle Mars, but without her talent.

The theatre at Valladolid is of quite a happy design, and though the interior is only decorated with a simple coat of white with adornments in *grisaille*, the effect is pretty; the decorator has had the curious idea of painting windows, with a clever imitation of fine spotted muslin curtains, on the walls of the stage-box. These windows in the first tier of boxes look very odd; the balconies and fronts of the boxes are not solid, but have turned balusters, which enable one to see whether the women have small feet and good shoes, and even whether they have slender ankles and well-adjusted stockings; this is not at all a drawback in the case of Spanish women, who are nearly always irreproachable in this respect. I see from a charming article by my substitute on the paper (for the press finds its way even into these barbarous regions) that the galleries of the new Opéra-Comique have been built on this system.

Outside Valladolid, the character of the landscape changes; the *landes* once more appear, only they have a feature unknown to those of Bordeaux, in the shape of clumps of stunted evergreen oaks; while their pine-trees spread out wider and approach the parasol shape. For the rest, they have the same aridity, solitude and desolate appearance; here and there stand a few heaps of ruins, honoured by the name of villages, burnt and devastated in the civil wars, in which wander a few ragged and sullen-looking inhabitants. The sole touch of the picturesque is added by some of the women's petticoats: these skirts are of a brilliant canary-yellow, embellished by many-coloured embroideries representing birds and flowers.

Olmedo, where one stops for dinner, is completely in ruins; whole streets are deserted, and others are blocked by tumble-down houses; grass grows in the open spaces. Like those accursed cities spoken of in the Scriptures, Olmedo will soon have no inhabitants save the flat-headed viper and the purblind owl, and the dragon of the desert will trail his scaly belly over the stones of its altars.

A ring of ancient dismantled fortifications girdles the city, while the kindly ivy casts its green mantle over the nakedness of its gutted and fissured towers. The ramparts are bordered with tall, beautiful trees. Nature does her best to repair the ravages of time and war. The depopulation of Spain is appalling; in the time of the Moors it numbered thirty-two million inhabitants; now it possesses at the outside ten or eleven million. Unless some fortunate change occurs, which is hardly probable, or unless marriages are supernaturally fruitful, towns which were once flourishing will be utterly abandoned, and their ruins of brick and hardened clay will melt insensibly into the earth, which swallows up all things, cities and men alike.

In the room where we were dining, a great big woman, built like a regular Cybele, was pacing up and down, carrying under her arm an oblong basket, covered with a cloth, from which came forth little plaintive squeaky whimperings, almost like those of a very young baby. This puzzled me greatly, for the basket was so small that it surely could not have contained any but a microscopic infant phenomenon, a Lilliputian fit for a show at a fair. It was not long before the riddle was solved: the wet-nurse (for that is what she was) drew from the basket a little coffee-coloured puppy, sat down in a corner and gravely put this new-fangled suckling to her breast. She was a *pasiega* on her way to Madrid to hire herself out as a wet-nurse, and was afraid that her milk might dry up.

After Olmedo, the scenery is not very varied: all I noticed was a wonderful effect of light before we arrived at sunset: the luminous rays fell sideways upon a mountain range in the distance, so that every detail stood out with extraordinary precision; the sides, which were bathed in shadow, were almost invisible; the sky was tinged with a leaden hue. A painter who reproduced this effect would be accused of exaggeration and inaccuracy. This time the *posada* was much more Spanish than those we had hitherto seen: it consisted of a vast stable, surrounded by white-washed chambers, each containing four or five beds: it was bare and wretched, but not unclean: the characteristic and proverbial dirt had not yet appeared; in the dining-room there was even the unheard-of luxury of a series of engravings representing the adventures of Télémaque—not the charming vignettes with which Nanteuil and his friend Baron illustrated the story of the melancholy son of Ulysses, but those horrible coloured daubs with which the Rue St. Jacques has flooded the universe. We started again at two in the morning, and as soon as the earliest gleams of daylight enabled me to distinguish anything, I saw a sight which I shall never forget in all my life: we had just changed horses at a village, called, I believe, St. Mary of the Snows, and were climbing the low foothills of the range we were about to cross; they might have been the ruins of some Cyclopean city: huge sandstone blocks rose on every side, assuming the shape of buildings, and outlined against the sky forms like those of some fantastic Babel. Here a flat stone, falling across two other rocks, looked deceptively like a Druidic *peulven* or dolmen; beyond this, a row of pinnacles, shaped like the shafts of columns, produced the impression of porticoes and propylaea; or again, there was nothing but a chaos, an ocean of sandstone, congealed at its most turbulent moment; the grey-blue tone of these rocks still further increased the strangeness of the prospect. At every turn mountain springs spurted forth in a cloud of spray from the cracks between the rocks, or distilled in tears of crystal; a thing that delighted me particularly was the melting snow as it gathered in the hollows, forming little lakes bordered with emerald turf, or set in a ring of silver, formed by the snow which had resisted the action of the sun. From time to time rose stone pillars, which serve to indicate the road when the snow spreads its treacherous mantle over the good road and precipices alike, and produce a curiously monumental effect; on every side torrents foam and babble; the road bestrides them with those bridges of mortarless stone so frequent in Spain; one comes upon them at every turn.

The mountains rose higher and higher; as soon as we had crossed one, we were faced by another and still higher one, as yet unseen; the mules were no longer enough for us, and we had to have recourse to oxen, which enabled us to get down from the coach and climb the rest of the Sierra on foot. I was really intoxicated by this keen, pure air; I felt so light, so joyful and so full of enthusiasm, that I shouted aloud and skipped like a kid; I longed to throw myself head first down all those charming precipices, so blue, so vaporous and so velvety; I should like to have been whirled away by the waterfalls, to dip my feet in every spring, to cull a branch from every pine, to wallow in the sparkling snow, to mingle with all nature and melt like an atom into this immensity.

The lofty summits glittered and sparkled beneath the sun's rays like a dancer's skirts beneath a shower of spangled silver; others had their heads wrapped in the clouds, and melted into the sky by insensible gradations—for there is nothing which so much resembles a mountain as a cloud; here were precipices, curves, tones and shapes of which no art, whether of pen or pencil, could give any idea; mountains come up to all one's dreams: which is no mean praise. Only one imagines them to be bigger; their immensity is only noticeable by comparison; if one looks hard, one sees that what one took from a distance for a blade of grass is a pine-tree sixty feet high.

At the turn of a bridge, which would have been very convenient for an ambush of brigands, we saw a small column with a cross: it was a monument to a poor devil who had ended his days in this narrow gorge as a consequence of *man airada* (a deed of violence). From time to time we met travelling *Maragatos* with their sixteenth-century costume, a leather jerkin buckled tight to the figure, wide breeches and a broad-brimmed hat; Valencians with their white linen trousers, resembling the full skirt of the Klephts, with handkerchiefs knotted round their heads, white footless gaiters with a blue border like the ancient *Knemis*, and a long piece of stuff (*capa de muestra*) with horizontal stripes of brilliant colours, draped over the shoulder in a most elegant manner.

What one could see of their skin was as brown as a Florentine bronze. We also saw trains of mules harnessed in the most charming style, with bells, fringes and gaily-coloured horse-cloths, and their *arrieros* armed with carbines. We were enchanted; the longed-for picturesque was offering itself in abundance.

The higher we climbed, the deeper and broader became the strips of snow; but a ray of sunshine bathed the whole mountain in moisture like a lovely mistress smiling through her tears. On every side there trickled little rills, scattered like the disordered tresses of a naiad, and clearer than a diamond. By dint of climbing we at last reached the higher crest, and sat down on the plinth of the pedestal of a great granite lion, which marks on the slope of the mountain the boundary of Old Castile. Beyond lies New Castile.

We took it into our heads to pluck a delicious pink flower, of whose botanical name I am ignorant, but which grows in the crevices of the sandstone; so we climbed upon a rock which, we are told, was the spot where Philip II used to sit and watch how the building of the Escorial went on. Either the tradition is apocryphal, or Philip had devilish good eyes.

The coach at last caught us up, after dragging itself painfully up the precipitous slopes. The oxen were unharnessed, and we descended the other side at a gallop: we stopped for dinner at Guadarrama, a little village crouching at the foot of the mountain, where the only curiosity is a granite fountain set up by Philip II. At Guadarrama, by an odd inversion of the natural order of the courses, they served us up for dessert a soup made with goat's milk.

Madrid, like Rome, is surrounded by a tract of waste land, so arid, dry and desolate that nothing can give any idea of it: not a tree, not a drop of water, not a green plant, not a trace of moisture, nothing but yellow sand and iron-grey rocks. As one gets farther away from the mountains, they are not even rocks, but large stones; at long intervals occurs a dusty *venta*, a cork-coloured church-tower showing its nose on the edge of the horizon, or great melancholy-looking oxen drawing wagons such as have already been described; a peasant on horseback or riding a mule, with his carbine across his saddle-bows, his hat pulled over his eyes and a wild expression; or else long trains of dirty-white asses carrying loads of chopped straw, tied up in nets of grass rope and that is all; the ass heading the file, the *colonel*, always wears a little tuft of silk or feathers to show his superiority in the hierarchy of the long-eared tribe.

After some hours, made longer by our impatience to arrive, we at last caught quite a distinct glimpse of Madrid. A few minutes afterwards, we entered the Spanish capital by the Puerta de Hierro: the coach at first followed an avenue planted with stunted pollard trees, and flanked with brick turrets which serve to draw up water. Apropos of water—though this is not a happy way of passing from one subject to another—I forgot to tell you that we had crossed the Manzanares by a bridge worthy of a more serious river; we then drove along by the palace of the Queen, one of those buildings which are said, by general consent, to be "in good taste." The vast terraces upon which it rises give it quite a grand appearance.

After enduring the Customs examination, we went and took up our quarters in the Calle del Caballero de Gracia, near the Calle de Alcalá and the Prado, at the Fonda de la Amistad, where it so happened that Madame Espartero, Duchess of Vittoria, was staying; and our most pressing business was to send Manuel, our body-servant, an enthusiastic *aficionado* and devotee of the national sport, to take tickets for the next bullfight.

PART II

The Gate of the Sun at Madrid

VII. The Bullfight

WE had to wait another two days. Never did days seem longer; to beguile my impatience I read more than ten times the notice posted at the corner of the principal streets; the notice promised wonders and miracles; eight bulls from the most famous grazing grounds: *picadores*, Sevilla and Antonio Rodriguez, *espadas*, Juan Pastor, also called El Barbero, and Guillén; ending up by forbidding the public to throw orange-peel and other missiles that might injure the combatants into the arena.

The word *matador* is hardly ever used in Spain for the one who kills the bulls; they call him *espada* (sword), which is nobler and has more character; nor do they say *toreador*, but rather *torero*. I offer this useful piece of information, in passing, to those who go in for local colour in songs and light opera. The bullfight is called a *media* (half) *corrida*, for there used to be two every Monday, one in the morning, the other at five in the evening, which made up a whole *corrida*: the one in the evening has alone been preserved.

It has been said and repeated on all sides that the taste for bullfights was dying out in Spain, and that civilization would soon cause them to disappear; if it does, so much the worse for civilization, for a bullfight is one of the finest spectacles that the imagination of man could devise; but this day is still far off, and the tender-hearted writers who assert the contrary have only to be transported one Monday, between four and five o'clock, to the Puerta de Alcalá, in order to convince themselves that the taste for this "cruel" amusement is still far from extinct.

Monday, the bullfight day, or *dia de toros*, is a public holiday; nobody works; the whole town is in a stir; those who have not yet taken their tickets hurry off to the Calle de Carretas, where the box-office is situated, in the hope of finding a vacant place; for by an arrangement which cannot be praised too highly, the enormous amphitheatre is entirely occupied by numbered stalls, a custom which might well be imitated in the French theatres; the Calle de Alcalá, the artery into which the crowded streets of the city debouch, is full of people on foot, on horseback and in carriages; on these solemn occasions the most fantastic and extravagant barouches and carriages are brought out of their dusty coach-houses, and the strangest teams, the most phenomenal mules, are brought to light; the carriages recall the Neapolitan *corricoli*; great red wheels, a body without springs, adorned with paintings of a more or less allegorical character, and lined with faded old damask or serge, with silk trimmings and fringes, and, added to all this, a certain rococo appearance which produces the most amusing effect; the conductor sits on the shaft, from which position he can most comfortably harangue and flog his mule, thus leaving one more place free for his fares. The mule is embellished with as many feathers, pompons, tufts, fringes and bells as can possibly be crowded on to the harness of any quadruped. A barouche generally contains a *manola* and her friend, with her *manolo*, not to mention a cluster of *muchachos* hanging on behind. They all drive like the wind, in a tempest of shouts and dust. There are also coaches with four and five mules, the like of which are now only to be found in Van der Meulen's pictures of the conquests and hunting parties of Louis XIV. Every sort of vehicle is laid under contribution, for it is the height of style among the *manolas*—that is to say, the *grisettes* of Madrid—to ride to the bullring in a carriage; they pawn their very mattresses in order to have money for that day, and, without being exactly virtuous for the rest of the week, they are certainly still less so on Sundays and Mondays; one also sees the country-people arriving on horseback, with their carbines across their saddle-bows; others on asses, alone or with their wives; not to mention the carriages of the fashionable world, and a host of honest citizens and *señoras* in their mantillas, all hastening up in a hurry: for here comes a detachment of the mounted National Guard, advancing with trumpeters before it to clear the ring, and nobody would miss the clearing of the arena for worlds, or the hasty flight of the alguacil, as soon as he has thrown the ring-attendant the key of the *toril* in which the horned gladiators are locked up. The *toril* is opposite the *matadero*, where the slaughtered beasts are skinned. The bulls are brought on the previous day, under cover of night, to a meadow near Madrid, known as *El Arroyo*, to which *aficionados* (enthusiasts for the sport) are fond of walking out; this walk is not without its dangers, for the bulls are at large, and their drivers have their work cut out to look after them; they are next induced to enter the *encierro* (the bulls' stable attached to the arena), by some old bulls, trained for this purpose, who are placed among the wild herd.

The Plaza de Toros (bullring) stands on the left, outside the Puerta de Alcalá, which is, by the way, rather a fine gate, in the style of a triumphal arch, with trophies and other heroic ornaments; the outside of the vast ring, with its whitewashed walls, has nothing remarkable about it: since all tickets are taken in advance, the public enters without disorder. Everybody climbs up to his place and seats himself according to his number.

The internal arrangement is as follows: all round the arena, which is of truly Roman proportions, runs a circular palisade of planks, six feet in height, painted blood-red, and provided on each side with a wooden ledge, about two feet from the ground, upon which the *chulos* and *banderilleros* step when they have to leap over to the other side because they are too hard pressed by the bull. This palisade is called *las tablas*. Four doors open in it, for the service of the ring, the entry of the bulls, the removal of dead bodies, etc. After this barrier there is another one, rather higher, forming with the other a sort of corridor for the *chulos* who are tired, the picador *sobre-saliente* (understudy), who has always to be there, all ready dressed and equipped, in case the principal is wounded or killed; besides the *cachetero* and a few *aficionados*, who manage, by means of persistence, to slip into this privileged corridor, the entry to which is as much sought after in Spain as that of the greenroom at the Opera can possibly be in Paris.

It frequently happens that the maddened bull leaps the first barrier, so the second is also fitted with rope netting intended to prevent him from leaping still farther; several carpenters with axes and hammers hold themselves in readiness to repair whatever damage may be done to the enclosures; so it may be said that accidents are impossible. All the same, it has happened that bulls *de muchas piernas* (with agile legs), as they are called in technical language, have leapt the second enclosure, in proof of which we have one of the engravings in the *Tauromaquía* of Goya, the famous artist of the *Caprichos*, an engraving which represents the death of the Alcalde of Torrezón, miserably gored by a leaping bull.

After this second enclosure begin the tiers of seats intended for the spectators: those next to the netting are called *barrera* seats, those in the middle *tendido*, and the rest, backing on the first tier of the *grada cubierta*, have been given the name of *tabloncillos*. These steps, recalling those of the Roman amphitheatres, are of bluish granite, and have no roof but the sky. Immediately after them come the covered seats, *gradas cubiertas*, arranged as follows: *delantera*, or front seats; *centro*, or middle seats; and *tabloncillo*, or seats with a back. Above them rise the boxes, known as *palcos*; and *palcos por asientos* (omnibus boxes), a hundred and ten in number. These boxes are very large, and will hold twenty persons. The *palco por asientos* differs from the ordinary *palco* in this respect, that one can take a single place in it, like a balcony stall at the opera. The boxes of the *Reina Gobernadora* (Queen Regent) and the *innocente Isabel* (the little queen) are decorated with silken draperies and closed with curtains. Beside it is the box of the *ayuntamiento* (the town council) which presides over the ring and settles any difficulties that may arise.

The arena, thus arranged, contains twelve thousand spectators, all comfortably seated and seeing perfectly, which is absolutely indispensable in the case of a spectacle appealing solely to the eye. This vast enclosure is always full, and those who cannot obtain places in the *sombra* (the shady side) would rather be roasted alive on the sunny steps than miss a *corrida*. Those who have fashionable aspirations are bound to have their box *a los Toros* (the bullring) just as, in Paris, they have a box at the *Italiens*.

When I emerged from the corridor to take my place, I felt quite giddy and bedazzled. The arena was bathed in torrents of light, for the sun is an improved chandelier which has the advantage of having no oil to leak, and it will be a long time before even gas outshines it; a vast hum floated over the arena like a mist of sound. On the sunny side, thousands of fans and little round parasols with handles made of reeds fluttered and caught the light; one might have taken them for swarms of many-coloured birds about to take to flight: there was not a single empty place. I assure you that it is a splendid spectacle in itself to see ten thousand spectators in a theatre so vast that God alone can paint its roof with the gorgeous blue which he draws from the vase of eternity.

The mounted National Guard, who had very fine horses and uniforms, rode round the bullring, preceded by two alguacils in full dress—a plumed hat in the Henri IV style, black tight-fitting tunics and mantles, and high boots—driving before them a few persistent enthusiasts (*aficionados*) and a few loitering dogs. As soon as the ring was cleared, the two alguacils went to fetch the *toreros*, consisting of *picadores*, *chulos*, *banderilleros* and the *espada*, the chief actor in the drama, who entered to the sound of a flourish of trumpets. The *picadores* were riding blindfolded horses, for the sight of the bull might scare them and make them plunge dangerously. The costume of the *picadores* is most picturesque: it consists of a short jacket, which does not button up, made of orange, flesh-pink, green or blue velvet, loaded with gold or silver embroidery, spangles, fripperies, fringes, filigree, buttons and every sort of trimming, especially on the epaulets, where the stuff completely disappears under a glittering, phosphorescent confusion of interlaced arabesques; a waistcoat in the same style, a frilled shirt, a gay, negligently knotted cravat, a silk sash and breeches of tawny buckskin padded and strengthened inside with sheets of metal, like postillions' boots, in order to defend the legs from goring; a grey hat (*sombrero*) with a very wide brim and a low crown, embellished with an enormous bunch of favours; a big bag, or flash, of black ribbon, called, I believe, the *moño,* tying up the hair at the back of the head, completes the costume. The *picador* is armed with a lance, shod with an iron point one or two inches long; this cannot wound the bull dangerously, but suffices to goad or direct him. A leather thumbstall fitted to the hand of the *picador* prevents the lance from slipping; the saddle is very high, both behind and before, and resembles the plated steel harness into which the knights of the Middle Ages fitted themselves for jousting; the stirrups are wooden and shaped like the toe of a boot, resembling Turkish stirrups; the rider's heel is armed with a long pointed iron spur, like a dagger; an ordinary spur would not suffice to guide horses which are often half dead.

The *chulos* have a very sprightly, gallant air, with their short satin breeches of green, blue or pink, having silver embroidery down all the seams, their flesh-coloured or white silk stockings, their jackets bedizened with designs and a pattern of foliage, their sashes drawn tightly round the body, and their little *montera* tipped rakishly over one ear; on their arm they bear a cloth cloak (*capa*) which they unfold and flutter before the bull so as to enrage, confuse or mislead him; they are well-built, slender, lissom young men, as opposed to the *picadores*, who are generally conspicuous for their great stature and athletic build: the latter require skill, the former agility.

The *banderilleros* wear the same costume, and their special function is to plant in the bull's shoulders a species of arrow with a barbed iron point, embellished with cut paper; these arrows are called *banderillas*, and are intended to goad the bull to fury, and make him so exasperated that he offers himself properly to the sword of the *matador*. Two *banderillas* have to be stuck in at once, and for this it is necessary to pass both arms between the horns of the bull, a delicate operation during which any distraction of the attention would be dangerous.

The *espada* only differs from the *banderilleros* in his costume, which is richer and more ornate, and sometimes of crimson silk, a colour for which the bull has a peculiar dislike. His arms are a long sword with its hilt shaped like a cross, and a piece of scarlet cloth, mounted upon a staff which runs across it; the technical name for this species of floating shield is *muleta*.

You are now acquainted with the theatre and the actors; we will next show you them at work.

The *picadores*, escorted by the *chulos*, march up and salute the municipal box, from which the keys of the *toril* are thrown down to them; the keys are picked up and handed to the alguacil, who carries them over to the ring-attendant, and then makes off at a gallop amid the gibes and shouts of the crowd, for the alguacils, and indeed all the representatives of justice, are hardly more popular than the gendarmes and police are in France. Meanwhile the two *picadores* go and station themselves on the left of the entrance to the *toril*, facing the Queen's box, for the entry of the bull is one of the most curious events in the *corrida*; they are posted at short intervals, with their backs to the *tablas*, firmly planted in their saddles, grasping their lances in their hands, and prepared to give a valiant reception to the savage beast; the *chulos* and *banderilleros* stand at a distance, or scatter themselves about the arena.

All these preparations, which sound longer in the description than in reality, whet one's curiosity to the highest degree. Every eye is anxiously fixed on the fateful door, and among all these twelve thousand glances, not a single one is turned in another direction. The most beautiful woman in the world would not receive the favour of a glance at such a moment.

For my part, I confess that my heart was constricted as it were by an invisible hand; my temples were buzzing, and hot and cold sweats broke out on my back. It is one of the most violent emotions I have ever experienced.

The trumpets shrilled out a flourish, the two wings of the red door swung back with a crash, and the bull rushed into the arena amidst a tremendous burst of cheering.

He was a magnificent beast, almost black, with a glossy coat, great dewlaps, a square muzzle, sharp, polished, crescent-shaped horns, muscular legs, lashing incessantly with his tail, and bearing between his shoulders a bunch of ribbons of the colours of his *ganaderia* (stud), attached to his hide by a tag. He paused for moment and snuffed the air once or twice, dazzled by the brilliant light and astonished at the din, then he caught sight of the first *picador*, and charged him with a furious rush.

The *picador* who was the object of the attack was Sevilla. I cannot resist the pleasure of describing here the famous Sevilla, who is indeed the ideal of his kind. Imagine a man of about thirty, of fine appearance and bearing, as strong as a Hercules, as bronzed as a mulatto, with magnificent eyes and a countenance like one of Titian's Caesars; the jovial serenity and disdain expressed in his features and port have something really heroic; he was wearing that day an orange jacket with silver lace and embroidery, which has remained indelibly imprinted upon my memory in every detail; he lowered the point of his lance, braced himself and met the charge of the bull so victoriously that the fierce brute staggered and passed on, bearing with him a wound that soon streaked his black hide with trickles of blood; he paused undecided for a few moments, then charged the second *picador*, who was posted a little beyond, with redoubled fury.

Antonio Rodriguez gave him a good thrust with his lance, tearing open a second wound by the side of the first, for they may only stab them in the shoulder; but the bull turned back upon him with lowered head, plunging his horn right into the horse's belly. The *chulos* ran up, waving their cloaks, and the stupid animal, drawn off and distracted by this fresh allurement, rushed after them at full speed; but the *chulos*, stepping on the shelf which we have mentioned above, leapt lightly over the barrier, leaving the animal very astonished at finding nothing in sight.

The bull's horn had ripped open the horse's belly, so that his entrails were pouring out and slipping down almost to the ground; I thought the *picador* would retire and take another; not at all: he touched the horse's ear to see whether it were a mortal blow; the horse had only come unstitched; these wounds, though a horrible sight, are curable; the bowels are put back into place, a few stitches are put in, and the poor beast can be used for another *corrida*; he touched him with the spur, and went off at a hunting pace to take up his position farther off.

The bull was beginning to understand that nothing but lance-thrusts awaited him in the direction of the *picadores*, and began to feel the need of returning to his pastures. Instead of making his entry without delay, after a short rush he returned to his *querencia* with imperturbable obstinacy; the *querencia*, in the jargon of the fancy, is whatever corner of the ring the bull chooses for his refuge, and returns to after his *cogida*; the *cogida* is the name given to an attack by the bull, and the *suerte* to an attack by the *torero*, which is also called the *diestro*.

A cloud of *chulos* came up, waving their brilliantly coloured *capas* before his eyes; one of them carried his insolence so far as to roll up his mantle and throw it on to the bull's head, so that he looked like the sign over the *Boeuf à la mode* shops, which anyone may have seen in Paris. The angry bull got rid of this untimely adornment as best he could, by tossing the innocent piece of cloth into the air and trampling upon it savagely as soon as it came down to the ground. Profiting by this renewal of his fury, a *chulo* began to tease him and draw him over towards the *picadores*; on finding himself face to face with his enemies, the bull hesitated, then, making up his mind, he rushed on Sevilla with such impetus that the horse rolled over with his hoofs in the air, for Sevilla's arm is a bronze buttress which nothing can bend. Sevilla fell beneath the horse, which is the best way, for the man is thus protected from being gored, the body of his mount serving him as a shield. The *chulos* intervened, and the horse escaped with a slash on his hind quarters. They picked up Sevilla, who remounted with the utmost calm. The horse of Antonio Rodriguez, the other *picador*, was less fortunate: he was gored in the chest so violently that the horn was buried in him to its full extent, and entirely disappeared in the wound. While the bull tried to free his head, which was held fast in the horse's body, Antonio seized hold of the shelf on *las tablas*, over which he climbed by the aid of the *chulos*; for when the *picadores* are thrown, they are so weighed down by their iron-shod boots that they are scarcely more able to move than the knights of old, wedged into their armour.

The poor beast was left to himself, and began to stagger across the arena as if he were drunk, entangling his feet in his own entrails; streams of black blood gushed violently from his wound, streaking the sand with jerky zigzags which betrayed his irregular gait; at last he came and collapsed near the *tablas*. He raised his head two or three times, rolling his already blue and glazing eyes, and drawing back his lips whitened with foam, so as to disclose the teeth in his shrunken gums; his tail thumped feebly against the ground; his hind legs twitched convulsively and gave a last kick, as if he would have cracked with his hard hoof the thick skull of death. His last death struggle was hardly at an end when the attendant *muchachos*, seeing that the bull was occupied over on the other side, ran up to remove his saddle and bridle. He stayed there stripped, lying on his side, a brown mass outlined against the sand. He was so thin and flat that he might have been taken for a silhouette cut out of black paper. I had previously observed at Montfaucon what strangely fantastic forms the horse assumes in death: of all animals, it is surely the one whose corpse is the saddest sight. Its head, so nobly and purely modelled, with its contours defined and its planes thrown into relief by the dread hand of death, seems to have been the habitation of human thought; the dishevelled mane, the scattered tail, have a touch of the picturesque and poetic. A dead horse is a corpse; all other animals which life has abandoned are mere carrion.

I lay stress upon the death of this horse, for it caused me the most painful sensation I experienced during the bullfight. What is more, he was not the only victim: fourteen horses were left dead in the arena that day, five of which were killed by a single bull.

The *picador* returned, with a fresh horse, and there were a few more attacks with more or less happy results. But the bull was beginning to flag, and his rage was dying down; the *banderilleros* came up with their paper-trimmed goads, and the bull's neck was soon adorned with a collar of cut paper, the efforts which he made to get rid of them only fixing them more securely. A little *banderillero* named Majarón placed his darts with great courage and success, and sometimes he even cut a caper before retiring; so he was loudly applauded. When the bull had seven or eight *banderillas* upon him, the iron of which tore his hide, while the paper rustled round his ears, he began to run to and fro with fearful bellowings. His black muzzle was white with foam, and in his mad rage, he gored so fiercely at one of the gates that it broke away from its hinges. The carpenters, who had kept an eye on his movements, at once put the door back in its place; a *chulo* drew him off towards the other side, and was so sharply pursued that he had only just time to leap the barrier. The bull, exasperated and enraged, made a mighty effort and got across *las tablas*. All those who were in the corridor leapt into the arena with wonderful alacrity, and the bull came back through another door driven by the spectators in the front row, who struck at him with their sticks and hats.

The *picadores* retired, leaving the field free for the *espada*, Juan Pastor, who went and saluted the municipal box and asked permission to kill the bull; permission was granted, so, throwing his *montera* (hat) into the air, as if to show that he was about to stake his all on the stroke, he walked deliberately up to the bull, hiding his sword beneath the red folds of his *muleta*.

The *espada* fluttered the scarlet stuff repeatedly, upon which the bull made a blind rush; he was able, by a feint, to avoid the rush of the savage beast, but it soon returned to the charge, goring madly at the light stuff, which it displaced, but could not pierce. The right moment had come; the *espada* planted himself right in front of the bull, waving his *muleta* in his left hand, and holding his sword horizontally, with its point level with the animal's horns; it is hard to find words to express the agonized suspense and frenzied attention aroused by this situation, which is worth all the plays of Shakespeare; in a few seconds' time, one of the actors will be killed. Will it be the man or the bull? There they both are, face to face and alone; the man has no arms of defence; he is dressed as if for a ball: light shoes and silk stockings; a woman's pin could pierce his satin coat; a strip of cloth, a fragile sword, and that is all; in this duel the bull has all the material advantage: he has two terrible horns, as sharp as daggers, an immense weight of impetus, a brute rage unconscious of danger; but the man has his sword and his nerve, and twelve thousand eyes fixed upon him: soon the lovely young women will be applauding him with the tips of their white fingers.

The *muleta* was drawn aside, disclosing the breast of the *matador*; the bull's horns were no more than an inch from his body; I thought he was lost! A flash of silver passed, quick as thought, between the two crescent horns, the bull sank upon his knees with a bellow of pain, bearing the handle of the sword between his shoulders, like St. Hubert's stag bearing the crucifix among his branching antlers, as represented in Albrecht Dürer's wonderful engraving.

A thunder of applause burst from the whole amphitheatre; the *palcos* of the nobility, the *gradas cubiertas* of the bourgeoisie, the *tendido* of the *manolos* and *manolas,* shouted and vociferated with all the ardour and impetuosity of the south: *Bueno! bueno! Entusiasmo para el Barbero!* The blow struck by the *espada* is, indeed, very highly esteemed and is called the *estocada a vuela pies;* the bull dies without losing a drop of blood, which is the height of elegance, and by falling on his knees he seems to recognize the superiority of his adversary. The *aficionados* say that the inventor of this blow was Joaquín Rodriguez, a celebrated *torero* of the last century.

When the bull is not killed on the spot, a mysterious little being dressed in black, who has taken no part in the *corrida*, is seen to leap the barrier: he is the *cachetero*. He approaches with furtive steps, watches the last convulsions, sees whether the bull is still able to rise—as sometimes happens—and stabs him treacherously from behind with a cylindrical dagger ending in a lancet, severing the spinal cord, and destroying life with the speed of lightning; the right place is behind the head, a few inches from the groove between the horns.

A military band announced the death of the bull; one of the doors opened, and four mules in magnificent harness, with feathers, bells and woollen tufts and little red and yellow flags—the Spanish colours—galloped into the arena. The function of this team is to remove the dead bodies, which are fastened to the end of a rope terminating in a hook. First they took away the horses, and then the bull. These four dazzling, jingling mules, dragging at a furious pace across the sand all those bodies which had been running so bravely a while ago, had an odd, savage appearance which to a certain extent concealed the dismal nature of their functions: an attendant came up with a basket of earth, and scattered it in the pools of blood, in which the *toreros'* feet might have slipped. The *picadores* once again stationed themselves on one side of the door, the band played a flourish, and another bull rushed into the arena; for there are no intervals in this show; nothing interrupts it, not even the death of a *torero*. As we have said, their understudies are there, ready dressed and armed, in case of accident. It is not our intention to describe one after the other the deaths of the eight bulls which were sacrificed that day; but we shall speak of a few variants and remarkable incidents.

The bulls are not always very ferocious; some of them, even, are very gentle and would like nothing better than to lie down quietly in the shade. One can see by their good-natured, easygoing appearance that they prefer their pastures to the ring: they turn their backs on the *picadores*, and allow the *chulos* to wave their many-coloured cloaks before their noses, with the utmost stolidity; even the *banderillas* are not enough to rouse them from their apathy; so violent means are perforce resorted to: the *banderillas de fuego*. These are a kind of fireworks, which go off a few minutes after they are stuck into the shoulders of the *cobarde*, or cowardly bull, exploding with a great show of sparks and detonations. By this ingenious invention the bull is at once goaded, scorched and stunned: even if he were the most *aplomado*, or leaden, of bulls, he must make up his mind to get into a rage. He makes all sorts of wild plunges, of which one would hardly think such a heavy beast was capable; he bellows, foams and twists himself in every direction in order to rid himself of these intruding fireworks, which scorch his ears and singe his hide.

The *banderillas de fuego* are, however, only allowed as a last resource; when they have to be resorted to, it is almost a stigma of dishonour upon the fight; but when the alcalde hesitates too long before waving his handkerchief, as a sign that permission is granted, there is such an uproar that he is simply forced to yield. The shouts and vociferations, the yells and stamping are beyond belief. Some shout *banderillas de fuego*, others *Perros! perros!* (the dogs). The bull is overwhelmed with insults: he is called a brigand, a murderer, a thief; he is offered a place in the shade, and made the object of a thousand often very witty jests. Soon a chorus of thumping with sticks is added to the shouting, which is no longer enough. The floors of the *palcos* creak and split, and the whitewash on the ceilings falls in scales of white, like snow mingled with dust. The exasperation is at its height: *Fuego al alcalde! Perros al alcalde!* (Fire for the alcalde! Set the dogs on the alcalde!), yells the infuriated crowd, shaking their fists at the municipal box. At last the blest permission is granted and calm is restored. During these blackguarding matches—forgive the term, I know of no better one—most comical jests are often made. We will report one which was very concise and pointed: a splendidly attired *picador* in a brand-new costume was taking it easy on his horse and doing nothing, in a part of the ring where there was no danger; *pintura, pintura!* (he is posing for his portrait!) shouted the crowd, who had observed his ruse.

The bull is often so spiritless that even the *banderillas de fuego* are insufficient. He returns to his *querencia* and will not make his entry. Once more a shout is set up of *perros! perros!* (the dogs! the dogs!). Then, on a sign from the alcalde, the dogs are introduced. They are splendid beasts, pure-bred and of extraordinary beauty; they go straight up to the bull, who tosses half a dozen of them, to be sure, but in the end this cannot deter one or two of the strongest and bravest from seizing him by the ear. Once they have taken hold, they are like leeches; they could be thrown right over without making them loosen their hold. The bull tosses his head and dashes them against the barriers: it is no use. When this has lasted some time, the *espada* or the *cachetero* plunges a sword into the flank of the victim, which staggers, bends his knees and sinks to the ground, where he is finished off. Sometimes, too, they use a sort of instrument called a *media luna* (half-moon) which hamstrings his hind legs and makes him incapable of any resistance; it then ceases to be a fight and becomes a revolting butchery. It often happens that the *matador* fails in his blow; the sword meets with a bone and glances off it, or else it enters the windpipe and makes the bull vomit blood in great spurts, which, according to the laws of bullfighting, is a serious fault. If the beast is not finished off by the second blow, the *espada* is overwhelmed with hooting, hissing and insult, for the Spanish public is very impartial; it applauds the bull or the man, according to their respective merits. If the bull disembowels a horse and throws a man, *bravo toro!* If it is the man who wounds the bull, *bravo el torero!* But it cannot tolerate cowardice either in man or beast. A poor devil who was afraid to go up and plant the *banderillas* on a very savage bull aroused such an uproar that the alcalde had to promise to have him put in prison before order could be restored.

During this same *corrida*, Sevilla, who is a splendid horseman, was much applauded for the following feat: a peculiarly strong bull caught his horse under the belly and, raising his head, lifted it right off the ground. In this perilous position, Sevilla never even wavered in his saddle or lost his stirrups, but held up his horse so well that it came down again on its feet.

It had been a good fight: eight bulls and fourteen horses had been killed, and a *chulo* slightly wounded; one could not have hoped for anything better. Each fight ought to bring in from twenty to twenty-five thousand francs; this is a grant made by the Queen to the great hospital, where the wounded toreros find every care that can be imagined; a priest and a doctor are in waiting in a room at the Plaza de Toros, ready to minister, one to the soul, the other to the body; they used formerly to say mass for their intentions during the fight, and I think they still do so. You see that nothing is neglected, and that the impresarios are full of forethought. When the last bull is killed, everybody leaps into the arena to see him closer at hand, and the spectators retire, discussing the merits of the different *suertes* or *cogidas* which have impressed them most.

And the women, you will say, what are they like? For that is one of the first questions which a traveller is asked. I must confess that I have no idea. I have a vague impression that there were some very pretty ones near me, but I will not affirm it with any confidence.

Let us go to the Prado to clear up this important point.

VIII. Madrid

WHEN one speaks of Madrid, the first two ideas which this word suggests to the imagination are the Prado and the Puerta del Sol: since we are close at hand, let us go to the Prado, for it is time for the promenade to begin. The Prado is made up of several walks and side-paths, with a paved road in the middle for carriages, and is shaded by stunted pollard trees, the roots of which are bathed in a little brick-bordered pool to which water is brought by channels at watering-times; if it were not for this precaution, they would soon be destroyed by the dust and scorched up by the sun: the promenade begins at the convent of Atocha, passes before the gate of this name, the Puerta de Alcalá, and ends at the Puerta de los Recoletos. But fashionable society keeps to the part bounded by the Fountain of Cybele and the Fountain of Neptune, from the Puerta de Alcalá to the Carrera de San Jeronimo. Here is to be found a wide space called the *salón,* edged by a row of chairs, like the main walk of the Tuileries; in the direction of the *salón* there is a side-path bearing the name of *Paris*; this is the local Boulevard de Gand, the rendezvous of fashion in Madrid, and as the imagination of the fashionable world is not precisely distinguished by its picturesqueness, they have chosen the dustiest, the least shady and most inconvenient part of the whole promenade; the crowd in this narrow space, squeezed between the *salón* and the carriage-road, is so great that one often finds it hard to raise one's hand to one's pocket for one's handkerchief; one has to keep in file and follow the stream, as in a queue outside a theatre (in the days when theatres had queues). The only reason for adopting this spot must have been that from there one can see the people driving along the road in their carriages and greet them (it is always respectable for a pedestrian to bow to a carriage). The equipages are not very brilliant; most of them are drawn by mules, whose dark chests, fat bellies and pointed ears produce a most ungraceful effect; one might take them for the mourning-coaches which follow funerals: even the Queen's coach is quite a simple bourgeois affair. An Englishman with a few millions would certainly despise it; there are no doubt, a few exceptions, but they are rare. What are charming are the lovely Andalusian saddle-horses, on which the dandies of Madrid show themselves off. It would be impossible to see a more elegant, noble and graceful sight than an Andalusian stallion, with his lovely plaited mane, his long, bushy tail hanging down to the ground, his harness ornamented with red tufts, his arched head, his sparkling eye and his neck swelling like the breast of a pouter pigeon. I saw one ridden by a woman which was pink (the horse, not the woman), like a rose of Bengal washed over with silver, and marvellously beautiful: what a difference between these noble beasts, which have preserved their fine primitive outlines, and those locomotive engines made of muscle and bone which are called English racers, and have nothing of the horse left save four legs and a backbone to mount a jockey on!

The general view of the Prado is really one of the most animated that could be seen, and it is one of the finest promenades in the world, not in its position, which is quite ordinary, in spite of all the efforts made by King Charles III to correct its defects, but on account of the astonishing crowd which collects there every evening, from half past seven to ten o'clock.

One sees very few women's hats on the Prado; with the exception of a few sulphur-yellow pancakes which must once have adorned some learned ass, there are nothing but mantillas. So the Spanish mantilla is a reality; I had imagined that it only existed in the songs of M. Crével de Charlemagne: it is made of black or white lace, more usually black, arranged at the back of the head over the top of the comb; a few flowers arranged on the temples complete this head-dress, which is the most charming that can be imagined. In a mantilla, a woman must be as ugly as the three cardinal virtues not to look pretty; unfortunately it is the only part of the Spanish costume which has been preserved; the rest is in the French style. The lower folds of the mantilla float over a shawl, an odious shawl, and the shawl is itself accompanied by some sort of ordinary stuff dress, which in no way recalls the full Spanish petticoat. I cannot help being astonished at such blindness; and I cannot understand how it is that these women, who are usually full of perception when their beauty is concerned, cannot see that their supreme attempts at elegance only succeed in making them look like provincial *merveilleuses*—a very poor result; their ancient costume is so perfectly appropriate to Spanish women's style of beauty, proportions and habits, that it is really the only possible one. The fan to some extent counteracts these pretensions to Parisianism. A woman without a fan is a thing which I have not yet seen in this happy country; I have seen some who wore satin slippers with no stockings, but they carried a fan; the fan follows them everywhere, even to church, where you meet groups of women of all ages, kneeling or squatting on their heels, fervently praying and fanning themselves, and crossing themselves from time to time in the Spanish style, which is much more complicated than ours, and performed by them with a precision and rapidity worthy of Prussian soldiers. Flirting a fan is an art totally unknown in France. Spanish women excel in it; the fan is opened, shut and turned between their fingers so lightly and vivaciously that a prestidigitator could not do it better. Some fashionable women form collections of great value; we saw one which numbered no less than a hundred of them in different styles; there were fans of every land and every age; in ivory, tortoise-shell, sandalwood, spangles, paintings in *gouache* of the time of Louis XIV and Louis XV, rice-paper from China or Japan—nothing was missing; several of them were scattered with rubies, diamonds and other precious stones: this is a tasteful luxury and a charming craze for a pretty woman; as the fans open and close, they make a little hissing noise which is repeated more than a thousand times a minute, so that its note pierces through the confused hum which floats over the promenade in a manner strange to a French ear. When a woman meets somebody of her acquaintance, she makes a little sign to him with her fan, and throws him, as she goes by, the word *agur* (adieu), which is pronounced *avour*. And now let us come to the Spanish beauties.

What we understand in France by the Spanish type does not exist in Spain, or at least I have not yet found it. When we speak of a *señora* or a mantilla we usually imagine a long, pale, oval face, great black eyes beneath velvety eyebrows, a slender, rather arched nose, a mouth as red as a pomegranate, and, over all, a warm, golden tone justifying the words in the song: "She is as yellow as an orange." This is the Arab or Moorish type, not the Spanish. The Madrileñas are charming in the full sense of the word: three out of four of them are pretty; but they in no way answer to one's previous ideas of them. They are little, dainty, well made, with slender feet, rounded figures and busts of rather a rich contour; but their skin is very white; their features are delicate and irregular, their mouths are small, and they are perfect copies of certain portraits of the Regency. Many of them have light auburn hair, and you can hardly take two turns up and down the Prado without meeting seven or eight blondes of every shade of colouring, from ash-blond to a violent red, like the beard of Charles V. It is a mistake to believe that there are no fair women in Spain. Blue eyes are frequent, but are not so much admired as black ones.

At first we found it rather hard to become accustomed to seeing women in low-necked dresses, as if for a ball, with bare arms, satin shoes on their feet, flowers in their hair and fans in their hands, walking alone in a public place; for here a man does not offer his arm to a woman unless he is her husband or a relative of her family: he is content to walk side by side with her, while it is daylight, at least, for when night has fallen, the etiquette is less rigid, especially with foreigners, who are not accustomed to it.

We had heard a great deal in praise of the *manolas* of Madrid! The *manola* is an extinct type, like the *grisettes* of Paris, or the *trasteverine* of Rome; she still exists, it is true, but shorn of her original character; she no longer wears her daring, picturesque costume; common calico has taken the place of the vividly coloured skirts embroidered with extravagant patterns of foliage; the hideous leather shoe has replaced the satin slipper, and, horrible to think of, the skirt has been made two good inches longer. In the old days they lent variety to the Prado by their vivacious movements and curious costume; nowadays it is hard to distinguish them from lower middle class women and shopkeepers' wives. I hunted for the true-born *manola* in every corner of Madrid, at the bullfight, in the gardens of Las Delicias, at the Nuevo-Recreo, at the Festival of St. Anthony, and I never met with a perfect example. Once, as I was wandering through the Rastro quarter, the *Temple* of Madrid, after stepping over a large number of beggars who were lying asleep on the ground among horrible rags, I found myself in a little deserted alley, and there I saw, for the first and last time, the longed-for *manola*. She was a tall, well-built girl, about twenty-four years of age, the highest limit of age which can be reached by a *manola* or a *grisette*. She had a bronzed complexion, a steady, sad gaze, rather thick lips and a touch of the African in the shape of her face. An enormous braid of hair, so black that it was blue, and plaited like the reeds of a basket, was wound round her head and fastened up by a great high comb; bunches of coral beads hung from her ears, her brown neck was adorned with a collar of the same material; a black velvet mantilla framed her head and shoulders, her dress was as short as those of the Swiss girls in the canton of Berne, and made of embroidered cloth, showing slender, muscular legs in well-adjusted black silk stockings; the shoe was of satin, in the ancient style; a red fan fluttered like a scarlet butterfly in her fingers loaded with silver rings. The last of the *manolas* turned the corner of the alley and disappeared from before my eyes, amazed at having seen for once a costume by Duponchel, a fancy dress from an opera ball, walking about in the real, living world!

I also saw on the Prado a few *pasiegas* (mountain women) of Santander in their national dress; the *pasiegas* are celebrated as the best wet-nurses in Spain, and their love of children is as proverbial as the honesty of the Auvergnat is in France; they wear a thickly pleated skirt of red cloth, edged with a broad braid, a tight black velvet bodice, also braided with gold, and on their heads a gay Indian kerchief in vivid colours, the whole accompanied by silver jewellery and other barbarous adornments; these women are very beautiful and give a most striking impression of strength and height. The habit of dandling babies in their arms gives them a carriage which accentuates the curves of the figure and throws their shoulders well back, an attitude which suits their full bust. To have a *pasiega* in full costume is a mark of luxury, like having a klepht riding behind one's carriage.

I have said nothing of the men's costume: look at the fashion plates of six months ago, in some tailor's window or reading-room, and you will have a perfect idea of them. Paris is the thought which occupies all their minds, and I remember seeing on a shoeblack's booth: "Boots cleaned here in the Parisian fashion" (*al estilo de Paris*). Gavarni and his delightful drawings: that is the modest aim which the modern hidalgos set before them: they do not know that none but the fine flower of Parisian elegance can attain to it. In due justice to them, however, we will say that they are much better dressed than the women: their shoes are as shiny, their gloves are as white as shoes or gloves can be. Their coats are in good style and their trousers praiseworthy. But their ties have not the same purity, and their waistcoats—the only part of modern custom in which the fancy can be displayed—are not always in irreproachable taste.

There is a trade in Madrid of which Paris has no conception: I mean the retailers of water; their shop consists of a *cantaro* of white earth, a little rush or tin basket containing two or three glasses, a few *azucarillos* (porous sticks of sugar flavoured with caramel) and sometimes a couple of oranges or lemons; others have little barrels covered with leaves, which they carry on their backs; and some of them—along the Prado, for instance—even open bars, painted and crowned with brass figures of Fame carrying flags, which are in no way outdone by the magnificence of the *coco*-venders of Paris. These water-sellers are usually young Galician *muchachos* in snuff-coloured jackets, with knee-breeches, black gaiters and a pointed hat; there are also a few Valencians with their wide white linen trousers, their piece of cloth thrown over the shoulder, their bronzed legs and their blue-edged *alpargatas*. A few women and little girls, with no distinctive costume, also trade in water. According to their sex, they are known as *aguadores* or *aguadoras*; in every corner of the city are to be heard their shrill cries, pitched in every possible note, and varied in a hundred thousand ways: *agua, agua; quien quiere agua? agua helada, fresquita como la nieve!* (water, water; who wants water? iced water as cool as snow!). This goes on from five o'clock in the morning to ten o'clock at night; these cries have inspired Bretón de los Herreros, a well-known poet of Madrid, with a song entitled *L'Aguadora,* which has been a great success throughout the whole of Spain. The thirst of Madrid is really extraordinary: all the water of the fountains, all the snow of the mountains of Guadarrama do not suffice for it. Many jests have been made about the poor Manzanares and the dried-up urn of its naiad; I should like to see what figure any other river would cut in a town devoured by such a thirst: the Manzanares is drained from its very source; the *aguadores* wait anxiously for the smallest drop of water, the slightest damp which makes its appearance between its parched banks, and carry it off in their *cantaros* and fountains; the washerwomen wash the linen with sand, and in the very middle of the stream a Mahometan would not find enough water for his ablutions. You remember, no doubt, Méry's delightful feuilleton on the thirst of Marseilles; multiply it by six, and you will have but the faintest idea of the thirst of Madrid. A glass of water costs a *cuarto* (about a farthing). What Madrid needs most, after water, is a light for its cigarettes; and so the cry of *fuego, fuego* is raised on every side, and mingles constantly with that of *agua, agua*. There is an implacable struggle between the two elements, each of which strives to make more noise than the other: this fire, more inextinguishable than that of Vesta, is carried by young rascals in little bowls full of charcoal and fine ashes, with a handle to prevent one from burning one's fingers.

But now it is half past nine, the Prado is beginning to empty, and the crowd is going off towards the cafés and wine-shops along the great Calle de Alcalá and the neighbouring streets.

The cafés of Madrid strike us, who are accustomed to the dazzling, fairy-like luxury of the Paris cafés, as regular twenty-fifth-rate public-houses; the style of their decorations felicitously recalls those shanties in which bearded women or living sirens are displayed; but this absence of luxury is made up for by the excellence and variety of the refreshments served. We must confess that Paris, so superior in everything else, is behindhand in this respect: the art of the lemonade-maker is still in its infancy. The most celebrated cafés are the Café de la Bolsa, at the corner of the Calle de Carretas; the Café Nuevo, which is the meeting-place of the *exaltados*; the Café of (I forget the name), the accustomed centre for people of moderate political opinions, known as *cancrejos*, or crayfish; that of the Levant, quite near the Puerta del Sol; this does not mean that the rest are not good; but these are the most frequented. Do not let us forget the Café del Principe, next door to the theatre of the same name, a habitual rendezvous of artists and men of letters.

If you wish, we will go into the Café de la Bolsa, ornamented with little plates of looking-glass, with a curved lower edge, forming designs such as one sees in certain German glasses; here is the list of *bebidas heladas, sorbetes* and *quesitos*: the *bebida helada* (iced drink) is contained in glasses distinguished into *grande* and *chico* (large and small), and offers a very great variety; there is the *bebida de naranja* (orange), *limón* (lemon), *fresa* (strawberry) and *guindras* (cherry), which are as superior to those horrible decanters of genuine gooseberry and citric acid with which they are not ashamed to serve you in the most brilliant cafés in Paris as real sherry is to the original wine of Brie: it is a sort of liquid ice, or snowy pulp of the most exquisite flavour: the *bebida de almendra blanca* (white almonds) is a delicious drink, unknown in France, where, under the pretext of barley-water, one swallows goodness knows what medicinal compounds; one is also given iced milk half filled with strawberry or cherry, which enables your throat to enjoy all the snows and hoar-frosts of Greenland while your body is drinking in the torrid zone. During the day, when the ices are not yet ready, you have *agraz*, a kind of drink made of green grapes, and contained in bottles with disproportionately long necks; the slightly acid flavour of *agraz* is highly agreeable; you may also drink a bottle of *cerveza* (beer) *de Santa Barbara con limón*, but this requires certain preparations: you are first brought a bowl and a great ladle, like those with which they stir punch, then a waiter advances, bearing the bottle, sealed with wire, which he uncorks with infinite care; the cork flies out, and he pours the beer into the basin, into which a decanter of lemonade has first been emptied. Then it is all stirred up with the ladle, one fills one's glass and drinks. If this mixture is not to your taste, you have only to go into the *horchaterias de chufas*, which are generally kept by Valencians. The *chufa* is a little berry, a sort of almond, which grows near Valencia; they roast them, pound them and compose an exquisite drink, especially when it is blended with snow; this preparation is extremely refreshing.

To make an end of the cafés, let us say that the *sorbets* (water-ices) differ from those of France in having a firmer consistency, while the *quesitos* are hard little ices, moulded in the form of a cheese; they are of all kinds, apricot, pine-apple and orange, as in Paris; but there are also some made with butter (*manteca*) and with the half-formed eggs taken from the bodies of hens which have been killed, a Spanish specialty, for it is only at Madrid that I have heard of this curious refinement They also serve *spumas* of chocolate, coffee and other flavours; these are a kind of extremely light iced whipped cream, dusted with very fine powdered cinnamon and accompanied by *barquillos*, or wafers rolled into the shape of an elongated horn, through which one takes one's *bebida* as through a siphon, by sucking it slowly at one end, a little refinement which enables one to relish the coolness of the drink longer: coffee is not drunk out of cups, but glasses; moreover, it is not very often used. All these details may perhaps strike you as tedious; but if you were exposed, as we are, to a temperature of from thirty to thirty-five degrees, you would find them of the greatest interest. One sees far more women in the cafés of Madrid than in those of Paris, though cigarettes and even Havana cigars are smoked there. The newspapers most frequently seen in them are the *Eco del Comercio,* the *Nacional* and the *Diario,* which announces daily the public amusements, the times of masses and sermons, the temperature, lost dogs, young peasant-girls desirous of hiring themselves out as wet-nurses, *criadas* (servant-girls) in search of a place, etc. But now it is striking eleven o'clock; it is time to go home; there are only a few late strollers passing along the Calle de Alcalá. Nobody is left in the streets save the *serenos,* with their lanterns slung at the end of a pike, their stone-coloured cloaks and their rhythmical cry: nothing is to be heard save a chorus of crickets chirping out their disyllabic plaint in their little cages bedecked with glass. They are fond of crickets in Madrid; every house has one of its own, hanging in the window in a tiny wire or wooden cage; they have also an odd passion for quails, which are kept in open-work baskets of osier; their incessant *piou-piou-piou* is a pleasant change from the *cri-cri* of the crickets; as Bilboquet remarks those who like that sort of thing will be pleased by it.

The Puerta del Sol is not a gate, as one might imagine, but a church-front, painted pink, and embellished with a clock-face, which is lit up at night, and a great sun with golden rays, whence its name of Puerta del Sol. Before this church there is a sort of square or open space, across which the Calle de Alcalá cuts lengthways, with the Calles de Carretas and de la Montera at right angles to it. The post office is a big regular building standing at the corner of the Calle de Carretas, with its frontage on the square. The Puerta del Sol is the meeting-place of the loungers of the town, and it would seem that there are many of them, for from eight o'clock in the morning there is a dense crowd. All these grave figures stand there wrapped in their cloaks, though it is abominably hot, under the frivolous pretext that what protects them from the cold also protects them from the heat. From time to time one sees a finger and thumb, as yellow as gold, peep out from the straight, motionless folds of the cloak and roll up in a cigarette-paper a few pinches of a chopped cigar; and soon there rises from the mouth of the grave figure a cloud of smoke, which proves that he is able to breathe, a fact which his complete immobility might have led one to doubt. Apropos of *papel español para cigaritas*, be it noted in passing that I have not yet seen a single book of it; the natives use ordinary letter-paper cut into small pieces; those liquorice-coloured booklets with gaily coloured grotesque designs diversified by *letrillas* or comic *romances* (songs) are exported to France for the benefit of lovers of local colour. Politics are the usual topic of conversation; the theatres and the war occupy their imaginations to a large extent, and more strategy is evolved at the Puerta del Sol than on all the battle-fields and in all the campaigns in the world. Balmaseda, Cabrera, Palillos and other more or less important insurgent leaders are constantly under discussion; deeds of theirs are related that make one shudder, cruelties that have long since gone out of fashion and come to be thought bad taste by the Caribs and Cherokees. During Balmaseda's last raid, he advanced to within twenty leagues of Madrid, and, having taken a village near Aranda by surprise, he amused himself by breaking the teeth of the *ayuntamiento* and the alcalde, ending up his sport by having horseshoes nailed to the feet and hands of the Constitutional priest. When I betrayed my astonishment at the perfect calm with which they listen to this news, the answer was that it happened in Old Castile, and so they need not trouble about it. This answer sums up the whole situation in Spain, and gives the key to many things which strike us as incomprehensible when seen from France. And indeed to an inhabitant of New Castile, what happens in Old Castile is as devoid of interest as what goes on in the moon. From the political point of view, Spain does not yet exist: it still consists of "the Spains," Castile and Leon, Aragon and Navarre, Granada and Murcia, etc.; peoples speaking different dialects and unable to bear each other. Like the simple-minded foreigner that I was, I exclaimed at such a refinement of cruelty; but they pointed out that it was a Constitutional priest, which went far towards mitigating the offence. Though to us, accustomed as we are to the colossal battles of the Empire, the victories of Espartero seem but poor affairs, they frequently serve as a text for the politicians of the Puerto del Sol. After one of these triumphs, in which two men have been killed, three prisoners taken, and a mule captured with a load consisting of a sabre and a dozen cartridges; there are illuminations and a distribution of oranges and cigars among the army, producing an enthusiasm easy to describe. Formerly, and even today, noble lords would go to the shops near the Puerta del Sol, ask for a chair, and stay there for most of the day, conversing with the customers, much to the annoyance of the shopkeeper who was the victim of this mark of familiarity.

Let us, if you will, go into the post office and see whether there are any letters from France; this anxiety about letters is almost a morbid one; you may be sure that on arriving at a town, the first building visited by the traveller is the post office; in Madrid, letters addressed *Poste restante* are all marked with a number; the number and the name of the person are inscribed on a list which is posted up on the pillars; there is the January pillar, the February pillar and so on; one looks for one's name, notes the number, and goes and asks for one's letter at the place where they are deposited, where it is handed out without further ado. If letters are not withdrawn, they are burnt at the end of a year. Under the arcades in the court-yard of the post office, shaded by great blinds of woven esparto-grass, have been installed all kinds of reading-rooms, like those under the arches of the Odéon in Paris, where one may read the Spanish and foreign newspapers; postage is not very expensive, and in spite of the innumerable dangers to which the mails are exposed along the roads, infested as they are by insurgents and brigands, the service is carried on as regularly as possible; it is also on these pillars that notices are posted by poor students, offering to clean a gentleman's boots in order to finish their course of rhetoric or philosophy.

Let us now stroll about the city at random, for chance is the best of guides; the more so, since Madrid is not rich in architectural splendours, and one street is as interesting as another; the first thing you see when you raise your eyes at the corner of a house or street, is a little earthenware plate on which is written *Manzana. vizitac. gener.* (Manzanares; general survey). These plates once served to number the houses grouped in islands or blocks; nowadays there are figures on them all, as in Paris; you would be surprised, too, at the number of fire-insurances with which the house-fronts are bedizened, especially in this country where there are no fire-places and fires are never lit. Everything is insured, up to the public buildings and churches; they say it is the civil war which is the cause of this great eagerness to be insured; since nobody is certain that he will not be more or less grilled alive by Balmaseda or somebody else, everyone tries to save at least his house.

The houses in Madrid are built of lath and brick and of compressed clay, except for the jambs, corners and supports, which are sometimes of grey or blue granite, the whole being carefully plastered and painted in rather fanciful colours, pale green, powder-blue, pinkish buff, canary, rose-pink and other more or less anacreontic hues; the windows are framed in ornamental or architectural designs, which are painted round them, with a mass of scrolls, plaits and little Cupids with flower-pots, and are fitted with broad-striped blue and white Venetian blinds, or woven esparto-grass mats which they water, so that the breeze as it passes through them may be cooled and charged with moisture. The quite modern houses are content with white rough-cast or a cast of lime-wash, as in Paris. The projecting balconies and *miradores* (gazebos) do something towards breaking the monotony of the straight lines and clear-cut shadows, and varying the naturally flat appearance of this style of building, in which relief is always indicated by painting and treated in the style of theatrical decoration; illuminate all this with brilliant sunshine, place here and there in the sun-bathed streets a few long-veiled *señoras* holding their unfurled fans against their cheeks to serve as parasols; a few sunburnt, wrinkled beggars draped in tattered stuff and rags of the consistency of tinder; a few half-naked Valencians with the build of Bedouins; among the roofs arrange the little humped cupolas and bulbous pinnacles, ending in leaden balls, of a church and a convent, and you will have quite a strange prospect, which may at last convince you that you are no longer in the Rue Laffitte and have really left the asphalt, even if the lacerated condition of your feet, due to the sharp cobble-stones of the streets of Madrid, had not already convinced you of this.

One thing which is really surprising is the frequence of the following inscription: *Juego de villar,* which occurs every twenty steps. Lest you may imagine that there is something mysterious about these three sacramental words, I hasten to translate them; they merely mean:

Billiards. I cannot imagine what the devil is the use of so many billiard tables; the whole universe might have a game here. After the *juegos de villar*, the most frequent inscription is that of *despacho de vino* (wine-shop). They sell Val de Peñas and full-bodied wines. The bars are painted in brilliant colours, adorned with draperies and foliage. The *confiterias* and *pastelerias* are also very numerous and quite attractively decorated; Spanish preserves deserve a special mention: those known by the name of Angel's Hair (*Cabello de Angel*) are exquisite. The pastry is as good as it can be in a country where there is no butter, or at least where it is so dear, and of such poor quality that one can hardly use it; it is something like what we call *petits fours*. All these shop-signs are written in abbreviated characters with interlaced letters, which make it hard at first for them to be understood by foreigners, who are great readers of signs if ever there were any.

The inside of the houses is spacious and convenient; the ceilings are lofty and space is nowhere grudged; in Paris a whole house would be built in the well of some of these staircases; you go through long suites of rooms before arriving at the part which is really inhabited; for these rooms are furnished with nothing but whitewashed plaster, or a flat wash of yellow or blue picked out with coloured stripes and panels in imitation of woodwork. Smoky, blackened pictures, representing the beheading or disembowelling of some martyr—which are favourite subjects with Spanish painters—hang upon the walls, mostly without frames, and all crumpled upon their stretchers. Floors are unknown in Spain; at least I have never seen one there. All the rooms are paved with brick; but as these bricks are covered with reed mats in winter and rush ones in summer, they are not so very uncomfortable; these mats of reeds and rushes are plaited with great taste. The savages in the Philippines or the Sandwich Islands could not do better. There are three things which are, in my opinion, an exact thermometer of the level of a race's civilization: pottery, the art of weaving straw, osier or what not, and the manner of harnessing beasts of burden; if the pottery is fine, pure in outline and as correctly proportioned as the antique, with the natural yellow or red tone of the clay; if the baskets and mats are fine, marvellously plaited, enhanced with wonderfully chosen coloured arabesques; if the harness is embroidered, stitched, adorned with bells, woollen tufts and designs of the choicest kind, you may be sure that the race is a primitive one, still very close to a state of nature: civilized peoples do not know how to make a pot, a mat, or a set of harness. As I write, I have before me the *jarra*, hanging by a piece of twine from a pillar, in which the water is cooling for me to drink: it is an earthen pot worth twelve *cuartos*, that is to say, about six or seven French *sous*; its outline is charming and I know nothing purer, except the Etruscan. The spreading top is formed like a four-leafed clover, each leaf hollowed into a channel, so that one can pour out one's water from whichever side one grasps the vase; the grooved handles, with a little moulding are attached with the perfection of elegance to the delightfully graceful neck and sides; really nice people prefer to these charming vases those abominable, bulging, pot-bellied, hump-backed English pots and pans, covered with a thick coat of glaze, which might be taken for riding-boots covered with white polish. But, talking about boots and pottery, we have wandered rather far from our description of the houses; let us return to it without further delay.

The few pieces of furniture in Spanish dwelling-houses are in shocking taste, recalling the "Messidor" or "Pyramid" style. Empire shapes still flourish in their full purity. You still find here those mahogany pilasters ending in a Sphinx's head of greenish bronze, those copper beadings and frames of Pompeian garlands which have long since vanished from the face of the civilized world; not a single piece of carved wooden furniture, not a table inlaid with mother-of-pearl, not a lacquered cabinet, nothing; old Spain has completely disappeared: nothing is left but a few Persian carpets and damask curtains. On the other hand, there are a quantity of really extraordinary wicker chairs and sofas; the walls are bedaubed with false columns and cornices, or washed over with tinted distemper. Scattered about on tables and what-nots are little biscuit or porcelain figures representing troubadours, Matilde and Malek-Adel, and other equally ingenious but out-of-date subjects; spun-glass poodles, electro-plated torches stuck with candles, and a hundred other splendours which it would take too long to describe, but which are sufficiently hinted at in what I have just said; I have not the heart to speak of the atrocious coloured engravings which misguidedly aspire towards adorning the walls.

There are perhaps a few exceptions, but very few. Do not run away with the idea that the houses of people of the upper classes are furnished more richly and in better taste. These descriptions which are scrupulously accurate, apply to the houses of people with a carriage, and eight or ten servants; the blinds are always down, the shutters half closed, so that the rooms are filled with a sort of tempered light to which one must grow accustomed before discerning their contents, especially when one comes in from outside; those who are in the room can see perfectly, but those who come in are blind for eight or ten minutes, especially when one of the preceding rooms is lit up. It is said that clever mathematicians have based upon this optical effect calculations resulting in perfect security, in an apartment so arranged, for an intimate tête-à-tête.

The heat is excessive in Madrid, and sets in suddenly, with no spring to form a transition; so with regard to the temperature of Madrid, the saying runs: three months of winter, nine months of hell. It is impossible to protect oneself from the deluge of fire except by staying in the lower rooms, which are in almost complete darkness, and in which continual watering maintains a certain dampness. This need for coolness has given rise to the fashion for *bucaros*, an odd, uncivilized taste which would not appeal to our French ladies who affect fashionable airs, but seem a most tasteful refinement to the fair Spaniards.

The *bucaros* are a sort of pot made of red American earth, rather like the kind of which the stems of Turkish pipes are made; they are of all shapes and sizes; some of them are picked out with gilded beadings and powdered with coarsely painted flowers; no more of them are made in America, so *bucaros* are beginning to become scarce, and in a few years' time will be as hard to find, and as fabulous in price, as old Sèvres; then everybody will have them.

When they want to use the *bucaros*, seven or eight of them are placed on marble-topped tables or brackets and filled with water, then the ladies go and sit on the sofa and wait for them to take effect, so as to enjoy this pleasure in a suitable state of repose. First the clay takes on a darker tinge; the water filters through its pores, and it is not long before the *bucaros* break into a perspiration, and diffuse an odour resembling the smell of wet plaster, or that of a damp cellar which has not been opened for a long time. This sweating of the *bucaros* is so profuse that by the time an hour has passed, half the water has evaporated; what remains in the jar is as cold as ice and has taken on a sickening flavour of well or cistern, which is considered exquisite by *aficionadas*. Half-a-dozen *bucaros* would be enough to saturate the air of a boudoir with damp enough to be noticeable as you enter; it is a sort of cold vapour-bath. Not content with inhaling the perfume and drinking the water, some people chew small fragments of *bucaros*, crunch them to a powder and end by swallowing them.

I saw a few evening parties or *tertulias* which have nothing remarkable about them; there is dancing to the piano, as in France, but if possible it is even more dismal and lamentable. I cannot understand why people who dance so little do not frankly make up their minds not to dance at all, which would be simpler and quite as amusing; the fear of being accused of a bolero, a fandango or a cachucha reduces the women to complete immobility. Their costume is very simple by comparison with that of the men, who are always dressed like fashion-plates. I observed the same thing at the palace of Villahermosa, at a charity performance in aid of the Foundlings, or *Niños de la Cuna*, at which were present the Queen-Mother, the little Queen and all the great and fashionable world of Madrid. Women who were doubly duchesses and four times marchionesses were wearing clothes that a Parisian milliner would scorn to wear to a dressmakers' party; they have forgotten how to dress in the Spanish style, but have not yet learnt how to dress like Frenchwomen, and if they were not so pretty, they would often be in danger of appearing ridiculous. Once alone, at a ball, I saw a woman in a full pink satin Spanish skirt, trimmed with five or six flounces of black silk lace, like the one worn by Fanny Elssler in *Le Diable Boiteux*; but she had been to Paris, where she had discovered the Spanish costume. These *tertulias* cannot cost very much to those who give them. Refreshments are conspicuous by their absence; no tea, no ices, no punch; but on a table in the first drawing-room are arranged just a dozen glasses of perfectly pure water, with a plateful of *azucarillos*; but one would generally be considered indiscreet and gluttonous if one were to carry one's Sardanapalian luxury so far as to sugar one's water; this is what happens in the richest houses: it is not due to avarice, but such is the custom; besides, the monastic sobriety of the Spaniards is perfectly adapted to this sort of diet.

As for morals, it takes more than six weeks to understand the character of the people and the usages of its society. Yet novelty produces an impression upon one which grows dim during a long visit. It appeared to me that in Spain the women had the upper hand, and enjoyed greater liberty than in France. The bearing of the men towards them seemed to me most humble and submissive; the latter pay them the strictest and most scrupulously punctilious attentions, and express their ardour in verses of every metre, rhyming, assonanced, *sueltos* (blank verse) and others; the moment they lay their hearts at the feet of a beauty, they may no longer dance with anyone under the age of a great-great-grandmother. They are only allowed to converse with women of fifty of recognized ugliness. They may no longer visit at houses where there is a young woman: a most assiduous visitor suddenly disappears, to return at the end of a year or six months; his mistress had forbidden him that house; yet he is received as if he had called the day before; this is quite a recognized custom. So far as one can judge at first sight, Spanish women are not fickle in love, and the love-affair into which they enter often last several years. After spending a few evenings in a certain circle, one can easily distinguish pairs of lovers at a glance. If one wishes to entertain Señora A., Señor B. must be invited, and *vice versa*: husbands are wonderfully civilized, and equal to the most easy-going Parisian husbands; there is not a sign of the old Spanish jealousy which has been the subject of so many dramas and melodramas. To complete the destruction of our illusions, everybody speaks French perfectly, and, thanks to a few men of fashion, who spend the winter in Paris and frequent the greenroom at the Opera, the most insignificant ballet-girl, the most obscure super, is perfectly well known in Madrid. I found there something which perhaps does not exist in any other place on earth: a passionate admirer of Mlle. Fitzjames, whose name will serve as a transition to lead us from the *tertulia* to the theatre.

The pieces at the Teatro del Principe are fairly conveniently distributed: it presents dramas, comedies, *saynetes* and interludes. I saw a piece by Don Antonio Gil y Zarate played there, named *Don Carlos el Hechizado* (the bewitched), which was constructed quite in the Shakespearian style. Don Carlos strongly resembles Louis XIII in *Marion de Lorme*, and the scene with the monk in the prison is an imitation of the visit of Claude Frollo to Esmeralda, in the dungeon where she is waiting for death. The rôle of Carlos is played by Julian

Romea, a wonderfully talented actor, unrivalled by anybody, to my knowledge, except Frederick Lemaître, in quite the opposite style; truth and illusion could be carried no further; Matilde Diez is also an actress of the highest order; she interprets her parts with the most delicate and subtle shades, and surprisingly acute discrimination. I have only one fault to find with her—namely, the extreme volubility of her delivery, which is no fault in Spanish eyes. Don Antonio Guzmán, the comic actor, would not be out of place on any stage; he strongly recalls Legrand, and at times Arnal. They also give fairy plays at the Teatro del Principe, interspersed with dances and ballets. I saw played there, under the title of *La Pata de Cabra*, an imitation of *Pied de Mouton*, which was once given at the Gaieté. The arrangement of the dances was extraordinarily poor: the chief dancers were not as good as the merest understudies at the Opera; on the other hand, the supers display unusual intelligence; the ballet of Cyclops is executed with a rare precision and finish: as to the *baile nacional*, no such thing exists. We had been told at Vittoria, Burgos and Valladolid that the good dancers were at Madrid; at Madrid they told us that genuine cachucha-dancers were only to be found in Andalusia, at Seville. We shall see about that; but I am afraid that where Spanish dances are concerned, I shall have to come back to Fanny Elssler and the Noblet Sisters. Dolores Serral, who made such a stir in Paris, where we were among the first to call attention to the passionate audacity, the willowy voluptuousness and impetuous grace which distinguish her dancing, appeared at the Madrid theatre several times without producing the least effect, so lost is all sense and understanding of the old national steps in Spain. When they perform the *Jota aragonesa* or the *bolero*, all the people of fashion get up and go; nobody is left but foreigners and the lower classes, in whom it is always harder to extinguish the poetic instincts. The most popular French playwright in Madrid is Frédéric Soulié; almost all the pieces translated from the French are attributed to him; he seems to have succeeded to the popularity of M. Scribe.

We are now well-informed in this respect and have only to finish with the public buildings: this will soon be done. The palace of the Queen is a big building, very square and solid, in fine well-fitted stone, with plenty of windows, a corresponding number of doors, Ionic columns, Doric pilasters—all that constitutes a tasteful edifice. The immense terraces which support it, and the snow-laden mountains of the Sierra Guadarrama against which it stands out, add distinction to its outlines, which might otherwise be dull and common. Velásquez, Maella, Bayeu and Tiepolo have painted its fine ceilings with compositions of a more or less allegorical character; the grand staircase is very fine, and Napoleon considered it superior to that of the Tuileries.

The building in which the Cortes are held is a medley, in the most abominable taste, of columns in the style of Paestum and lions with manes like wigs: I should doubt whether good laws could be passed among such architecture; in the middle of the square, opposite the Hall of the Cortes, stands a bronze statue of Miguel Cervantes; it is no doubt laudable to erect a statue to the immortal author of *Don Quixote*, but it might well have been a better one.

The monument to the victims of the *Dos de Maio* (May 2nd) stands on the Prado, not far from the picture gallery; when I saw it, I thought for an instant that I had been carried back to the Place de la Concorde at Paris and saw, as by some fantastic mirage, the venerable obelisk of Luxor, which I had never before suspected of roving; it is a sort of grey granite cippus, surmounted by an obelisk of reddish granite somewhat similar in tone to that of the Egyptian Needle; the effect is rather fine and is not lacking in a certain mournful dignity. It is a pity that the obelisk is not whole; inscriptions in honour of the victims are carved in letters of gold on the sides of the pedestal. The *Dos de Maio* is a heroic and glorious episode, turned by the Spaniards to frivolous uses; one sees nothing on all sides but engravings and pictures with it as their subject. You will easily believe that they do not represent us in a flattering light: we are made as repulsive as the Prussians of the Cirque-Olympique.

The armoury does not come up to one's expectations. The Artillery Museum in Paris is incomparably richer and fuller. In the Madrid Armoury there are but a few complete suits of armour composed entirely of genuine pieces. Helmets of an earlier or later date are placed upon cuirasses in a different style. The explanation given of this disorder is that, at the time of the French invasion, all these curious relics were hidden in the attics, where they became so jumbled and mixed that it has not since been possible to put them together and set them up again with any certainty. Hence it is almost impossible to rely upon the information given by the custodians. For the coach of Joan the Mad, mother of Charles the Fifth, we were shown a carved wooden carriage of wonderful workmanship, which evidently could not go back earlier than the reign of Louis XIV. Charles V's light carriage, with its leather cushions and curtains, seemed to us far more probable. There are very few Moorish arms: one or two shields, a few yataghans, and that is all. The most curious things there are a large number of curiously shaped saddles adorned with embroidery, gold and silver stars and a scalework of steel plates; nothing is known for certain about their date and the person to whom they belonged. The English greatly admire a sort of triumphal cab of hammered iron presented to Ferdinand about 1823 or 1824.

Let us mention in passing, just to put them on record, a few fountains in a corrupt but rather amusing rococo style; the Bridge of Toledo, in bad taste, very rich and ornate, adorned with vases surmounted by flames, egg-shaped ornaments and rosettes; a few churches oddly striped with different colours and crowned with Muscovite pinnacles; and then let us turn towards the Buen Retiro, a royal residence situated a few steps away from the Prado; we Frenchmen, who have Versailles and Saint-Cloud, and used to have Marly, are hard to please in the matter of royal residences; the Buen Retiro seems to us like a well-to-do grocer's dream come true; there is a garden full of common but glaring flowers, little pools adorned with shell-work, and worm-eaten shrubberies with fountains in the style of a provision-dealer's shop-window, slimy green lakes upon which float wooden swans painted a glossy white, and other marvels in doubtful taste. The natives go into ecstasies over a certain summer-house built of round blocks, the inside of which has pretensions to the Hindu style; the first Turkish garden—a simple-minded patriarchal Turkish garden, with kiosks made of coloured panes of glass, through which one looked out upon the blue, green and red landscapes—was very superior both in taste and magnificence; above all, there is a certain chalet, which is really the most absurdly comical thing imaginable. By the side of it there is an outhouse, adorned with a stuffed she-goat and kid, besides a sow, carved in grey stone, suckling little pigs of the same material. A few steps from the chalet the guide slips away and opens the door mysteriously, and when at last he calls you and allows you to go in, you hear a dull noise of cog-wheels and balanced weights, and find yourself face to face with some awful mechanical figures, churning butter, spinning at the wheel, or rocking with their wooden feet wooden babies lying in carved cradles; in the neighbouring room the sick grandfather is lying in bed, with his medicine on the table beside him; fidelity to nature has been carried so far as to place beneath the camp-bed an indescribable vessel very faithfully reproduced; such is the faithful catalogue of the chief splendours of the Retiro; all this mediocrity is somewhat relieved by a fine bronze equestrian statue of Philip V, in an attitude resembling the statue in the Place des Victoires.

We will not speak here of the museum; it will be the subject of a special study; the limits of a single letter do not allow us to linger over it. Suffice it to say that it is extremely rich: it abounds in Titians, Raphaels, Paolo Veroneses, pictures by Rubens and Velásquez, Ribera and Murillo: the pictures are very well lighted, and the architecture of the building does not lack style, especially inside. The front, which overlooks the Prado, is in rather bad taste; but on the whole the construction does honour to the architect Villanueva, who planned it. Having seen the museum, go and see the natural-history section with its mastodon or *dinothereum giganteum*, a marvellous fossil with bones like bars of bronze, which must be at least the Biblical behemoth; a mass of virgin gold weighing sixteen pounds; the Chinese gongs, the note of which, whatever one may say, is very like that of a cauldron which somebody has kicked; and a series of pictures showing all the variations which may arise from crossing the white, black and copper-coloured races. Do not forget three wonderful pictures by Murillo in the Academy: the Foundation of Santa Maria Mayor (two subjects), St. Elizabeth washing the heads of persons with a skin disease, two or three splendid Riberas, a charming woman in Spanish costume, lying on a sofa, by good old Goya, a burial scene by El Greco, some portions of which are worthy of Titian, and a fantastic sketch, again by El Greco, representing monks doing penances, which surpass all the most mysteriously funereal dreams of Lewis or Ann Radcliffe. Having done this, one can take mules or a carriage, and go off to the Escorial or Toledo, feeling that one has conscientiously fulfilled one's function as a traveller.

IX. The Escorial

To go to the Escorial, we hired one of those fantastic carriages bedizened with Cupids in grisaille, and other adornments in Pompadour style, of which we have already had occasion to speak; all harnessed to four mules and embellished with a *zagal* in quite a good fancy dress. The Escorial is situated seven or eight leagues from Madrid, not far from Guadarrama, at the foot of a mountain chain; nothing more arid and desolate could be imagined than the country through which one has to drive on the way to it: not a tree, not a house; great hill-sides unfolding one beyond the other; parched ravines, which the presence of several bridges show to be watercourses, and here and there a glimpse of blue mountains crowned with snow or cloud; the landscape, such as it is, is not lacking in grandeur: the absence of all vegetation gives the lines of the country an extraordinary austerity and freedom; the further one gets from Madrid, the larger grow the stones with which the plain is starred, which aspire towards becoming rocks; these grey-blue stones, breaking out all over the scaly ground, look like warts on the wrinkled back of an age-old crocodile; they cut the outline of the hills into a thousand strange patterns, giving them an appearance like the ruins of giant buildings.

Half-way there, at the end of a fairly steep ascent, one finds a poor, solitary house, the only one which one comes across in a distance of eight leagues, opposite a fountain from which a pure icy water filters drop by drop; as many glasses of water are drunk as the spring will yield, the mules are breathed, and then a fresh start is made; it is not long before you see that architectural leviathan, the Escorial, thrown into relief against the misty mountain background by a brilliant ray of sunshine. The effect at this distance is very fine; it might be taken for a vast Oriental palace. The stone cupola and the balls at the end of every pinnacle contribute very largely towards the illusion; before reaching it, one drives through a great olive-wood full of crosses, oddly perched in the most picturesque fashion on masses of great rocks; once the wood is passed, you debouch into the village, and find yourself face to face with the colossus, which loses greatly by being seen close at hand, like all colossi in this world. The first thing that struck me was the vast quantity of swallows and martins circling in the air in countless numbers, and filling it with their shrill, strident cries. These poor little birds seemed scared by the deathly silence reigning in this Thebaid, and were making an effort to introduce a little noise and animation.

Everybody knows that the Escorial was built as the result of a vow made by Philip II at the siege of St. Quentin, where he was obliged to bombard a church of St. Lawrence; he promised the saint that he would compensate him for the church he was taking away from him by a larger and more beautiful one, and he kept his word better than is the habit of earthly kings; after the Pyramids of Egypt, the Escorial, begun by Juan Bautista and furnished by Herrera, is surely the greatest mass of granite existing upon earth: in Spain it is known as the eighth wonder of the world; every country has its eighth wonder, which makes at least thirty eighth wonders of the world.

When I come to give an opinion of the Escorial, I am excessively perplexed. So many serious and highly placed persons—who, I prefer to think, had never seen it—have spoken of it as a masterpiece and a supreme achievement of human genius, that a poor devil of a wandering journalist like me will seem to be deliberately straining after originality, and taking a pleasure in running counter to accepted ideas; none the less, in my very soul and conscience, I cannot help considering the Escorial to be the dullest and most dismal building imagined for the mortification of their fellow-men by a gloomy monk and a suspicion-haunted tyrant. I am well aware that the Escorial was destined for an austere religious purpose, but gravity is not the same thing as aridity, melancholy is not depression, contemplation is not tedium, and it is always possible happily to unite beauty of form with lofty ideals.

The Escorial is arranged in the shape of a gridiron, in memory of that of St. Lawrence. Four towers, or square pavilions, represent the feet of the instrument of martyrdom; these pavilions are united by wings of the building, which form the frame; other buildings cross from one side to the other, in imitation of the bars of the gridiron; the palace and the church are built in the handle. This strange idea, which must have been a great hindrance to the architect, is not easily grasped at a glance, though it is very clear on the plan; and if one had not been warned of it, one would certainly not have noticed it. I do not blame this childish symbolism, which was in the taste of the time; for I am convinced that laying down limits, far from injuring an artist of genius, is a help to him, increases his strength, and enables him to find resources of which he would not have dreamed; but it seems to me that they might have been turned to a much better purpose. Those who love "good taste and sobriety" in architecture, must find the Escorial perfect, for the only line used is the straight line, the only order the Doric, the poorest and most melancholy of all.

The Escorial

The first thing which strikes you very unpleasantly is the ochreous yellow tone of the walls, which one might suppose to be built of compressed clay, if the joints of the stones, marked by lines of glaring white, did not prove the contrary. There could be no more monotonous sight than these six or seven-storied buildings, with no mouldings, no pilasters and no columns, but with little crushed-looking windows, looking like the cells of a hive. It is the ideal of a barracks or a hospital; the only merit of it all is that it is built of granite. But this merit is thrown away, for at a hundred yards' distance it might be taken for potter's clay. Above it all crouches heavily a humped dome, for which I can find no better comparison than the dome of the Val-de-Grâce, with no ornament save a multitude of granite balls. All round it, that nothing may be lacking to complete the symmetry, have been raised buildings in the same style, that is to say, with a number of little windows and not the slightest ornament; these buildings communicate with one another by bridge-shaped galleries thrown across the road leading down to the village, which is now a mere mass of ruins. All the approaches to the edifice are flagged with granite, and its bounds are marked by little walls three feet high, embellished with the inevitable balls at every angle and intersection. The façade does not stand out in any way from the bulk of the edifice, and in no way breaks its aridity, so that it is hardly perceptible, in spite of its gigantic size.

One first enters a vast court-yard, at the opposite side of which rises the portal of a church, having nothing remarkable about it save some colossal statues of the prophets, with gilt ornaments and rose-tinted faces. This court-yard is flagged, damp and chilly; grass grows green in the corners; you have only to set foot in it for weariness to descend upon your shoulders like a leaden mantle; your heart sinks; you feel that all things are at an end, and that for you all joy is dead. Twenty paces from the door, you scent an indefinable odour, icy and sickly, of holy water and sepulchral vaults, from which blows a draught laden with pleurisy and catarrh. Though there are thirty degrees of heat outside, your marrow congeals in your bones; you feel that a living warmth can never more rekindle in your veins the blood which has turned more chilly than a viper's. These walls, impenetrable as the tomb, can never permit the air of the living to filter through their thick partitions. Well! In spite of this cloistered and Muscovite chill, the first thing I saw upon entering the church was a Spanish woman kneeling on the stone pavement, beating her breast with one hand, while she fanned herself with the other with at least equal fervour; the fan, I perfectly well remember, was as green as water or the leaf of an iris, and makes me shiver all down my back when I think of it.

The guide who led us round the interior of the edifice was blind, and it was really marvellous to see the precision with which he would stop before the pictures, pointing out the subject and the painter without hesitating or ever making a mistake. He took us through an infinite number of corridors, equalling in complexity the *Confessional of the Black Penitents* or the *Castle in the Pyrenees* by Ann Radcliffe. The name of this good man is Cornelio; he is the best-tempered fellow in the world, and seems to take quite a joy in his infirmity.

The interior of the church is bare and depressing. Enormous mouse-grey pilasters of coarse granite, with grains of mica looking like kitchen salt, rise towards the frescoed vaulting with its misty azure tones, ill-assorted with the chilly and poverty-stricken colour of the architecture: the retable, carved and gilt in the Spanish fashion, with very fine paintings, does something towards correcting this meagre decoration, in which everything is sacrificed to some mysterious, insipid ideal of symmetry; the gilt bronze statues kneeling on both sides of the retable, representing, I think, Don Carlos and the princesses of the royal family, are effective in the grand style; the choir, facing the high altar, is a vast church in itself; the stalls which surround it, instead of flowering with exuberant, fantastic arabesques like those of Burgos, share in the general rigidity, having as their sole decoration just a few mouldings. We were shown the place where for fourteen years the gloomy Philip II, a king born to be a grand inquisitor, used to come and sit: it is the stall standing in the corner; in the panelling opens a door, which communicates with the interior of the palace. Though I do not plume myself upon my devotional fervour, I have never entered a Gothic cathedral without experiencing a deep, mysterious sentiment, an unusual emotion, or without a vague fear that, on walking round a great clustering pillar, I might come upon the Eternal Father in person, with his long, silver beard, his crimson mantle, and his azure robe, gathering up the prayers of the faithful in the folds of his tunic. In the church of the Escorial one is so weighed down and crushed, one feels oneself so completely dominated by a gloomy, inflexible power, that the uselessness of prayer appears a proven fact. The God of such a temple will never suffer himself to be prevailed upon.

After going round the church, we went down into the Pantheon. This is the name given to the vault in which the bodies of the kings are laid; it is an octagonal chamber thirty-six feet in diameter and thirty-eight feet in height, situated exactly below the high altar, in such a way that when the priest is saying mass, his feet are upon the keystone of the vault; one descends to it by a staircase of granite and coloured marble, closed by a fine bronze grille. The walls of the Pantheon are entirely lined with jasper, porphyry and other equally precious marbles. Niches are hollowed out in the walls, with funerary monuments of antique forms intended to contain the bodies of the kings and queens who have left issue; in this vault reigns a deathly and penetrating chill; as the flickering light of the torch falls upon the polished marbles, they send back reflections as of glass; they look as if water were streaming down them, and one might imagine that one was in a grotto beneath the sea. The monstrous edifice weighs upon you with its whole mass; it surrounds you, it seizes you in its grasp and stifles you; you feel yourself held fast, as if by the tentacles of a gigantic polypus of granite. The dead contained within these funerary urns seem deader than any others, and it is hard to believe they will ever succeed in rising again. Here, as in the church, you receive a sinister and despairing impression; in all these dismal vaults there is no single hole through which you can see the sky.

In the sacristy there still remain a few good pictures (the best of them have been transferred to the Royal Museum at Madrid)—among others, two or three unusually perfect paintings on wood of the German school: the ceiling of the grand staircase is painted in fresco by Luca Giordano, with an allegorical representation of Philip II's vow and the foundation of the convent; the acres of wall-space painted in Spain by Luca Giordano are something truly prodigious, and we moderns, who are left breathless in the middle of even the shortest task, find it hard to conceive how such works are possible; Pellegrini, Luca, Gangiaso, Carducho, Romolo Cincinnato and many others have all painted cloisters, vaults and ceilings in the Escorial. That of the library, by Carducho and Pellegrini, is a fresco in beautiful pale and luminous tones; the composition is rich, and its twining arabesques are in the best of taste. The library of the Escorial has this peculiarity, that the books are arranged on the shelves with their backs to the walls and their edges turned towards the spectator; I do not know the reason of this oddity. It is particularly rich in Arabic manuscripts, and must contain priceless and completely unknown treasures. Now that the conquest of Africa has made Arabic a fashionable language in common use, it is to be hoped that this rich mine will be explored in every direction by our young Orientalists; the other books seemed to me in general to be works on theology and scholastic philosophy. We were shown a few vellum manuscripts with margins adorned with designs and miniatures; but since it was Sunday and the librarian was not there, this was all we could manage, and we had to go away without seeing a single *incunabulum*, a disadvantage which my companion felt much more keenly than I did, for unfortunately I have not a passion for bibliography, or for anything else.

In one of these corridors is placed a life-sized white marble Christ, attributed to Benvenuto Cellini, and a few very strange, fantastic paintings in the style of the Temptations of Callot and Teniers, but much more ancient. At any rate, nothing more monstrous could be imagined than these interminable low, narrow corridors of grey granite which run through the building like veins in the human body; one really needs to be blind to find one's way about them; one goes up and down stairs and round thousands of corners, and one would only have to walk about them for three or four hours to wear the soles of one's shoes quite through, for the granite is as rough as a file and as stubborn as emery paper. When one is upon the dome, one sees that the balls which look no larger than bells from below, are really of enormous dimensions, and might be used for monstrous geographical globes. A vast horizon stretches out at your feet, and you can take in at a glance the country lying between you and Madrid; on either side rise the mountains of Guadarrama. In this way you can see the whole plan of the building; you look right down into the courts and cloisters, with their rows of arcades rising one above the other, their fountains, or central pavilions; the roofs appear like ridges as in a bird's-eye view.

At the time when we made the ascent of the dome, there was a stork with three little ones on top of one of the chimneys, in a great nest of straw, like an inverted turban; this interesting family formed the oddest silhouette you can imagine; the mother stood on one leg in the middle of the nest with her neck sunk between her shoulders, and her beak resting majestically upon her breast, like a philosopher in meditation; the little ones were stretching out their long beaks and necks to ask for food; I hoped I was to witness one of those sentimental scenes of natural history in which one sees the great white pelican drawing blood from her side to feed her little brood; but the stork appeared to be but little moved by these demonstrations of hunger, and stood as motionless as the stork in the woodcut which adorns the frontispiece of books brought out by Cramoisi; this melancholy group added still more to the utter solitude of the place, and gave an Egyptian touch to this pile of buildings worthy of the Pharoahs. On our way down we saw the garden, in which there is more architecture than vegetation; there are great terraces and beds of clipped box, forming designs like the sprays on old damask, with a few fountains and pools of greenish water; a tedious, solemn garden, as starchy as a Spanish collar (*golilla*) and in all ways worthy of the frowning building to which it is attached.

They say that on the outside wall alone there are eleven hundred and ten windows, which is a cause of great wonderment to the bourgeois; I have never counted them, preferring to believe it, rather than devote myself to such a task; but there is nothing improbable in it, for I have never seen so many windows in one place; the number of doors is equally fabulous.

I came away from this desert of granite, this monkish necropolis, with an extraordinary sensation of satisfaction and relief; I felt as if I were being reborn, and might once again be young and rejoice in God's creation, all hope of which I had lost beneath these funereal vaults. The warm, luminous air enfolded me like a fine, downy woollen stuff, and infused a new warmth into my body, chilled by that atmosphere of death; I was delivered from that architectural nightmare which I had thought would never end. I advise those persons who have the idiocy to maintain that they are bored to go and pass three or four days at the Escorial; there they will discover what real tedium means, and will find amusement for the rest of their lives in the thought that they might be in the Escorial, but are not.

When we returned to Madrid there was a stir of pleased surprise among our friends, who were glad to see us still alive. Few people come back from the Escorial; they die of consumption in two or three days, or if by chance they are English, they blow their brains out. Luckily we have strong constitutions, and, as Napoleon said of the cannon ball which tried to knock him over, the building which is to be the death of us is not yet built. What was no less surprising was to see that we had brought back our watches; for along the Spanish roads there are always persons very anxious to know the time; and since there are neither clocks nor sundials, they are of course bound to consult travellers. Talking about thieves, we will here relate a story of which we came near to being the heroes. The coach from Madrid to Seville, by which we had intended to start, but in which no places were left, was stopped in La Mancha by a band of insurgents or robbers—which is the same thing; the robbers divided the spoils, and were preparing to carry off the prisoners into the mountains in order to extort ransom from their families (might one not think this had happened in Africa?), when another and larger band came up, which thrashed the first, robbed them of their prisoners and carried the latter off to the mountains for good.

On the way there, one of the travellers drew his cigar-case out of a pocket which they had forgotten to search, took one, struck his tinder-box, and lit it. "Would you like a cigar?" he said with true Castilian politeness to one of the bandits. "They are Havanas." "*Con mucho gusto,*" replied the bandit, flattered by this courtesy; and there stood the traveller and the brigand, with their cigars together, drawing at them and puffing out the smoke in order to light them the more quickly. They fell into conversation, and, from one thing to another, the robber began, like all tradesmen, to complain of his business; times were hard, business was going badly, a lot of respectable people kept interfering and spoiling trade; they stood in queues to rifle the wretched diligences, and three or four bands had often to squabble over the spoils of a single galley or mule-train. Lastly, travellers were so sure of being robbed that they only took with them what was strictly necessary, and wore their poorest clothes. "See," he said with a melancholy gesture of discouragement, displaying a worn-out cloak, worthy to cover Honesty herself, "is it not shameful to be forced to steal such rags? Could the most respectable man living be worse dressed? We take the travellers as hostages, of course, but nowadays relations are so hard-hearted that they cannot make up their minds to loosen their purse-strings; we are responsible for the expense of feeding them, and, moreover, after a month or two it costs us a charge of powder and shot to blow our prisoners' brains out; this is always unpleasant when one has got used to people; and it is for this that we have to sleep on the ground, eat acorns, and sometimes bitter ones, drink melted snow, make enormous journeys along abominable roads and risk our necks at every turn."

Thus spoke the brave bandit, more disgusted with his profession than a Parisian journalist when his turn comes round to write a feuilleton.

"Well!" said the traveller; "if you do not like your profession, and make so little out of it, why do you not take to another?"

"I have thought of doing so, and my companions are of the same way of thinking; but what can one do? We are hunted down and pursued; we should be shot like dogs if we went near any village; we have to go on living in the same way."

The traveller, who was a man with a certain amount of influence, remained awhile in thought.

"So you would gladly give up your profession if you received an *indulto* (amnesty)?"

"Certainly," replied the whole band; "do you suppose it is fun being a robber? We have to work like blacks and lead the life of a dog. We had just as lief be honest."

"Very well," replied the traveller, "I undertake to obtain your pardon, on condition that you give us back our liberty."

"Let it be as you have said: go to Madrid; here is a horse and money for the journey, and a safe-conduct so that our companions may let you pass. Come back quickly; we will wait for you at such-and-such a place with your friends, whom we will treat as well as we can."

The man went to Madrid, obtained a promise that the bandits should receive an *indulto*, and came back to look for his comrades in misfortune; he found them sitting down peacefully with the brigands, eating sugar-cured La Mancha ham and frequently embracing a wineskin full of Val de Peñas, which had been stolen specially for them, as a delicate attention! They were singing and enjoying themselves heartily, and would rather have turned robbers like the rest than gone back to Madrid; but the leader of the band remonstrated with them severely and recalled them to a sense of their situation, and the whole troop set off arm-in-arm for the town, where both travellers and robbers were received with enthusiasm, for brigands captured by the stage-coach are a rare curiosity.

Toledo

X. Toledo

WE had exhausted the sights of Madrid, we had seen the Palace, the Armoury, the Buen Retiro, the Museum and Academy of Painting, the Teatro del Principe, the Plaza de Toros; we had strolled on the Prado, from the fountain of Cybele to the Fountain of Neptune, and a slight feeling of boredom was creeping over us. And so, in spite of a temperature of thirty degrees, and all kinds of alarming tales of insurgents and *rateros*, we set out boldly on the way to Toledo, the city of beautiful swords and romantic daggers.

Toledo is one of the most ancient cities, not only in Spain, but, if the chroniclers are to be believed, in the whole universe. The more moderate of them fix the date of its foundation before the Flood. (Why not in the days of the pre-Adamite kings, a few years before the creation of the world?) Some attribute the honour of laying the first stone of it to Tubal, others to the Greeks; one party to the Roman consuls Telmon and Brutus; another to the Jews, who entered Spain with Nebuchadnezzar; relying on the etymology of *Toledo*, which comes from *Toledoth*, a Hebrew word meaning generations, because the twelve tribes had contributed towards building and peopling it.

However this may be, Toledo is most certainly a wonderful old city, situated a dozen leagues from Madrid; that is to say, of course, Spanish leagues, which are longer than a nine-column feuilleton, or a day on which one has no money, the two longest things we know. One reaches it either by a light carriage, or by a little coach which runs twice a week; the latter method is preferable, as being safer, for on the other side of the Pyrenees, as used to be the case in France, one makes one's will even before the shortest journey. This terror of brigands must be exaggerated, for in the course of a very long pilgrimage through the provinces with the most dangerous reputation, we never saw anything to justify this panic. Nevertheless, fear adds greatly to the pleasure, it keeps you alert and saves you from boredom: you are performing a heroic action, you are exerting superhuman courage; the scared, anxious look of those who are left behind raises you in your own estimation. The commonest thing in the world, a journey by coach, becomes an adventure, an expedition; you start, it is true, but you are not sure that you will get there—or come back again. This is always something in a civilization as advanced as that of modern times, in the prosaic and unlucky year 1840.

One leaves Madrid by the Gate and Bridge of Toledo, all decked with flaming vases, scrolls, statues and rosettes, in poor taste but producing quite a stately effect; we pass on the right the village of Caramanchel, where Ruy Blas went to seek the "little blue flower of Germany" for Marie de Neubourg (nowadays Ruy Blas would not find even the poorest forget-me-not in this cork-coloured hamlet built on a pumice-stone soil); and one enters a vile road leading into an interminable dusty plain, all covered with wheat and barley, the pale yellow of which adds still further to the monotony of the landscape. A few ominous crosses which stretch their gaunt arms here and there, a few pointed steeples which reveal the existence of an unseen village in the distance, some dried-up ravines crossed by a stone bridge, are the only things which give variety to the scene. From time to time one meets a peasant on his mule, with his carbine at his side; a *muchacho* driving before him two or three asses loaded with jars or chopped straw, bound round with grass ropes; a poor emaciated, sunburnt woman, dragging along a sullen-looking child, and that is all.

As we drove on, the landscape became more and more deserted, and it was not without a feeling of inward satisfaction that we caught sight, on a bridge of mortarless stone, of the five guards in green uniforms who were to act as our escort, for an escort is needed on the journey from Madrid to Toledo. Might one not imagine that one was in the heart of Algeria, and that Madrid was surrounded by a Mitidja inhabited by Bedouins?

A halt is made for lunch at Illescas, a town or village—we can hardly say which—where one sees a few traces of old Moorish buildings, and the houses have windows filled with gratings of elaborate ironwork and surmounted by crosses.

Lunch consists of a soup with garlic and eggs in it, the inevitable tomato omelette (*tortilla*), roasted almonds and oranges, washed down by a fairly good Val de Peñas, which is, however, thick enough to cut with a knife, reeking of pitch and the colour of blackberry syrup. The cookery is not the bright side of Spain, and the inns have not improved noticeably since Don Quixote, whose pictures of omelettes full of feathers, horny haddock, rancid oil and chick-peasie fit to use as musket-bullets, are still absolutely truthful; but I am sure I do not know where one would find nowadays the five fat pullets and monstrous geese at the wedding-feast of Gamacho.

From Illescas onwards, the country grows rougher, and the result is a still viler road; it is one series of quagmires and death-traps. This does not prevent them from driving full tilt; Spanish postillions are like the Morlach coachmen of Dalmatia; they do not care in the least what goes on behind them, and provided they reach their destination, if only with the pole and the front wheels, they are satisfied. However, we arrived without difficulty, amidst a cloud of dust kicked up by our mules and the horses of our guard, and entered Toledo, panting with curiosity and thirst, through a magnificent Arab gate with an elegantly curved arch and granite pillars with balls on top of them, richly bedizened with texts from the Koran; this gate is called the Puerta del Sol; it is russet in hue, with the tones of something cooked and preserved, like a Portugal orange, and stands out in splendid relief against a limpid sky of lapis lazuli. In our misty climates, one cannot really form any idea of these violent colours and harsh outlines, and the paintings of them which people bring back will always appear exaggerated.

On driving through the Puerta del Sol, one finds oneself on a sort of terrace, from which a most extensive view can be enjoyed; one looks out over the *Vega*, dappled and striped with trees and cultivated fields, which owe their freshness to a system of irrigation introduced by the Moors. The Tagus, crossed by the Bridge of Saint Martin and the Bridge of Alcantara, rolls its rapid yellow waters almost all round the town, which lies in a bend of it. Below the terrace shimmer before one's eyes the gleaming brown roofs of the houses, and the towers of convents and churches, with their chequered roofs of green and white earthenware tiles; in the distance are to be seen the red hills and gaunt precipices which close in the horizon of Toledo. The peculiarity of this view is that it is entirely devoid of atmosphere or of that mist in which wide prospects are always bathed in our country; the transparence of the air leaves the lines perfectly clear-cut, and enables one to descry the slightest detail from a considerable distance.

As soon as our luggage had been examined, our most urgent business was to look for some kind of *fonda* or *parador*, for the eggs of Illescas were already far behind us; we were led through alleys so narrow that two laden asses could not have not passed each other if they met, to the Fonda del Caballero, one of the most comfortable places in the city. There, by scraping together what little Spanish we knew, eked out by a pathetic pantomime, we succeeded in conveying to our hostess, a gentle, charming woman of a most interesting and distinguished appearance, that we were dying of hunger, a fact which always seems greatly to surprise the natives, who live on air and sun, in the economical fashion of chameleons.

The whole kitchen staff began to bestir itself, the innumerable little pots, in which the highly flavoured ragouts of the Spanish cuisine are distilled and sublimated, were pushed up to the fire, and they promised us dinner by the end of an hour. We profited by this hour to examine the *fonda* in greater detail.

It was a fine building—some ancient mansion, no doubt—with an inner court paved with a mosaic of coloured marbles, and adorned with white marble well-heads, and troughs lined with earthenware tiles for washing glasses and bowls.

These court-yards are called *patios*; they are usually surrounded by columns and arcades, with a fountain in the middle. A canvas *tendido* (awning), which is drawn back at night, so as to admit the cool night air, forms the ceiling of this kind of inside-out drawing-room. All round it, at the level of the first story, runs a balcony of elegantly wrought iron, on to which open the windows and doors of the apartments, which one only enters to dress, dine or take one's siesta. The rest of the time is spent in this court-yard-saloon—into which they bring down the pictures, the chairs, the sofas and the piano, and adorn it with pots of flowers and orange-trees in tubs.

Our inspection was hardly finished when Celestina (the odd and capricious servant at the inn) came, humming a song, to tell us that dinner was served. The dinner was quite passable: cutlets, eggs with tomato, chicken fried in oil, trout from the Tagus, with a bottle of Peralta, a sweet full-flavoured wine with a slight muscat aroma which is quite pleasant.

When our meal was finished, we straggled about the town, preceded by a guide, a barber by trade, who showed round tourists in his spare time.

The streets of Toledo are extremely narrow; one could join hands from one window to the opposite one, and nothing would be easier than to step from one balcony to another, if one was not kept in order and prevented from indulging in these aerial familiarities by most handsome grilles and fine bars of that rich ironwork with which they are so lavish beyond the Pyrenees. This lack of breadth would draw cries of astonishment from all partisans of civilization, whose dreams are all of immense open spaces, vast squares, disproportionate streets and other more or less progressive improvements; yet nothing is more reasonable than these narrow streets in a torrid climate, and the architects who are making broad gashes in the solid mass of Algiers will soon begin to notice this. At the bottom of these narrow clefts, cut in just the right places round the blocks and islands of houses, one enjoys a deliciously cool shade, and wanders about the ramifications and pores of this human accretion, which is called a town but reminds one of some haunt of deep-sea monsters; the molten lead which Phoebus Apollo ladles out from high heaven during the noontide hours can never reach you; the projecting roofs serve as a parasol.

If you are obliged, to your cost, to cross some *plazuela* or *calle ancha* exposed to the glare of the dog-days, you will soon appreciate the wisdom of our forbears, who would not sacrifice to any mysterious ideal of stupid regularity; the flags are like those plates of red-hot metal upon which showmen make geese and turkeys dance a breakdown; wretched dogs, with no shoes or *alpargatas*, rush across them with plaintive howls. If you lift the knocker on a door, you burn your fingers; you can feel your brains boiling in your brain-pan like a stew-pot on the fire; your

A Romantic in Spain

nose turns cardinal, your hands put on tan gloves, and you evaporate in sweat. You see how much use these great squares and broad streets are. All those who have walked down the Calle de Alcalá at Madrid between noon and two o'clock will be of my way of thinking. Besides, in order to make the streets spacious, the houses are cramped, whereas the opposite plan strikes me as the more reasonable. Of course it is understood that this remark only applies to warm countries where it never rains and carriages are very rare. Narrow streets in our rainy climates would be sinks of abomination. In Spain women go out walking, even for long distances, in black satin slippers—for which I admire them, especially in Toledo, where the streets are paved with little polished, shiny, pointed stones, which seem to have been carefully arranged sharp side uppermost; but their little arched, wiry feet are as tough as a gazelle's hoofs, and they trip along as gaily as can be over these cobble-stones cut into facets like a diamond, which wring cries of anguish from travellers accustomed to the soft asphalt of Seyssel and the elastic bitumen of Polonceau.

The houses of Toledo are of an austere and imposing appearance; they have but few windows in their façades, and these windows are as a rule grated. The doors, ornamented with bluish granite pillars with balls on top of them—a decoration which is frequently met with—have a thick, solid appearance which is still further increased by the huge nails with which they are starred. They have at once something of the convent, the prison, the fortress and even the harem, for the Moors have passed this way. By a rather odd contrast, some of these houses are adorned outside with paintings, either in fresco or in distemper, of imitation bas-reliefs, scenes in monochrome, flowers, shells and wreaths, with vases, medallions, Cupids and all the mythological lumber of the last century. These houses, which recall those panels painted over doors in the Pompadour style, produce the strangest and most comical effect among their forbidding-looking sisters of feudal or Moorish origin.

We were led through an inextricable network of little alleys, where my friend and I walked in single file, like the geese in the ballad, for lack of space to take each other's arm, till we came to the Alcázar, which stands like an acropolis at the highest point of the city; and after some discussion we went in, for the first impulse of people whom one asks for anything is to refuse, whatever the request may be: "Come back tonight, or tomorrow; the custodian is asleep; the keys have been mislaid; you must have a permit from the Governor." These are the answers which one first receives; but by exhibiting the magic *peseta*, or, in cases of extreme difficulty, the shining *duro*, one always manages in the end to force one's way in.

The Alcázar, built on the ruins of the ancient Moorish palace, is nowadays itself ruined; it is like one of those marvellous architectural dreams which Piranesi tries to embody in his magnificent engravings; it is by Covarrubias, a little-known artist very superior to the dull, heavy Herrera, whose fame has been very much overrated. The façade is adorned and enriched with arabesques in the purest Renaissance style, and is a masterpiece of elegance and nobility. The burning Spanish sun, which turns marble red and tinges stone with saffron hues, has clothed it in a robe of rich, vigorous colouring, very different from the leprous black with which the passing centuries encrust our ancient buildings. To use the expression of a great poet, Time has passed its skilful thumb over the marble ribs and over-rigid contours, giving to the already soft and flowing lines of the carving a supreme touch of polish and a final perfection. I particularly remember a great staircase of fairy-like elegance, with its marble columns, balustrades and steps already half broken down, leading up to a floor which opens on an abyss, for this part of the building has fallen in. This wonderful staircase, which might belong to a king's palace, leads to nothingness, but has something strange and enchanting about it.

The Alcázar is built upon a great terrace surrounded by ramparts with crenellations in the Eastern style, from the top of which one looks out upon an immense view, a truly magical panorama: here the cathedral pierces the heart of the sky with its spire of incalculable height; beyond its glints in a ray of sunlight the church of San Juan de los Reyes; the Bridge of Alcantara, with its tower-shaped gate, bestrides the Tagus with its bold arches; on the bank of the stream Juanello's *Artificio* rears one above the other its tiers of red brick arcades, which one might take for the ruins of some Roman building, and the massive towers of the *Castillo* of Cervantes (this Cervantes has nothing to do with the author of *Don Quixote*), perched on the rugged, formless rocks which fringe the river-bank, frets the horizon with yet another notch, deeply indented as it is by the spiny summits of the mountain ranges.

A wonderful sunset completed the picture: the sky shaded by insensible gradations of tone from the most brilliant red to orange, and then to pale lemon, ending in a strange blue like a greenish turquoise, which in its turn died away in the west into the lilac hues of night, whose shades already shed their freshness over all that side.

With my elbows on an embrasure of the battlements, looking down upon a bird's-eye view of this city where I knew not a soul, where my name was absolutely unknown, I had fallen into a state of deep meditation. Before all these objects, all these forms, which I looked upon but should probably never see again, I was seized with doubts of my own identity; I felt so absent from myself, so far removed from my sphere, that it all seemed an hallucination, a strange dream from which I should be awakened with a start by the shrill, quavering music of some vaudeville, as I leant on the edge of a box at some theatre. By one of those sudden transitions of ideas which occur so frequently in day-dreams, I thought of what my friends might be doing at that time, I wondered if they noticed my absence, and whether by chance, at that very moment, as I bent over the battlements of the Alcázar at Toledo, my name was fluttering in Paris on the lips of some faithful and beloved friend. Apparently the inner answer was not in the affirmative, for in spite of the splendour of the sight, I felt my soul overcome by an immeasurable sadness; and yet I was fulfilling the dream of my whole life, I was touching with my hand one of my most ardently cherished desires: I had talked so much, in my beautiful salad days of romanticism, about my good Toledo blade, that I was curious to see the place where they were made.

Nothing less was required to draw me away from my philosophic meditation than a proposition from my friend that we should go and bathe in the Tagus. Bathing is too rare a curiosity in this land, where in summer they water the river-beds, to neglect such an opportunity. Taking the guide's word for it that the Tagus was a serious river, having enough moisture in it to dip one's cup in, we hurried down from the Alcázar, in order to avail ourselves of the lingering daylight, and made our way towards the river. We crossed the Plaza de la Constitución, round which stand houses which, with their great woven-grass awnings, rolled back or half lifted by the projecting balconies, have a most picturesque appearance, quite Venetian or mediaeval, and passed under a fine Arab gate with a round brick arch, arriving at the Bridge of Alcantara, near which there is a good bathing-place, by a very steep and precipitous zigzag road, winding down under the rocks and walls which encircle Toledo.

Night fell while we were on our way down, for in southern climates it follows suddenly upon the day; this did not prevent us from groping our way into this venerable river, made famous by the languorous poem of Queen Hortense, and by the sand of gold which it washes down in its crystal waves, if we are to believe the poets, the hired attendants and the travellers' guides.

Having finished our bath, we hurried up so as to arrive before the closing of the gates. We sipped a glass of *horchata de chufas* and iced milk, with an exquisite flavour and aroma, and had ourselves guided back to our *fonda*.

Our bedroom, like all Spanish bedrooms, was of whitewashed plaster, hung with those yellowed pictures, thick with dirt, those mystic daubs painted like ale-house signs, which one so often meets with in the Peninsula, the country with the greatest number of bad pictures in the world; we say this without prejudice to the good ones.

We made haste to go to sleep as quickly and as soundly as possible, so as to wake up early the next day and go and see the cathedral before the service began.

The Cathedral of Toledo is justly considered to be one of the finest and, above all, the richest in Spain. Its origins are lost in the night of antiquity; and, if one is to believe local writers, it goes back to St. James the Apostle, first Bishop of Toledo, who is said to have recommended the site to his disciple and successor Elpidius, a hermit of Mount Carmel. Elpidius constructed a church on the spot pointed out to him, and placed it under the invocation and title of St. Mary, while this divine lady was still living in Jerusalem. "Signal felicity! Illustrious blazon of the Toledans! Most excellent trophy of their glories!" exclaims in a lyrical effusion the author from whom we extract these details.

The Blessed Virgin was not ungrateful, and, according to the same legend, came down, body and soul, to visit the Church of Toledo, bearing in her own hands a beautiful chasuble in *cloth of heaven* for the blessed St. Ildefonso. "Behold how this Queen doth requite them!" exclaims our author again. The chasuble is in existence, and one can see, sunk in the wall, a stone still preserving the imprint of the divine foot which was planted upon it. An inscription in the following terms bears witness to the miracle:

Quando la Reina del cielo
Puso los pies en ci suelo
En esta piedra los puso.
(When the Queen of Heaven planted her feet on the ground, it was on this stone that she placed them.)

The legend further relates that the Blessed Virgin was so pleased with her statue, and thought it so well made, so well-proportioned and so like her, that she kissed it and conferred upon it the gift of working miracles. If the Queen of the Angels were to come down and visit our churches today, I doubt whether she would be tempted to embrace her images.

More than two hundred writers of the most serious and honourable character relate this story, which is at least as well authenticated as the death of Henry IV; as for me, I feel no difficulty in believing this miracle, and am perfectly ready to include this story among the number of genuine facts. The church continued to exist in the same state till the time of St. Eugenius, sixth Bishop of Toledo, who enlarged and beautified it, as far as his means allowed, under the title of Our Lady of the Assumption, which it still preserves to this day; but in the year 302, the period of the cruel persecution which the Emperors Diocletian and Maximin inflicted upon the Christians, the prefect Dacian ordered the sacred building to be demolished and razed, so that the faithful no longer knew where to seek and find the bread of salvation. Three years later, when Constantine came to the throne, the persecution ceased, the prelates returned to their see, and the Archbishop Melantius began to rebuild the church, still on the same spot. A little later, about the year 312, the Emperor Constantine, having been converted to the faith, ordered, among other heroic works to which his Christian zeal impelled him, that the basilica of Our Lady of the Assumption, destroyed by Dacian, should be repaired and built at his expense as sumptuously as possible.

Toledo had then as its archbishop Marinus, a learned man of letters, who was on intimate terms with the Emperor; this circumstance ensured him full liberty of action, and he spared nothing to build a church that should be remarkable for its grand and sumptuous architecture; it was this church which lasted throughout the whole period of the Goths; which was visited by the Virgin, turned into a mosque during the conquest of Spain, and became a church again when Toledo was recaptured by King Alonso VI; the plan of it was carried off to Oviedo by order of King Alonso the Chaste, in order that the church of San Salvador might be built there on the same lines in the year 803. Our author adds that those who may be curious to know what were the shape, size and splendour of the Cathedral of Toledo in the days when the Queen of the Angels came down to visit it, have only to go and see that of Oviedo, and they will be content. For our part, we greatly regret that we were unable to give ourselves this pleasure.

Finally, during the happy reign of St. Ferdinand, when Don Rodrigo was Archbishop of Toledo, the church assumed the wonderful and magnificent form which it wears today, which is, they say, that of the Temple of Diana at Ephesus. O naïve chronicler! Allow me to disbelieve every word of this; the temple at Ephesus was not as fine as the Cathedral of Toledo! Having said a pontifical mass in the presence of the King and the whole court, Archbishop Rodrigo laid the first stone one Saturday in the year 1227; the work went on with great ardour until it had received those last touches which raised it to the highest pitch of perfection attainable by human art.

Forgive us this short historical digression. We are not in the habit of indulging in them, and shall soon return to our humble mission of descriptive tourist and literary photographer.

The outside of Toledo Cathedral is much less rich than that of the Cathedral of Burgos: there is no riot of ornament, no arabesques, no statues spreading collar-wise round the doorways; but solid buttresses, sharp, clear-cut angles, a thick armour of hewn stone, a sturdy-looking tower which has none of the delicate filigree of the Gothic; and the whole is clothed in russet tones, the colour of a browning roast or of a skin tanned like that of a pilgrim from Palestine; the interior, on the other hand, is carved and elaborated like a grotto of stalactites.

The door through which we entered is of bronze, and bears the following inscription: *Antonio Zurreno, del arte de oro y plata, faciebat esta media puerta* (Antonio Zurreno, of the craft of the gold and silversmiths, made this half of the door). The impression which one receives is extraordinarily strong and imposing; the church is made up of five naves; the central nave soars up to an amazing height, so that the others appear to bow their heads at its side and kneel in token of adoration and respect; the enormous mass is upheld on eighty-eight pillars as thick as towers, each one made up of sixteen tapering columns bound together; a transverse nave cuts the great nave between the choir and the high altar, forming the arms of the cross. All this architecture is most consistent and complete in style, a merit which is rare in Gothic cathedrals, for they are usually built at several different periods; the original plan has been carried out from beginning to end, except for the arrangement of certain chapels, which in no way disturb the harmony of the general impression. Through the stained-glass windows, sparkling with emerald, sapphire and ruby, and set like jewels in a framework of stone, chased like the metal of a ring, there filters a soft, mysterious light which moves one to a religious ecstasy; when the sun is too violent, grass blinds are lowered over the windows, maintaining a cool penumbra which makes the churches of Spain so propitious for meditation and prayer.

The high altar or retable might pass for a church in itself; it is a vast accumulation of little columns, niches, statues, leafy scroll-work and arabesques, of which but a feeble idea could be given by the minutest description; the whole construction, which rises as high as the vaulting and runs all round the sanctuary, is painted and gilt with a richness passing imagination. The warm, tawny tones of the antique gilding form a splendid foil for the threads and sparkles of light caught in passing by the mouldings and projecting ornaments, and produce wonderful effects of the most picturesque opulence. The paintings on a background of gold which adorn the panels of this altar equal in richness of colour the most brilliant Venetian canvases; this union of colour with the severe and almost hieratic forms of mediaeval art is but rarely met with; some of these pictures might be taken for works of Giorgione in his first manner.

The choir, or *silleria*, stands opposite the high altar, according to the Spanish usage; it consists of three rows of carved wooden stalls, marvellously sculptured and elaborately fretted with carvings of historical, allegorical and sacred subjects. Gothic art verging on the Renaissance has produced nothing purer, more perfect or of a finer design. This alarmingly detailed work is attributed to the patient chisels of Philip of Burgundy and Berruguete. The archbishop's stall, raised above the others and arranged like a throne, marks the centre of the choir; this prodigious piece of woodwork is crowned by columns of jasper with tones of gleaming brown, and on the entablature stand alabaster figures, also by Philip of Burgundy and Berruguete, but in a freer and more flowing style, which is wonderfully elegant and effective. Enormous bronze book-stands covered with gigantic missals, great carpets of woven grass, and two organs of colossal dimensions placed opposite each other, one on the right and the other on the left, complete the decorations.

Behind the retable is to be found the chapel in which are buried Don Alvaro de Luna and his wife, lying side by side in two magnificent alabaster tombs; the walls of this chapel are decorated with the arms of the Constable and the shells of the Order of Santiago, of which he was the Grand Master. Near by, in the vaulting of that part of the nave which is called the *trascoro*, may be noticed a stone with a funerary inscription: it belongs to a noble Toledan, whose pride revolted against the idea that his tomb might be trodden under foot by persons of humble station and doubtful extraction: "I will not have boors walking over my belly," he said on his death-bed, and since he left great possessions to the Church, his strange whim was gratified by placing his body in the masonry of the vaulting, where it is sure that nobody will walk over him.

We will not attempt to describe the chapels one by one, it would take a volume to do so: we will be content to mention the tomb of a cardinal, executed in the Arab style with a delicacy that cannot be imagined; we can find no better comparison than to liken it to lace on a grand scale, and will go on without more delay to the Mozarabic or Musarabic Chapel (both words are used)—one of the most curious in the cathedral. Before describing it, let us explain what is meant by the words Mozarabic Chapel.

At the time of the Moorish invasion, the inhabitants of Toledo were forced to surrender after a two years' siege; they tried to obtain the most favourable terms of capitulation, and among the articles agreed upon was the following: to wit, that six churches should be retained for those Christians who might desire to live among the barbarians. These churches were those of St. Mark, St. Luke, St. Sebastian, St. Torquatus, St. Olalla and St. Justa. By this means the faith was preserved in the city for four hundred years, the period of the Moorish domination, and for this reason the faithful Toledans were called Mozarabians, that is to say, mingled with the Arabs. During the reign of Alonso VI, when Toledo was restored to Christian rule, Richard, the papal legate, desired to make them abandon the Mozarabic for the Gregorian rite, and was supported in this by the King and the Queen, Doña Constanza, who preferred the Roman rite. All the clergy were up in arms and protested violently; the faithful were highly indignant, and there was very nearly a mutiny and an uprising of the people; the King, alarmed at the course which events were taking, and fearing that the worst extremities might ensue, calmed them down as best he could, and proposed to the Toledans a curious middle course, quite in the spirit of the times, which was accepted with enthusiasm by both parties: the partisans of the Gregorian and of the Mozarabic rites were each to choose a champion and make them fight it out, so that God should decide in what terms and by what rite he would prefer to be praised. And indeed, if the judgment of God was to be accepted, surely it must be in liturgical matters.

The Mozarabian champion was named Don Ruiz de la Matanza; the day was fixed. The Vega was chosen as the scene of the combat. The victory was for some time dubious; but in the end Don Ruiz won the upper hand and rode out of the lists victorious, amid the joyful shouts of the Toledans, who went off to the churches to kneel and give thanks to God, weeping for joy and throwing their caps into the air. The King, Queen and court were greatly vexed at this triumph. They came to the rather tardy conclusion that it was an impious, rash and cruel thing to

solve a theological question by a bloody combat, and maintained that the point ought to be decided by a miracle; so they proposed a fresh test, which the Toledans, trusting in the excellence of their rite, were pleased to accept. The test, which was preceded by a general fast and prayers in all the churches, consisted in placing on a lighted pyre a copy of the Roman use and another of the Toledan; the one which remained in the flames without being burnt was to be considered the better and more pleasing to God.

The test was carried out exactly, down to the smallest detail. A pyre of dry and blazing wood was raised in the square called Zocodover, which had never witnessed such a crowd of spectators since it had been a square; the two breviaries were cast into the fire, each party raising their eyes and arms towards Heaven and praying to God for the liturgy in which he preferred them to serve him; the Roman rite was thrown out, with its leaves all scattered by the violence of the flames, and came out of the trial intact, but a little singed. The Toledan remained majestically in the midst of the flames, on the spot where it had fallen, without moving or suffering any damage. There are a few enthusiastic Mozarabians who even claim that the Roman missal was entirely consumed. The King, the Queen and the legate Richard were but ill pleased, but it was impossible to go back upon the judgment; and so the Mozarabic rite was saved and ardently followed for long years by the Mozarabians, their sons and grandsons; but at last all understanding of the text was lost and nobody could be found capable of saying or following the services which had been the object of such a lively dispute. Don Francisco Ximenes, Archbishop of Toledo, not wishing such a memorable usage to fall into desuetude, founded a Mozarabic chapel in the cathedral, had the black-letter rituals translated and printed in common type, and instituted priests whose special function it was to say these services.

The Mozarabic chapel, which is still in existence today, is adorned with Gothic frescoes of the highest interest; they have as their subject the battles between the Toledans and the Moors; they are in perfect preservation, and their colours are as fresh as if they had only been finished the day before; an archeologist would find in them a quantity of curious information about armour, costumes, equipment and

architecture, for the principal fresco represents a view of old Toledo which must have been extremely accurate. In the frescoes at the sides are painted in great detail the ships which brought the Arabs to Spain; an expert might obtain from them useful information for the confused history of naval affairs in the Middle Ages. The arms of Toledo, five sable stars on a field of silver, are repeated in several parts of this chapel, with its elliptical vaulting, closed, in the Spanish fashion, by a grille of fine workmanship.

The Chapel of the Virgin is lined throughout with wonderfully polished porphyry, jasper, and yellow and purple breccia, and is of a richness surpassing the splendours of the *Thousand and One Nights;* many relics are preserved in it, among others a reliquary presented by St. Louis, in which is contained a piece of the true cross.

In order to obtain a breathing-space, we will, if you please, go and take a turn in the cloister, framing in its elegant, severe arcades fine masses of verdure which preserve their freshness in the shadow of the church, in spite of the devouring heat of the season; all the walls of this cloister are covered with immense frescoes in the style of Van Loo, by a painter named Bayeu. These compositions, with their facile composition and pleasing colour, are not in keeping with the style of the building, and must undoubtedly have taken the place of ancient paintings effaced by the passage of time, or considered by people of good taste at that period to be too Gothic. A cloister is in its right place by the side of a church; it effects a happy transition between the calm of the sanctuary and the stir of the city. One may wander, dream or muse in it without being forced to take part in the prayers and rites of worship; Catholics enter the church, Christians more often remain in the cloister. This tendency of the mind has been grasped by Catholicism, with its psychological insight. In religious countries, the place which is most elaborately decorated and enriched with gilding and flowers is the cathedral; it is there that the shadow is coolest and the peace most profound; the music there is better than at the theatre, and, as a spectacle, its pomp is unrivalled. It is the focus, the centre of attraction, like the Opera in Paris. We northern Catholics, with our Voltairian places of worship, have no idea of the luxury, the elegance and the comfort of Spanish churches; these churches are well-appointed and full

of life, without the chilly, deserted aspect of our own: in them the faithful can be at home with their God.

The sacristies and chapter-houses of the Cathedral of Toledo are of more than royal magnificence; nothing could be nobler or more picturesque than these vast halls decorated with a solid and austere luxury of which the church alone knows the secret. They are a mass of carven woodwork in walnut or black oak, *portières* of tapestry or Indian damask, brocaded curtains with broad, sweeping folds, storied wall-hangings, Persian carpets and frescoes; we will not attempt to describe them one after the other, we will merely speak of one apartment, decorated with wonderful frescoes of religious subjects in the German style, so skilfully imitated by the Spaniards, which are attributed to Berruguete's nephew, if not to Berruguete himself, for these astounding men of genius pursued their careers in the three arts simultaneously. We will also mention a ceiling by Luca Giordano, in which a whole world of angels and allegories swarms in the most distorted and foreshortened attitudes, producing a curious optical effect. From the centre of the vault shoots a ray of light, which, though painted on a plane surface, from whatever side one looks at it, seems to strike down perpendicularly upon one's head. It is here that the treasure is kept, that is to say, the fine copes of brocade, of tufted cloth of gold, of silver damask; the marvellous point-lace, the silver-gilt reliquaries, the diamond monstrances, the gigantic silver chandeliers, the embroidered banners, all the materials and accessories for the representation of that sublime Catholic drama called the Mass.

In the presses of one of these halls is kept the wardrobe of the Blessed Virgin, for statues of cold marble or alabaster do not satisfy the impassioned piety of southern peoples; carried away by their piety, they heap the object of their worship with ornaments of extravagant richness; nothing can be too beautiful, too brilliant or too ruinous; beneath this flood of jewellery both form and figure disappear; little do they care. The great thing is that it should be absolutely impossible to hang another pearl from the ears of the marble idol, to set a bigger diamond in the gold of its crown, or to trace another jewelled spray upon the brocade of its robe.

No queen of old—not even Cleopatra, who drank pearls—no empress of late imperial days, no mediaeval duchess, no Venetian courtesan in the days of Titian, had ever a more glittering jewel-case or a richer trousseau than Our Lady of Toledo. We were shown a few of her robes: one of them is covered so completely that one is unable to guess at the fabric, with foliage and arabesques of fine pearls, among which are some of priceless size and value—among others, several rows of black pearls of unheard-of rarity; this astounding robe is covered with jewelled constellations of suns and stars, almost too brilliant for the eye to bear; and it is worth several million francs.

Our inspection ended with an ascent of the tower, the top of which is reached by steep ladders, placed one above the other, of a somewhat discouraging appearance. Almost half-way up, one passes through a sort of storehouse, in which one comes upon a series of gigantic puppets, painted and dressed in the fashion of the eighteenth century, which are used for some procession or another in the style of the procession of the Tarasque. The magnificent view over which one looks out from the top of the spire is a great compensation for the fatigue of the ascent. The whole city is outlined before one with the clear-cut accuracy of those plans carved in cork by M. Pelet, which were admired at the last industrial exhibition. This comparison may no doubt appear most prosaic and not very picturesque, but really I could not find a better or more accurate one. These hump-backed, distorted blue granite rocks which shut in the Tagus, and encircle the horizon of Toledo on one side, add still further to the strangeness of the landscape, inundated and overwhelmed with a crude, pitiless, blinding light, tempered by no reflections, and increased still more by the quivering intensity of a sky without cloud or mist, white-hot like iron in a furnace.

The heat was appalling, like that of a kiln, and one needed a perfect passion of curiosity to prevent one from renouncing all exploration of antiquities in this Senegambian temperature; but we had still all the ferocious ardour of Parisian tourists with an enthusiasm for local colour. Nothing discouraged us; we only stopped to drink, for we were thirstier than the sands of Africa, and soaked up water like dry sponges. I really do not know how it was that we did not become dropsical; not to speak of wine and ices, we consumed seven or eight jars of water a day. *Agua! agua!* was our unceasing cry, and a chain of *muchachos*, passing jars from hand to hand between our room and the kitchen, hardly sufficed to quench the blaze. Had it not been for this persistent watering, we should have crumbled into dust, like sculptors' clay models when they neglect to damp them.

Having gone round the cathedral, we resolved, in spite of our thirst, to go to the church of San Juan de los Reyes, but it was not till after long parleying that we succeeded in getting the keys, for the church of San Juan de los Reyes has been closed for five or six years, and the convent of which it forms a part is deserted and falling into ruins.

San Juan de los Reyes stands on the banks of the Tagus, quite near the bridge of St. Martin; its walls have that fine orange tone characteristic of old buildings in climates where it never rains. The outside is decorated with a collection of statues of kings in noble, chivalrous attitudes and with the proudest bearing; but this is not the most remarkable thing about San Juan de los Reyes, for all mediaeval churches have a host of statues. The walls are covered from top to bottom with a multitude of chains hanging from hooks: these are the fetters of the Christian prisoners set free by the conquest of Granada. These chains, hung up at once as ornaments and votive offerings, give the church a strange and repellent resemblance to a prison.

In this connexion we were told an anecdote which we will relate here, for it is short and characteristic. The dream of every *jefe político* in Spain is to have an *alameda* in his town, just as every prefect in France dreams of a Rue de Rivoli for his. Well, the dream of the *jefe político* of Toledo was to obtain the pleasure of a promenade for those under his administration; the site was chosen, and it was not long before the earthworks were completed, thanks to the co-operation of the convict workmen; all that the promenade lacked were the trees, but these cannot be improvised, so the *jefe político* had the judicious idea of replacing them by stone stumps connected by iron chains. Since money is very scarce in Spain, the ingenious administrator, who was nothing if not resourceful, bethought him of the historic chains of San Juan de los Reyes, and said to himself: "By Jove, the very thing!" And the chains of the captives delivered by Ferdinand and Isabella the Catholic were attached to the stones of the *alameda*. Each of the craftsmen who had carried out the work received a few fathoms of this heroic ironwork; a few intelligent persons (they are to be found everywhere) raised an outcry at this vandalism, and the chains were restored to the church. As for those given to the workmen in payment, they had already been forged into ploughshares, mule's shoes and other utensils. This story is perhaps a calumny, but it has every sign of trustworthiness: we tell it as it was told to us. Let us return to our church. The key was hard to turn in the rusty lock. Having surmounted this slight obstacle, we entered a derelict cloister of wonderful elegance; from the flowered capitals of the slender, lithe, straight columns sprang arches adorned with mouldings and carved ornaments of extreme delicacy; along the walls ran long inscriptions in praise of Ferdinand and Isabella, in Gothic characters mingled with flowers, foliage and arabesques; a Christian imitation of the text and verses of the Koran used by the Moors as an architectural adornment. How sad that so precious a building should be abandoned to its fate!

By dint of a few kicks at the doors, which were barred by worm-eaten planks or blocked by rubbish, we managed to make our way into the church, which is built in a charming style, and, save for a few barbarous mutilations, seems as if it had been completed yesterday. Gothic art has produced nothing more exquisitely harmonious, more elegant or delicate. All round it runs a gallery carved in open-work and pierced like a fish-slice, with its irregular balconies suspended from clustering pillars, and following their ins and outs in every detail; the decoration is completed by gigantic leafy volutes, eagles, chimeras, heraldic monsters, coats of arms, scrolls and emblematic inscriptions in the style of those in the cloister. The choir, facing the retable, at the other end of the church, is supported upon an effective, boldly springing, elliptical arch.

The altar, which was undoubtedly a masterpiece of sculpture and painting, has been pitilessly overthrown. These useless ravages sadden one's soul and make one doubt the intelligence of man: how can ancient stones be any obstacle to new ideas? Cannot a revolution take place without demolishing the past? It seems to us that the *Constitución* would have lost nothing if it had left standing the church of Ferdinand and Isabella the Catholic, that noble queen who believed the word of genius and endowed the universe with a new world.

Venturing on to a half broken-down staircase, we made our way into the interior of the convent: the refectory is fairly spacious and has nothing remarkable in it save a ghastly picture over the door; it is made still more hideous by being covered with a coat of filth and dust, and represents a decaying corpse, with all the horrible details so willingly treated by the brush of Spanish artists. A lugubrious symbolic inscription, one of those menacing Biblical texts which are such a grim warning to human insignificance, is written up beneath this sepulchral picture—a singular choice for a refectory. I do not know whether all the stories of monkish gluttony are true, but, for my part, I should have but a poor appetite in a dining-room decorated like this.

Above it, on each side of a long corridor, are ranged the deserted cells of the vanished monks, like the combs in a beehive; they are all exactly alike, with rough whitewashed walls. This whiteness greatly impairs the poetry of one's impression, for it allows no visions of terror and grotesque fancy to lurk in the dark corners. The inside of the church and the cloister are likewise painted white, which gives them a new and fresh appearance in contrast with the style of architecture and the condition of the buildings. The absence of moisture and the fierce heat have prevented plants and weeds from germinating in the crevices of the stones and rubble, and these remains have not even the green mantle of ivy with which time covers the ruins in northern climates. We wandered long in the derelict building, along endless corridors and up and down breakneck staircases, just like any hero of Ann Radcliffe, but all the ghosts we saw were two wretched lizards, who made off as fast as their legs could carry them; for, being Spaniards, they were doubtless unacquainted with the French proverb, "The lizard is the friend of man." Besides, to walk like this through the very veins and members of a great building from which life has departed is one of the keenest pleasures that can be imagined; one keeps expecting to meet, round the corner of some cloister, an old monk with his gleaming brow and eyes sunk in shadow, walking gravely along with his arms crossed on his breast, on his way to some mysterious service in the desecrated and abandoned church.

We turned back, for there was nothing else of interest to see, not even the kitchens, to which our guide led us down with a Voltairian smile which would not have been disowned by a subscriber to the *Constitutionnel.* The church and cloisters are of unusual splendour; the rest is of the most severe simplicity: all is for the soul, nothing for the body.

At a short distance from San Juan de los Reyes stands, or, rather, does not stand, the celebrated mosque-synagogue, for, if one had no guide, one might go past it twenty times without suspecting its existence. Our bear-leader knocked at a door cut in a most uninteresting-looking wall of red compressed clay; after some time, for Spaniards are never in a hurry, they came and opened it, and asked if we had come to see the synagogue; when we answered in the affirmative, they showed us into a sort of court-yard full of rank vegetation, in the midst of which an Indian fig-tree spread its branches, with their deeply indented leaves of a green as brilliant and intense as if they had been varnished. On the opposite side stood a ramshackle barn looking more like a farm-building than anything else. They took us into this tumble-down shanty. We were never so surprised; we were in the heart of the East; the delicate columns with their capitals spreading out turban-wise, the Turkish arches, the texts from the Koran, the flat ceiling with cedar-wood panelling, the light coming from above—nothing was wanting. There were traces of ancient painting which, though almost effaced, stained the wall with strange colours and added still further to the singularity of the impression. This synagogue, turned by the Arabs into a mosque, and by the Christians into a church, is nowadays used by a joiner as both workshop and residence. He has set up his bench in the place where the altar stood; this desecration is quite recent. There are still some vestiges of the retable to be seen, together with the inscription on black marble which records the consecration of this edifice for Catholic worship.

And, talking about synagogues, we will here relate the following curious anecdote: The Jews of Toledo, probably in order to mitigate the horrors with which they inspired the Christian peoples, as the slayers of their God, used to pretend that they had not given their consent to the death of Jesus Christ, for the following reason: when Jesus was brought to trial, the council of priests, presided over by Caiaphas, sent to consult the tribes, in order to know whether he was to be set free or put to death; the question was laid before the Jews of Spain, and the synagogue of Toledo pronounced in favour of acquittal. This tribe is therefore not stained with the blood of the righteous, and does not merit the execration aroused by the Jews who voted against the Son of God. The original answer of the Toledan Jews, with a Latin translation of the

Hebrew text, is preserved, they say, in the Vatican archives. As a reward, they were permitted to build this synagogue, which is, I think, the only one that was ever tolerated in Spain.

We had been told about the ruins of an ancient Moorish pleasure-house, the palace of Galiana; in spite of our fatigue, we made them take us there on leaving the synagogue, for we were pressed for time, and had to set out for Madrid once more on the morrow.

The palace of Galiana lies outside the city, in the Vega, and to reach it one crosses the Bridge of Alcantara; after a quarter of an hour's drive through fields and standing crops, through which run thousands of little irrigation channels, we arrived at a group of trees of a fresh green, at the foot of which was working a watering-wheel of an ancient and almost Egyptian simplicity. The water was drawn up in earthen jars, attached to the spokes of the wheel by reed ropes, and poured into a channel of rounded tiles, which led to a reservoir; from thence it was easily carried by trenches to the points where moisture was required.

Through the foliage of the trees could be seen the indistinct outline of an enormous heap of ruddy brick; this was Galiana's palace.

Through a low door we made our entry into this pile of ruins inhabited by a family of peasants; one could not possibly imagine anything blacker, smokier, more cavernous and more filthy. The dwellings of the Troglodytes were princely by comparison, and yet the charming Galiana, the lovely Moor with her long eyes stained with henna, and her brocaded robe starred with pearls, had trodden this broken-down floor with her tiny slippers; she had leant over this window-sill, gazing far out over the Vega at the Moorish horsemen as they practised hurling the *djerid*.

We bravely continued our explorations, and mounted by rickety ladders to the upper stories, clinging hand and foot to the tufts of dried grass which hung like beards from the frowning chin of the old walls.

On reaching the roof, we observed a strange phenomenon; we had gone in with white trousers on, but we came out with them black—but a black which hopped, swarmed and crawled: we were covered with little tiny fleas which had leapt upon us in solid swarms, attracted by our cold northern blood. I should never have believed that there were so many fleas in the whole world.

A few conduit pipes which brought water to the baths are the only traces of magnificence that time has spared; the mosaics of glass and enamelled earthenware, the miniature marble columns with their capitals covered with gilding, sculpture and texts from the Koran, the alabaster basins, the stones pierced with holes through which the perfumes filtered—all this has disappeared. Absolutely nothing is left save great skeleton walls and heaps of brick, all crumbling into dust; for unluckily these marvellous edifices, which recall the fairy-like scenes of the *Thousand and One Nights*, are only built of brick and compressed clay, covered with a crust of stucco or plaster. All this lacework, all these arabesques are not, as is generally believed, carved in marble or stone, but modelled in plaster, which enables them to be reproduced in infinite numbers and without great expense. It is due to the preserving dryness of the Spanish climate that buildings constructed in such fragile materials should have survived down to our day.

The legend of Galiana has worn better than her palace. She was the daughter of King Galafer, who loved her more than all the world and had a pleasure-house built for her in the Vega, with delightful gardens, kiosks, baths, fountains and lakes which rose and fell with the waxing and waning of the moon, either by magic or by one of those hydraulic artifices so well known to the Arabs. Galiana was her father's idol, and passed her life as pleasantly as could be in this charming retreat, spending her time in music, poetry and dancing. Her most painful task was to evade the gallant attentions and adoration of her suitors. The most assiduous and determined of them all was a certain petty king of Guadalajara, named Bradamant, a Moorish giant, valiant and fierce; Galiana could not endure him, and, as the chronicler says: "What matters it that the knight be of fire if the lady be of ice?" None the less, the Moor was undaunted, and his passionate desire to see Galiana and speak to her was so keen that he had a covered way hollowed out between Guadalajara and Toledo, by which he came to visit her every day.

In those days Charles the Great, the son of Pepin, came to Toledo, being sent by his father to bring aid to Galafer against Abderrahman, King of Cordoba. Galafer lodged him in Galiana's very palace, for the Moors willingly allow their daughters to be seen by great and illustrious persons. Charles the Great had a tender heart beneath his cuirass of iron, and it was not long before he fell madly in love with the Moorish princess. At first he tolerated Bradamant's attentions, for he was not yet sure that he had touched his fair one's heart; but in spite of her reserve and modesty, Galiana could not long hide from him the preference of her inmost soul; so he began to show his jealousy, and demanded the removal of his swarthy rival. Galiana, who, the chronicler says, was already French to the eyes, and, moreover, hated the petty king of Guadalajara, gave the prince to understand that she and her father were equally annoyed by the Moor's persistence and that she would gladly be rid of him. Charles did not need to be told this twice; he challenged Bradamant to single combat, conquered him, giant though he was, and, cutting off his head, he presented it to Galiana, who considered this a tasteful gift. This piece of gallantry advanced the French prince very far in the affections of the beautiful Moor, and their love increased on both sides, till Galiana promised to embrace the Christian religion, in order that Charles might marry her; this was carried out with no difficulty, for Galafer was delighted to give his daughter to such a great prince. In the meantime Pepin died and Charles returned to France, bearing Galiana with him; she was crowned queen and welcomed with great rejoicings. Thus it was that a Moorish woman was adroit enough to become a Christian queen, "and although it is attached to an old building," adds the chronicler by way of a concluding remark, "the memory of this story deserves to be preserved in Toledo."

Our first need was to rid ourselves of the microscopic denizens who were streaking the folds of our once white trousers with their bites; luckily the Tagus was not far off, and we took Princess Galiana's fleas straight there, using the same method as foxes, which plunge into the water up to the muzzle, holding between their teeth a piece of bark, only to let it float away with the current when they feel that it is peopled by a sufficient crew; for as these infernal little beasts are gradually overtaken by the water, they take refuge on it in masses. We ask the ladies to pardon this creepy, picaresque detail, which would be more in place in the life of Lazarillo de Tormes or Guzmán de Alfarache, but a journey in Spain would not be complete without it, and we hope to be excused in the name of local colour.

The banks of the Tagus are lined on that side with precipitous rocks which are hard of approach; and it was not without difficulty that we climbed down to the place where we were to effect this wholesale drowning. I struck out swimming, doing the side-stroke as perfectly as possible, in order to be worthy of so famous and dignified a river as the Tagus; and after a few strokes, I reached some tumble-down buildings and shapeless remains of masonry, which rose only a few feet above the level of the river. On the bank, in exactly the same position, stood an old ruined tower with a row of round-topped arches, in which were hanging prosaically some clothes hung up by the washerwomen to dry in the sun.

I was merely in the *baño de la Cava*, known to Frenchmen, in other words, as the Bath of Florinda, and the tower which I had opposite to me was King Rodrigo's tower: it was from the balcony of this window that Rodrigo watched the young girls bathing from behind a curtain, and saw the fair Florinda measuring her leg and that of her companions, to find out whose was the roundest and most shapely! See from what causes great events arise! If Florinda had had clumsy calves or a badly turned knee, the Arabs would never have come to Spain. Unluckily Florinda had a dainty foot, slender ankles and the whitest and most shapely leg in the world. Rodrigo fell in love with the imprudent lady of the bath and seduced her. Count Julian, the father of Florinda, was furious at this outrage and, in order to avenge it, betrayed his country, calling the Moors to his aid. Rodrigo lost this famous battle, so often celebrated in the collections of traditional ballads (*romanceros*), and came to a miserable end in a coffin filled with vipers, in which he had laid himself in order to do penance for his crime. Poor Florinda was branded with the shameful name of *La Cava* and overwhelmed with the execration of the whole of Spain; but what a wild and singular idea to go and place a young girls' bathing-place opposite the tower of a young king.

Since we have begun talking about Rodrigo, let us here relate the legend of the Grotto of Hercules, which is inevitably bound up with the history of the hapless Gothic prince. The Grotto of Hercules is a cellar which extends, they say, three leagues outside the walls, and the door of which, carefully shut and padlocked, comes out in the Church of San

Ginés, at the highest point of the city; on this spot once stood a palace founded by Tubal; Hercules restored it, enlarged it and set up in it his laboratory and school of magic, for Hercules, whom the Greeks afterwards turned into a god, was originally a mighty magician. By means of his art he built an enchanted tower, with talismans and inscriptions, on which it was told how, so soon as anyone should penetrate within these magic precincts, a fierce and barbarous race would conquer Spain.

Fearing lest this dread prognostication might come true, all the kings, and especially the Gothic ones, added new bolts and padlocks to the mysterious door; not that they had any positive faith in the prophecy, but, like wise men, they were anxious not to interfere with these spells and sorceries. Rodrigo was more curious or more needy, for his debauches and prodigalities had drained him of money; so he was ready to risk the hazard, hoping to find considerable treasures in the enchanted vault; he approached the grotto, at the head of a few resolute men supplied with torches, lanterns and ropes; he came to the door hollowed out of the living rock and closed by a lid covered with padlocks, with a tablet upon which one read in Greek characters: "The king who shall open this vault and succeed in discovering the wonders it contains shall see both good and evil fortune." Other kings had been alarmed at the choice, and had not dared to proceed further; but Rodrigo, risking ill fortune so that he might have a chance of the good, ordered that the padlocks should be broken, the locks forced and the cover wrenched up; those who boasted themselves to be the boldest descended first, but soon returned with their torches extinguished, pale and scared, and those who were able to speak told how they had been affrighted by a terrible vision. In spite of this, Rodrigo would not renounce his intention of breaking the spell; so, placing the torches in such a way that the draught from the cavern could not put them out, he placed himself at the head of the band and boldly entered the grotto. He soon came to a square chamber, of rich architecture, in the middle of which was a bronze statue of lofty stature and terrible appearance. This statue had its feet upon a column three cubits high, holding in its hand a mass of arms with which it smote heavy blows upon the pavement, producing the noise and draught which had thrown the first comers into such terror. Rodrigo, with the courage of a Goth and the resolution of a Christian, who trusts in God and is not amazed by the enchantments of the heathen, walked straight up to the colossal figure and asked its leave to visit the wonders which were there.

In token of consent the brazen warrior ceased to strike the ground with his mass of arms: they were able to perceive what was in the chamber, and it was not long before they came upon a coffer, on the lid of which was written: "He who shall open me shall look upon marvels." Seeing the submissiveness of the statue, the king's companions recovered from their fright, and, encouraged by this auspicious inscription, were already making ready to fill their cloaks and their pockets with gold and diamonds; but nothing was found in the coffer save a roll of cloth, on which were painted troops of Arabs, some on foot, the others on horseback, with turbans on their heads and carrying shields and lances, and an inscription, the gist of which was as follows: "He who cometh so far and doth open this coffer shall ruin Spain and be overthrown by nations like unto these." King Rodrigo tried to dissemble the grievous impression which he felt, lest he might add to the dismay of the others; and they looked further to see if there were not some compensation for these disastrous prophecies. Raising his eyes, Rodrigo perceived upon the wall, to the left of the statue, a tablet saying: "Wretched king! Thou hast entered here to thine undoing!" And to the right there was another, whose meaning was: "Thy place shall be taken by strange nations and thy people shall suffer heavy chastisement." Behind the statue was written: "I appeal to the Arabs," and in front of it: "I do my duty."

The king and his courtiers retired full of sorrow and dark forebodings. That very night there was a raging tempest, and the ruins of the Tower of Hercules fell to the ground with a terrible crash; it was not long before events justified what had been foretold by the magic grotto, and the turbans, lances and strangely shaped shields of the Arabs painted on the roll of cloth in the coffer appeared in very deed upon the luckless soil of Spain. And all this because Rodrigo looked upon the leg of Florinda and descended into a cave.

But night is now falling; we must return to the *fonda*, eat our supper and go to bed, for we have still to see the hospital of Cardinal Don Pedro Gonzalez de Mendoza, the arms factory, the remains of the Roman amphitheatre and a thousand other places of interest, for we are leaving tomorrow evening. For my part, I am so tired of these sharp-pointed cobble-stones that I should like to turn myself upside-down and walk on my hands for a while, like clowns, to rest my aching feet. O cabs of civilized lands! O omnibuses of the era of progress! I called upon you in my anguish; but what could you have done in the streets of Toledo?

The hospital of the cardinal is a big building of ample, austere proportions, which it would take too long to describe. We will walk quickly through the court-yard, surrounded by columns and arcades, which has nothing of interest in it save two wells with white marble curbs, and go straight into the church to examine the cardinal's tomb, carved in alabaster by the amazing Berruguete, who, during the eighty years of his life, covered the land with masterpieces of varied style but unvarying perfection. The cardinal is lying on his tomb in his pontifical vestments; death has pinched his nose with its thin fingers, and the last contraction of the muscles, in the attempt to hold back the fleeting soul, has constricted the corners of his mouth and sharpened his pointed chin; no death-mask was ever more sinister in its fidelity; and yet the beauty of the work is so great that one forgets how repellent it is to look upon. Little children in attitudes of grief support the plinth and the cardinal's coat of arms; the most docile, pliant terra-cotta could not produce an effect of greater freedom and softness; it is not carved, it is moulded!

There are also in this church two pictures by Domenico Theotocopuli, called El Greco, a strange, extravagant painter who is hardly known outside Spain. His mania, as you know, was the fear of being taken for an imitator of Titian, whose pupil he was; this anxiety threw him into the most fantastic affectations and caprices.

One of these pictures, representing the Holy Family, must have made poor El Greco very unhappy, for at the first glance one would take it for a genuine Titian. The ardent tones of the colour, the brilliant hues of the draperies, that lovely amber-yellow light which gives warmth even to the coldest tones of the Venetian painter, all combine to deceive the most practised eye; only the touch is less broad and liquid. What little reason was left to El Greco must entirely have foundered in the dark seas of madness after finishing this masterpiece;

there are not many painters nowadays who are capable of going mad for such a reason.

The other picture, of which the subject is the Baptism of Christ, belongs entirely to El Greco's second manner: an abuse of black and white, violent contrasts, peculiar colours, contorted attitudes, and draperies creased and crumpled in wanton folds; but it is all inspired by a depraved energy, a morbid power which reveal the great painter and the madman of genius. Few pictures have interested me as much as those of El Greco, for the worst of them have always something unexpected, which soars beyond the possible in such a way as to startle you and make you dream.

From the hospital we went on to the arms factory. It is a huge building, symmetrical and tasteful, founded by Charles III, whose name occurs on all buildings of public utility: the factory is built quite near the Tagus, whose waters are used to temper the blades and turn the wheels of the machines. The workshops occupy the sides of a great court-yard surrounded by porticoes and arcades, like nearly all court-yards in Spain. Here the iron is heated; there it is brought under the hammer; beyond that it is tempered; in this chamber are the whetstones for sharpening and proving the blades; in another are made the sheaths and hilts. We will not pursue this investigation further, for it would teach our readers nothing in particular; we will only say that old horseshoes and mules' shoes enter into the composition of these justly celebrated blades and are carefully collected for this purpose.

To show us that Toledo blades still deserved their reputation, we were taken to the testing-room: a workman of tall stature and colossal strength took a sword of the most ordinary variety, a straight cavalry sabre, thrust it into a bar of lead fixed to the wall, and bent the blade in every direction as if it had been a whip, so that the hilt almost touched the point; the elastic, supple temper of the steel enabled it to bear this test without breaking. Next, the man took his stand before an anvil, and struck such a well-directed blow upon it that the blade cut some way into it: this exhibition of strength reminded me of the scene in one of Walter Scott's novels, in which Richard Coeur de Lion and King Saladin practise cutting through iron bars and cushions.

The Toledo blades of today are as good as those of yore; it is not the secret of their temper which is lost, but that of the design; all that is lacking in modern work, if it is to stand comparison with the ancient, is this little thing, so despised by progressive persons! A modern sword is nothing but a tool, a sword of the sixteenth century was at once a tool and a jewel.

We had counted upon finding in Toledo some old arms, daggers, poniards, broadswords, rapiers and other curiosities, suitable for arranging in trophies along some wall or on some dresser, and with this aim in view we had learnt by heart the names and marks of sixty swordsmiths of Toledo, collected by Achille Jubinal, but no opportunity arose for putting our learning to the test, for there are no more swords at Toledo than there is leather at Cordoba, lace at Malines, oysters at Ostend, or *pâté de foie gras* at Strasbourg; it is in Paris that all specialities are to be found, and, if one comes across a few in foreign countries, it is because they come from Mlle. Delaunay's shop on the Quai Voltaire.

We were also shown the remains of the Roman amphitheatre and lake for naval spectacles, which look exactly like a ploughed field, as is the case with all Roman remains in general. I have not enough imagination to go into ecstasies over non-existent things, bristling with so many problems; I leave this to the antiquaries, and I would rather tell you about the walls of Toledo, which are visible to the naked eye and produce a wonderfully picturesque effect. The buildings are most harmoniously adapted to the irregularities of the ground; it is often hard to say where the rocks end and the ramparts begin; every civilization has taken a hand in the work; this part of the wall is Roman, that tower is Gothic and these battlements are Arab. The whole of this part between the Puerta Cambrón and the Puerta Visagra (*via sacra*), where the Roman road probably ran, was built by the Gothic king Wamba. Each of these stones has its history, and if we desired to tell it all, we should need a volume instead of an article; but it does not go beyond our competence as travellers to tell once again how fine a figure Toledo makes on the horizon, seated on its throne of rocks, with its girdle of towers and diadem of churches: one could not imagine a stronger or more austere outline, adorned with richer colour, or in which the mediaeval character is more faithfully preserved. I remained gazing at it for more than an hour, trying to sate my eyes with the lines of this wonderful prospect and engrave them upon my memory: night fell, alas! too soon, and we went off to bed, for we were to start at one o'clock in the morning, in order to avoid the excessive heat. In fact, our coachman arrived exactly at midnight, and we climbed on to the wretched cushions of our carriage, heavy with sleep and in an advanced state of somnambulism. The terrible jolting caused by the Toledo cobble-stones, which are like caltrops, soon roused us enough to enjoy the fantastic appearance of our nocturnal caravan. The walls were so close together that the carriage, with its great scarlet wheels and extravagantly shaped body, appeared to cleave its way through floods of houses which closed up again behind it! A *sereno*, with the bare legs, full breeches and striped handkerchief of the Valencians, walked in front of us, carrying on the end of his lance a lantern whose flickering gleams called forth a constantly changing play of light and shadow, such as Rembrandt might not have disdained to reproduce in some of his fine etchings of night-watches and patrols; the only noise one heard was the silvery tinkle of the bells round our mules' necks, and the creaking of our axles. The citizens slept as deeply as the statues in the chapel of *los Reyes nuevos*. From time to time our *sereno* would push his lantern under the nose of some fellow sleeping right across the road, and stir him up with the butt-end of his lance; for wheresoever sleep overtakes a Spaniard, he stretches his cloak on the ground, and slumbers with perfect philosophy and imperturbability. Before the gate, which was not yet open, and where we were kept waiting for two hours, the ground was strewn with sleepers snoring in every possible key, for the street is the only bedroom which is not devoured by beasts, and to get into bed one requires the resignation of an Indian fakir. At last the damned gate turned on its hinges, and we returned along the same road as we had come by.

XI. On the Road Again

WE had to pass through Madrid again and take the coach for Granada; we might have gone and waited for it at Aranjuez, but we should have run the risk of finding it full, so we decided in favour of the former course.

Our guide had taken the precaution, the previous evening, of sending a mule on ahead, to wait for us half-way and relieve the one which was drawing our carriage; for it is doubtful whether we could have covered the distance between Toledo and Madrid in a day without this precaution, owing to the unbearable heat of this dusty, shadeless road running past interminable fields of wheat.

We arrived about one o'clock at Illescas half baked—not to say entirely—and without further accidents. We longed for the end of this road which was only new to us in that we were travelling in the opposite direction.

My companion preferred to sleep, and I, being now more at home with Spanish cooking, started fighting for my dinner against countless swarms of flies. The landlady's daughter, a nice little girl of twelve or thirteen, with eyes like an Arab, stood by my side with a fan in one hand and a little broom in the other, trying to keep off the teasing insects, which returned to the charge with renewed fury and buzzing as soon as she slackened or ceased her movements. By her aid, I managed to cram into my mouth a few morsels fairly free from flies; and when my appetite was somewhat appeased, I started a dialogue with my fly-chaser, though of necessity it was greatly limited by my ignorance of language. However, by the aid of my dictionary in diamond-type, I managed to keep up quite a fair conversation for

a foreigner. The little thing told me that she could read and write
every kind of print, and even Latin, and could also play the *pandero*
quite well, so I insisted upon her giving me a sample of her talent;
she did so with a very good grace, to the detriment of my friend's
sleep, for he was at last awakened by the tinkle of the copper plates
and the dull thrumming of the ass's-hide, lightly tapped by the little
musician's thumb.

The fresh mule was harnessed to the carriage, so we had to
continue on our way; and it really requires great moral courage to
start in a temperature of thirty degrees, from a *posada* where one is
in sight of several rows of jars, pots and *alcarrazas* covered with beads
of perspiration. Water-drinking is a voluptuous pleasure which I
have known only in Spain; it is true that the water there is light,
limpid and exquisitely flavoured. The prohibition of wine-drinking
to which Mahometans are subject is a prescription quite easy to
follow in such climates.

Thanks to the eloquent harangues addressed to our mule by the
calesero, and the skill with which he pelted its ears with little stones, we
drove at a fairly good pace. At awkward moments he would call her
vieja, revieja (old, doubly old), an insult to which mules are particularly
sensitive, either because it is always accompanied by a thump on the
back with the butt-end of the whip, or else because it is intrinsically
humiliating. The timely repetition of this epithet brought us to the gates
of Madrid at five o'clock in the evening.

We already knew Madrid, and saw nothing new there save the
Corpus Christi procession, which has lost much of its ancient
splendour since the suppression of the convents and religious
confraternities. The ceremony, however, is not lacking in solemnity.
The route of the procession is strewn with fine sand, and the streets are
kept shady and cool by *tendidos* of sail-cloth stretched from one house
to another; the balconies are decked with flags, and filled with pretty
women in gala dress; it is the most charming sight imaginable. The
incessant flutter of the fans as they open and shut, or quiver and flirt
their wings like butterflies about to settle, the turns of the arm which
the women give as they settle their mantillas and adjust the fall of an
ungraceful fold, the glances they cast at acquaintances from one

window to another, the pretty movement of the head and graceful gesture which accompany the *agur* by which the *señoras* respond to the gentlemen saluting them, the picturesque crowd mingled with Gallegos, Pasiegas, Valencians, *manolas* and venders of water; all this makes up a scene of charming animation and gaiety. The *Niños de la Cuna* (Foundlings), dressed in their blue uniforms, walk at the head of the procession. We saw very few pretty faces in this long procession of children; and even marriage, with all its conjugal carelessness, would find it hard to produce anything uglier than these love-children. Next come the banners of the parishes, the clergy, the silver reliquaries, and, under a canopy of gold, the *corpus Dei* in a blaze of diamonds, of a brilliancy almost unbearable to the eye.

The proverbial piety of the Spaniards seemed to me much abated, and in this respect one might have thought oneself in Paris, at the time when it was considered in good taste to show one's opposition by not kneeling in the presence of the Blessed Sacrament. As the canopy drew near, the men hardly did more than touch the brim of their hats. Catholic Spain exists no longer. The Peninsula has arrived at the stage of Voltairian and liberal ideas on "fanaticism." To demolish convents seems to it the height of civilization.

One evening, being near the post office at the corner of the Calle de Carretas, I saw the crowd hurriedly scattering and a constellation of glittering lights coming down the Calle Mayor: it was the Blessed Sacrament, being conveyed in its coach to the bed-side of some dying man, for in Madrid God no longer goes on foot. The object of this flight was evidently to avoid kneeling.

And as we are talking about religious ceremonies, we may say that in Spain the cross on the pall is not white as in France, but of a sulphur-yellow, which is quite as funereal. They do not use a hearse to remove the body, but a hand-bier.

We found Madrid unbearable, and the two days we had to pass there seemed to us like two centuries. Our dreams were all of orange and lemon-trees, of cachuchas, castanets, dancing skirts and picturesque costumes; for everybody was giving us marvellous accounts of Andalusia, with that bragging and bombast which is as incurable a habit of the Spaniards as of the Gascons in France.

At last the longed-for moment arrived, for all things come round, even the day for which one longs; and we set off in a most comfortable coach, drawn by a sleek and vigorous team of shaven mules, who went at a great pace. This coach was lined with nankeen, and decked with curtains and green Venetian blinds. It seemed to us the height of elegance after the abominable galleys, *sillas volantes* and coaches in which we had so far been jolted about; and it would really have been very comfortable, had it not been for the kiln-like temperature which was burning us to a cinder, in spite of our constantly fluttering fans and the extreme lightness of our clothes. And so in our travelling Turkish bath there was a perpetual litany of "*Ay! que calor!* I am suffocating! I am melting!" and other exclamations of the same sort. However, we bore our troubles in patience, and let the sweat stream down our noses and temples without too many curses, for at the end of our fatigues, we had the prospect of Granada and the Alhambra, the dream of every poet; Granada, the very name of which causes the stoutest bourgeois in the civic guard, the most typical elector and militarist, to break into admiring epithets and dance on one foot.

The country round Madrid is dismal, bare and scorched, though less stony on this side than on the way from Guadarrama; the successive stretches of land, distorted rather than broken, unfold themselves one after the other with no particular features of interest, save the dusty, chalky villages which are scattered here and there among the general aridity, and which one would not notice if their square church-towers did not attract one's attention. Pointed spires are rare in Spain, and the tower with four sides is the most ordinary form. Suspicious-looking crosses stretched their arms where two roads joined, and from time to time there passed an ox-cart with the driver sleeping wrapped up in his cloak, or a wild-looking peasant on horseback with his carbine across his saddle-bows.

The sky at noon is the colour of melted lead; the ground a dusty grey with specks of glittering mica, and the faintest tinge of blue in the far distance. Not a single group of trees, not a shrub, not a drop of water in the parched beds of the torrents; nothing to rest the eye or refresh the imagination. In order to find a little shelter from the sun's devouring rays, one must keep to the narrow band of scant blue shadow cast by the walls. It is true that July was at its height, and this is not exactly the time to travel coolly in Spain; but, in our opinion, one ought to visit countries at their extreme season: Spain in summer, Russia in winter.

We met with nothing worthy of special mention till we came to the royal residence (*sitio real*) of Aranjuez. It is a country-house built in brick, with stone groins, producing a red and white effect, with high-pitched slate roofs, pavilions and weathercocks, recalling the style of building prevalent under Henri IV and Louis XIII, the Palace of Fontainebleau or the houses on the Place Royale, Paris. The Tagus, which one crosses by a suspension bridge, keeps the vegetation in a condition which is the admiration of the Spaniards, and enables the trees of the north to reach a vigorous development: one sees at Aranjuez elm, ashes, birches and aspens, which are as curious down there as Indian figs, aloes and palms would be here.

They showed us a gallery specially built so that Godoy, the famous Prince of Peace, might go by it from his house to the castle. As one leaves the village, one sees on the left a bullring of somewhat monumental proportions.

While they were changing mules, we ran to the market to buy a supply of oranges and take an ice, or rather a lemon-flavoured sorbet of snow, at one of those open-air *refresco*-shops which are as common in Spain as bars are in France. Instead of drinking half a pint of blue wine or a liqueur-glass of brandy, the peasants and vegetable-women in the market take a *bebida helada*, which costs no more, and at any rate does not cloud and stupefy their brains. This absence of drunkenness makes the lower orders very superior to the corresponding classes in our so-called civilized countries.

The name Aranjuez, formed of the two words *Ara Jovis*, is a sufficient indication that this residence stands on the site of a former temple of Jupiter. We had no time to see the inside of it, but we did not regret this much, for all palaces are alike. The same is true to courtiers; originality is only found among the people, and the lower orders seem to have retained a licence for poetry.

From Aranjuez to Ocaña the landscape, though not remarkable, is at least more picturesque. The ground on both sides of the road is broken by the beautiful lines of the hills, with the light falling full upon them, and as often as some favouring breeze blows away the whirlwind of dust in which the coach gallops along, wrapped in its cloud, like a god, you may catch a glimpse of them. The road, though in bad condition, is a fairly good one, thanks to this marvellous climate, in which it never rains, and to the scarcity of carriages, almost all the transport being by means of beasts.

We were to dine and sleep at Ocaña, and wait there for the *correo real* (royal mail) so that we might avail ourselves of its escort, for we were soon going to enter La Mancha, which was then infested by bands of *palillos*, strolling players and other honest men whom one would rather not meet.

We stopped at a nice-looking hostelry with a pillared *patio* covered with a superb *tendido*; the cloth of which it was made was single in some parts and double in others, forming symmetrical designs by means of the varying degrees of transparency. The maker's name and address at Barcelona were written most legibly in this way. Myrtles, pomegranates and jasmines planted in red earthenware pots lent gaiety and fragrance to this inner court, with its mysterious half-light filtering through the awning. The patio is a charming invention; in it one enjoys more fresh air and space than in one's room; one can walk about or read in it, sit alone or join the others. It is a neutral ground for meetings, where, without the boredom of formal visits and presentations, one ends by making acquaintances and forming ties; and when, as at Granada or Seville, there is the added charm of a fountain or running water, I know of nothing more delightful, especially in a country where the thermometer constantly stands at a Senegambian level.

While waiting for our food, we went to take a siesta; this is a habit which one is simply bound to adopt in Spain, for the heat, from two to five o'clock, is something of which a Parisian can form no idea. The pavements are burning, the iron door-knockers grow red-hot, a deluge of fire seems to rain down from heaven, the wheat bursts open in the ear, the earth cracks like the enamel of an over-heated saucepan, the grasshoppers send up a livelier chirp than ever as they rub their bodies, and what little air reaches you seems to be blowing from the brazen mouth of a hot-air pipe; the shops are shut, and not all the money in the world would persuade a tradesman to sell you anything. There is nobody in the streets but dogs and Frenchmen, according to the popular saying, which is not very flattering to us. As to the guides, even if you were to give them Havana cigars or a ticket for the bullfight, the two most tempting things in the eyes of a Spanish hired servant, they would refuse to take you to the smallest building. The only thing left is to sleep, like everybody else, and one soon resigns oneself to this; for what can one lonely man do, awake amidst a sleeping nation?

Our rooms were whitewashed and exquisitely clean. The insects of which we had been given such creepy descriptions had not yet appeared, and our slumbers were not troubled by any four-legged nightmares.

At five in the afternoon we got up and went for a turn, while waiting for supper. Ocaña is not rich in antiquities, and its chief claim to renown is the desperate attack made by the Spanish troops on a French redoubt during the war of invasion. The redoubt was taken, but almost the whole of the Spanish battalion was left on the field. They buried these heroes each where he fell. They had kept their ranks so well, in spite of a deluge of grape-shot, that they can still be recognized by the regular intervals between the graves. Diamante wrote a play called *The Hercules of Ocaña*, composed, no doubt, in honour of some powerful athlete, like Goliaths of the Cirque-Olympique. Passing through Ocaña recalled this to our minds.

The harvest was drawing to an end at a time when our wheat is scarcely beginning to yellow, and they were carrying the sheaves on to the great threshing-floors of trodden earth, looking like a riding-school, in which the horses and mules tread the corn from the ear with their hoofs. The beasts are harnessed to a sort of sleigh on which, in an attitude of bold, proud grace, stands the man whose duty it is to direct operations. He needs a cool head and steady nerves to maintain his position on this frail machine, drawn by three or four horses which he whips with all his might. A painter of the school of Léopold Robert would turn these scenes of biblical and primitive simplicity to good use. Here, as in Italy, he would find no lack of fine, sunburnt heads, sparkling eyes, Madonna-like faces, characteristic costumes, golden light, azure skies and sunshine.

The sky that evening was of a milky blue tinged with rose; the fields lay before us, as far the eye could reach, like a vast sheet of pale gold, in which appeared here and there, like islands in an ocean of light, ox-wagons almost disappearing beneath the sheaves. The impossible idea of a picture without shadow, so long pursued by the Chinese, had become a reality. All was radiance and light; the darkest tones were no deeper than a pearl-grey.

At last we were served with a tolerable supper—at least, our appetite made us think it tolerable—in a low room ornamented with little paintings on glass, giving an oddly rococo and Venetian effect. After supper my friend Eugène and I, being poor smokers, and only able to take a very concise share in the conversation, owing to the necessity of expressing all we had to say in the two or three hundred words we knew, went up to our room, rather depressed at the various stories about robbers which we had heard told at table, and which seemed all the more terrible for being only half understood.

We had to wait till two o'clock in the afternoon for the arrival of the *correo real,* for it would not have been prudent to start without it. We had also a special escort of four horsemen armed with blunderbusses, pistols, and great sabres. They were men of tall stature, with characteristic faces, framed in enormous black whiskers, with pointed hats, broad red sashes, velvet breeches and leather gaiters, looking far more like robbers than gendarmes; so that it was most ingenious to take them with us, in case we met any.

Twenty soldiers, crowded into a galley, followed the *correo real.* A galley is an unsprung cart with two or four wheels; a mat of twisted grass ropes takes the place of a plank bottom. This succinct description will enable you to understand the position of these wretched creatures who were obliged to stand up and cling to the sides of the cart to save themselves from falling on top of each other. Add to this a speed of ten miles an hour, the stifling heat, and a sun directly overhead, and you will agree that it takes a heroically good temper to consider the situation amusing. And yet these poor soldiers, barely covered by their ragged uniforms, with empty bellies, and nothing to drink save the lukewarm water in their bottles, shaken as they were like rats in a trap, did nothing but go into shouts of laughter and sing all the way. The sobriety of the Spaniards, and the patience with which they endure fatigue, border on the miraculous. In this respect they have remained Arabs. It would be impossible to carry disregard of the material side of life further. But these soldiers, with no bread and no shoes, possessed a guitar.

All that part of the kingdom of Toledo through which we were driving is terribly arid, being affected by the proximity of La Mancha, the country of Don Quixote, and the most desolate and sterile province in Spain.

We had soon left La Guardia behind us, an insignificant and most wretched-looking little village. At Tembleque we bought a few dozen pairs of garters, for pretty legs in Paris, cherry-pink, orange, or sky-blue in colour, embellished with gold or silver thread, and with mottoes woven into the fabric that would have shamed the most gallant doggerel of Saint-Cloud. Tembleque is famous for its garters, as Châtellerault in France is for penknives.

While we were bargaining over our garters, we heard beside us a harsh, throaty, menacing growl like that of a mad dog; we turned hastily round in some apprehension, for we did not know how to address a Spanish mastiff, and we saw that this noise was not made by a dog, but by a man.

Never has a more abominable monster sprung from a nightmare kneeling on the chest of a delirious patient. Quasimodo was a Phoebus beside him. A square brow, hollow eyes glittering with a wild brilliancy, a nose so flat that nothing but the nostrils indicated its position, a lower jaw sticking out two inches beyond the upper one, such, in a few words, is the portrait of this scarecrow, whose profile was as concave as the crescents drawn in the Almanac of Liège, with the man in the moon's face in them. This poor wretch's profession was to have no nose and to imitate a dog, which he performed to admiration, for he was more snub-nosed than a death's-head, and made more noise by himself alone than all the school-children at the Barrière du Combat in their luncheon hour.

Puerto Lapiche consists of a few squat, more than half-ruined hovels, perched on the slope of a crumbling, crevassed hill-side, made friable by drought, and fantastically scarred by land-slides. Aridity and desolation could go no further. Everything is the colour of cork and pumice-stone.

The fire of heaven seems to have passed over it; lastly, a grey dust, as fine as pounded stone, is dredged over the picture. This poverty is all the more heart-rending for the implacable brilliance of the sky, which emphasizes its destitution. The cloudy melancholy of the north is nothing to the glaring misery of hot countries.

When one sees these wretched huts, one is seized with pity for the thieves, who are obliged to live by marauding in a region where, for ten leagues round, one would not find enough fuel to cook a boiled egg. The stage-coaches and convoys of galleys are quite insufficient as a resource, and the poor brigands who prowl about La Mancha are often forced to content themselves with supping off a handful of those sweet acorns which were the delight of Sancho Panza. What can they take from people who have neither a penny nor a pocket to put it in, and whose only utensils are a saucepan and a jug? To loot such villages as these seems to me one of the most dismal fancies that could enter the head of an out-of-work robber.

A little beyond Puerto Lapiche, one enters La Mancha, where we saw on our right two or three windmills, which are given out to be those which victoriously withstood the shock of Don Quixote's lance, but, for the time being, were listlessly turning their limp sails under the breath of a fitful wind. The *venta*, where we stopped to drain two or three jars of cool water, also boasts of having harboured the immortal hero of Cervantes.

We will not weary our readers by a description of this monotonous road through a flat, stony, dusty region, varied here and there by olive-trees, with their sickly greenish-grey foliage, where one meets nothing but sallow, emaciated, mummified peasants with rusty hats, short breeches and gaiters of thick, blackish-grey cloth, with a ragged coat slung over their shoulders, and driving before them a mangy sort of ass with a coat hoary with age, limp ears and a lamentable appearance; where one sees nothing outside the villages but half-naked children, as dark as mulattoes, who watch with a wild and startled gaze as one passes by.

We reached Manzanares at midnight, dying of hunger. The courier before us had availed himself of his rights as previous occupant, and his influence with the staff of the inn, to exhaust all the provisions, consisting, it is true, of three or four eggs and a piece of ham. We set up the most piercing and pathetic wails, declaring that, in default of other food, we should set fire to the house and roast the landlady herself. Thanks to this energy, we obtained by two o'clock in the morning a supper for which they had had to rouse half the village. We had a piece of kid, some eggs with tomato, some ham and goat's-milk cheese, with quite a passable little white wine. We all dined together in the court-yard, by the light of three or four brass lamps, rather like funeral lamps of antiquity, the flames of which, blown by the night air, cast fantastic lights and shadows, making us look like werewolves and ghouls tearing to pieces the dug-up corpse of a child. To give the meal a thoroughly uncanny effect, a tall, blind woman came up to the table, guided by the noise, and began to sing verses to a plaintive, monotonous tune, like the incantation of a sibyl. On hearing that we were foreigners, she improvised some eulogistic stanzas in our honour, which we requited with a few reals.

Before getting back into the carriage, we took a turn in the village and went for a walk, groping our way rather, it is true, but anything was better than staying in the court-yard of the inn.

We went as far as the market-place, not without treading on a few people who were sleeping in the shadow under the open sky. In summer-time they usually sleep in the streets, some on their cloaks, others upon a horse-cloth; some on a sack full of chopped straw (these are the sybarites), others simply on the bare bosom of Mother Cybele, with a stone for their pillow.

The peasants who had arrived during the night slept higgledy-piggledy in the middle of their queer vegetables and uncivilized-looking wares, between the legs of their asses and mules, waiting for daylight, which was not long in coming.

A feeble ray of moonlight illuminated indistinctly in the darkness some sort of ancient crenellated building, on which one recognized, from the whiteness of the plaster, defence-works put up during the last civil war, and as yet unmellowed by the lapse of time. As conscientious travellers, this is all we can say about Manzanares.

We got back into the carriage; sleep overcame us, and when we opened our eyes again we were in the neighbourhood of Val de Peñas, a village renowned for its wine; the earth and the hills, starred with pebbles, were of a singularly crude shade of red, and we began to distinguish on the horizon lines of mountains jagged like saws, and quite sharply outlined in spite of the great distance.

Val de Peñas is quite ordinary, and owes all its reputation to its vineyards. Its name, valley of stones, is perfectly justified. We stopped there for luncheon, and by an inspiration from heaven, I had the idea of drinking first my own chocolate and then that intended for my friend, who was not yet awake, and, in view of future privations, I crammed my cups with as many *buñuelos* (a sort of little fritter) as they would hold, so as to make a fairly substantial kind of soup; for I had not yet arrived at the camel-like sobriety which I afterwards achieved, after long practice in abstinence worthy of an anchorite of primitive days. I was not yet acclimatized, but had brought an inordinate appetite from France, which inspired the natives with respectful astonishment.

PART III

The Grand Plaza, Granada

XII. Val de Peñas to Granada

AFTER a few minutes we set off again at full speed, for we had to follow close upon the *correo real* so as not to lose the benefit of its escort. As I leant out of the carriage to take a last look at Val de Peñas, my cap fell off on to the road; a *muchacho* of twelve or fifteen saw it, and in order to get a reward of a few pence, picked it up and began to run after the diligence, which had already gone some distance; however, he caught it up, though he was running bare-foot on a road paved with sharp, cutting stones. I threw him a handful of *sous*, which must certainly have made him the wealthiest ragamuffin in the whole country-side. I only record this insignificant incident because it is characteristic of the nimbleness of the Spaniards, the best walkers in the world, and the most agile runners that one could see. We have already had occasion to speak of the running footmen called *zagales*, who can follow galloping carriages for leagues at a stretch without appearing tired, or even perspiring.

At Santa Cruz they offered to sell us all sorts of little knives and *navajas*; Santa Cruz and Albaceyte are famous for this fancy cutlery. The *navajas* are of a very characteristically Arab and barbarous style, having pierced copper handles with circles of red, green or blue showing through the holes; the fish-shaped blades, which are always very sharp, are embellished with coarse but boldly executed niello-work; most of them bear mottoes, such as: *Soy de un solo* (I belong to one only); or *cuando esta vivora pica, no hay remedio en la botica* (when this viper stings, there is no antidote at the chemist's). Sometimes the blade has three parallel grooves picked out with red paint, which give it a most formidable appearance. The length of these *navajas* varies from three inches to three feet; a few *majos* (peasant dandies) have knives which when opened are as long as a sabre; a spring joint or a ring which one can turn supports and steadies the blade. The *navaja* is the Spaniards' favourite weapon, especially among the lower orders; they wield it with incredible dexterity, making a shield of their cloak, which they roll round the left arm. It is an art which, like fencing, has its own rules, and there are as many masters of knife-play in Andalusia as there are fencing-masters in Paris. Everyone who uses the knife has his own secret thrusts and special ways of stabbing; they say that adepts of the art can recognize the *artist* responsible for a wound from the look of it, just as we recognize a painter by his touch.

The ground began to rise and fall more often and more abruptly; we kept driving up and down hill. We were approaching the Sierra Morena, which forms the boundary of the kingdom of Andalusia. Behind this line of purple mountains was hidden the paradise of our dreams. The stones were already giving place to rocks, and the hills to groups of mountains rising tier above tier; thistles six or seven feet high bristled at the edge of the road like the halberds of invisible soldiers. Though I claim not to be an ass, I am very fond of thistles (a taste which I share, moreover, with butterflies), and this variety surprised me; it is a splendid plant, from which one might obtain charming decorative designs. Gothic architecture itself has no more clear-cut or finely chiselled arabesques and scrolls of leafage. From time to time, in the fields close by, we caught sight of large yellowish patches, as if a sack of chopped straw had been emptied there; but when we drove close by this straw, it rose in a cloud and flew off with a whirring noise; it was a mass of locusts at rest: this was quite an Egyptian touch.

It was about here that, for the first time in my life, I really suffered from hunger: Ugolino in his tower could have been no more starved than I was; and unlike him, I had not got four sons to eat. The reader, who saw me swallowing two cups of chocolate at Val de Peñas, is perhaps astonished at this untimely starvation; but Spanish cups are the size of a thimble, and contain at the most two or three spoonfuls. My grief was increased a hundredfold at the *venta* where we separated from our escort, by seeing a magnificent omelette, intended for the men's dinner, all golden in a ray of sun which entered by way of the chimney; I prowled round it like a devouring wolf, but it was too well guarded for anyone to succeed in carrying it off. Fortunately a lady from Granada, who was in the coach with us, took pity on my anguish, and gave me a few slices of sugarcured La Mancha ham, and a piece of bread, which she had kept in reserve in one of the carriage pockets. May she be requited a hundredfold for this ham in the next world!

Not far from this *venta*, to the right of the road, stood some pillars on which the heads of three or four malefactors were exposed to view: this is always a reassuring sight, and proves that one is in a civilized country.

The road rose in a series of zig-zags. We were about to pass through the *Puerta de los Perros*; this is a narrow gorge, a breach in the mountain wall, leaving just room for a torrent and the road which skirts it. The *Puerta de los Perros* (Gate of Dogs) is so called because through it the conquered Moors left Andalusia, carrying with them the fortune and civilization of Spain. Spain, which comes in contact with Africa, as Greece does with Asia, is not suited for European manners. The genius of the East keeps appearing in every guise, and it is perhaps a pity that the country has not remained Moorish and Mahometan.

Nothing grander or more picturesque could be imagined than this gate of Andalusia. The gorge cuts its way through immense red marble rocks laid with an almost architectural regularity in a series of gigantic courses; these enormous blocks, with their wide horizontal fissures, like veins of marble in the mountain, are a sort of anatomical chart of the earth in which its structure is laid bare for our study, and their proportions would make the most enormous granite structures of Egypt seem microscopic. In the crevices cling evergreen oaks and huge cork-trees, looking no bigger than tufts of grass on an ordinary wall. As one approaches the bottom of the gorge, the vegetation grows denser and denser, forming an impenetrable thicket through which can be seen the waters of the torrent sparkling like diamonds here and there. The rocks fall sheer down from the edge of the road, so it has been thought prudent to furnish it with a parapet, otherwise the carriage, which always descends at a gallop, and is very difficult to guide on account of the frequent sharp turns, might easily turn a somersault at least five or six hundred feet into the depths.

It was in the Sierra Morena that the Knight of the Woeful Countenance, in imitation of Amadis on the Roca Pobre, accomplished the famous penance which consisted in turning head-over-heels upon the sharpest rocks in his shirt, and that Sancho Panza—commonplace matter-of-fact reason by the side of noble madness—found the valise of Cardenio, so well furnished with ducats and fine shirts! One cannot take a step in Spain without coming upon the memory of Don Quixote, so profoundly national is the work of Cervantes, and so completely do his two figures sum up in themselves the whole of the Spanish character: exalted chivalry and the spirit of adventure, combined with great practical common sense and a sort of jovial good nature, full of caustic shrewdness.

At Venta de Cardona, where we changed mules, I saw a pretty little baby of dazzling fairness lying in its cradle, like a little waxen Jesus in the crib. When Spaniards have not yet become bronzed by the sun they are in general extremely fair.

As soon as one has crossed the Sierra Morena the aspect of the country undergoes an entire change; it is as if one had suddenly passed from Europe into Africa: vipers return to their holes, leaving their slanting trails in the fine sand of the road, and the aloes begin to brandish their great spiny sabres on the edge of the ditches.

These spreading fans of thick, fleshy, blue-grey leaves at once impart a different aspect to the landscape. One feels that one has really got to another place, and is indeed no longer in Paris; the difference of climate, architecture and costume does not cause such a sense of strangeness as the presence of the huge vegetation of these torrid regions, which we only see, as a rule, in hot-houses. Laurels, evergreen oaks, cork-trees and figs, with their glossy, metallic foliage, have something free, sturdy and wild about them, which points to a climate in which nature is more powerful than man, and is able to do without him.

Before us stretched the fair realm of Andalusia in a vast panorama. This view had the grandeur and semblance of the sea; ranges of mountains, flattened by the distance, broke like a long blue swell in curves of infinite softness. The intervening spaces were bathed in broad drifts of golden mist, while here and there a brilliant ray of sunshine cast a wash of gold over some nearer hill, shot with a thousand hues like a pigeon's breast. Other mountain heights had fantastically crumpled contours like those stuffs in old pictures which are yellow on one side and blue on the other. All this was flooded with a glittering, resplendent light, the same, perhaps, as that which illuminated the earthly paradise! The light streamed down in liquid gold and silver upon this sea of mountains, throwing up at every obstacle a spangled phosphorescent spray. It was vaster than the most immense perspective of the Englishman John Martin, and a thousand times more beautiful. An infinity of light is far sublimer and more miraculous than an infinity of darkness!

As we gazed upon this marvellous picture, which changed with every turn of the wheels, displaying to us some fresh magnificence, we saw appearing on the horizon the pointed roofs of La Carolina, with its symmetrical pavilions, a sort of model village or agricultural phalanstery, built in olden days by Count Florida Blanca, and settled by him with Germans and Swiss, whom he brought into the country at great cost. This village was all built at the same time, and sprang into life at the inspiration of a single will; so it has that dull regularity from which those dwellings are free which group themselves together little by little at the whim of chance and time. Everything is as straight as a plumb-line, and from the middle of the *plaza* one can see the whole village: here is the market and the Plaza de Toros, there are the church and the alcalde's house. It is very well arranged, certainly, but I should prefer the most wretched village that had sprung up by chance. Moreover, this colony was not a success: the Swiss became homesick, and died like flies at the very sound of the bells: they were obliged to stop ringing them. However, they did not all die, and the population of La Carolina still preserves traces of its German origin. At La Carolina we had a proper dinner washed down by an excellent wine, and were not obliged to ask for double portions; we no longer rode in company with the mail, for the roads were perfectly safe on that side.

Aloes of more and more African proportions continued to appear at the side of the road, while on the left a long festoon of flowers of the brightest pink, gleaming amidst emerald foliage, outlined the whole course of a dried-up streamlet. Taking advantage of a halt at which we changed horses, my companion ran over to the flowers and brought back a large bunch; they were oleanders of incomparable freshness and brilliancy. The question addressed by M. Casimir Delavigne to the Greek river: *Eurotas, Eurotas, que font tes lauriers-roses?* (Eurotas, Eurotas, what of your oleanders?), might be addressed to this stream, whose name I do not know and which perhaps has none.

Like the laughter of ruby lips followed by sad reflections, the oleanders were succeeded by great olive-woods, whose pale foliage recalls the powdered tresses of northern willows, and harmonizes wonderfully with the ashen tinge of the soil. This foliage, with its soft, austere and sober tone, was most judiciously chosen by the ancients, with their subtle appreciation of natural analogies, as the symbol of peace and wisdom.

It was about four o'clock when we arrived at Bailén, famous for the disastrous capitulation which bears its name. We were to pass the night there, and, while waiting for our supper, we went for a walk in the town and the surrounding country with the lady from Granada and a very pretty girl, who was going to Malaga for the sea-bathing, accompanied by her father and mother; for the customary reserve of the Spaniards very soon gives way to a well-bred and cordial familiarity as soon as they are sure that you are neither commercial travellers, tight-rope dancers nor venders of pomade.

The church of Bailén, which can hardly have been built before the sixteenth century, surprised me by its strange colour. The marble and stone, pickled, as it were, by the Spanish sun, instead of turning black, as they do under our wet skies, had taken on ruddy tones of extraordinary warmth and vigour, tending even towards saffron and crimson, the hues of a vine-leaf in late autumn. Beside the church, above a little wall gilded with touches of the warmest light, a palm-tree, the first I had ever seen in the open country, unfolded its leaves abruptly against the dark blue of the sky. This unexpected palm-tree was like a sudden revelation of the East as one turned a corner, and produced a singular effect upon me. I expected to see the ostrich-like necks of camels outlined against the sunset glow, and the white burnouses of the Arabs in a caravan.

There were some rather picturesque ruins of ancient fortifications which had a tower sufficiently well preserved for one to be able to climb up on to it by the aid of one's feet and hands, taking advantage of the projecting stones. We were rewarded for our trouble by a most magnificent view. The town of Bailén, with its tiled roofs, red church and white houses crouched at the foot of the tower like a flock of goats, formed a wonderful foreground; beyond them, the fields of wheat rippled with golden waves, and right in the background, over several ranges of mountains, one saw the distant crests of the Sierra Nevada, gleaming as if they had been cut out of silver. The veins of snow, sparkling in a chance ray of light, sent back gleams like a rainbow, and the sun, like a great golden wheel, of which its disk was the axle, radiated its flaming rays like spokes in a sky tinged with every hue of agate and aventurine.

The inn where we were to sleep consisted of a great building forming only a single room, with a chimney-piece at each end, a ceiling of blackened woodwork coated with a sooty film by the smoke, racks down both sides for the horses, mules and asses, and for the travellers a few little rooms beside it, containing a bed made of three planks laid on two trestles and covered by linen slips with a few scraps of woollen flock floating between them, which innkeepers, with the cool effrontery which characterizes them, allege to be mattresses; this did not prevent us from snoring like Epimenides and the seven sleepers all in one.

We started early in the morning, in order to avoid the heat, and again saw the lovely oleanders, as radiant as glory and as fresh as love, which had delighted us on the previous day. Soon our way was barred by the Guadalquivir with its turbid yellowish water; we crossed it by a ferry and took the road toward Jaen. The Tower of Torrequebradilla was pointed out to us upon our left, illuminated by a ray of light, and it was not long before we caught sight of the strange silhouette of Jaen, the capital of the kingdom of this name.

An enormous, ochre-coloured mountain, as tawny as a lion's hide, dissolving into gold-dust beneath the light, and bronzed by the sun, rises abruptly in the middle of the town; the massive towers and long lines of the ancient fortifications trace picturesque, fantastic angles on its gaunt sides. The cathedral, a huge architectural pile, looking from a distance bigger than the town itself, rises proudly like an artificial mountain by the side of the natural one. This cathedral, in the Renaissance style of architecture, boasts the possession of the actual handkerchief upon which Saint Veronica received the imprint of Our Lord's face, and was built by the Dukes of Medina-Celi. It is undoubtedly fine, but from afar we had dreamed that it would be older and, above all, more curious.

On the way from the *parador* to the cathedral I looked at the playbills; on the previous evening they had played *Mérope*, and on that evening they were to give *El Campanero de San Pablo, por el ilustrísimo Señor Don José Bouchardi*, or, in other terms, *The Bellringer of St. Paul's*, by my friend Bouchardy. A performance at Jaen, an uncivilized town where they never go about without knives at their belts and carbines across their shoulders—this is indeed fame, and but few of the great geniuses of our day could boast a like success. If in the past we borrowed a few masterpieces from the Spanish theatre we certainly pay them back in the same coin with our vaudevilles and melodramas.

Having gone round the cathedral, we returned, like the other travellers, to the *parador*, the appearance of which seemed to promise us an excellent meal: there was a café attached to it, and it had all the appearance of a civilized European establishment. But, as we sat down to table, somebody noticed that the bread was as hard as a millstone, and asked for some fresh. The inn-keeper could not be induced to change it. While we were arguing the point, somebody else noticed that the food had been warmed up, and must already have been served up some long time before. We all set up the most piteous complaints and demanded a new and entirely original dinner.

Here is the answer to the riddle: the coach before us had been stopped by brigands in La Mancha, so the travellers, having been carried off to the mountains, had been unable to eat the meal prepared for them by the innkeeper at Jaen. So as not to lose his money, he had kept the dishes and warmed them up for us, but his expectations were disappointed, for we all left the table and went off to eat elsewhere. This unlucky dinner must have been served up for the third time to the next set of travellers to arrive.

We took refuge in a dingy *posada*, where, after a long wait, we were served with a few cutlets, some eggs and a salad, in chipped plates, with odd glasses and knives. The feast was a poor one, but it was seasoned with so many bursts of laughter and jests about the comical fury of the innkeeper when he saw his clients walk out in a procession, and the fate of the unlucky wretches to whom he was sure to serve up his skinny fowls, after a third turn in the frying-pan to freshen them up, that it quite made up to us for everything, even for our meagre fare. When once the first ice of reserve is broken, Spaniards have a childish, simple gaiety, which is most charming. The least thing makes them laugh till the tears come into their eyes.

It was at Jaen that I saw the largest number of picturesque national costumes: most of the men had blue velvet breeches trimmed with silver filigree buttons, Ronda gaiters with fancy designs in stitching, cords and arabesques in a darker shade of leather. It is the height of elegance to fasten only the first button of the gaiters at the top and bottom so as to show the calf. The costume is completed by wide sashes of yellow or red silk, a brown cloth jacket gay with trimming, a blue or dark brown cloak, a broad-brimmed pointed hat embellished with velvet and tufts of silk, and is something like what used to be worn by Italian brigands. Others wore what is called a *vestido de cazador* (hunting-costume), all of tawny doeskin and green velvet.

A few women of the people wore red capes which touched in high lights and dots of glittering scarlet on the darker background of the crowd. The fantastic costumes, bronzed faces, sparkling eyes, spirited expression, and calm impassive carriage of these *majos*, of whom there are more here than anywhere else, give the population of Jaen an aspect which is rather African than European, an illusion which is greatly added to by the burning heat of the climate, the dazzling whiteness of the houses, which are all whitewashed in Arab fashion, the brownish tone of the ground and the unchanging azure of the sky. There is a Spanish proverb about Jaen, "ugly city, bad people," which no painters will consider true. For to most people in Spain, as in France, a fine city is one which is perfectly four-square and has a sufficient complement of lamp-posts and bourgeois.

On leaving Jaen, one enters a valley which stretches as far as the Vega of Granada. The first part of it is arid; gaunt mountains, crumbling with drought, scorch you like burning mirrors with the radiation from their whity surface; there is no trace of vegetation save a few pale tufts of fennel. But soon the valley closes in and grows deeper, the streams begin to trickle, vegetation revives, and shade and coolness reappear. The *rio* of Jaen fills the valley-bottom, along which it rushes between stones and rocks which impede it at every moment and bar its way. The road skirts it and follows its every bend, for in mountain regions the torrents are quite the cleverest engineers at tracing the course of roads, and the best thing one can do is to trust to their guidance.

A peasant's house at which we stopped to drink was surrounded by two or three channels of running water dividing some distance away into little rills which watered a mass of myrtles, pistachio-trees, pomegranates and trees of every kind and of an extraordinarily vigorous growth. It was so long, since we had seen a real green that this garden, though uncultivated and three parts wild, seemed to us an earthly paradise in miniature.

The young girl who gave us water, in one of those charming porous clay pots which make the water so cool, was very pretty, with her eyes elongated almost to the temples, her tawny skin and African mouth, full and scarlet as a lovely carnation, her flounced skirt and her velvet shoes, of which she seemed very conscious and proud. This type, which occurs frequently in Granada, is evidently Moorish.

At a certain point the valley contracts, and the rocks draw so close together that they leave barely room for the *rio* to pass. In former days carriages were forced to go down and drive along the very bed of the torrent, which was not without danger on account of the holes, the stones and the level reached by the water, which must be very much swollen in winter. In order to obviate this disadvantage, one of the rocks has been pierced from one side to the other, making quite a long tunnel, in the style of a railway viaduct. This is quite a considerable piece of work and only dates from a few years back.

From this point onwards, the valley opens out, and the road is no longer blocked. About here a gap of a few leagues occurs in my reminiscences. Overcome by the heat, which the approach of stormy weather made really suffocating, I ended by falling asleep. When I awoke, night, which comes so suddenly in southern climates, had completely fallen; an abominable wind raised a whirl of burning dust; this wind must be a very near relation to the African sirocco, and I cannot think how it was we were not asphyxiated. All outlines disappeared in this fog of dust; the sky, which is usually so brilliant on a summer night, was like the vault of an oven, and it was impossible to see two steps in front of us. We made our entry into Granada at about two o'clock in the morning, and alighted at the Fonda del Comercio, a so-called hotel on the French model, where there were no sheets on the beds, and we slept on the table in our clothes; but these little tribulations affected us but slightly; we were in Granada, and in a few hours' time we were going to see the Alhambra, and the Generalife.

Our first care was to make our servant find us a *casa de pupilos*, that is to say, a private house where they take boarders; for since we were to stay some time in Granada, the meagre hospitality of the Fonda del Comercio would no longer do for us. This servant, named Louis, was a Frenchman from Farmoutiers in Brie. He had deserted at the time of the French invasion under Napoleon, and had been living in Granada for more than twenty years. His physique was the queerest you can imagine: his great height—five feet eight inches—made the most curious contrast with his small head, as wrinkled as an apple, and no bigger than your fist. Cut off from all communication with France, he had preserved his old Brie patois in all its native purity; he talked like Hodge in the comic opera and seemed to be for ever repeating speeches from M. Etienne's plays. In spite of his long residence in the country, his thick head had refused to equip itself with a new language; he barely knew the most indispensable phrases. He had nothing Spanish about him but the *alpargatas* and the little Andalusian hat with a turned-up brim. This concession was a great grief to him, and he avenged himself by overwhelming the natives he met with every kind of comical abuse, in the Brie patois of course, for Master Louis was afraid of a blow above all things, and he cherished his skin as if it had really been worth something.

He took us to a very decent house in the Calle de Parragas, near the Plazuela de San Antonio, a few steps from the Carrera del Darro. The mistress of this boarding-house had lived for a long time in Marseilles and spoke French, a decisive inducement to us, for our vocabulary was still very limited.

We were installed in a whitewashed room on the ground floor, of which the only furniture was a many-coloured rosette on the ceiling; but this room had the charm of opening on to a *patio* surrounded by white marble columns with Moorish capitals which had no doubt come from some old demolished Arab palace. A little basin with a fountain in it was hollowed out in the middle of the court, and kept it cool; a great woven-grass mat, forming the *tendido*, tempered the sun's rays and scattered stars of light here and there over the pebbled squares of the pavement.

It was here that we took our meals, read and lived. We hardly went into our room except to dress and sleep. Without the *patio*, an architectural feature recalling the ancient Roman *cavaedium*, the houses of Andalusia would be uninhabitable. The sort of vestibule leading into it is usually paved with little pebbles of different colours, forming designs in a rough mosaic, which represent sometimes pots of flowers, sometimes soldiers, Maltese crosses or merely the date at which the house was built.

From the top of our house, upon which was a sort of *mirador*, could be seen through groups of trees, clearly outlined against the blue of the sky on the crest of a hill, the massive towers of the fortress of the Alhambra, clothed by the sun in ruddy hues of extreme warmth and intensity. The silhouette was completed by two great cypresses standing side by side, the black points of which rose high into the blue above the red walls; these cypresses are never out of sight: whether one climbs the snow-streaked sides of El Mulhacen, or wanders across the Vega or in the Sierra de Elvira, one always finds them on the horizon, dark and immobile amid the flood of bluish or golden vapours with which distance softens the roofs of the city.

Granada is built on three hills, at the end of the plain called the Vega: the Vermilion Towers, so called on account of their colour (*Torres Bermejas*), which they allege to be of Roman, or even of Phoenician origin, occupy the first and least elevated of these eminences; the Alhambra, which is a city in itself, covers the second and highest hill with its square towers, connected by high walls and immense foundations, enclosing within them gardens, woods, houses and open spaces; on the third mound is situated the Albaicin, separated from the others by a deep ravine, choked with vegetation, cactuses, colocynths, pistachio-trees, pomegranates, oleanders and tufts of flowers, at the bottom of which rolls the Darro, with the rapidity of an Alpine torrent.

The Darro, which washes down gold in its waters, runs through the city, sometimes open to the sky, sometimes beneath bridges so long that they deserve rather to be called tunnels, and goes to join the Genil, which is content to wash down mere silver, in the Vega, a little way from the Alameda. This course of the torrent through the city is called the Carrera del Darro, and from the balcony of the houses along its edge one enjoys a magnificent view. The Darro frets constantly at its banks, and causes frequent land-slides; and an ancient rhyme sung by the children alludes to this mania for carrying everything away, for which it gives a grotesque reason. Here is the poem in question:

Darro tiene prometido
El casarse con Genil
Y le ha de llevar en dote
Plaza Nueva y Zacatin
(The Darro has promised to marry the Genil,
Bringing with it as a dowry
the Plaza Nueva and Zacatin).

The gardens known as the *carmenes del Darro,* of which such enchanting descriptions are given in Spanish and Moorish poetry, are situated on the edge of the Carrera, as one goes up in the direction of Los Avellanos.

The city is thus divided into four large quarters: the Antequeruela, which occupies the lower slopes of the hill, or rather mountain, crowned by the Alhambra; the Alhambra and its appendage the Generalife; the Albaicin, once a vast fortress, but nowadays a ruined and depopulated quarter; and Granada proper, which lies in the plain around the cathedral and the *plaza* called the Vivarambla, and forms a separate quarter.

Such is, roughly, the topographical plan of Granada, which is cut right across by the Darro; it is skirted by the Genil, which washes the edge of the Alameda, and sheltered by the Sierra Nevada, of which one catches a glimpse at the end of every street; the transparent atmosphere brings it so near that it looks as if one could touch it with one's hand from the lofty balconies and *miradores.*

The general appearance of Granada in many ways falls short of the idea which one has formed of it in advance. In spite of oneself, in spite of the many disappointments one has already experienced, one had not reckoned with the fact that three or four hundred years and whole seas of bourgeois have passed over the scene of so many deeds of romance and chivalry. One pictures to oneself a city half Moorish and half Gothic, in which open-work spires are mingled with minarets, and gables alternate with flat roofs; one expects to see carved and storied houses, with coats of arms and heroic mottoes, fantastic buildings with the stories projecting one beyond the other, with jutting beams and windows decked with Persian carpets and blue and white pots—in fact, the original of a scene at the Opera, representing some marvellous mediaeval scene.

The people one meets with in modern costume, frock-coated like men of property and wearing hats shaped like blunderbusses, produce an unpleasant effect upon you, in spite of yourself, and seem more ridiculous than they are; they really cannot go out walking, for the greater glory of local colour, in the Moorish burnous of Boabdil's day, or the iron armour of the time of Ferdinand and Isabella the Catholic: like nearly all the middle-class population of the Spanish towns, they consider it a point of honour to show that they are not in the least picturesque, and to prove their civilization by their strapped-down trousers. This is the cause which they have at heart; they are afraid of appearing barbarous and behind the times, and when one belauds the wild beauty of their land, they apologize humbly for having as yet no railways, and being without factories driven by steam. One of these honest citizens, in whose presence I was extolling the attractions of Granada, answered: "It is the best-lighted city in Andalusia; observe how many lamp-posts we have; but what a pity they are not supplied with gas."

Granada is gay, smiling and animated, though greatly fallen from its past glory. The number of inhabitants is increasing, and they cleverly act the part of a large population; the carriages are finer and more numerous than in Madrid. The impetuous Andalusian character fills the street with a life and movement unknown to the grave Castilians who, as they walk the streets, make no more noise than their own shadow: what we have said applies in particular to the Carrera del Darro, the Zacatin, the Plaza

Nueva, the Calle de los Gomeles leading to the Alhambra, the Plaza del Teatro, the approaches to the Promenade and the chief arterial streets. The rest of the city is furrowed in every direction by an inextricable tangle of alleys three or four feet wide, too narrow to admit carriages, which recall in every particular the Moorish streets in Algiers. The only noise one hears in them is the hoof of an ass or mule striking a spark from the gleaming cobble-stones of the pavement, or the monotonous thrumming of a guitar as it drones in the depths of an inner courtyard.

The balconies decked with sun-blinds, pots of flowers and shrubs, the vine-trails straying from one window to another, the oleanders tossing their brilliant sprays of flowers over the garden-walls, the fantastic play of sun and shadow, recalling Decamps' pictures of Turkish villages, the women seated on the door-steps, the half-naked children playing and tumbling over each other, the asses coming and going in their harness loaded with feathers and woollen tufts, give these streets, which nearly always run uphill, and are sometimes broken by a few steps, a characteristic aspect which is not lacking in charm, and the unexpectedness of which more than makes up for what it lacks in regularity.

Victor Hugo says of Granada, in that charming poem in the *Orientales*: *Grenade peint ses murs de plus vives couleurs* (Granada paints her walls in yet more vivid hues).

This detail is very apt. Houses of any wealth are painted outside in the most fantastic fashion, with sham architecture, ornaments in monochrome and imitation reliefs. They have panels, cartouches, painted panels over the doors, flaming vases, volutes, medallions of tiny roses, egg- and rosette-shaped ornaments, pot-bellied Cupids, carrying all sorts of allegorical utensils against an apple-green, flesh-pink or pinkish-fawn background: the most extreme expression of the rococo style. It is at first hard to take these painted semblances for real houses. You feel as if you were for ever walking about the wings of a theatre. We had already seen painted house-fronts of this sort in Toledo, but they do not approach those of Granada in their riot of decoration and strangeness of colour. For my part, I do not dislike this fashion, which cheers the eye and forms a happy contrast with the chalky tinge of the whitewashed walls.

We were speaking just now about the middle classes and their French costumes, but fortunately the lower classes do not follow the Paris fashions; they have retained the pointed hat with a velvet brim, trimmed with silk tufts, or with a flower-pot crown and broad facings in the style of a turban; the jackets embellished with embroideries and cloth appliqué in all kinds of colours, at the elbows, cuffs and collar, with a vague reminiscence of Turkish coats; the red or yellow sash; the trousers with a front-flap, supported by filigree buttons or South American column-stamped coins welded to a hook; the leather gaiters open up the side and showing the leg; but it was all more brilliant, more florid, more ornate, more festive, more loaded with tinsel and tawdry trimmings than in other provinces. One also sees a number of costumes known by the name of *vestido de cazador* (hunting-costume) of Cordoba leather and blue or green velvet, set off with tagged cords. It is the height of style to carry in the hand a rod (*vara*) or white stick, with a bifurcated tip, four feet high, upon which one leans negligently when one stops for a chat. No self-respecting *majo* would dare to appear in public without this *vara*. Two coloured handkerchiefs, with their ends falling from the jacket pockets, a long *navaja* thrust through the belt, not in front, but in the middle of the back, are the pinnacle of elegance for these lower-class exquisites.

This costume so attracted me that my first care was to order myself one. I was taken to the house of Don Juan Zapata, a man with a great reputation for national costumes, who cherished a hatred for black jackets and frock-coats which was at least equal to my own. Finding in me one who shared his antipathies, he gave free play to his bitter sentiments, and poured into my bosom his elegies on the decadence of art. He recalled with a grief which woke an echo in myself the happy days when a stranger dressed like a Frenchman would have been hooted in the streets and pelted with orange-peel, when *toreadores* wore jackets embroidered with fine gold and worth more than five hundred pesetas, and young men of good family wore trimmings and cords of exorbitant price.

"Alas, sir, it is only the English who buy Spanish costumes now," he said, as he finished taking my measurements.

This Señor Zapata felt about his suits rather as Cardillac did about his jewels. It was quite a grief to him to deliver them to his clients. When he came to try on my costume, he was so dazzled by the brilliance of the pot of flowers which he had embroidered in the middle of the back, on a background of brown cloth, that he went mad with joy and began to behave in the most extravagant fashion. Then suddenly the thought of leaving this masterpiece in my hands pierced through his hilarity, and plunged him in sudden gloom. Under pretext of some alteration, he wrapped the coat up in his handkerchief, handed it to his apprentice— for a Spanish tailor would consider himself dishonoured if he carried his own parcel—and made off as if he was being carried away by devils, darting at me a sly and ironical glance. On the next day he returned alone, and, drawing the money I had given him from a leather purse, he told me that it hurt him too much to part with his coat, and that he would rather return me my *duros*. It was only when I represented to him that this costume would give a high idea of his talent, and make his reputation in Paris, that he consented to give it up.

The women have the good taste not to abandon the mantilla, the most delicious head-dress that could frame a Spanish face; they walk about the streets and on the promenade, with loose hair, a red carnation on each temple, and their black laces arranged about them, and glide along by the walls flirting their fans with incomparable grace and vivacity. A woman's hat is a curiosity in Granada. Fashionable ladies have indeed some jonquil-yellow or poppy-red affair stowed away in a bandbox which they keep in reserve for occasions of great state; but such occasions, thank God, are very rare, and these horrible hats only see the light on the Queen's birthday or at solemn school ceremonies. May your hats never invade "the city of the Caliphs," and may the terrible threat contained in the words *modista francesa,* painted in black at some street corner, never be carried into effect. Serious minds, as they are called, will doubtless think us very frivolous, and laugh at our picturesque grievances, but we are among those who believe that varnished boots and waterproof coats contribute very little towards civilization, and we even consider civilization itself a thing of very little worth. It is a grievous spectacle for the poet, the artist and the philosopher to see form and colour disappearing from the world, to see lines growing blurred and colours confused, and a most disheartening uniformity invading the universe under some vague pretext of progress. By the time everything is exactly alike, travelling will become entirely useless, and, by a happy coincidence, it is precisely then that railways will be at the height of their activity. What use will it be to make a long journey at the rate of twenty-five miles an hour, only to see more Rues de la Paix lighted by gas, and filled with comfortable bourgeois? We believe that such was not God's design, when he moulded each country in a different way, gave it its own vegetation, and peopled it with special races, dissimilar in conformation, complexion and language. It is a misinterpretation of the spirit of Creation to desire to impose the same livery upon men of every climate, and this is one of the thousand errors of European civilization; one is quite as uncivilized in a swallow-tailed coat—and much uglier. What a fine figure Sultan Mahmud's Turks cut, to be sure, since the reform of the old Asiatic costume, and how boundless is the progress of enlightenment among them!

In order to reach the promenade, one follows the Carrera del Darro, and crosses the Plaza del Teatro, in which stands a funeral column set up in memory of Joaquín Maiquez by Julian Romea, Matilde Diez and other dramatic artists, and upon which stands the front of the Arsenal, a rococo building, daubed with yellow and adorned with statues of grenadiers painted mouse-grey.

The Alameda of Granada is surely one of the pleasantest places in the world: it is called the *Salón*; a curious name for a promenade: picture to yourself a long wall with several rows of trees of a verdure unique in Spain, finishing at both ends in monumental fountains, whose basins bear upon their shoulders curiously misshapen and delightfully barbarous aquatic deities. These fountains, unlike the ordinary run of such contrivances, pour out their waters in broad sheets which evaporate in fine rain and moist spray, diffusing a delicious freshness. Along the side alleys flow rills of crystalline transparency imprisoned in beds of pebbles. A great parterre, adorned with fountains, and filled with shrubs and flowers, myrtles, rose-bushes, jasmines and all the wealth of the Flora of Granada, occupies the space between the Salón and the Genil, and extends as far as the bridge built by General Sebastiani at the time of the French invasion. The Genil makes its way in its marble bed from the Sierra Nevada through forests of laurels of incomparable beauty. Glass and crystal are similes too dense and opaque to give any idea of the purity of this water, which lay but yesterday in sheets of silver on the white shoulders of the Sierra Nevada. It is a torrent of molten diamonds.

In the evening, between seven and eight o'clock, the male and female exquisites of Granada meet at the Salón: the carriages file along the edge of the pavement, for the most part empty, for Spaniards are very fond of walking, and, in spite of their pride, will condescend to go without a carriage. Nothing can be more charming than to see groups of young women and girls walking to and fro in mantillas, with bare arms, real flowers in their hair, satin shoes on their feet and fans in their hands, followed at a short distance by their friends and admirers, for in Spain it is not the custom to give one's arm to ladies, as we have already remarked in speaking of the Prado at Madrid. This habit of walking alone adds an ease, elegance and independence to their carriage which our women, who are always clinging to somebody's arm, have not got. As painters say, the effect "tells." This constant separation of the men from the women, at least in public, is a foretaste of the East.

The Alameda of Granada at sunset is a spectacle of which northern peoples can form no idea: the Sierra Nevada, the jagged outlines of which enfold the city on this side, takes on hues which cannot be imagined. All the cliffs and crests turn rosy as they are caught by the light, but it is a dazzling, ideal, fabulous rose, washed with silver, shot with rainbow and opal gleams which would make the purest tones of the painter's palette appear muddy; shades of mother-of-pearl, ruby-like transparencies, veins of agate and aventurine which might challenge all the fairy jewellery of the *Thousand and One Nights*. The valleys, the crevasses and irregularities, all those parts to which the rays of the setting sun do not penetrate, are of a blue which might rival the azure of sky and sea, of lapis lazuli and sapphire; this contrast between the tone of the lights and shadows is prodigiously effective: the mountain seems to have clothed itself in a vast robe of changing-hued silk, spangled and ribbed with silver; little by little the resplendent colours die away and melt into purple half-tones, the shadows invade the lower slopes and the light withdraws to the higher summits; and the whole plain is long since sunk in gloom before the silver diadem of the Sierra has ceased to sparkle in a serene sky beneath the farewell kiss of the sun.

The strollers on the promenade take yet another turn or two before they disperse, some to take a water-ice or an *agraz* at Don Pedro Hurtado's café, the best shop for ices in Granada, others to betake themselves to the *tertulia*, where they will meet their friends and acquaintances.

In Granada this is the gayest and most animated time of day. The open-air shops of the venders of water and ices are lit up with a host of lamps and lanterns: the standard lamps and altar lights before the images of the Madonna vie with the stars in number and brilliancy, which is saying a great deal; and, if it is a moonlight night, one can read the most microscopic print with ease. The light is blue, not yellow, that is all.

Thanks to the lady who had saved me from dying of starvation in the diligence, and who introduced us to several of her friends, we were soon well known in Granada society, and had a charming time there. We could not have had a more cordial, open-hearted and amiable reception; after five or six days, we were quite on intimate terms, and, according to the Spanish usage, we were called by our Christian names: in Granada I was Don Teofilo, and my friend had the title of Don Eugenio, while we were allowed the liberty of calling the women and girls of the families in which we were received by theirs: Carmen, Teresa, Gala, etc. This familiarity is quite consistent with the politest manners and the most respectful attentions.

So we went to a *tertulia* every evening, in one home or another, from eight o'clock till midnight. The *tertulia* is held in the *patio* surrounded by columns of alabaster, and beautified with a fountain, the basin of which is surrounded by pots of flowers and tubs with bushes in them on whose leaves the drops fall pattering down. The walls are hung with six or eight lamps, the galleries are furnished with straw or wicker sofas and chairs; guitars lie here and there; the piano stands in one corner, and the card-tables are set up in another.

On entering, everybody goes up and greets their host and hostess, who, after the usual courtesies, invariably offer you a cup of chocolate, which it is the right thing to decline, and a cigarette, which one sometimes accepts. Having performed these duties, you go and join a group in the corner of the *patio* which attracts you most. The parents and elderly people play *trecillo*; the young men talk to the young ladies, recite the verses they have written during the day, are scolded and made to do penance for the crimes which they may have committed on the previous day, such as dancing too often with a pretty cousin or casting too ardent a glance towards some forbidden balcony, and other trifling *peccadilloes*. If they have been very good, they are given in exchange for the rose which they have brought with them, a carnation from the lady's breast or hair, and when everybody goes up to the balcony to hear the band beating the tattoo, their pressure of the hand is answered by a glance of the eye and a slight squeeze of the fingers. Love seems to be the only occupation in Granada. You have hardly spoken to a girl more than twice or three times, when the whole town hails you as *novio* and *novia*, that is to say, an engaged couple, and assails you with innocent banter about your supposed passion; this makes you a little uneasy, all the same, for it causes visions of matrimony to pass before your eyes. This gallantry is more apparent than real; in spite of the languorous looks, the burning glances, the tender or passionate conversations, the caressing diminutives and the *querido* (dear) which is prefixed to one's name, one ought not to think oneself too highly favoured. If a woman in good society were to say to a Frenchman a quarter of what a young girl of Granada says to one of her many *novios* without any serious intention, he would believe that his hour of triumph was coming that very night—in which he would be mistaken; if he allowed himself a little too much freedom he would soon be called to order, and given to understand that he must state his matrimonial intentions in the presence of the grandparents. This virtuous freedom of speech, so different from the stiff, artificial manners of the northern nations, is preferable to our verbal hypocrisy, which conceals a great coarseness of action. At Granada, it is thought quite extraordinary to pay attentions to a married woman, and considered quite usual to pay one's court to a young girl. In France, the opposite is the case; nobody ever speaks a word to unmarried girls. It is this which causes unhappy marriages; in Spain, a *novio* sees his *novia* two or three times a day, talks to her without being listened to, escorts her to the promenade and comes at night to converse with her through the grating of the balcony, or the window on the ground-floor. He has enough time to get to know her, and study her character; and does not, as the saying goes, buy a pig in a poke.

When conversation languishes, one of the ladies' admirers takes down a guitar and begins to sing some gay Andalusian melody, plucking at the cords with his fingers and marking the rhythm on the body of the instrument with the palm of his hand; or he sings some curiously modulated comic stanzas, interspersed with "ays" and "olas", producing a strange impression. A lady sits down to the piano, plays a piece by Bellini, who seems to be the Spaniards' favourite composer, or sings a song by Bretón de los Herreros, the great librettist of Madrid. The evening winds up with a little impromptu ball, at which, alas! they dance neither jotas nor fandangos nor boleros, for these are left to peasants, servants and gypsies, but quadrilles and rigadoons, and sometimes the waltz. One evening, however, at our request, two daughters of the house were good enough to dance the bolero; but they first closed the windows and door of the patio, which are usually left open, lest they might be accused of bad taste and local colour. The Spaniards are usually annoyed when one talks to them about the cachucha, castanets, *majos, manolas,* monks, smugglers and bullfights, though at heart they are very fond of these things, which are really national and characteristic. They ask you, with an air of evident vexation, whether you do not think them as advanced in civilization as you are, for the deplorable mania for imitating England or France has penetrated everywhere. The Spain of today is at the stage of Voltaire-Touquet and the *Constitutionnel* of 1825, that is to say, hostile to all colour and poetry. It is understood, of course, that we are talking of the so-called enlightened class living in the towns.

When the quadrilles are over, one takes leave of one's host and hostess, by saying to the lady *a los pies de vd,* and to the husband *beso a vd la mano,* upon which they reply *buenas noches* and *beso a vd la suya,* with a *hasta mañana* (till tomorrow) as a last farewell on the door-step, which pledges you to return. The Spaniards remain polite and ceremonious in their very familiarity. Even the lower classes, peasants and vagabonds, treat one another with an exquisite urbanity which is very different from the coarseness of our rabble; it is true that an offensive word might be followed by a stab, and this makes people very circumspect in their speech. It may be remarked that the once proverbial French politeness has disappeared since we left off carrying swords. The laws against duelling will end by making us the rudest people in the universe.

On one's way home, one comes upon young gallants muffled in their cloaks under the windows and balconies engaging in *pelar la paba* (plucking the turkey), that is to say, conversing with their *novias* through the bars. These nocturnal interviews often last till two or three in the morning, which is not at all surprising, for the Spaniards spend part of the day sleeping. One may also happen to stumble upon a serenade composed of three or four musicians, but usually of the lover alone, singing verses to his own accompaniment on the guitar, with his hat pulled over his eyes and his foot on a step or stone. In the olden times, two serenades would not have been tolerated in the same street; the first arrival counted upon being left alone and would not allow the thrum of any guitar but his own to break the silence of the night. These pretensions were upheld at the point of the rapier or the knife, unless, indeed, the watch happened to pass by; when the two rivals would join forces and charge the patrol, reserving their private quarrel for later settlement. The touchiness of serenaders has been greatly mollified, and everyone may *rascar el jamón* (scrape the ham) with the tranquil mind under the walls of his fair one.

If it is a dark night, one has to be careful not to plant one's foot on the stomach of some honourable hidalgo rolled up in his mantle, which serves him as garment, bed and house. During the summer nights, the granite benches of the theatre are covered with a mass of riff-raff who have no other refuge. Each one has his own step, which is, as it were, his room, where one is always sure to find him. They sleep there under the blue dome of heaven, with the stars for a night-light, safe from the bugs, and defying the bites of mosquitoes by the horny consistency of their tanned skin, bronzed by the fires of the Andalusian sun, and certainly as black as the darkest mulatto.

Such was the life we led, with but few variations: the morning was given up to walks about the city, or a stroll in the Alhambra or the Generalife, and afterwards to an obligatory call upon the ladies with whom we had passed the evening. When we only came twice a day they called us ingrates, and indeed we were received with such kindness that we really felt ourselves to be wild, uncivilized beings and extremely neglectful.

We had such a passion for the Alhambra that, not satisfied with going there every day, we wanted to stay there altogether, not in the neighbouring houses, which are let for high rents to English people, but in the palace itself; and thanks to the influence of our friends in Granada, though we were not formally granted permission, they promised to wink at our presence. We stayed there four days and four nights, which were without the least doubt the most delicious moments in my life.

On our way to the Alhambra we will pass, if you please, through the Vivarambla, where the valiant Moor, Gazul, once fought with bulls, and the houses, with their timbered balconies and miradores bear a vague resemblance to hen-coops. The fish-market occupies one corner of the *plaza*, the middle of which forms an open space surrounded with stone benches, and peopled with moneychangers, sellers of water-jars, earthen pots, water-melons, haberdashery, songs, knives, rosaries and other minor open-air industries. The Zacatin, which has retained its Moorish name, connects the Vivarambla with the Plaza Nueva. This street, flanked by side-alleys, and shaded by sail-cloth awnings, is filled with all the stir and hum of the commercial life of Granada: hatters, tailors, bootmakers, venders of stuffs and trimmings, occupy nearly all the shops, to which the refinements of modern luxury are as yet unknown, and which recall the ancient pillars of the Paris markets. The Zacatin is crowded at all hours. Sometimes appears a strolling troupe of students from Salamanca, playing on guitars, tambourines, castanets and the triangle, and singing spirited comic verses; sometimes appears a horde of gypsy-women with their flounced blue dresses powdered with stars, their long yellow shawls, their dishevelled hair and great amber or coral necklaces round their necks; or a string of asses laden with enormous jars and driven by a peasant from the Vega, as sunburnt as an African.

The Zacatin leads into the Plaza Nueva, of which a whole side is occupied by the superb Palacio de la Cancilleria, remarkable for its rusticated columns and the rich severity of its architecture. Having crossed the Plaza, one begins to mount upwards along the Calle de los Gomeres, at the end of which one finds oneself at the edge of the precincts of the Alhambra, facing the Gate of Pomegranates, called Bib-Leuxar by the Moors, and having on its right the Torres Bermejas, built, as learned men maintain, on Phoenician foundations, and nowadays inhabited by potters and basket-makers.

Before going any further, we must warn our readers, in case they may consider that our descriptions, though scrupulously accurate, do not come up to the ideas which they have formed of the Alhambra, that this fortress-palace of the ancient Moorish kings does not look in the least like what one had imagined. One expects to find terraces rising tier above tier, minarets, with a lacework of carving, and endless vistas of columns. In reality there is nothing of the sort; outside, one only sees massive brick-red or toast-coloured towers, built at different periods by the Arab princes; inside, it is nothing but a series of halls and galleries, decorated with the utmost delicacy, but with nothing grand about them. Having made these reservations, let us continue on our way.

On passing through the Gate of Pomegranates, one finds oneself within the walls of the fortress and under the jurisdiction of a special governor. Two roads lead through a wood of lofty trees. Let us take the one on the left, which leads to the fountain of Charles the Fifth; it is the steeper of the two but the shorter and more picturesque. Little streams rush down pebble-paved channels, diffusing a fresh coolness at the foot of the trees, which are almost all of northern varieties, with foliage of a brilliant green which is delightful only a few steps from Africa. The sound of purling waters is mingled with the shrill chirping of a hundred thousand grasshoppers or crickets, whose unceasing music, in spite of the coolness of the spot, inevitably calls up thoughts of the torrid south. Water gushes out on every side, from beneath the trunks of the trees, and through the cracks in the old walls. The hotter it grows, the more copious become the springs, for it is the snow that feeds them. This mixture of water, snow and fire makes the climate of Granada peerless in all the world, a regular earthly paradise, and though we are no Moors, one may, whenever we seem absorbed in a profound melancholy, apply to us the Arab proverb, "He is thinking of Granada."

At the end of the road, which leads steadily uphill, one comes to a great monumental fountain shoring up a terrace, and dedicated to the Emperor Charles the Fifth, with a quantity of mottoes, coats of arms, victories, Imperial eagles and mythological medallions in the Romano-Germanic style, rich, but heavy and powerful. Two escutcheons with the arms of the House of Mondéjar indicate that Don Luis de Mendoza, the Marquis of this name, put up this monument in honour of the red-bearded Caesar. This fountain supports with its solid masonry the earth of the inclined plane which slopes up to the Gate of Judgment, through which one enters the Alhambra properly so called.

The Gate of Judgment was built by King Yusef-Abul-Hajjaj about the year AD 1348: it owes this name to the Musulman habit of administering justice at the gate of their palaces; which has the advantage of being very majestic, and allowing nobody to penetrate into the inner court-yards; for M. Royer-Collard's maxim, "Private life should be enclosed by a wall", was invented centuries ago in the East, the land of the Sun, from whence come all light and wisdom.

The term tower, rather than gate, should be applied to this building erected by the Moorish King Yusef-Abul-Hajjaj, for it is really a great square tower, fairly high, and pierced with a great arch hollowed out in the form of a heart, to which a repellent and cabalistic appearance is given by the hieroglyphics of a key and a hand, which are sunk in two separate stones. The key is a symbol deeply venerated among the Arabs, owing to a verse of the Koran which begins with the words, *He has opened*, and many other symbolical interpretations; the hand is intended to avert the evil eye or gettatura, like the little coral hands worn in Naples as a pin or charm against ill-omened glances. There was an ancient prophecy saying that Granada would never be taken until the hand grasped the key; to the shame of prophecy it must be admitted that the two hieroglyphs are still in the same place, and that it was outside a conquered Granada that Boabdil, *el rey chico*, as he was called on account of his small stature heaved the historic sigh, the *suspiro del Moro*, which has given its name to a rock in the Sierra de Elvira.

This massive crenellated tower, washed with orange and red against a glaring background of sky, having behind it an abyss of vegetation, the precipitous slope of the city and, in the distance long ribbon-like mountains veined with a thousand lines, like African porphyries, forms a really majestic and splendid entrance to the Arab palace. Beneath the Gate is a guard-room, and poor ragged soldiers take their siesta on the very spot where the caliphs, seated on divans of gold brocade, with black eyes immobile in their marble countenances and their fingers lost in the folds of their silky beards, heard with a solemn dreamy air the complaints of the faithful. An altar is placed against the wall, surmounted by an image of the Virgin, as if to sanctify this former haunt of the worshippers of Mahomet from the very entrance.

Passing through the gate, one comes out into a vast open space called the Plaza de los Algives; in the middle is a well, with its brim

The Court of Lions, The Alhambra

surrounded by a sort of wooden scaffolding covered with grass matting beneath which one can go and drink, for a *cuarto*, great glasses of water, diamond-clear, icy cold and exquisitely flavoured. One side of the Plaza is surrounded by the Torre Quebrada, the Torre del Homenaje, the Torre del Armería and the Watch Tower (Torre de la Vela), from which a bell announces the hours for the distribution of water, besides a stone parapet upon which one can lean and admire the marvellous prospect lying before one; the other side is occupied by the palace of Charles the Fifth, a great Renaissance building which one would admire anywhere else; but one curses it here, when one considers that it covers a corresponding area of the Alhambra, which was pulled down on purpose to make room for its bulky mass. And yet this Alcázar was designed by Alonso Berruguete; the trophies, bas-reliefs and medallions on the façade are carved with a bold, spirited and patient chisel; the circular court with its marble columns, where the bullfights must have been held, is indeed a magnificent piece of architecture, but *non erat hic locus*.

One enters the Alhambra by a corridor situated at the corner of the palace of Charles the Fifth, and after taking a few turns, one comes to a great court-yard known indiscriminately by the name of *Patio de los Arrayanes* (Court of the Myrtles), of the *Alberca* (the Reservoir) or of the *Mezouar*, an Arabic word meaning the women's bath.

As one emerges from dim passages into this large enclosure bathed in light one has an impression similar to that which one has at the diorama. You feel as if an enchanter's wand had transported you into the heart of the East, four or five centuries ago. Time, which changes all things in its advance, has in no way modified the appearance of these scenes, where no surprise would be caused by the appearance of the Sultana "Chain of Hearts" and the Moor Tarfé.

In the middle of the court-yard is hollowed out a great reservoir three or four feet deep, in the shape of a parallelogram, bordered by two beds of myrtles and shrubs, and finishing at both ends in a sort of gallery, with slender columns, supporting Moorish arches of great delicacy. Fountains with their jets of water, of which the overflow runs off into the reservoir by a marble-lined drain, are placed beneath each gallery to complete the symmetry of the decoration. On the left are the archives, and the room to which, be it said to the shame of the inhabitants of Granada, is relegated, among rubbish of every sort, the magnificent Alhambra vase, nearly four feet high, and all covered with ornaments and inscriptions; a monument of inestimable rarity, which alone would be the glory of a museum, but which Spanish negligence allows to go to rack and ruin in a wretched back room. One of the wings which form the handles has recently been broken. On this side, too, are the passages leading to what was once the mosque, converted into a church at the time of the Conquest, under the invocation of St. Mary of the Alhambra. On the right are the apartments of the attendants, where the head of some dusky Andalusian maidservant, framed in a narrow Moorish window, produces quite a pleasingly Oriental effect. In the background, above an ugly roof of pantiles, replacing the cedar beams and gilded tiles of the Arab roof, rises the stately Torre de Comares, with its vermilion crenellations silhouetted against the wonderful limpidity of the sky. This tower contains the Hall of the Ambassadors, and communicates with the *Patio de los Arrayanes* by a sort of antechamber known from its shape as *La Barca*.

The antechamber to the Hall of the Ambassadors is worthy of its purpose: the bold line of its arches, the variety and complication of its arabesques, the mosaic of its walls, the workmanship of its stucco vaulting, as intricate as the roof of a stalactite grotto, and painted in blue, green and red, of which traces are still visible, form a whole which is charming in its fantastic originality. On each side of the door leading to the Hall of the Ambassadors, in the very jamb of the arch, above the facing of glazed tiles which adorn the base of the walls with triangles of bold colour, are hollowed two white marble niches in the form of chapels, carved with extreme delicacy. It was there that the Moors of old used to put off their slippers before going in, as a sign of respect, rather as we take off our hats in august spots.

The Hall of Ambassadors, one of the largest in the Alhambra, occupies the whole interior of the Patio de los Comares. The cedar-wood ceiling displays those mathematical intricacies which are so familiar to Arab architects: all the pieces are inserted in such a way that their angles, both exterior and interior, compose an infinite variety of designs; the walls are concealed beneath a network of ornaments so close and so inextricably intertwined that one can find no better comparison than a series of thick laces laid one upon the other. Gothic architecture, with its stone lacework and the pierced ornamentation of its rose-windows, is nothing to this. Nothing can give one an idea of it save a fish-slice, or those stamped paper embroideries with which confectioners cover their sweetmeats. One of the characteristics of the Moorish style is that it has few projections and few raised silhouettes. All this decoration is carried out on plane surfaces, and the depth of the relief never exceeds four or five inches; it is like a sort of tapestry worked in the very wall itself. One peculiar feature distinguishes it; namely, the use of writing as a motive of decoration; it is true that Arabic writing, with its intricate and mysterious outlines, lends itself marvellously to this mode of employment. The inscriptions, which are nearly always *suras* from the Koran or eulogies of the various princes who built and adorned the halls, unroll their curves along the friezes, on the jambs of the doors, and around the arches of the windows, mingled with flowers, foliage, loops and all the rich ornamentation of Arab calligraphy. Those in the Hall of the Ambassadors mean "Glory to God, power and wealth to believers," or contain the praises of Abu-Nazar, who, "if he had been transported alive to heaven, would have surpassed the brilliance of the stars and planets," a hyperbolical affirmation which appears to us a little too Oriental. Other bands are loaded with eulogies of Abi-Abd-Allah, another sultan who set artists to work on this part of the palace. The windows are bedizened with poems in praise of the clearness of the water in the reservoir, the fresh green of the shrubs and the perfume of the flowers which adorn the court of the Mezouar, which, indeed, one can see from the Hall of the Ambassadors, through the door and the slender columns of the gallery.

The loopholes with an inner balcony, pierced in the walls at a great height from the ground, the roof of beams, with no other decorations but the zigzags and interlaced patterns formed by the arrangement of the pieces, give the Hall of the Ambassadors a more austere appearance than the other apartments in the palace, and one more in harmony with its purpose. From the end window one enjoys a marvellous view over the gorge of the Darro.

Having finished this description, we must destroy yet another illusion: all these splendours are neither in marble, alabaster, nor even stone, but merely in plaster! This is quite contrary to the ideas of fairy-like luxury which the very name of the Alhambra calls up in the most matter-of-fact imagination; but it is the absolute truth: with the exception of the columns, which are generally turned all in one piece, and are hardly more than six to eight feet high, a few slabs in the pavement, the basins of the fountains, and the little chapels for leaving slippers in, there is not a single scrap of marble used in the internal construction of the Alhambra. The same is true of the Generalife: no race, however, has carried to a higher pitch than the Arabs the art of modelling, hardening and carving plaster, which acquires beneath their hands the hardness of stucco without its shiny surface.

Most of these ornaments, then, are made in moulds, and repeated with little trouble as often as symmetry requires. Nothing would be easier than to reproduce exactly a hall in the Alhambra: all that would be necessary would be to take casts of all the decorative patterns. Two arches which had collapsed in the Hall of the Tribunal have been restored by workmen of Granada with a perfection which leaves nothing to be desired. If we were a bit of a millionaire, one of our fancies would be to make a duplicate of the Lion Court in one of our parks.

From the Hall of the Ambassadors one goes, by a corridor constructed in comparatively recent days, to the *tocador* or Queen's Dressing-room. It is a little pavilion situated on top of a tower, from which one enjoys the most wonderful panorama, and which used to serve as an oratory for the Sultanas. At the entrance, one notices a white marble slab pierced with little holes to give passage to the smoke of the perfumes burnt beneath the floor. Upon these walls one can still see fantastic frescoes executed by Bartolomé de Ragis, Alonso Perez and Juan de la Fuente. On the frieze are groups of Cupids and the interlaced monograms of Isabella and Philip V. It would be hard to dream of anything more elegant and charming than this little retreat with slender Moorish columns, and elliptical arches, hanging over a blue abyss, the bottom of which is dotted with the roofs of Granada; the perfumes of the Generalife, blooming like a great mass of oleanders on the brow of the neighbouring hill, are wafted hither on the breeze, with the plaintive screech of the peacocks strutting upon its dismantled walls. What hours I have passed there, in a serene melancholy which is so different from the melancholy of the North, with one leg hanging over the abyss, schooling my eyes to grasp each form, each outline of the wonderful picture spread out before them, which they will doubtless never see again! No description, no painting can ever equal this brilliance, this light, the brightness of these tones. The most ordinary tints take on the value of jewels, and everything is maintained in this key. Towards the end of the day, when the sun's rays fall slantwise, they produce effects beyond conception: the mountains sparkle like piles of rubies, topazes and carbuncles; a golden dust pours down between them, and if, as often happens in the summer, the peasants are burning off the stubble on the plain, the puffs of smoke rising slowly heavenwards catch magical gleams from the fiery setting sun. I am astonished that Spanish painters in general should have painted in such sombre tones and devoted themselves exclusively to imitating Caravaggio and other gloomy masters. The pictures of Decamps and Marilhat, who have painted nothing but places in Asia or Africa, give a much truer idea of Spain than all the paintings brought back from the Peninsula at great expense.

We will cross without a halt the garden of Lindaraja, now no more than a piece of waste land, strewn with rubbish and bristling with thorn-bushes, and enter for a moment the Baths of the Sultana, lined with a mosaic of glazed earthenware tiles, and enriched with plaster filigree-work, which would put the most complicated madrepores to shame. A fountain occupies the middle of the room; two alcove-like recesses are sunk in the wall; it was there that Chain-of-Hearts and Zobeida used to come and repose on squares of cloth of gold, after lingering over the delights and refinements of an Oriental bath. One can still see the tribunes or balconies fifteen feet above the ground, where the musicians and singers used to take up their place. The baths are great bowls of white marble cut in a single piece, placed in little vaulted closets lighted by pierced rosettes or stars. In order that we may not fall into tiresome repetitions we will not speak of the Hall of Secrets, where a singular effect of acoustics is to be observed and the corners are blackened by the noses of curious persons who go and whisper some nonsense there which is faithfully repeated in the other corner; of the Hall of the Nymphs, in which is to be seen above the door an excellent bas-relief of Jupiter caressing Leda in the form of a swan, which is remarkable for its freedom of composition and bold execution; of the apartments of Charles the Fifth, stripped outrageously bare, which have now nothing curious about them save their ceilings bedizened with the ambitious motto *non plus ultra*; and we will betake ourselves to the Court of the Lions, the most curious and best-preserved portion of the Alhambra.

The English engravings and the many drawings which have been published of the Court of the Lions give only a very partial and quite misleading idea of it: they are almost all of them out of proportion, and, overloaded as they are by the necessity for rendering the infinite detail of Arab architecture, they give the idea of a building of a much more imposing character.

The Court of the Lions is a hundred and twenty feet long, and sixty-three wide, and the galleries surrounding it do not exceed twenty-two feet in height. They are formed of a hundred and twenty-eight columns of white marble, arranged with symmetrical irregularity by groups of three and four; on these columns, of which the highly wrought capitals preserve traces of gold and colour, are supported arches of the utmost elegance and a very original shape.

As you enter, you are faced, at the other end of the parallelogram, with the Hall of the Tribunal, the vaulting of which contains an artistic curiosity of priceless rarity and worth; namely, some Arab paintings, perhaps the only ones which have come down to us. One of them represents the Court of the Lions itself with its fountain, gilt but quite recognizable; there are a few figures which one cannot make out clearly, owing to the dilapidated state of the paintings, but which seem to be engaged in a joust or passage at arms. The other has as its subject a sort of divan in which are assembled the Moorish kings of Granada, whose white burnouses, olive faces, red mouths and black, mysterious eyes can still be clearly distinguished. These paintings, it is alleged, are on prepared leather, stuck to cedar-wood panels, and go to prove that the precept of the Koran forbidding the representation of living beings was not always observed scrupulously by the Moors, even if the twelve lions of the fountain were not there to confirm this assertion.

On the left, in the middle of the gallery running along one of the long sides of the court-yard, is the Hall of the Two Sisters, in a corresponding position to the Hall of the Abencerrages. This name of the Two Sisters has been given to it because of two immense slabs of white marble of Machael, of equal size and exactly alike, which one sees in the pavement. The vault or cupola, which the Spaniards call by the very expressive name of a media-naranja (half orange), is a miracle of patient workmanship. It may be compared to a honeycomb in a beehive, the stalactites of a grotto or the clusters of soapy globules which children blow from a straw. These myriads of tiny vaults and domes, three or four feet deep, springing one from the other, with the constant intersection and break of their ribs, resemble the product of some chance crystallization rather than the work of a human hand: blue, red or green colouring still gleams in the hollows of the mouldings with a brilliancy almost as fresh as if it had only just been laid on. The walls, like those of the Hall of the Ambassadors, are covered from the frieze down to the level of a man's head with an incredibly delicate and complicated incrustation of plaster. The lower part of the wall is faced with tiles of glazed earthenware on which points of black, green and yellow form a mosaic pattern against a white ground. The middle of the apartment, according to the invariable custom of the Arabs, whose dwelling-places seem to be no more than great decorated fountains, is occupied by the basin and jet of a fountain. There are four beneath the colonnade of the Tribunal, the same number beneath the colonnade at the entrance, and another in the Hall of the Abencerrages, not to speak of the *Taza de los Leones*, which, not content with spouting water from the jaws of its dozen monsters, tosses another flood of it heavenward from the mushroom on top. All these streams of water drain back along channels hollowed between the slabs forming the floor of the halls and the pavement of the court-yard, to the foot of the Fountain of the Lions, where they are swallowed by a subterranean conduit. Here indeed is a style of dwelling in which one would not be inconvenienced by dust, but one wonders how these halls can have been habitable in winter. No doubt the great cedar doors were then closed, the marble floor was covered with thick carpets, fires of fruit-kernels and fragrant woods were kindled in the *braseros*, and thus they waited for the return of the fine season which in Granada is never long in coming.

We will not describe the Hall of the Abencerrages, which is almost similar to that of the Two Sisters, and has nothing remarkable about it but an ancient wooden door composed of a lozenge-shaped inlay, and dating from the time of the Moors. At the Alcázar in Seville may be noticed another, exactly in the same style.

The *Taza de los Leones* enjoys a marvellous reputation in Arab poetry; there are no praises that are not heaped upon these superb animals: I must admit that it would be hard to find anything less resembling lions than these products of African fancy: their paws are mere stocks, like those roughly shaped pieces of wood which are stuck in the bodies of cardboard dogs to make them stand upright; their muzzles, striped with horizontal lines, no doubt to represent their whiskers, are exactly like the snout of a hippopotamus; the eyes are of an excessively primitive design recalling the formless efforts of children. Yet if one accepts these twelve monsters not as lions, but as fabulous beasts, or a decorative caprice, they produce, together with the basin which they support, a picturesque and most elegant effect, which helps one to understand their fame, and the eulogies contained in the Arabic inscription of twenty-four twenty-two-syllabled verses which is carved on the walls of the bowl into which falls the water from the upper basin. We ask our readers to forgive the rather barbarous fidelity of the translation:

"O thou who dost behold the lions fixed in their place! Observe that they lack only life in order to be perfect. And thou to whose lot doth fall the heritage of this Alcázar and kingdom, accept it from the noble hands which have governed it without discontent and without resistance. May God save thee for the work which thou hast now completed, and preserve thee for ever from the vengeance of thine enemy! Honour and glory to thee, O Mahommed, our King, adorned with the lofty virtues by which thou hast conquered all things. May God never suffer this fair garden, the image of thy virtues, to have a rival which shall surpass it! The substance which tinges the basin of the fountain is like mother-of-pearl beneath the clear and sparkling water; its surface is like molten silver, for peerless are the limpid clearness of the water and the whiteness of the stone; they are like a drop of transparent essence upon a face of alabaster. Hard would it be to follow its course. Behold the water, and behold the basin; thou canst not tell whether it is the water that is still or the marble which doth flow. Like the prisoner of love, whose face is bathed in discomfiture and fear under the glance of the envious, even so the jealous water is angry with the stone, and the stone is full of envy for the water. Like unto this inexhaustible flood is the hand of our king, for he is liberal and generous as the lion is strong and valiant."

It was into the basin of the Fountain of the Lions that fell the heads of the thirty-six Abencerrages, when they were led into a trap by the Zegris. The rest of the Abencerrages would all have shared the same fate, had it not been for the devotion of a little page who ran, at the risk of his life, and warned the survivors, preventing them from entering the fatal court-yard. You are shown some great reddish stains on the bottom of the basin, left there by the victims as an ineffaceable indictment of the cruelty of their murderers. Unfortunately scholars maintain that the Abencerrages and the Zegris never existed. As regards this question, I am quite prepared to take the word of songs, popular traditions and M. Chateaubriand's story, and I firmly believe that these crimson stains are blood, and not rust.

We had set up our head-quarters in the Court of the Lions; our furniture consisted of two mattresses, which were rolled up in a corner during the day-time, a copper lamp, an earthenware jar and a few bottles of sherry which we set to cool in the fountain. We slept at times in the Hall of the Two Sisters, at times in that of the Abencerrages, and it was not without some slight apprehension that I lay down in my cloak and watched the pale rays of the moon falling through the openings in the vault upon the water in the basin and the gleaming pavement, and mingling, to their astonishment, with the yellow, flickering flame of a lamp.

The popular traditions collected by Washington Irving in his *Tales of the Alhambra* came back into my memory; the stories of the Headless Horse and the Hairy Phantom, gravely related by old Echeverria, seemed to me extremely probable, especially when the light was blown out. Legends appear much more possible at night, in the darkness shot with uncertain gleams, which lend a fantastic appearance to the vaguely looming objects: doubt is the son of the daylight, but faith is the daughter of the night, and what astonishes me, for my part, is that St. Thomas should have believed in Christ after putting his finger in his wound. I am not sure I did not see the Abencerrages walking the galleries by moonlight with their heads under their arms: however that may be, the shadows of the columns took on a devilishly suspicious shape, and the breeze as it passed through the arcades had a most convincing resemblance to the breathing of a human being.

One morning—it was a Sunday—about four or five o'clock, we felt ourselves being drenched, as we slept on our mattresses, with a fine, soaking rain. They had opened the conduits of the fountains earlier than usual, in honour of a Prince of Saxe-Coburg who had come to visit the Alhambra, and who, it was said, was to marry the young Queen as soon as she was of age.

We were hardly up and dressed when the Prince arrived with two or three of his suite. He was furious. In order to celebrate his visit with great dignity the custodians had fitted all the fountains with the most ridiculous mechanical and hydraulic devices that can be imagined. One of these inventions was intended to represent the Queen's journey to Valencia, by means of a little tin coach and some lead soldiers set in motion by the force of the water. You can imagine the Prince's satisfaction at this ingenious and constitutional refinement. The *Fray-Gerundio*, the satirical paper of Madrid, persecuted this poor prince with peculiar venom. It reproached him, among other crimes, with quarrelling too sharply over the reckoning of his account at inns, and with appearing at the theatre in the costume of a *majo*, with a pointed hat on his head.

A party of men and women from Granada came to spend the day in the Alhambra; there were seven or eight young and pretty women, and five or six gentlemen. They danced to the sound of the guitar, played at little games and sang in chorus, to a delightful tune, the song of Fray Luis de Leon, which has obtained a popular success in Andalusia. The fountains were dry, for they had started shooting up their silver jets too early in the morning, so the frolicsome young girls seated themselves in a ring on the alabaster rim of the basin in the Hall of the Two Sisters, and throwing back their pretty heads, they sang the refrain of the song in chorus.

The Generalife is situated a little way from the Alhambra, on a rounded spur of the same mountain. One approaches it by a sort of sunk road crossing the ravine of Los Molinos, all edged with the huge, glossy leaves of fig-trees, with green oaks, pistachio-trees, laurels and cistuses of an incredibly luxuriant growth. The ground on which one walks is composed of a yellow sand soaked with water and of extraordinary fertility. No road could be more enchanting to follow than this one, which looks as if it were cut through a virgin forest in America, so blocked is it with foliage and flowers, and so filled with the heady fragrance of aromatic plants. Vines spring from the crevices of the fissured walls and droop from every branch their fantastic tendrils and their leaves indented like an Arab ornament; the aloe spreads its fan of azured blades, the orange-tree contorts its knotty stem, and clings with its finger-like roots to the gashes in the cliffs. All is filled with flowers blooming in a dense disorder full of unexpected charms. A stray branch of jasmine mingles a white star with the scarlet flowers of the pomegranate, a laurel stretches across the road to embrace a cactus, in spite of its thorns. Nature, left to her own devices, seems to glory in her seductions, as if she wished to show how even the most exquisite and cunning art lags far behind her.

After a quarter of an hour's walking, one arrives at the Generalife, which is, as it were, merely the *casa de campo*, the rustic pavilion of the Alhambra. The outside, like that of all Eastern buildings, is very simple: great walls with no windows, surmounted by a terrace with an arcaded gallery, the whole crowned with a little modern belvedere. Nothing is left of the Generalife save the arcades and some great arabesque panels, unluckily encrusted with coats of whitewash which have been renewed with desperately persistent cleanliness. Little by little the delicate sculptures, the marvellous incised lines of this fairy-like architecture are obliterated and blocked up till they disappear. What is nowadays only an indistinctly vermiculated wall was once a transparent lacework as fine as the ivory leaves carved for fans by the patient Chinese. The brush of the whitewasher has caused the disappearance of more masterpieces than the scythe of Time, if we may be allowed to use this mythological and out-of-date expression. In a room which is fairly well preserved, one may observe a series of dingy portraits of the Kings of Spain, which have no merit save a chronological one.

The real charm of the Generalife are its gardens and its waters. A marble-lined canal runs the whole length of the enclosure, bearing its swift and abundant waters under a series of leafy arches formed by gnarled and fantastically clipped yews. Orange-trees and cypresses are planted on both banks; at the foot of one of these cypresses of monstrous girth, which dates back to Moorish days, the favourite of

Boabdil, if the legend is to be believed, often proved that bolts and bars are but a feeble guarantee of the virtue of Sultanas. This much is certain, that the yew-tree is very thick and very old.

The prospect ends in a colonnaded gallery with fountains and marble pillars, like the Court of the Myrtles in the Alhambra. The canal makes a bend, and you enter other enclosures adorned with pools, whose walls preserve some traces of frescoes of the sixteenth century, representing rustic buildings and views. In the middle of one of these pools blooms like an immense bouquet a gigantic oleander of incomparable brilliance and beauty. At the time when I saw it, it was like an explosion of flowers, like the flower-piece of some display of vegetable fireworks; it had a resplendent, vigorous freshness of colour, which was almost loud, if this word may be used of colours, and would have made the hues of the reddest rose look pale! Its lovely flowers sprang with all the ardour of desire towards the pure light of the sky; its noble foliage, shaped on purpose by nature to form a crown of glory, wet with the spray from the fountains, sparkled like emeralds in the sun. Never has anything caused me such a keen sensation of beauty as this oleander at the Generalife.

The water is brought to the gardens by a sort of steep inclined plane, skirted by little walls in the style of a parapet, supporting channels of great curved tiles down which the streams rush, open to the air, with the gayest and liveliest prattle imaginable. On each level step copious jets shoot up from the middle of little basins, their crystal plume soaring up into the dense foliage of the laurel-grove, whose branches meet above them. The mountain streams with water on every side; at every step a spring gushes forth, and all the time one hears plashing at one's side some stream diverted from its course, on its way to feed a fountain or carry moisture to the foot of a tree. The Arabs carried the art of irrigation to a very high pitch; their hydraulic works bear witness to a very advanced civilization; these still exist today, and to them Granada owes the fact that she is the paradise of Spain, enjoying an eternal spring amidst an African temperature. An arm of the Darro was diverted by the Arabs, and brought nearly five miles to the hill of the Alhambra.

From the belvedere of the Generalife one has a clear view of the lie of the Alhambra, girdled with ruddy, half-ruined towers, and its stretches of wall which follow the swelling curves of the mountain up hill and down dale. The palace of Charles the Fifth, which cannot be seen from the direction of the town, outlines its square massy bulk, touched by the golden sun with a yellow gleam, against the diapered slopes of the Sierra Nevada, whose snowy ridge makes a fantastic gash in the sky. The spire of Santa Maria raises its Christian silhouette above the Moorish battlements. A few cypresses thrust themselves through the fissured walls, dark sighs of leafage among all this light and azure, like a melancholy thought amid the joy of a feast. The sides of the hill sloping down towards the Darro and the ravine of Los Molinos, are lost in a sea of verdure. It is one of the finest views that can be imagined.

On the other side, as if to form a contrast with all this freshness, rises a waste mountain, scorched, brown and stained with tones of ochre and burnt sienna, known as the *silla del Moro* from some remains of buildings standing on its summit. It was from here that King Boabdil used to watch the Arab horsemen jousting with the Christian knights on the Vega. The memory of the Moors is still a living one in Granada. They might have left the town yesterday, and if one may judge by what they have left behind, it is indeed a pity that they went. What Southern Spain requires is African, not European civilization, for the latter is not adapted to the burning climate and the passions which it inspires. The mechanism of constitutional government is only suited to the temperate zones; above thirty degrees of heat, constitutions melt or blow up.

Now that we have finished with the Alhambra and the Generalife, let us cross the gorge of the Darro and, taking the road which leads to the Monte Sagrado, let us visit the caves of the gypsies, of whom there are a fair number at Granada. The road is hewn in the side of the hill called the Albaicin, which overhangs it on one side. The gaunt, chalky-white slopes bristle with the palette-shaped leaves and lances, green as verdigris, of gigantic prickly pears and monstrous nopals; beneath the roots of these great, fleshy plants, which seem to serve as *chevaux de frise*, or a spiked fence, the dwellings of the gypsies are hollowed in the living rock. The entrance to these caves is whitewashed; instead of a door, a rope is stretched across them, upon which runs a piece of tattered tapestry. Inside swarms and pullulates the wild family; children with skins browner than Havana cigars play naked before the threshold, both sexes alike, and roll in the dust with shrill, guttural cries. The *gitanos* are usually blacksmiths, mule-clippers, veterinary surgeons and, above all, horse-dealers. They have a thousand recipes for producing fire and mettle in the most broken-winded worn-out beasts; a *gitano* would have made Rocinante gallop and Sancho's ass prance. But under cover of all this, their true profession is that of thieving.

The *gitanas* sell amulets, tell fortunes, and practise the shady trades customary among the women of their race: I have seen very few pretty ones, though their faces were remarkably typical and characteristic. Their swarthy skin sets off the clearness of their Eastern eyes, whose fire is tempered by a sort of mysterious melancholy, the memory, as it were, of an absent fatherland and a fallen greatness. Their mouths are rather thick-lipped and highly-coloured, recalling the full mouths of Africa; their narrow brows, and the arched forms of their noses, betray their common origin with the gypsies of Wallachia and Bohemia, and all the descendants of that strange race which pervaded the society of the Middle Ages under the generic term of Egyptians, and of which all these centuries have failed to break the mysterious succession. Almost all the women possess a natural majesty of port and a supple carriage, and hold themselves so erect from the hips that in spite of their rags; dirt and poverty, they seem conscious of the antiquity and purity of their unmixed descent, for gypsies only marry among themselves, and any children who might be born of passing unions would be cast from the tribe without pity. One of the claims put forward by the *gitanos* is that they are good Castilians and good Catholics, but I believe that at heart they have a touch of the Arab and Mahometan, a charge with they deny whenever they can, out of a lingering terror of the vanished Inquisition. A few deserted and half-ruined streets of the Albaicin are also inhabited by richer and less nomad *gitanos*. In one of these alleys, we caught sight of a little girl of eight, stark naked, who was practising dancing the *zorongo* on the sharp cobble-stones. Her sister, gaunt and emaciated, with eyes like glowing coals in a lemon-coloured face, was crouching on the ground beside her, with a guitar across her knees, thrumming at the chords with her thumb, and producing music not unlike the shrill chirping of the grasshoppers. The mother, richly dressed, with her neck loaded with glass beads, beat time with the tip of a blue velvet slipper, on which her eye dwelt with satisfaction. The savage attitude, the strange costume and extraordinary colour of this group would have made an excellent subject for a picture by Callot or Salvator Rosa.

The Monte Sagrado, which contains the miraculously discovered grottoes of the martyrs, has nothing very interesting about it. It is a convent with quite an ordinary church, under which is hollowed out the crypt. This crypt has nothing in it which produces a very vivid impression. It is composed of a jumble of little narrow corridors, seven or eight feet high and covered with whitewash. Altars adorned with more piety than taste have been set up in niches arranged for the purpose. It is there that the shrines and bones of these holy persons are enclosed behind gratings. I expected to see a dark, subterranean church, mysterious and almost alarming, with squat pillars and flattened vaulting, lit by the flickering gleam of a distant lamp—in fact, something like the ancient catacombs; and I was considerably surprised at the clean and attractive appearance of this whitewashed crypt, lit by skylights, like a cellar. Catholics of our rather superficial kind require the picturesque to stimulate our religious sentiments. The devout worshipper gives scarcely a thought to play of light and shade, or more or less skilfully planned architectural proportions; he knows that beneath this poorly shaped altar are the bones of saints who have died for the faith he professes, and that is enough for him.

The Charterhouse, now bereft of its monks, like all the convents in Spain, is a wonderful building, and it cannot be too much regretted that it has been diverted from its original purpose. We have never quite understood what harm these cenobites can have done, cloistered in a voluntary prison and living by austerities and prayers, especially in a country like Spain, where there is certainly no lack of land.

One goes up a double flight of steps to the doorway of the church, above which is a rather effective statue of St. Bruno. The decoration of this church is curious, consisting of plaster arabesques modelled in patterns of a truly prodigious variety and invention. It is as though the architects had intended to vie with the lacework of the Alhambra in lightness and intricacy, though in quite a different style. There is not a space the size of one's hand in the whole of this vast nave, that is not floridly diapered, covered with sprays and incised lines, and as dense as the heart of a cabbage; it would drive anyone crazy who tried to make an exact copy of it in pencil. The choir is lined with porphyry and precious marbles. A few poor pictures are hung here and there along the walls, making one regret the space they cover. The cemetery is beside the church; according to the Carthusian usage, no tomb or cross marks the place where lie the deceased brothers; the cells surround the cemetery, and are each provided with a little garden. In a piece of ground planted with trees, which no doubt served as a promenade for the monks, I was shown a sort of fish-pond with a border of sloping stones, on which a few dozen tortoises crawled awkwardly about, basking in the sun and quite happy at finding themselves safe, at last, from the stew-pot. The Carthusian rule binds the brethren never to eat meat, but tortoise is considered by the casuists to be fish. These were intended to serve as food for the monks. The revolution has saved them.

While we are by way of visiting convents, let us, if you please, enter the monastery of San Juan de Dios. The cloister is of the queerest kind, and in quite prodigiously bad taste; the walls are painted in fresco with various good deeds in the life of San Juan de Dios, framed with odd figures and fantastic ornaments outdoing the most extravagant and fantastic distortions of Japanese monsters and Chinese grotesques. There are sirens playing the violin, little she-monkeys dressing themselves up, flowers looking like birds, birds looking like flowers, lozenges of looking-glass, earthenware tiles, true-lover's knots, all in inextricable confusion. The church is fortunately of a different date, and is almost entirely gilded. The retable, supported by twisted columns, produces a rich and majestic effect. When the sacristan who acted as our guide saw that we were French, he questioned us about our country, and asked if it were true, as they were saying in Granada, that Nicholas, the Emperor of Russia, had invaded France and made himself master of Paris; such was the latest news. These wild absurdities were spread among the people by the partisans of Don Carlos in order to create a belief in an absolutist reaction on the part of the European powers, and to rally the failing spirit of their disorganized bands by the hope of speedy assistance.

In this church I saw a sight which impressed me; it was an old woman who was dragging herself on her knees from the door to the altar; she had her arms stretched out in a cross, as stiff as stocks, with her head thrown backwards, her eyes turned up till they showed nothing but the whites, her lips drawn back from her teeth, her face shiny and leaden-hued; it was ecstasy verging on catalepsy. Never has Zurbarán painted anything more ascetic and febrile in its ardour. She was performing a penance imposed by her confessor, and still had four more days to continue.

The convent of San Geronimo, converted into a barracks, contains a Gothic cloister with two tiers of arcades of rare beauty and character. The capitals of the columns are embellished with fantastic foliage and animals charming in their fantasy and execution. The desecrated and abandoned church offers this peculiarity, that all its architectural ornaments and reliefs are painted in monochrome like the vault of the Bourse, instead of being carried out in reality; here is buried Gonzalvo de Cordoba, nicknamed the Great Captain. His sword had been preserved there, but has lately been carried off and sold for two or three *duros*, the value of the silver mount of the hilt. It is thus that many objects of value either artistically or for their associations have disappeared with no profit to the thieves save the mere pleasure of evil-doing. They really might imitate our revolution in some other aspect than in its stupid vandalism. This is the feeling which possesses one every time one visits an empty convent, at the sight of so much useless ruin and devastation, of so many masterpieces of every kind lost beyond recall, of the gradual achievement of many centuries removed and swept away in an instant. It is granted to nobody to foretell the future; for my part, I doubt whether it will restore to us the heritage of the past, which we destroy as though we had something to put in its place. Even this something might be placed by the side of the rest, for the earth is not so covered with buildings that one is forced to build new ones on the ruins of the old.

Such were the reactions in which I was engaged as I walked through the former convent of San Domingo in the Antequeruela. The chapel is inconceivably overloaded with decorations of tinsel, gilding and trifling ornaments. It is a mass of twisted columns, volutes, rosettes, incrustations of coloured breccia, glass mosaics, mother-of-pearl and shell inlay, crystals, bevelled mirrors, radiant suns, transparencies, etc., all the most disordered, misshapen, deformed and baroque imaginings that the tortuous taste of the eighteenth century, with its horror of the straight line, could possibly inspire. The library, which has been preserved, is composed almost exclusively of folios and quartos, bound in white vellum, with the title written by hand in black or red ink. They are mostly theological treatises, dissertations of the casuists and other scholastic productions of little interest to mere men of letters. A collection of pictures from monasteries has been formed in the convent of San Domingo which has nothing of remarkable quality in it, with the exception of a few fine, ascetic heads and some scenes of martyrdom which seem to have been painted by the tormentors, so vast is the erudition in torture which is displayed in them; it proves that the destroyers are fine experts in painting, for they have succeeded admirably in keeping all that is good for themselves. The court-yards and cloisters are of wondrous beauty, adorned with fountains, orange-trees and flowers. How marvellously it is all arranged for dreaming, meditation and study! And what a pity it is that the convents were inhabited by monks, and not by poets! The gardens, left to themselves, have taken on a rustic and uncultivated appearance. The paths are invaded by luxuriant vegetation; on all sides nature regains possession of her rights; as each stone falls, she replaces it with a tuft of grass or flowers. The most remarkable feature of these gardens is a pleached alley of great laurels, paved with marble and flanked on each side with a long seat of the same material with a sloping back. Fountains stationed at intervals maintain a refreshing cool beneath this dense green, at the end of which one enjoys a magnificent view of the Sierra Nevada, through the windows of a charming Moorish mirador, forming part of the remains of the old Arab palace which are built into the convent. They say that this pavilion used to communicate by long subterranean passages with the Alhambra, at some distance away. The idea, at least, is very deeply rooted in Granada, where the most trifling Moorish ruin is always endowed with ten or twelve miles of underground passages and a hidden treasure protected by some spell or another.

We would often go to San Domingo and sit in the shade of the laurels, or bathe in a swimming-bath, in which, if the mocking songs are to believed, the monks used to disport themselves merrily with the pretty girls they used to entice there or carry off. It should be observed that it is in the most Catholic countries that holy things, priests and monks are treated most lightly; Spanish epigrams and stories about monks have nothing to envy the jests of Marot or Béroalde de Verville in licence, and from the way in which religious rites are parodied in old plays, one might almost think that the Inquisition had never existed.

And, talking about baths, we will here mention a small detail to prove that the art of arranging bathing establishments, though carried to such a pitch by the Arabs, has fallen greatly from its high estate at Granada. Our guide took us to some baths which were fairly nicely arranged, with cubicles opening off a *patio* shaded by a roof of vines, the greater part of which was occupied with a reservoir of the most limpid water. So far all was well, but whatever do you imagine the bath-tubs were made of? Copper, zinc, wood or stone? Not at all, you are quite wrong; we will tell you, for you will never guess. They were enormous clay jars, like those in which oil is stored; these newfangled baths were sunk in the ground up to about two-thirds of their height. Before putting ourselves in these jars, we had them lined with a white sheet, a cleanly precaution which struck the bath-attendant as very odd, and which we had to impress upon him several times before we were obeyed, so great was his astonishment. He explained this whim to himself by a pitying shrug of the shoulders and head, muttering to himself the one word *Ingleses!* We squatted in our jars with our heads sticking out rather like potted partridges, and looking pretty absurd. It was not till then that I understood the story of Ali Baba, or the Forty Thieves, which had always seemed a little difficult to believe, and made me doubt for a moment the veracity of the *Thousand and One Nights.*

There are, indeed, some old Moorish baths in the Albaicin, a swimming-bath roofed with a vault pierced with little star-shaped lights; but they are not properly equipped, and one would only find cold water there.

Such, on the whole, are the notable sights of Granada which one can see during a stay of a few weeks. Distractions are few in number: the theatre is closed during the summer; the bullring has no regular program; there are no casinos or public resorts, and one finds no French or foreign newspapers except at the Lyceum, where the members hold meetings on certain days, at which they read speeches and poetry, or sing or play pieces, written, as a rule, by some young poet belonging to the society.

Everyone is conscientiously engaged in doing nothing: compliments, cigarettes, the composition of four and eight-lined stanzas and, above all, cards suffice to fill life pleasantly. One does not find here that frenzied restlessness, that need for action and movement which vex the people of the North. The Spaniards struck me as very philosophic. They attach only the slightest importance to the material side of life, and are totally indifferent to comfort. The thousand artificial needs created by northern civilizations seem to them to be childish and inconvenient refinements. And indeed, since they are not bound to protect themselves incessantly from the climate, the joys of the English home do not inspire them with the least envy. What does it matter whether the windows fit properly, to people who would pay for a draught or a breath of air, if it were to be had? Favoured with a beautiful sky, they have reduced existence to its simplest expression; this sobriety and moderation in all things ensure them great liberty and extreme independence; they have time to live, and the same can hardly be said of us. The Spaniards have no idea of working first, in order to rest afterwards; they would far rather do the opposite, which, indeed, seems to be more reasonable. A workman who has earned a few reals quits his work, throws his fine embroidered jacket over his shoulder, takes his guitar and goes off to dance or make love to the *majas* of his acquaintance until he has not a single *cuarto* left; then he resumes his work. An Andalusian can live gloriously on three or four *sous* a day; for this sum he can have the whitest of bread, an enormous slice of watermelon and a liqueur glass full of anisette; he will have nothing to pay for his lodging save the trouble of stretching his cloak on the ground under some colonnade or arch of a bridge. Work in general is, in the eyes of the Spaniards, a humiliating thing unworthy of a free man, a perfectly natural and reasonable idea in my opinion, for when God desired to punish man for his disobedience he could find no greater torment to inflict upon him than that he should earn his bread by the sweat of his brow. Pleasures won, as ours are, by dint of toil, fatigue, mental tension and application, would seem to them too dearly bought. Like all simple peoples living very near to the state of nature, they have right-minded ideas which lead them to despise mere conventional enjoyments. To anyone arriving from Paris or London, those two whirlpools of devouring activity and feverish, overwrought existence, life as it is led in Granada is a strange spectacle, a life that is all leisure filled up with conversation, the siesta, the promenade, the music and the dance. One is surprised to see the tranquil happiness of these faces, the peaceful dignity of their expression. None of them have that fussy appearance which one notices about passers-by in the streets of Paris. Everyone takes things easy, choosing the shady side of the road, stopping to chat with his friends and betraying no haste to get anywhere. The certainty that they cannot earn any money quenches all ambition: there are no careers open to the young men. The most adventurous of them go away to Manila or Havana, or take service in the army; but owing to the lamentable financial situation, they sometimes go years and years without hearing a word about pay. Convinced of the uselessness of their efforts, they do not try to seek an impossible fortune, and pass their time in a charmed idleness encouraged by the beauty of the country and the burning heat of the climate.

I noticed hardly any haughty reserve in the Spaniards: there is nothing so misleading as the reputation attributed to individuals or races. I found them, on the contrary, extremely simple and good-tempered; Spain is the real land of equality, if not in words, at least in deeds. The poorest beggar lights his *papelito* from the *puro* of the noble lord, who allows him to do so without the least affectation of condescension; the great lady steps smilingly over the wastrels lying like tattered bundles across her doorway, and when she travels she does not turn up her nose at drinking out of the same glass as the *mayoral*, the *zagal* and the *escopetero* who escort her. Foreigners find it very difficult to get used to this familiarity, especially the English, who have their letters served up to them on dishes, from which they pick them up with tongs. One of these estimable islanders, on his way from Seville to Xeres, sent his *calesero* (coachman) to dine in the kitchen. The man, who considered in his own mind that he was doing a heretic great honour by putting his elbows on the same table with him, made no remonstrance, and concealed his wrath as carefully as the traitor in a melodrama; but half-way along the road, seven or eight miles from Xeres, in a horrible desert, full of quagmires and thorn-bushes, our friend tipped the Englishman neatly out of the carriage, shouting to him, as he whipped up his horse: "Milord, you thought me unworthy to sit at your table; but I, Don Balbino Bustamente y Orozco, do not consider you high-class enough to sit on the seat of my carriage. Good evening!"

The servants, both male and female, are treated with an easy familiarity very different from our affected politeness, which seems to remind them at every word of their inferior position. A small example will prove this statement. We had gone in a party to the country-house of Señora X; in the evening they wished to dance, but there were far more ladies than gentlemen; Señora X sent for the gardener and another servant, who danced all the evening with no embarrassment, self-consciousness or eager servility, as if they had really belonged to our society. They asked the prettiest and most titled ladies to dance in turn, and these accepted the invitation with the best possible grace. Our democrats are still far removed from this practical equality, and our wildest republicans would be shocked at the idea of standing up in a quadrille opposite a peasant or a footman.

These observations, like all rules, are subject to an infinite number of exceptions. There are no doubt many active, hard-working Spaniards, sensitive to all the refinements of life, but such is the general impression which a traveller receives after a stay of some length, an impression which is often juster than that of native observers, who are less keenly and intimately affected by the novelty of what they see.

Our curiosity about Granada and its buildings was now satisfied, and as we kept coming upon the prospect of the Sierra Nevada at the end of every street, we resolved to become more closely acquainted with it, by attempting the ascent of El Mulhacen, the highest peak in the chain. Our friends at first attempted to dissuade us from this plan, which was not without some attendant danger; but when they saw that we were quite determined, they recommended us a hunter named Alexander Romero, who, they said, knew the mountain from end to end, and would be capable of acting as our guide. He came to see us at our *casa de pupilos*, and his frank, manly countenance at once impressed us favourably: he wore an old velvet waistcoat, a red woollen girdle and white linen gaiters like those worn by the Valencians, showing his wiry, muscular legs, as brown as Cordoba leather. For shoes he wore *alpargatas* of plaited rope; a little Andalusian hat, turned rusty by exposure to the sun's rays, a carbine and a powder-horn slung across his shoulder, completed his equipment. He took charge of the preparations for the expedition, and promised to bring us by three o'clock the next day the four horses we required, one for my travelling companion, another for me, a third for a young German who had joined our caravan and a fourth for our servant, who was to preside over the culinary department of the expedition. As for Romero, he was to go on foot. Our provisions consisted of ham, roast chickens, chocolate, bread, lemons, sugar, and, above all, of a great leathern wallet known as a *bota,* full of excellent Val de Peñas wine.

The horses were outside the house at the appointed time, with Romero trying to ram in our door with the butt-end of his carbine. Still hardly awake, we got into the saddle and our procession moved off; our guide went ahead of us as a forerunner to point out the road. Though it was already light, the sun had not yet appeared, and the low, rolling, foot-hills we had passed stretched around us, fresh, limpid and blue, like the waves of a still ocean. Granada grew dim and distant in the misty atmosphere. When the ball of fire appeared on the horizon, all the mountain-tops blushed like young girls at the appearance of a lover, and seemed to display a modest confusion at being seen is their morning undress. So far we had only climbed quite gentle slopes, unfolding one beyond the other and offering no real difficulty. The spurs of the mountain melt into the plain by skilfully graduated curves, so as to form a preliminary plateau which is always easily accessible. We had arrived upon this first plateau. The guide decided that we must breathe our horses, give them their food and have our own breakfast. We took up our position at the foot of a rock, near a little spring with diamond-clear water glittering beneath the emerald grass. Romero, with the skill of an American savage, improvised a fire by means of a handful of brushwood, and Louis made us some chocolate which, reinforced by a slice of ham and a sip of wine, made up our first meal in the mountains. While our dinner was being cooked, a magnificent viper passed beside us, and seemed surprised and displeased with us for camping on his domain; he betrayed his feelings by a rude hiss which earned him a good stab in the belly with a sword-stick. A little bird, which had looked on at this scene with an air of great interest, no sooner saw that the viper had got the worst of it, than he ran up with the feathers of his neck standing on end, with wings flapping and eyes ablaze, screaming and chirping in an extraordinary state of excitement, drawing back every time a fragment of the poisonous beast gave a convulsive writhe, but soon returning to the charge and giving it a few pecks, after which he rose three or four feet into the air. I do not know what this serpent can have done to the bird in his lifetime, or what grudge we had furthered by killing it; but I have never seen a greater demonstration of joy.

We started off again. From time to time we met strings of little asses descending from the upper regions, loaded with snow which they were carrying to Granada for the day's consumption. The leaders saluted us, as they passed by, with the consecrated formula of *vayan ustedes con Dios*, and our guide called out to them some jest about their wares, which would never get as far as the town with them but would have to be sold to the Superintendent of the Watering Department.

Romero kept ahead of us, leaping from rock to rock as lightly as a chamois, and shouting: *Bueno camino* (Good road). I should be quite curious to know what the good fellow understood by a bad road, for there was no sign of a track. To right and left, as far as we could see, descended lovely precipices of a deep, misty, azure blue, varying in depth from fifteen hundred to two thousand feet, a difference which did not trouble us very much, it is true, for a few dozen fathoms more or less did not affect the situation in the least. I remember with a shudder a certain place where we had to cross, which was three or four gunshots long and two feet broad, like a natural plank thrown between two abysses. As my horse was at the head of the file, I had to be the first to cross by this kind of tight rope, which would have given pause to the most resolute acrobats. In some places the path was so narrow that my mount had barely space to plant his hoofs, and each of my legs hung over a different abyss: I sat motionless in my saddle as if I had been carrying a chair balanced on the tip of my nose. The few minutes I spent in crossing seemed very long.

When I think about this incredible climb in cold blood, I am amazed, as one is at the memory of a confused dream. We passed by roads where a goat would have hesitated to set its foot, and climbed slopes so steep that our horses' ears touched our chins, over rocks and stones which slid from under our feet, and along terrifying precipices. We followed a zigzag course, taking advantage of the slightest irregularity of the ground, making small but steady progress, and rising by degrees towards the summit, the goal of our ambition, of which we had lost sight since starting the ascent; for each plateau hides the upper one from one's eyes. Every time our beasts stopped to draw breath, we turned in our saddles to gaze at the vast panorama formed by the circular canvas of the horizon. The mountain-tops beyond which we had climbed were outlined as on a great map. The Vega of Granada and the whole of Andalusia lay before us like a sea of azure in which a few points of white, touched by the sun, represented the sails. The neighbouring summits, bald, bare, seamed and fissured from top to bottom, had tones of ashy green, Egyptian blue, lilac and pearl-grey in the shadow, and the warmest and most wonderful hues in the light, like orange-peel or a lion's skin, or like burnished gold. Nothing gives such an idea of chaos, of a universe still in the hands of the Creator, as a chain of mountains seen from on high. One might imagine that some race of Titans had tried to build there one of those towers of enormity, those prodigious *Lylacqs* which throw God into alarm; that they had stacked up materials and started gigantic terraces, when some unknown breath overthrew and scattered like a storm their inchoate temples and palaces. One might think oneself amidst the ruins of some antediluvian Babel, or the remains of a pre-Adamite city. These enormous blocks, these piled-up masses worthy of the Pharaohs, suggest the idea of a vanished race of giants, and the age of the world is clearly inscribed in the deep wrinkles on the hoary brow and crabbed face of these age-old mountains.

We had reached the haunts of the eagle. We perceived some of these noble birds perched at long intervals on solitary rocks, with eyes towards the sun, in that state of contemplative ecstasy which takes the place of thought in animals. One of them was hovering at a great height, and seemed to hang motionless in the midst of an ocean of light. Romero could not resist the pleasure of sending him a bullet as a sort of visiting-card. The shot carried away one of his great wing-feathers, but the eagle, with ineffable majesty, went on his way as if nothing had reached him. The feather circled slowly down, and at last reached the earth, where it was picked up by Romero, who stuck it in his hat.

Snow began to appear in the shadow of the rocks in slender streaks, and in scattered patches; the air grew rare, the cliffs became more and more abrupt; soon the snow lay before us in vast sheets and enormous heaps, and the sun's rays no longer availed to melt it. We were above the source of the Genil, which we could see like a blue ribbon frosted with silver, rushing hurriedly down in the direction of its beloved city. The plateau upon which we were standing rises about nine thousand feet above sea-level, and is dominated by no peaks but Veleta and El Mulhacen, which rise yet another thousand feet into the unplumbed abyss of the sky. It was here that Romero decided we were to pass the night.

We unharnessed our horses, who were tired out; Louis and the guide tore up bushes, roots and broom to keep up our fire, for though there were from thirty to thirty-five degrees of heat on the plain, there was a coolness on these heights which the sunset was bound to change into a stinging cold. It might have been about five o'clock, my companion and the young German wished to profit by what light was left to climb alone and on foot the highest mound. For my part I preferred to stay behind and, stirred to the soul by this grand and sublime spectacle, I began to scribble in my note-books a few verses, which, if not very well turned, had at least the merit of being the only alexandrines composed at such a height. Having finished my stanzas, I made some excellent ices for our dessert out of snow, sugar, lemon and brandy. Our encampment was quite picturesque; the saddles of our horses served as seats, our cloaks as carpets and a great heap of snow sheltered us from the wind. In the middle sparkled a fire of broom which we fed by throwing on to it from time to time a branch which writhed and hissed as the sap spurted out in many-coloured jets. Above us the horses stretched out their thin heads, with gentle, mournful eyes, to catch a few wafts of heat.

The night was advancing with great strides. The lower mountains had disappeared first, one after the other, and like a fisherman who flies before the rising tide, the light was leaping from summit to summit as it withdrew towards the heights to escape the shadow rising from the depths of the valleys, and drowning all things in its blue-tinged waves. The last ray which rested on the peak of El Mulhacen paused a moment in hesitation, then, spreading its golden wings, it soared like a bird of flame up into the depths of the sky, and disappeared. The darkness was complete, and the wide-flung reflection from our hearth sent dancing shadows grimacing over the rocky walls. Eugène and the German did not reappear, and I began to grow anxious: they might have fallen over a precipice, and been swallowed up in a heap of snow. Romero and

Louis were already asking me to sign a statement to the effect that they had not murdered or robbed those two honest gentlemen and that, if the latter were dead, it was at least their own fault.

In the meantime we were rending our bosoms with the shrillest and most savage howls to show them the way to our wigwam, in case they could not see the flames. At last a gunshot, repeated by all the mountain echoes, informed us that we had been heard, and that our companions were now not far off. They appeared, indeed, after a few minutes, jaded with fatigue, and maintaining that they had seen Africa distinctly across the sea, which is quite possible, for the air is so pure in this climate that one's view may extend to a distance of thirty or forty leagues. We had a very merry supper, and by playing tunes on our wineskin as if it were bagpipes, we made it almost as flat as the wallet of a Castilian beggar. It was agreed that each of us was to watch in turn, so as to keep up the fire, and this was faithfully carried out. But the circle, which started with quite a large circumference, grew narrower and narrower. As the hours went by, the cold increased in intensity, and we ended by getting right into the fire, to such an extent that we burnt our shoes and trousers. Louis broke into lamentations; he regretted his *gaspacho* (cold garlic soup), his house, his bed and even his wife; he vowed, by all his gods, that never again would he be ensnared into climbing mountains, maintaining that they are more interesting from below than from on high, and that one must be raving mad to risk breaking one's bones a hundred thousand times, and getting one's nose and ears frost-bitten in the middle of August, in Andalusia, within sight of Africa. He never ceased moaning and grumbling like this all night, and we could not succeed in reducing him to silence. Romero, who said nothing, was only dressed in linen, and had nothing to wrap himself in but a narrow strip of stuff.

At last the dawn appeared; we were enveloped in a cloud, and Romero advised us to begin our descent if we wished to be back in Granada by night. As soon as it was light enough to distinguish things, I noticed that Eugène was as red as a well-boiled lobster, and he simultaneously noticed the same thing about me, which he felt it his duty not to hide from me. The young German and Louis had also turned cardinal; Romero's skin alone had retained the tan shade of a boot-top, and his bronzed legs, though bare, had not undergone the slightest alteration. It was the biting cold and the rarefaction of the air which had turned us red in this fashion. Going up is nothing, for one can see what is above one, but coming down, with the abyss before one's eyes, is quite another matter. At first sight, we thought it could not be managed, and Louis began to scream like a jay being plucked alive. However, we could not stay for ever on El Mulhacen, an uncomfortable place if ever there was one, and, with Romero as our leader, we began the descent. To describe the roads, or rather, the absence of roads, by which this devil of a fellow led us, would be impossible if we are not to be accused of bragging; never has such a series of death-traps been set up for a steeplechase, and I doubt if the boldest of gentlemen-riders has ever outdone our exploits on El Mulhacen. The slopes of a switchback are gentle by comparison. We spent almost all the time standing up in our stirrups and throwing ourselves back against our horses' haunches, so as not to keep flying over their heads in a parabola. All the outlines of the view ran into a blur before our eyes; the streams appeared to flow backwards towards their sources, the rocks tottered and rocked upon their bases, the most distant objects seemed only two paces away, and we had lost all sense of proportion, an effect which does occur in the mountains, where the vast masses and vertical planes prevent one from judging distances any longer by the ordinary means.

In spite of all these obstacles, we arrived in Granada without a false step on the part of our horses; but they could not muster more than a single shoe between them. Andalusian horses—though these, indeed, were poor jaded brutes—have no equal for mountain work. They are so docile, so patient and intelligent that the best thing to do is to leave the reins loose on their necks.

Our return was awaited with impatience, for they had seen from the city the fire which we had lit like a beacon on the plateau of El Mulhacen. I wanted to go and describe our perilous expedition to the charming Señoras B., but I was so tired that I fell asleep on a chair with my stocking in my hand, and remained in the same position without waking until ten the next morning. A few days later we left Granada, heaving a sigh no less profound than that of King Boabdil.

XIII. Granada to Malaga

A RUMOR calculated to raise a stir in every corner of a Spanish town had suddenly run round Granada, to the great joy of the *aficionados*. The new bullring at Malaga was at last finished, after costing the contractor five million reals. In order to inaugurate it solemnly by exploits worthy of the great days of the art, the great Montes of Chiclana had been engaged with his team, and was to fill the bill for three consecutive days; Montes, the first *espada* in Spain, the brilliant successor of Romero and Pepe-Illo. We had already been present at several bullfights, but had not had the good fortune to see Montes, who was prevented by his political opinions from appearing in the ring in Madrid; and to leave Spain without seeing Montes was as uncivilized and barbarous a thing to do as to leave Paris without seeing Mlle. Rachel. Though, according to the itinerary which we had sketched out, we ought to have gone to Cordoba, we could not resist this temptation, and we resolved to go out of our way to Malaga, in spite of the difficulty of the road, and the small amount of time left us for doing it.

There is no stage-coach from Granada to Malaga; the only means of transport are *galeras* or mules: we chose mules, as being safer and more expeditious, for in order to arrive on the very morning of the bullfight we had to take to the by-ways of the Alpujarras.

Our friends in Granada recommended us a *cosario* (leader of a convoy) named Lanza, a fine-looking fellow, an honest man and an intimate friend of the bandits. In France this would seem rather a poor recommendation, but things are different beyond the mountains. The muleteers and drivers of *galeras* know the robbers, drive bargains with them, and in consideration of a tax of so much a head per traveller or per convoy, according to circumstances, they obtain a free passage, and are not stopped. These arrangements are observed on both sides with scrupulous probity, if such a word is not out of place in speaking of transactions of this kind. When the chief of the band controlling the road retires with an *indulto* (amnesty), or for any reason cedes his business and clientele to some other, he takes care to present officially to his successor the *cosarios* who pay him the "black tax", lest they might be molested by mistake; in this way travellers are sure of not being robbed, while the robbers avoid the risks of an attack and a struggle which is often dangerous. Everybody gets what he wants.

One night, between Alhama and Velez, our *cosario* was drowsing upon the neck of his mule, at the tail-end of the train, when all of a sudden he was roused by piercing cries; he saw the glint of blunderbusses at the edge of the road. There could be no further doubt, the convoy was being attacked. Surprised to the last degree, he leapt from his mount, struck up the mouth of the blunderbusses with his hand, and told them his name.—"I beg your pardon, Señor Lanza," said the brigands, quite taken aback by their mistake. "We had not recognized you; we are honest fellows, incapable of such an indelicacy; our honour would not allow us to take so much as a cigar from you."

If one is not with a man known on the road, one must drag after one a strong escort, armed to the teeth, which is very costly and offers less security, for as a rule the *escopeteros* are retired robbers.

In Andalusia, when one is travelling on horseback and going to a bullfight, it is the custom to wear national costume. So our little caravan was quite picturesque, and cut quite a good figure as we left Granada. I joyfully seized the opportunity of dressing up out of carnival, and, leaving off my horrible French garments for a time, put on my *majo's* costume: pointed hat, embroidered jacket, velvet waistcoat with filigree buttons, red silk sash, breeches and gaiters open at the calf. My travelling companion wore his costume of green velvet and Cordoba leather. Others wore the *montera*, and a black jacket and breeches adorned with silk trimmings of the same colour, with a yellow tie and belt. Lanza was conspicuous for the luxury of his silver buttons, made of Spanish-American two-column pesetas, with a hook welded to them, and the solid-silver embroideries on his second jacket, slung on his shoulder like a hussar's dolman.

The mule allotted me for a mount was shaved half-way up its body, which enabled me to study its muscular system as conveniently as on an anatomical chart. The saddle was composed of two gaily coloured blankets folded double so as to soften the projecting vertebrae and the sloping angle of the backbone as much as possible. On either side hung two objects resembling wooden troughs and not unlike rat-traps, which served as stirrups. The harness was so loaded about the head with pompons, tufts and ornaments that it was quite hard to distinguish through their straggling filaments the sullen, cantankerous profile of the ill-tempered beast.

On the road the Spaniards regain their old-world originality, and shed all traces of foreign imitations; the national character reappears in its entirety in these trains crossing the mountains, which cannot be very different from desert caravans. The roughness of the roads, which are barely more than tracks, the savage grandeur of the surroundings, the picturesque costume of the *arrieros*, the fantastic harness of the mules, horses and asses walking in file, all transport you thousands of miles away from civilization. Travelling becomes a reality, an action in which you take your part. In a stage-coach, one ceases to be a man, one is merely a thing without life, a bundle; you differ very little from your trunk. You are tossed from side to side, and that is all. You might as well stay at home. What constitute the pleasure of a traveller are obstacles, fatigue or even danger. What charm can there be in a journey when one is always sure to arrive and find horses ready, a downy bed, an excellent supper and all the comfort one enjoys at home? One of the great misfortunes of modern life is the absence of the unexpected, the lack of adventure. Everything is so well regulated, so well fitted into its place and ticketed, that chance is no longer possible; another century of improvements, and everybody will be able to foresee from the very day of his birth all that will happen to him up to the day of his death. There will be a complete annihilation of the human will. No more crime; no more virtue; no more character; no more originality. It will be impossible to distinguish a Russian from a Spaniard, an Englishman from a Chinaman, a Frenchman from an American. We shall even be unable to recognize each other, for everybody will be alike. Then an immense tedium will descend upon the universe, and suicide will decimate the population of the globe, for curiosity, the chief incentive to life, will be extinct.

A journey in Spain is still a perilous and romantic enterprise; one has to put forth one's strength and be brave, patient and strong; one risks one's life at every step; privations of every kind, the absence of the things most indispensable for existence, the danger of the roads, which are really impassable to anybody but Andalusian muleteers, a heat that is infernal, a sun that would split one's skull, are the least of the drawbacks; you have also the insurgents, the robbers and the hotel-keepers, arrant rogues whose honesty is regulated by the number of carbines you carry with you. Danger surrounds you, follows and precedes you; you hear nothing on all sides but whispered tales of terror and mystery. "Yesterday the bandits supped in this *posada*."—"A caravan has been carried off and taken to the mountains by brigands to hold it to ransom."—"*Palillos* are ambushed at such-and-such a spot which you will have to pass." No doubt there is much exaggeration in all this; but, however incredulous one may be, one is forced to believe something when one sees at every turn of the road wooden crosses bearing such inscriptions as "Here they killed a man", "Here died by violence..."

We had left Granada in the evening and were to ride all night. The moon was not long in rising, silvering with its rays the cliffs upon which it shone. The shadows of the rocks stretched out in fantastic outlines along the road we were following, and produced strange optical effects. In the distance we heard the bells on the asses, which had gone on ahead with our luggage, tinkling like the notes of musical glasses or some *mozo de mulas* singing love-songs with those guttural tones and gliding changes of pitch which always sound poetical by night in the mountains. It was charming, and it will be appreciated if we quote two stanzas here, which were probably improvised, and thanks to their graceful quaintness, have remained graven on our memory.

"*Son tus labios dos cortinos*
De terciopelo carmesi;
Entre cortina y cortina,
Niña, dime que si

Atame con un cabello
A los banco, de tu cama,
Aunque el cabello se rompa,
Seguro está que non me vaya. "
(Thy lips are two curtains
Of crimson velvet;
Between curtain and curtain,
Little one, say "Yes."
Bind me with a hair
To the frame of your bed;
Though the hair may break,
It is sure that I shall stay.)

We had soon passed Cacín, where we forded a pretty torrent a few inches deep, whose clear waters shimmered over the sand like the scales of a silvery fish, and rushed like an avalanche of silver spangles down the rapid slopes of the mountain.

From Cacín onwards, the road became horribly bad. Our mules were wading up to the belly in stones, throwing up a spray of sparks from each hoof. We went uphill and downhill, hugging precipices, zigzagging and striking off at angles, for we were among the Alpujarras, those solitary fastnesses, those steep and savage ranges from which, they say, the Moors could never be completely expelled, and where a few thousand of their successors live concealed from every eye.

At a turn in the road, we had a real fright for a moment. We saw, by the aid of the moonlight, seven tall fellows draped in long cloaks, with pointed hats on their heads, and *trabucos* on their shoulders, standing motionless in the middle of the road. The adventure for which we had been hunting so long had presented itself in the most romantic way possible. Unfortunately the bandits greeted us most politely with a respectful *Vayan ustedes con Dios.* They were the very opposite of robbers, being *migueletes*—that is to say, gendarmes. A bitter disappointment for two enthusiastic young travellers who would gladly have offered their luggage as the price of an adventure!

We were to sleep at a little village called Alhama, perched like an eagle's nest on the crest of a precipitous rock. Nothing could be more picturesque than the sharp angles which the road is forced to make as it follows the irregularities of the mountain-side to reach this falcon's aerie. We arrived about two o'clock in the morning, thirsty, hungry and jaded with fatigue. The thirst was quenched with three or four jars of water, the hunger appeased by a tomato omelette, in which there were not too many feathers for a Spanish omelette. A somewhat stony mattress, like a sack of walnuts, was stretched out on the ground and undertook the task of lulling us to rest. By the end of two minutes I was sleeping the sleep attributed to the just, dutifully imitated by my companion. Day overtook us in the same attitude, as motionless as two lumps of lead.

I went downstairs to the kitchen to beg for some food, and thanks to my eloquence, I obtained some cutlets, a chicken fried in oil, half a water-melon and, for dessert, some Barbary figs which the innkeeper's wife stripped of their prickly skins with great dexterity. The water-melon did us a lot of good; this rosy pulp in its green rind has something cool and refreshing about it which is pleasant to see. One has hardly got one's teeth into it before one is soaked to the elbow with a slightly sweetened water with a most agreeable flavour, quite unlike the juice of our cantaloup melons. We required these refreshing slices to temper the heat of the peppers and spices with which all Spanish dishes are seasoned. On fire within, and roasted without, such was our condition; the heat was appalling. As we lay on the brick floor of our bedroom, we left our imprint upon it in patches of sweat; the only means of obtaining a little comparative coolness is to stop up all the windows and doors and remain in absolute darkness.

None the less, in spite of this broiling temperature, I boldly slung my jacket over my shoulder and went to take a turn in the streets of Alhama. The sky was white like molten metal; the pebbles of the pavement shone as if they had been waxed and polished; the whitewashed walls scintillated as with points of mica; a pitiless, blinding light poured down into every recess. The shutters and doors cracked with the drought, the panting earth gaped, the vine-twigs writhed like green wood in the fire. Add to all this the heat radiating from the neighbouring rocks, like burning glasses reflecting back the sun's rays with redoubled heat. To complete my torture, I was wearing thin-soled shoes through which the pavement scorched the soles of my feet. Not a breath of air, not a puff of wind strong enough to stir a piece of down. Nothing more savage and melancholy could be imagined.

As I wandered at random about these solitary streets, with their chalk-white walls broken by an occasional window, stopped up with wooden shutters of quite an African appearance, I arrived, without meeting, I will not say a soul, but so much as a body, at the chief square of the town, which is very quaint and picturesque. An aqueduct bestrides it with its stone arches. It is situated upon a plateau hewn in the mountain-top, and has no pavement but the rock itself, with grooves cut in it to prevent the feet from slipping. The whole of one side ends in a precipice overhanging abysses at the bottom of which one can distinguish among masses of trees some mills turned by a torrent so foamy that it looks like soapy water.

The time fixed for our departure was approaching, and I returned to the *posada* drenched with perspiration as if it had poured with rain, but pleased at having done my duty as a traveller in a temperature that would have baked an egg hard.

The caravan set out again by the vilest, though the most picturesque of roads, on which none but mules could keep a footing; I let the reins lie on my beast's neck, judging him to be better able to guide himself than I was, and trusting entirely to him to pass the difficult places. Several rather sharp tussles in which I had already engaged with him in order to make him walk beside my companion's mount, had convinced me of the uselessness of my efforts. The proverb "as stubborn as a mule" is of a truthfulness to which I can bear witness. Touch a mule with a spur, and he stops; slash him with a switch, and he lies down; check him with the reins, and he breaks into a gallop; a mule on the mountains is quite unmanageable, he feels his importance and takes advantage of it. Often in the very middle of the road, he suddenly stops, raises his head in the air, stretches out his neck, draws back his lips so as to expose his gums and long teeth, and heaves inarticulate sighs, sobs convulsively, and utters a dreadful clucking sound which is horrible to listen to, like the scream of a child being murdered. You might half-kill him during these singing exercises with out making him budge an inch.

We were riding through a regular Campo Santo. The crosses commemorating murders were becoming alarmingly frequent; in likely places one sometimes counted three or four of them within less than a hundred steps; it had ceased to be a road, and become a cemetery. We must admit, however, that if we had the habit in France of perpetuating the memory of violent deaths by crosses, certain streets in Paris would have no cause to envy the Velez-Malaga road. Many of these sinister monuments bear dates which are already of long standing; but the fact remains that they keep the imagination of the traveller on the alert, draw his attention to the slightest sounds, cause him to keep a sharp look-out and prevent him from having a moment's boredom; at every turn in the road, one has only to come upon a suspicious-looking rock, or a dangerous group of trees, to say to oneself: "Perhaps a ruffian is hidden there, taking aim at me and trying to make me the pretext for another cross, for the edification of passers-by and future travellers!"

Once across the passes, the crosses became less frequent; we were travelling through mountain scenery of a grand, austere character, the summits indented by great archipelagos of mist, in an entirely desert region where one came upon no sort of habitation save the hut of rushes sheltering a water-seller or a vender of brandy. This brandy is colourless, and is drunk out of elongated glasses filled up with water, which it turns white like eau-de-Cologne.

It was sultry, stormy weather, and the heat was suffocating; a few large drops, the only ones which had fallen for the last four months from the implacable lapis-lazuli sky, dappled the thirsty sand and made it look like a panther-skin; still it could not make up its mind to rain, and the vaulted heavens resumed their immutable serenity. The sky was so consistently blue during my stay in Spain, that I find in my note-book an entry to this effect: "Saw a white cloud," as if that were a notable event. We men of the north, whose mist-laden horizon offers an ever-varying pageant of form and colour, in which the wind builds mountains, isles and palaces of cloud, for ever overthrowing them and rebuilding them anew, can have no idea of the profound melancholy inspired by this azure sky which one finds always hanging overhead, as uniform as eternity. In one little village through which we passed, everybody had come out on to the door-step to enjoy the rain, just as we go indoors at home to take shelter from it.

Night had fallen almost suddenly, with no twilight, as it does in hot countries, and we cannot have been very far from Velez-Malaga, where we were to sleep. The mountains softened into gentler slopes, and died away into little pebbly plains crossed by streams fifteen or twenty feet wide and a foot deep, fringed with giant reeds. The funeral crosses began to appear in larger numbers than ever, their whiteness making them clearly visible in the blue night mist. We counted three of them within the space of twenty feet. Moreover, it is a remarkably deserted spot, suitable for an ambush.

It was eleven o'clock by the time we entered Velez-Malaga, where the windows shone merrily, and the sound of voices and guitars rang through the streets. Young girls were sitting on the balconies singing stanzas, accompanied from below by their *novios*; at the end of each stanza there was a lengthy burst of laughter, exclamations and applause. Other groups were dancing the cachucha, the fandango and the jaleo at the street-corners. The hollow thrum of the guitars rose like the hum of bees, the castanets pattered and clacked: all was joy and music. One might almost suppose that pleasure was the only serious business of the Spaniards; they throw themselves into it with a wonderful candour, dash and fire. No people could look less unhappy; a traveller finds it difficult to believe in the seriousness of political affairs, and can hardly imagine that the country has been ravaged and laid waste by ten years of civil war. Our peasants are far from possessing the happy-go-lucky inconsequence, the jovial bearing and the elegant costume of the Andalusian *majos*. As far as education is concerned, they are far inferior. Almost all Spanish peasants can read, and have their minds stored with poems which they sing or recite without spoiling the metre; they are perfect riders, and skilled in handling the knife and the carbine. It is true that the wonderful fertility of the soil and the beauty of the climate enable them to dispense with the brutalizing toil which in less favoured countries reduces man to the level of a machine or a beast of burden, and deprives him of the divine gifts of strength and beauty.

It was not without an inner contentment that I tied up my mule to the palings of the *posada*.

Our supper was of the simplest kind; all the serving-men and maids of the hostelry had gone to the dance, and we had to be content with a mere *gaspacho*. This *gaspacho* is worthy of a special description, and we shall here give the recipe, which would have made the hair of the late Brillat-Severin stand on end. You pour some water into a soup tureen, and to this water you add a dash of vinegar, some cloves of garlic, some onions cut into quarters, some slices of cucumber, a few pieces of *pimiento*, a pinch of salt; then one cuts some bread and sets it to soak in this pleasing mixture, serving it cold. At home, a dog of any breeding would refuse to sully its nose with such a compromising mixture. It is the favourite dish of the Andalusians, and the prettiest women do not shrink from swallowing bowlfuls of this hell-broth of an evening. *Gaspacho* is considered highly refreshing, an opinion which strikes me as rather rash, but, strange as it may seem the first time one tastes it, one ends by getting used to it and even liking it. As a most providential compensation we had a decanter of an excellent dry white Malaga wine to wash down this meagre repast, and drained it conscientiously to the last drop, thus restoring our strength, exhausted by a nine hours' spell upon indescribable roads at a temperature like that of a kiln.

At three o'clock, our convoy moved off; the sky was overcast; a warm mist softened the horizon line, a moist breeze made me conscious that the sea was near, and it was not long before one could see it drawn along the edge of the sky in a line of hard blue. A few foam-flecks floated here and there on the swelling sea, and the waves, breaking in great uniform scrolls, died away on sand like boxwood sawdust. On our right rose high cliffs; at times the rocks left a way open before us, at times they barred the road, and we turned aside to climb round them. The straight route is not often followed by Spanish roads; the obstacles would be so difficult to remove, that it is better to go round them than over them. The famous motto *linea recta brevissima* (the straight line is the shortest) would be utterly untrue in this case.

As the sun rose, it dispersed the mists like idle smoke; the sea and sky resumed their azure rivalry, in which none can decide which wins the day; the cliffs once more took on their hues of bronze, iris, amethyst and burnt topaz; the sand again began to sparkle and the water to shimmer in the glaring light. Far, far away, almost on the horizon, five fishing-boats fluttered their sails in the breeze like the wings of a dove.

At long intervals there began to appear on the gentler slopes little white houses like bits of sugar, with flat roofs and a sort of peristyle formed of a trellis supported at each end by a square pillar, and in the middle by a massive pylon of a rather Egyptian design. The *aguardiente* shops grew more numerous; they were still built of rushes, but were now made more attractive by a whitewashed bar daubed with a few streaks of red; the road, which from this point onwards followed a well-defined route, began to be edged with a line of cactuses or aloes, broken here and there by gardens and houses, before which women sat mending nets, while children played about naked and shouted: "*Toro! toro!*" as they saw us go by on our mules. Our *majo's* costume made them take us for the owners of *ganaderias*, or *toreros* of Montes' team.

Ox-drawn wagons and strings of asses followed closer upon each other. The stir which is always perceptible as one approaches a great city now began to make itself felt. Mule-trains converged from all directions, bearing spectators to the opening of the bullring; we had met many of them in the mountains, coming from a distance of eighty or ninety miles round; *aficionados* are as far superior in passion and ardour to patrons of the arts as a bullfight is in interest to a performance at the Opera; nothing stops them, neither the heat of the journey, its difficulty nor its dangers; provided they get there and find seats near the *barrera*, so that they can aim a blow at the bull's haunches, they think themselves amply repaid for their pains. Where is the tragic or comic author who can boast of exerting a like attraction? This does not prevent the moralists from maintaining with sickly sentiment that the taste for this barbarous amusement, as they call it, is declining in Spain from day to day.

Nothing stranger and more picturesque can be imagined than the surroundings of Malaga. One feels as if one has been transported to Africa: the dazzling whiteness of the houses, the deep indigo tones of the sea, the glaring intensity of the light, all add to the illusion. Along each side of the highway enormous bristling aloes brandish their cutlasses; gigantic cactuses with their vivid green palette-shaped leaves and distorted stumps writhe hideously like monstrous serpents, or like the humped backs of stranded whales; the springing column of a palm spreads here and there its leafy capital beside some European tree, surprised to find itself in such company, and watching uneasily, as it would seem, the fearsome vegetation of Africa which creeps about its feet.

An elegant white tower rose outlined against the azure sky: it was the lighthouse of Malaga; we had reached our journey's end. It might have been about eight in the morning; the bustle of the city was at its height, sailors went to and fro, loading and unloading, with rare animation for a Spanish town, the ships at anchor in the port; the women with their heads and bodies draped in great scarlet shawls, forming a marvellous frame for their Moorish faces, walked rapidly along, dragging after them some brat, stark naked or in its shirt. The men hurried along muffled in their cloaks, or with their jackets slung on their shoulder, and, strangely enough, all this crowd was going in the same direction, namely, towards the Plaza de Toros.

We halted at the Parador de los Tres Reyes, a comparatively luxurious house, shaded by a beautiful vine with its branches twining in and out of the bars of the balcony, and possessing a great room where the proprietress sat enthroned behind a counter loaded with crockery, almost like a Parisian café. A very pretty servant, a charming example of the lovely women of Malaga, who are famous throughout all Spain, showed us to our rooms, but caused us a moment of lively anxiety by telling us that all places for the bullfight were sold, and that we should have great difficulty in getting any. Fortunately Lanza, our *cosario*, found us two *asientos de preferencia* (numbered seats), on the sunny side, it is true; but we did not mind that at all, we had long ago sacrificed our fresh complexions, and a layer of tan more or less on our bronzed and yellow faces mattered but little. The bullfights were to continue for three consecutive days. The tickets for the first day were crimson, for the second green and for the third blue, to avoid any confusion, and prevent lovers of the sport from appearing twice with the same card.

During our luncheon a touring company of students came up; there were four of them, more like models for Ribera or Murillo than theological students, so ragged they were, so ill-shod and so dirty. They sang some comic stanzas, accompanying themselves on the tambourine, the triangle and the castanets; the one who played the *pandero* was quite a virtuoso in his own line; he made the ass-skin ring upon his knees, his elbows and his feet, and, when all these means of percussion were insufficient, he stretched out the tambourine with its copper disks and rattled it over the head of some *muchacho* or old woman. One of them, who was the orator of the party, passed around the hat, pouring out all kinds of jests with the utmost volubility, to excite the generosity of the assembly. "A little *real*," he would cry, throwing himself into the most imploring attitudes, "so that I may finish my studies, become a priest and live with nothing to do!" When he had obtained a small coin, he stuck it on his forehead, beside those he had already extorted, exactly like the dancing-girls who cover their perspiring faces, at the end of the dance, with the sequins and piastres thrown them by the ecstatic Osmanlis.

The bullfight was announced for five o'clock, but we were advised to go to the ring before one o'clock, for the corridors would soon be choked with people and we should be unable to reach our stalls, though they were numbered and reserved. So we snatched a hasty luncheon and betook ourselves to the Plaza de Toros, preceded by our guide Antonio, a lean fellow outrageously squeezed into a broad red girdle which made his thinness still more conspicuous, a condition which he wittily attributed to unhappy love.

The streets were packed with a crowd, which grew still denser as we drew near the bullring; the water-sellers, the venders of iced *cebada*, fans and paper parasols, the cigar-sellers, and coachmen were making an appalling din; a confused roar rose from the city like a mist of noise.

After going a roundabout way through the narrow, tortuous streets of Malaga, we at last arrived at the happy spot, the outside of which has nothing remarkable about it. A detachment of soldiers had great difficulty in controlling the crowd, which tried to break into the ring; though it was one o'clock at the latest, the tiers of seats were already filled from top to bottom, and it was only by dint of much elbowing and exchange of abuse that we managed to reach our stalls.

The bullring at Malaga is of truly antique proportions, capable of containing twelve or fifteen thousand spectators within its vast funnel, of which the arena forms the bottom, while the ornaments which crown it rise as high as a five-storied house. This gives some idea of what a Roman arena was like, and of the attraction of those terrible games in which men wrestled at death-grips with wild beasts, beneath the eyes of a whole people.

No stranger or more brilliant spectacle could be imagined than that offered by these immense tiers of seats covered by an impatient crowd, endeavouring to while away the hours of waiting by every kind of absurd prank, and *andaluzadas* of a most lively originality. Modern costumes were few in number, and those who wore them were greeted with laughter, hooting and hissing: the spectacle was greatly enhanced by this: the brilliant colours of the jackets and girdles, the scarlet draperies of the women, the fans striped with green and pale yellow, prevented the crowd from presenting that black, funereal appearance which it always has in our country, where dark hues predominate.

There were a fair number of women there, and I noticed many pretty ones. The Malagueña is distinguished by the golden pallor of her uniform complexion—for the cheeks have no more colour in them than the brow—her face of an elongated oval, her bright pink lips, her finely cut nose and the brilliance of her Arab eyes, which one might imagine were stained with henna, so finely marked are the eyelids, prolonged as by a line drawn towards the temples. I do not know whether the effect is to be attributed to the severe folds of red drapery surrounding their faces, but they have a grave, passionate expression which gives them an Eastern touch, and is not shared by the Madrileñas, the Granadinas or the Sevillanas, who are prettier, daintier and more anxious to attract, and are always thinking about the effect which they produce. I saw some fine heads there, superb types by which the painters of the Spanish school have not profited sufficiently, and which would provide an artist of talent with a series of valuable and entirely novel studies. According to our ideas, it seems strange that women can look on at a show in which a man's life is in constant danger, blood flows in great pools and miserable exhausted horses entangle their feet in their own entrails; one might picture them to oneself as bold-eyed shrews with savage gesticulations, but one would be much mistaken: never did gentler or more Madonna-like faces bend over the infant Jesus with softer eyelids or more tender smiles. The varying fortunes of the bull's last agony are closely followed by these pale and charming creatures, whom an elegiac poet would be only too happy to take as his Elvire. The merits of the strokes are discussed by lovely lips that one would rather hear talk of nothing save love. It would be wrong to infer that they are cruel and hard-hearted from the fact that they gaze dry-eyed upon scenes of carnage which would make our sensitive Parisiennes turn faint; it does not prevent them from being kind, simple-hearted and compassionate towards the unfortunate; but habit is everything, and the bloody aspect of things, which is the most striking to foreigners, is the least interesting feature of it to the Spaniards, absorbed in the merits of each blow, and the skill displayed by the *toreros*, who do not run such great risks as one might at first imagine.

It was as yet no more than two o'clock, and the sun was flooding the whole of that side of the amphitheatre on which we were sitting, with a deluge of fire. How we envied the privileged persons who were sitting cool and fresh in the bath of shade cast by the upper boxes! After seventy miles on horseback across the mountains, to sit for a whole day beneath an African sun in a temperature of thirty-eight degrees, is indeed rather a gallant deed on the part of a poor critic, who for once had paid for his seat, and did not want to lose it.

The *asientos de sombra* (places in the shade) were showering all sorts of sarcasm upon us; they sent us water-sellers to prevent us from catching fire; they begged us to light their cigars at the glowing coals of our noses, and sent us offers of a little oil to help us finish frying. We answered as best we might, and when the shadow, moving round with the hours, relinquished one of them to the scorching sun, there were bursts of laughter and cheering without end.

Thanks to a few jars of water, several dozen oranges and two fans constantly in motion, we kept ourselves from bursting into flames, and were not yet quite grilled or overcome by apoplexy when the musicians came and took their seats in their gallery. A small band of cavalry exerted itself to clear the arena swarming with *muchachos* and *mozos*, who somehow managed to melt into the general mass, though it was mathematically impossible to fit in a single person more; but in some conditions a crowd is a wonderfully elastic thing.

A vast sigh of satisfaction went up from these fifteen thousand breasts, relieved of a load of suspense. The members of the *ayuntamieno* were greeted with frantic applause, and when they entered their box, the band began to play the national airs: *Yo que soy contrabandista,* the March of Riego, which the whole public sang together, clapping their hands and stamping with their feet.

We will not presume to relate here the details of a bullfight. We had occasion to give a conscientious description of one during our stay in Madrid, and only desire to report the principal events and remarkable feats of this bullfight, in which the same combatants held the ring without a rest for three days, during which twenty-four bulls were killed, and ninety-six horses left dead on the arena, with no other accident to the fighters than a slight scratch given by a bull's horn to the arm of a *capeador,* a wound which had nothing dangerous about it, and did not prevent him from appearing again in the ring on the morrow.

At five o'clock precisely, the doors of the arena were thrown open, and the team which was to perform marched in procession round the ring. At the head rode the three *picadores,* Antonio Sanchez and José Trigo, both of Seville, and Francisco Briones of Puerto Real, each with hand on hip and his lance poised on his foot, with the gravity of Roman generals riding up in triumph to the Capitol. The saddles of their horses were inscribed in gilt nails with the name of the proprietor of the ring: Antonio Maria Alvarez. Next came the *capeadores* or *chulos,* wearing three-cornered hats, and muffled in their vivid-coloured cloaks; the *banderilleros* followed hard upon them, dressed like Figaro. At the tail-end of the procession advanced in lonely majesty the *matadores* or *espadas,* as they say in Spain, Montes of Chiclana and José Parra of Madrid. Montes was with his faithful four, a matter of great importance for the safety of the fight, for at times of political dissension, it often happens that a Christino *torero* will not go to the aid of a Carlist *torero* who is in danger, and *vice versa.* The procession significantly wound up with the team of mules whose function it is to take away the dead horses and bulls.

The struggle was about to begin. The alguacil, in civil costume, whose duty it was to take the key of the *toril* to the ring-attendant, and who rode very badly on a spirited horse, opened the tragedy with quite an amusing farce: first he lost his hat, then his stirrups. His trousers, having no straps, rode up above the knee in the most grotesque fashion; and, the gate having been mischievously thrown open for the bull before he had had time to withdraw from the arena, his extreme terror made him still more ridiculous, owing to the way in which he turned and twisted on his horse. However, he was not thrown, to the great disappointment of the mob: the bull, dazzled by the floods of light streaming into the arena, did not notice him at first, and allowed him to get out without touching him with his horns. So the fight began amid a burst of mighty, Homeric, Olympian laughter; but it was not long before silence was restored, for the bull had soon ripped the horse of the first *picador* in two and unhorsed the second.

We had no eyes for anyone but Montes, whose name is proverbial throughout all the Spains, and whose prowess is the subject of a thousand tales of wonder. Montes was born at Chiclana, in the neighborhood of Cadiz. He is a man aged from forty to forty-three, a little below the average height, with a grave bearing and measured gait, and a pale olive-tinged complexion, with nothing remarkable about him but his mobile eyes, which seemed the only living feature in his impassive countenance; he seemed supple rather than robust, and owes his successes rather to his cool head, accurate eye and thorough knowledge of his art than to his muscular strength. After the first few steps which a bull takes into the arena, Montes knows whether he is short or long-sighted, whether he is "light" or "dark"—that is to say, whether he attacks openly or resorts to ruses—whether he is *de muchas piernas* or *aplomado*—light or heavy—whether he will close his eyes during the *cogida* or keep them open; thanks to these observations, made with the rapidity of thought, he is always equipped for defence. But he pushes cool temerity to its utmost limits, and has therefore received a good number of wounds during his career, as the scar which furrows his cheek bears witness, and has several times been carried from the ring with a serious wound.

That day he was clad in a costume of apple-green silk embroidered in silver with the utmost elegance and luxury, for Montes is rich, and if he continues to enter the arena, it is out of love of his art and a craving for emotion, for his fortune amounts to more than fifty thousand *duras*: a considerable sum if one thinks of the money which the *matadores* are bound to lay out on their costumes—a complete suit costing from fifteen hundred to two thousand francs—and on their constant journeys from one city to another, accompanied by their teams.

Unlike other *espadas*, Montes is not content to kill the bull when the signal is given for his death. He superintends the ring, directs the combat and comes to the aid of *picadores* or *chulos* who are in danger. More than one *torero* owes his life to Montes' intervention. There was one bull who would not let his attention be distracted by the cloaks which they waved before him, but kept goring the belly of a horse which he had overthrown, and trying to do the same to the rider, who was sheltered beneath the corpse of his mount. Montes took the savage brute by the tail, and waltzed him round three or four times, to his great disgust, amid the frantic applause of the whole audience, thus giving time for the picador to be helped to his feet. Sometimes he stands right in front of the bull with folded arms and steady eye, and the monster suddenly comes to a stop, dominated by his piercing gaze, as keen and cold as a sword-blade. The shouts and yells, roars and outbursts of stamping and cheering which go up are beyond imagination; everybody is seized with delirium, and a general frenzy runs through the fifteen thousand spectators on the benches, drunk with *aguardiente*, sunshine and blood; handkerchiefs are waved, hats are tossed into the air, and Montes, calm alone among the whole crowd, enjoys in silence a deep, restrained exultation, bowing carelessly like a man capable of other and greater feats. For applause like this I can conceive that a man might risk his life every minute; their reward is not too great. And you, singers with throats of gold, dancers with fairy feet, actors of every kind, emperors and poets who imagine that you have aroused enthusiasm, you have not heard the applause of Montes!

Sometimes the spectators themselves implore him to condescend to give one of these demonstrations of skill from which he always emerges victorious. A pretty girl blows him a kiss, crying: "Come, Señor Montes, come, Paquirro" (for that is his Christian name), "you who are so gallant, do some little thing (*una cosita*) for a lady." And Montes plants his foot on the bull's head and leaps over him, or else flutters his cloak before his muzzle, and then with a sudden movement wraps himself in it in such a way as to drape it elegantly in faultless folds; then he bounds aside and lets the beast charge past him with an impetus which it cannot check.

Montes' style of killing is remarkable for the precision, sureness and ease of the blow; with him, all idea of danger vanishes; he is so cool, so completely master of himself, he seems so certain of success, that the combat appears no more than play; perhaps there is even some loss of emotion. It is impossible to tremble for his life; he will strike the bull where he will, when he will and how he will. The risks of the duel are far too unequal; a less skilful *matador* sometimes produces a more moving effect by the risks and chances which he takes. This will no doubt seem a very refinement of barbarism, but the *aficionados*, all those who have witnessed bullfights and passionately admire a staunch and courageous bull, will surely understand us. An event which happened on the last day of the *corridas* will prove the truth of our assertion, and was rather a rash revelation to Montes of how far the Spanish public carried its spirit of impartiality as between man and beast.

A magnificent black bull had just been let loose in the ring. Connoisseurs had formed the highest opinion of him from the abrupt way in which he had rushed from the *toril*. He combined all the points of a fighting-bull; his horns were long and sharp, with well-curved points; his legs were slender, delicate and muscular, promising great agility; his ample dewlap and his well-developed flanks were a sign of enormous strength. For this reason he bore in the herd the name of Napoleon, that being the only name which could express his unchallenged superiority. Without the least hesitation he charged the *picador* stationed beside the *tablas*, overthrew him and his horse, which fell dead on the spot, then rushed at the second, who was equally unfortunate, and had barely time to be helped over the barrier, all bruised and tumbled by his fall. In less than a quarter of an hour, seven horses were lying on the sand with their bellies ripped open; the *chulos* would only wave their coloured capes in the distance, without losing sight of the palisades, and leapt over to the other side whenever Napoleon showed signs of approaching. Even Montes himself seemed uneasy, and once even placed his foot on the wooden shelf of the *tablas*, ready to vault them in case of a surprise or too hot a pursuit, a thing he had not done during the two previous *corridas*. The joy of the spectators was expressed by a clamour of exclamations, and the most flattering compliments were being showered upon the bull from every mouth. A fresh exploit on the animal's part inflamed the enthusiasm to the highest pitch.

A picador's *sobresaliente* (understudy)—for two or three of the principals had been put out of action—was awaiting with lowered lance the impact of the terrible Napoleon, who, careless of the stab which it inflicted on his shoulder, caught the horse under the belly, gave a first toss which brought him down with his forelegs upon the shelf of the palisade, and with the second lifted him by the hind quarters and threw him, rider and all, right over the barrier into the corridor of refuge which runs all round the ring.

This splendid feat was greeted with a thunder of cheers. The bull was master of the ring, round which he careered in triumph, amusing himself, in the absence of opponents, by turning over and tossing into the air the corpses of the horses which he had torn open. The supply of victims was exhausted, and by now there was nothing left in the ring stables to provide the *picadores* with fresh mounts. The *banderilleros* were perched on the *tablas*, not daring to come down and harass with their paper-decked darts this redoubtable fighter, whose rage certainly required no stimulus. The spectators grew impatient at this sort of *entr'acte*, and began to shout: *Las banderillas! Las banderillas! Fuego al alcalde!* Fire for the alcalde who will not give the order! Finally, at a sign from the governor of the ring, a *banderillero* left the group, planted two darts in the neck of the raging beast, and made off at full speed, but none too fast, for its horn shaved his arm and slashed open his sleeve. Thereupon, in spite of the uproar and hooting of the crowd, the alcalde gave the death-signal, and waved to Montes that he was to take his *muleta* and his sword, in defiance of all the rules of the ring, which require that a bull should have had at least four pairs of *banderillas* on him before he is handed over to the matador's death-stroke.

Instead of advancing, as was his custom, into the middle of the arena, Montes planted himself twenty paces from the barrier, in order to have a refuge in case of accident; he was very pale, and without indulging in any of the elegancies or displays of gallantry which have won him the admiration of Spain, he unfurled the scarlet *muleta* to attract the bull, which required no pressing to advance. Montes made three or four passes with the *muleta*, holding his sword pointed horizontally at the level of the bull's eyes, then all of a sudden the bull fell as though struck by a thunderbolt, and expired after one convulsive bound. The sword had entered its brow and pierced the brain, a blow forbidden by the rules of bullfighting, for the matador is bound to pass his arms between the animal's horns and give the death-blow between the nape of the neck and the shoulders, thus increasing the danger for the man and giving some chance to his brute opponent.

As soon as the public understood the stroke, for it had happened as quick as thought, a roar of indignation went up, from the *tendidos* to the *palcos*; a storm of insults and hissing broke out with an incredible uproar and tumult. Butcher, murderer, brigand, robber, galley-slave, hangman, were the gentlest of the epithets. "Send Montes to Ceuta! Throw Montes in the fire! Set the dogs on Montes! Death to the alcalde!" were the cries that rang out on every side. Never have I seen such fury, and I confess, to my shame, that I shared in it. Soon shouting was not enough; they began to pelt the poor devil with fans, hats, sticks, jars of water and fragments torn from the benches. There was yet another bull to kill, but its death passed unnoticed amid this horrible bacchanal, and it was José Parra, the second *espada*, who finished him off with two quite well-placed blows. As for Montes, he was livid, his face was green with rage, and his teeth drew blood from his white lips, although he affected a perfect composure, leaning with affected grace upon the hilt of his sword, the reddened point of which he had wiped in the sand in contravention of the rules.

On what things popularity depends! Never could anyone have imagined, on the two previous days, that so sure an artist, so completely master of his public as Montes, could be so ruthlessly punished for a breach of the rules, though it was undoubtedly called for by the most imperious necessity, in view of the extraordinary agility, vigour and rage of the animal. As soon as the *corrida* was at end he stepped into his carriage, followed by his team, and drove off, swearing by all his gods that he would never set foot in Malaga again. I do not know whether he has kept his word, or remembered the insult on the last day longer than his opening triumphs and ovations. I consider now that the public of Malaga was unjust to the great Montes of Chiclana, for his sword-thrusts had been superb, and in moments of danger he had given such thorough proofs of his heroic coolness and wonderful skill, that the delighted crowd had made him a present of all the bulls he had killed, and allowed him to make a cut in their ear, in sign of possession, so that they could not be claimed either by the hospital or the contractor.

Stunned, intoxicated and sated with violent emotions, we returned to our *parador*, hearing nothing in the streets along which we passed save praise of the bull and curses upon Montes.

That very evening, in spite of my fatigue, I let myself be taken to the theatre, desiring to pass with no transition from the bloody realities of the arena to the intellectual emotions of the stage. The contrast was striking; in the one place had been noise and crowds, in the other was silence and neglect. The theatre was almost empty, a few sparse spectators scattered here and there diversified the deserted benches, yet they were playing *The Lovers of Teruel*, a piece by Juan Eugenio Hartzenbusch, one of the most remarkable productions of the modern Spanish school. It is a touching poetical story of two lovers who remain unconquerably faithful to each other through countless temptations and obstacles: in spite of the efforts which the author makes, often with success, to vary a situation which is invariably the same, the subject would be too simple for a French audience; the passionate situations are treated with great ardour and spirit, though sometimes spoilt by a certain melodramatic exaggeration to which the dramatist too easily gives way. The passion of the Sultana of Valencia for Isabel's lover, Juan Diego Martinez Garces de Marsilla, whom she causes to be drugged with a narcotic and brought to the harem, the vengeance of this Sultana when she sees that she is disdained, the guilty letters of Isabel's mother, found by Rodrigo de Azagra—who uses them as a means of marrying the daughter, and threatens to show them to the injured husband—are rather strained situations, but introduce touching and dramatic scenes. The piece is written both in prose and in verse. So far as a foreigner can judge of the style in a language of which he never knows all the subtleties, Hartzenbusch's verse seemed to me better than his prose. It is easy, straightforward, animated, with varying pauses, and fairly sparing in those poetical redundancies into which the southern races are too often led by their facile prosody. His prose dialogues seem to be copied from modern French melodrama, and err on the side of heaviness and bombast. *The Lovers of Teruel*, with all its faults, is very superior, as a work of literature, to those translations adapted or distorted from our light drama which now flood the theatres of the Peninsula. It bears traces of a study of the ancient romances and the masters of Spanish dramatic art, and it is to be desired that the young poets on the other side of the mountains should follow in this way rather than waste their time in translating bad melodramas into more or less genuine Castilian.

The serious play was followed by a fairly comic *saynete*. The subject was an old bachelor who had engaged a pretty maid-of-all-work, as the small advertisements say in Paris. This hussy first brought in a great lout of a Valencian, six feet high, with enormous whiskers, a huge *navaja*, an insatiable appetite and an unquenchable thirst, and passed him off as her brother; next came an equally fierce-looking cousin, bristling all over with blunderbusses, pistols and other lethal weapons, followed by a smuggler uncle carrying on him a whole arsenal and a face to match, to the great terror of the poor old man—who had already repented of his licentious propensities. All these ruffianly types were interpreted by the actors with wonderful truth and spirit. At the end arrived a good soldier nephew and delivered his rascal of an uncle from this band of brigands who were living upon him, making love to his servant while they drank his wine, smoked his cigars and pillaged his house. The uncle promised for the future to have none but two old menservants. The *saynetes* are like our vaudevilles, but the plot is less complicated, and they sometimes consist of a few detached scenes like the interludes of the Italian comedy.

The performance wound up with a *baile nacional*, fairly satisfactorily executed by two couples of dancers. Spanish dancing-girls have not the finish, perfect correctness and grand style of Frenchwomen, but, in my opinion, they far surpass them in grace and charm; they work very little, and do not go in for those terrible exercises in flexibility which make a dancing-class like a torture-chamber, so they escape that leanness, like that of a horse in training, which gives our ballets such a macabre and anatomical touch; they preserve the rounded contours of their sex; they look like women dancing, not dancing-women, which is quite a difficult thing.

Their style has not the least relation to that of the French school. In the latter it is expressly laid down that the bust should be motionless and upright; the body takes hardly any part in the movements of the legs. In Spain, the feet hardly leave the ground; there are none of those wide circular or spreading movements of the legs, which make a woman look like a pair of compasses stretched to its limits, and are considered down there revoltingly indecent. It is the body which dances, with curving motions of the hips, bending sides and a waist which twists and turns with the suppleness of a serpent or an Egyptian dance-girl. When the body is thrown back, the dancer's shoulders almost touch the ground; the arms are faint and lifeless, with the flexibility and slackness of a trailing scarf; one would hardly believe that the hands could raise the clacking ivory castanets with their cords interwoven with gold; and yet at the given moment, this voluptuous languor is succeeded by bounds like those of a young jaguar, proving that these bodies, so silken soft, enclose muscles of steel. The Moorish dance-girls of today still follow the same system: their dancing consists in harmoniously seductive undulations of the body, hips and loins, with the arms thrown back over the head. Arab traditions are preserved in the national dances, especially in Andalusia.

Spanish male dancers, though not very good, have a dashing, bold and gallant bearing which I far prefer to the insipid, equivocal graces of our own. They do not appear to be thinking either of themselves or the public; their glances and smiles are all for their partners, with whom they always appear to be passionately in love, and whom they seem prepared to defend against all comers. They have a certain savage grace, and an insolent curve of the body which is very characteristic. If they wiped off their paint, they might make excellent *banderilleros* and leap from the boards of the theatre on to the sands of the arena.

The *malagueña*, or local dance of Malaga, has a poetry which is really charming. First appears the male dancer, with his sombrero pulled over his eyes, muffled in his scarlet cloak like an hidalgo wandering in search of adventures. Enter the lady, fan in hand and draped in her mantilla, with the air of a woman going to take a turn on the Alameda. The man tries to see the face of the mysterious siren; but the coquette plies her fan so skilfully, opening or shutting it adroitly, and turning it first one way and then another on a level with her pretty face, that the gallant, in disappointment, falls back a few paces and hits upon another stratagem. He rattles the castanets beneath his cloak. On hearing the sound, the lady listens; she smiles, her bosom flutters, the point of her little satin shoe beats time in spite of herself; she casts aside her fan and mantilla and appears in the gay costume of the dance, glittering with tinsel and spangles, a rose in her hair, a great tortoise-shell comb upon her head. Her partner throws away his mask and cloak, and the two of them execute a delightfully original dance.

As I returned along the edge of the sea, reflecting as in a mirror of burnished steel the pale face of the moon, I mused upon this striking contrast between the crowd in the arena and the empty theatre, the enthusiasm of the crowd for brutal realities, and their indifference to the speculations of the intelligence. Poet as I was, I began to envy the gladiator. I regretted that I had abandoned action for dreams. The night before, at the same theatre, they had played a piece by Lope de Vega, which had attracted an audience no greater than the work of the young writer: thus it is that the talent of ancient or of modern days is not worth a blow from the sword of Montes.

Moreover, the other theatres in Spain are scarcely better frequented than the one at Malaga, not even the Teatro del Principe in Madrid, where there is, however, a very great actor, Julian Romea, and an excellent actress, Matilde Diez. The old flow of dramatic genius in Spain seems to have been irretrievably checked, yet never did river pour in more ample streams along an ampler course; never was there such prodigious and inexhaustible fecundity. Our most productive writers of vaudevilles are far behind Lope de Vega, who had no collaborators, and whose works are so numerous that their exact number is unknown, and a complete copy scarcely exists. Calderón de la Barca, not to speak of his cloak-and-sword dramas, wrote numbers of *autos sacramentales*, a sort of Catholic mystery plays in which a fantastic depth of thought and strangeness of conception are combined with enchanting poetry and the most florid elegance. A series of quarto catalogues would be required even to mention the titles of the plays by Lope de Rueda, Montalban, Guevara, Quevedo, Tirso, Rojas, Moreto, Guilhen de Castro, Diamante and many others. The number of dramatic works written in Spain during the sixteenth and seventeenth centuries passes all imagination; one might as well count the leaves in the forest or the sands of the sea: they are almost all in verses of eight feet mingled with assonances, printed in two columns on quarto pages of wrapping-paper, with a rough engraving as frontispiece, and bound in quires of from six to eight pages. The booksellers' shops overflow with them; one sees thousands of them hanging up higgledy-piggledy among the poems and versified legends of the open-air book-stalls; the epigram on a too fertile Roman poet, whose body, they said, was burnt after his death on a pyre made up of his own words, can be applied without exaggeration to most Spanish dramatists. They display a fertility of invention, a wealth of incident and an intricacy of plot which can hardly be conceived. Long before Shakespeare, the Spaniards had invented the drama; their theatre is romantic in the full sense of the word; apart from a certain childish display of erudition, their plays owe nothing either to the Greek or the Latin, and, as Lope de Vega says in his *Arte nuevo de hacer comedias en este tiempo*:

> *"Quando he de escribir una comedia,*
> *Encierro los precepos con seis claves."*
> (When I have to write a comedy,
> I lock up the Rules with six keys.)

Spanish dramatists do not seem to have concerned themselves much with the delineation of character, though in every scene are to be found the keenest and most delicate strokes of observation; man is not studied philosophically, and in their dramas one but seldom meets with those episodical characters which are so frequent in the great English tragic poet, those sketches drawn from the life which only contribute indirectly to the action, and have no object save to represent a facet of the human soul, an original individuality, or to reflect the poet's thought. In Spain, the writer seldom allows us to catch a glimpse of his personality, except at the end of the piece, when he asks the pardon of the public for his defects.

The chief motive in Spanish plays is the "point of honour":

> *"Los casos de la honra son mejores,*
> *Porgue mueven con fuerza a toda gente*
> *Con ellos las acciones virtuosas,*
> *Que la virtud es donde quiera amada."*

(The problems of honour are the best
because they strongly move all men;
and side to side with them stand virtuous actions,
for virtue dwells wheresoever she is loved.)

Thus speaks Lope de Vega, who knew what he was talking about, and did not fail to follow his own precepts. The point of honour plays the same part in Spanish comedy as fate did in Greek tragedy. Its unyielding laws, its cruel necessities, easily gave rise to dramatic scenes of the highest interest. *El pundonor*, a kind of chivalrous religion with its own laws, subtleties and refinements, is far superior to 'Aνάγκη, the Fate of antiquity, whose blows fell blindfold and at random on guilty and innocent alike. One is often shocked, when one reads Greek tragedies, at the situation in which the hero is placed, when he is equally criminal whether he acts or not; the Castilian point of honour is always perfectly logical and consistent with itself. It is, moreover, no more than an exaggeration of every human virtue carried to the highest pitch of sensitiveness. In his most fearful bursts of rage or his most cruel deeds of vengeance, the hero maintains a noble and solemn attitude. It is always in the name of loyalty, of conjugal fidelity, of respect for ancestors or the stainless honour of his coat of arms that he unsheaths his great sword with the guard of iron, often against those whom he loves with his whole soul, but whom an imperious necessity obliges him to slay. From this clash of passion at odds with the point of honour, arises the interest of most plays of the ancient Spanish theatre, a deep, human interest keenly felt by the spectators, who would have acted exactly like the hero in similar circumstances. Given this fruitful material so deeply in harmony with the manners of the age, we must not be surprised at the prodigious facility of the old dramatists of the Peninsula. Another source abounding in equal interest found in deeds of virtue, chivalrous devotion, sublime renunciation, unchanging fidelity, superhuman passion or ideal delicacy prevailing over the most cunningly planned intrigues, or intricate plots. In cases like this the author's aim seems to have been to set before his audience a consummate model of human perfection. All the fine qualities that he can invent are heaped on the head of his princes or princesses; he makes them more careful of their purity than the snowy ermine, which would rather die than have a stain upon its unspotted coat.

A profound feeling for Catholicism and the manners of feudalism inspires the whole of this drama, which is truly national in origin, in subject and in form. The division into three days (*jornadas*) followed by Spanish dramatists is surely the most logical and reasonable. Exposition, plot and solution, such is the natural distribution of every properly conceived dramatic action, and we should do well to adopt it, instead of our division into five acts, handed down from antiquity, two of which, the second and the fourth, are so often useless.

It should not, however, be imagined that the ancient Spanish plays were invariably sublime. The grotesque, that indispensable element in mediaeval art, slips into them in the shape of the *gracioso* or *bobo* (idiot), who relieves the seriousness of the action by more or less risky jests or plays on words, and produces at the hero's side the effect of those deformed dwarfs in coats of many colours, playing with greyhounds taller than themselves, whom one sees beside some king or prince in the old portraits in the Galleries.

Moratín, the author of *El Si de las Niñas* and *El Café*, whose tomb one may see at Père-Lachaise in Paris, is the last flicker of Spanish dramatic art, just as the old painter Goya, who died at Bordeaux in 1828, was the last still recognizable descendant of the great Velásquez.

Now nothing is played any more on the Spanish stage but translations of French melodramas and vaudevilles. At Jaen, in the heart of Andalusia, they are playing *Le Sonneur de Saint Paul*, at Cadiz, a few steps from Africa, *Le Gamin de Paris*. The *saynetes* which were once so gay and original and full of highly flavoured local character, are now no more than imitations, borrowed from the repertory of the Théâtre des Variétés. And yet, not to mention Don Martinez de la Rosa and Don Antonio Gil y Zarate, who belong to a day that is not altogether recent, the Peninsula can muster several young men of talent and promise; but public attention, in Spain as in France, is distracted by the seriousness of public affairs. Hartzenbusch, the author of *The Lovers of Teruel*; Castro y Orozco, to whom we owe *Fray Luis de León*, or *The Age and Society*; Sorilla, who has successfully produced the drama of *El Rey y el Zapatero*; Bretón de los Herreros, the Duke of Rivas, Larra, who killed himself for love, Espronceda, whose death has just been announced in the papers, and who infused into his compositions a passionate and savage energy sometimes worthy of Byron, are (or, alas! in the last two cases one must say, were) writers of great merit, talented, elegant and facile poets, who might have ranked with the old masters, if they had not lacked that which is lacking to us all, assurance, a stable point of departure, a common stock of ideas shared with the public. The point of honour and the heroism of the old plays are no longer understood, or seem ridiculous, and the modern creed is not yet sufficiently formulated for poets to be able to interpret it.

So we must not blame the crowd too much if the meantime it flocks to the arena and seeks its emotions where they are to be found; after all, it is not the fault of the people if the theatres are not more attractive; so much the worse for us poets if we let ourselves be superseded by the gladiators. On the whole, it is healthier for both mind and heart to see a brave man kill a savage beast beneath the open heavens, than to hear a mountebank with no talent sing an obscene vaudeville or retail adulterated literature before the smoky footlights.

PART IV

The Great Mosque, Cordoba

XIV. Malaga to Seville

WE had tried mules; in order to complete our experience of the means of transport in the Peninsula, it remained to sample the *galera*. It so happened that one was starting for Cordoba. It was already laden with a Spanish family, and we filled it to overflowing. A short description of this agreeable conveyance would not be out of place here: picture to yourself a rather low wagon with four wheels and latticed sides, having no bottom but a network of grass ropes, in which boxes and bundles are heaped up regardless of their external angles. Over this are thrown two or three mattresses, or, to speak more correctly, two linen bags in which float a few stray flocks of almost uncarded wool; upon these mattresses the wretched travellers stretch themselves crosswise, in a position, if we may be forgiven such a vulgar comparison, resembling that of calves being carried to market. It is true that their feet are not tied together, but their position is hardly the more comfortable for that. The whole turn-out is covered with coarse canvas stretched over hoops, and is driven by a *mayoral* and drawn by four mules.

The family with whom we were travelling was that of quite a well-educated engineer, who spoke French well: they were escorted by a tall ruffian of uncouth appearance, once a brigand in José Maria's band, but now an overseer at the mines. This queer creature rode behind the galley, with a knife in his belt and a carbine on his saddle-bows. The engineer seemed to think a great deal of him; he extolled his honesty, for the man's previous occupation caused him no uneasiness on this score; it is true that in mentioning José Maria he several times repeated that he was a good, honest man. This opinion, which strikes us as slightly paradoxical when applied to a highwayman, is shared by the most respectable people in Andalusia. Spain has remained Arab in this respect, and bandits easily pass for heroes, an association of ideas which is less strange than it appears at first sight, especially in southern lands, where the imagination is so impressionable; a contempt for death, audacity, coolness, prompt and bold decision, skill and strength, the sort of dignity which attaches to a man in revolt against society, all these qualities, which have such a powerful action on minds as yet but partly civilized—are they not such as make up a great character? And is the popular admiration of these qualities in vigorous natures so mistaken, even if they are turned to a use which must be condemned?

The short cut which we were following went rather steeply up and down hill through a region broken with hills and scored with narrow valleys, at the bottom of which were the beds of dried-up torrents, bristling with enormous rocks which caused us the most excruciating jolts, and drew piercing shrieks from the women and children. As we drove along, we noticed a few sunset effects of wonderful poetry and colour. The mountains in the distance took on hues of extraordinary warmth and intensity, all crimson and purple, tinged with gold; the complete absence of vegetation gave the landscape, which consisted of nothing but rock and sky, a character of naked grandeur and savage harshness, the like of which is nowhere to be found, and which no painter has ever interpreted. We halted at nightfall for a few hours at a little hamlet consisting of three or four houses, to rest our mules and enable us to take a little food. Like the improvident French travellers we were, though a five months' stay in Spain ought to have made us wiser, we had brought no provisions from Malaga; so we were obliged to sup off dry bread and white wine, which a woman at the *posada* was kind enough to go and fetch for us, for Spanish larders and cellars do not share that abhorrence of a vacuum which Nature is said to entertain, and harbour emptiness with a clear conscience.

About one o'clock in the morning we set out again, and in spite of the appalling jolting, the overseer's children who were rolling all over us, and the banging of our wobbling heads against the sides of the cart, it was not long before we fell asleep. When next the sun tickled the tips of our noses with a ray like a golden wheat-ear, we were near

Caratraca, an insignificant little village not marked on the map, and having no distinguishing feature but some sulphur springs which are most efficacious for skin-diseases, and attract to this remote spot a somewhat dubious population with whom it is better to have no dealings. They gamble for infernally high stakes; and though it was as yet very early in the day, the cards and doubloons were already going as usual. There was something hideous in the sight of these sick men with their earthy faces, tinged with green, and rendered even uglier by greed, deliberately stretching out their twitching fingers to seize their prey. The houses in Caratraca, as in all Andalusian villages, are coated with whitewash; this, combined with the brilliant colour of the tiles, the wreathing vine-branches and the shrubs which surround them, give them a festive, prosperous appearance very different from the ideas about Spanish dirt prevalent in the rest of Europe, ideas which are false on the whole, and can only have arisen in connexion with some wretched hamlets in Castile, of which we possess the like, and worse, in Brittany and the Sologne.

In the court-yard of the inn my eye was caught by some rough frescoes representing bullfights, of a simplicity that was quite primitive; all round these paintings might be read *coplas* (verses) in honour of Paquirro Montes and his team. The name of Montes is highly popular in Andalusia, like that of Napoleon among us; his portraits adorn walls, fans and snuff-boxes, and the English, ever ready to exploit the fashion, whatever it may be, send out thousands of handkerchiefs from Gibraltar on which the features of the celebrated matador are printed in red, purple and yellow, accompanied by laudatory inscriptions.

Warned by our starving condition on the previous day we bought some provisions from our innkeeper, in particular a ham, for which he made us pay an exorbitant price. A great deal is said about highwaymen, but the danger is not on the roads: it is beside them, at the inn, where they can cut your throat and fleece you with impunity, while you have no pretext for resorting to weapons of defence, and letting fly with your carbine at the waiter who brings you your bill. I pity the bandits from bottom of my heart; such innkeepers as this do not leave much for them to do, and give them no chance at the travellers till they are like so many squeezed lemons. In other countries they make you pay dearly for the things which they sell you; in Spain you pay an extortionate price for utter destitution.

Our siesta at an end, they harnessed the mules to the galley; each of us returned to our place on the mattresses, the *escopetero* got on his little mountain horse, the *mayoral* provided himself with a store of tiny pebbles for throwing at his mules' ears, and we started off again. The region through which we were passing was wild without being picturesque; bare, seamed hill-sides, flayed, as it were, to the bone; stony watercourses, like scars left in the ground by the ravages of the winter rains; olive-woods whose pale foliage, dredged with flour-like dust, suggested no idea of freshness or verdure; here and there, on the mutilated flanks of a chalky tufa gorge, a tuft or two of fennel blanched by the heat; snake and adder trails in the dust of the road; overhead a burning sky like the roof of an oven; and not a breath of air, not a puff of wind! The grey sand kicked up by the hoofs of the mules fell back without forming a cloud in the air. A sun which would have heated iron white-hot beat on the awning of our galley, where we sat ripening like melons under glass. From time to time we got out and did a spell on foot to stretch our legs, keeping in the shadow of the horse or wagon, and climbed back to our places, crushing the mother and children a little, for we could only get to our corner by crawling on all fours under the low dome formed by the hoops of the galley. By dint of struggling through gorges and broken ground, and taking short cuts across fields, we lost sight of the right road. Our *mayoral,* in the hope of discovering where we were, went on as if he had known quite well where he was going; for the *cosarios* and guides will only admit that they are lost when they are at their wits' end, and have taken you twelve or fifteen miles out of the way. It is only fair to say that nothing was easier than to stray from this fabulous and almost untrodden road, a mere track interrupted at every step by deep gullies. We found ourselves in the midst of great fields dotted with olive-trees, whose stunted, distorted trunks writhed themselves into sinister shapes, where there was no trace of a human habitation, and no sign of a living creature; we had met nobody since morning but one half-naked *muchacho* driving half-a-dozen black pigs before him in a cloud of dust. Night fell. To put the last touch to our misfortunes, there was no moon, and all we had to guide us was the tremulous light of the stars.

The *mayoral* kept leaving his seat every moment, and getting down to feel the ground with his hands, to see if he could not come across a rut or wheel-track which might lead him back to the road; but his search was fruitless, and he was obliged, most unwillingly, to tell us that he was lost, and did not know where he was: he could not make it out, he had been this way twenty times, and could have gone to Cordoba blindfold. All this seemed to us a little suspicious, and it occurred to us that we were perhaps in danger of some ambush. Our situation was not particularly pleasant; here we were, overtaken by night in a remote spot, far from all human aid, in the midst of a region famous for sheltering more robbers than all the Spains put together. These reflections no doubt occurred with equal force to the mining-overseer and his friend, the former associate of José Maria, who should have been an expert in such matters, for they silently loaded their carbines with bullets, and likewise two others which were lying in the galley, and handed us one each without saying a word, which spoke volumes. By so doing, they left the *mayoral* unarmed, so that if he had been in league with the bandits, he would thus have been rendered powerless. However, after wandering about at random for two or three hours, we caught sight of a light in the far distance, gleaming beneath the branches like a glow-worm; we adopted it at once as our pole-star, and guided our course as straight as possible towards it, at the risk of upsetting every moment. At times an irregularity of the ground hid it from our sight. Then it seemed to us that all nature was extinguished; but once again the light would appear, and with it our hopes revived. At last we drew near enough to a farm to distinguish its window, the heaven in which shone our star, in the shape of a copper lamp. Ox-carts and farming-implements scattered here and there reassured us completely, for we might have fallen into some den of thieves or *posada de barateros*. The dogs scented our presence and barked furiously, so that the whole farm was soon astir. The peasants came out, gun in hand, to discover the cause of this night alarm, but seeing that we were honest travellers who had lost their way, they politely invited us to come in and rest ourselves in the farm-house.

It was these good people's supper-time. A wrinkled old woman, tanned and almost mummified, whose skin hung in creases at every joint like a hussar's boot, was preparing a gigantic *gaspacho* in a red earthenware bowl. Five or six greyhounds of the tallest breed, with lean flanks, broad chests and magnificent heads worthy of a royal hunting pack, were following the old woman's movements with the most unflagging attention and the saddest and most wondering air that can be imagined. But this delicious feast was not for them; in Andalusia it is men, not dogs, who eat this soup of bread-crusts soaked in water. Looking on at these appetizing preparations from a greater distance were some cats, looking more like Japanese monsters, owing to their absence of ears and tails, for in Spain they cut off these superfluous decorations. A bowl of the said *gaspacho,* two slices of our ham and a few bunches of pale amber grapes, made up our supper, for which we had to compete against the familiar encroachments of the greyhounds, which, under the pretext of licking us, were literally snatching the meat from our mouths; we got up and ate standing, plate in hand; but the devilish beasts stood up on their hind legs, and placed their front paws on our shoulders, thus bringing themselves level with the coveted morsel. If they did not remove it, they at least gave it a lick or two, thus taking toll of its first and most delicate flavour. These greyhounds must, we thought, have been lineal descendants of a famous dog, whose history Cervantes did not, however, include among his dialogues. This famous animal occupied the position of scullery-maid in a Spanish inn; now a maid who was scolded because the plates were not clean, would swear by all her gods that they had been washed *por siete aguas* (in seven waters). *Siete Aguas* was the dog's name, given him because he licked the plates so thoroughly that one would think they had been through seven waters; that day he must have been careless. The greyhounds at the farm were surely of this breed.

We were given a boy as our guide, who knew the roads perfectly, and led us with no further accident to Ecija, where we arrived at about ten in the morning.

The approach to Ecija is quite picturesque; one reaches it by a bridge, at the end of which stands a gate in the form of an arch of the triumphal type. This bridge spans a river which is none other than the Genil of Granada, and is blocked by mill-weirs and the ruins of ancient arches; on crossing it, one finds oneself in an open space planted with trees, adorned with two monuments in a baroque style. One of them consists in a gilded statue of the Blessed Virgin standing on a pillar, whose hollowed pedestal forms, as it were, a kind of chapel, embellished with pots of artificial flowers, votive offerings, garlands of pith flowers and all the trifling adornments of southern piety. The other is a gigantic St. Christopher, also of gilt metal, with his hand resting on a palm-tree—a walking-stick proportionate to his height—carrying on his shoulder, with prodigious muscular tension and an effort which would lift a house, a tiny infant Jesus of charming delicacy and daintiness. This colossus, attributed to the Florentine sculptor Torrigiani—the one who flattened Michelangelo's nose with a blow of his fist—is perched upon a pale pink granite pillar of the Salomonic order (the name given here to twisted columns), the spiral of which breaks out into extravagant scrolls and flowers half-way up. I am very fond of statues perched up like this; they produce more effect, being seen from a greater distance, and to more advantage. Ordinary pedestals have something massive and squat about them which takes away from the lightness of the figures supported by them.

Though Ecija lies outside the usual tourist-routes, and is not generally known, it is none the less a most interesting town, with a most original and characteristic appearance. The towers which form the sharpest angles in its outlines are neither Byzantine, Gothic nor Renaissance; they are Chinese or, rather, Japanese; you might take them for the turrets of some *miao* dedicated to Confucius (Kung-Tse), Buddha or Fo, for they are entirely covered with porcelain or earthenware tiles of the brightest shades of colour, and roofed with glossy green and white tiles arranged in a chequered pattern, which look extraordinarily curious. The rest of the buildings are equally fantastic, and the love of elaboration is pushed to its utmost limits. One sees nothing but gilding, incrustations, coloured marble and breccia, crumpled up like stuffs, nothing but festoons of flowers, true-lover's knots and chubby angels, all coloured and enhanced with an extravagant wealth of painting in the sublimest of bad taste.

The Calle de los Caballeros, in which are the residences of the nobles, and which contains the finest mansions, is really a miracle in its way; one finds it hard to imagine that one is in a real street, among houses inhabited by possible beings. Balconies, grilles and friezes, nothing is straight, everything is twisted and contorted, blossoming into flowers, scrolls and rosettes. You will not find a single square inch of surface that is not adorned with incised lines, festoons, gildings, relief-work or painting; all the most riotous, thickly incrusted exaggeration of what we call the rococo, with a massive, accumulated luxury which French good taste has always succeeded in avoiding even at the worst periods. This Dutch–Chinese–Pompadour style is an amusing surprise in Andalusia. The ordinary houses are of whitewashed plaster, with a dazzling whiteness which stands out marvellously against the dark blue of the sky. Their flat roofs, small windows and *miradores* made us think of Africa, though the idea was already sufficiently suggested by a heat of thirty-seven degrees Réumur, the usual temperature of the place during a cool summer. Ecija is nicknamed the frying-pan of Andalusia, and never was a nickname better deserved: it is situated in a hollow, surrounded by sandy hills, which shelter it from the wind, and project the sun's rays back upon it like a concentric arrangement of mirrors. Existence there consists in being fried; but this did not prevent us from visiting every corner of it while waiting for our luncheon. The Plaza Mayor presents a most original appearance, with its pillared houses, its rows of windows, its arcades and projecting balconies.

Our *parador* was quite comfortable, and they served us up an almost human meal, which we relished with a gluttony which was quite permissible after so many privations. After a long siesta in a big room well shuttered, darkened and watered, we were thoroughly rested, and when, about three o'clock, we got back into the galley, we wore a look of serenity and entire resignation.

The road from Ecija to La Carlotta, where we were to sleep, crosses rather an uninteresting region, with an arid, dusty look—at least, the season caused it to appear so—and has left only the slightest trace in our memory. At rare intervals appeared a few groves of olive-trees or sparse clumps of evergreen oaks, and one saw aloes with their blue-green foliage and characteristic effect. The mine overseer's dog (for we had quadrupeds in our menagerie, not to speak of children) put up a few partridges, two or three of which were brought down by my travelling companion. Such was the most remarkable incident in this stage of our journey.

La Carlotta, where we stopped for the night, is a hamlet of no importance. The inn occupies what once was a convent which was first turned into a barracks, as nearly always happens in times of revolution, for military life is the one which most easily fits into and feels at home in buildings arranged for monastic uses. Long arcaded cloisters formed a covered gallery round the four sides of the court-yards. In the middle of one of them gaped the black mouth of an enormous, very deep well, promising us the delicious treat of good, clear, cold water. As I leaned over the curb, I saw that the inside was all lined with plants of the loveliest green, which had grown between the crevices of the stones. One had to go and look down the wells to find a little freshness and greenery, for the heat was so great that one might have thought it was caused by a house on fire close by. The only thing that can give any idea of the temperature is that of hot-houses for growing tropical vegetation. The very air was afire, and every puff of wind seemed to be charged with incandescent molecules. I tried to go out and take a turn round the village, but an atmosphere like that of a Turkish bath met me at the door and forced me to turn back. Our supper consisted of chickens cut into joints and spread higgledy-piggledy on a layer of rice tasting as strongly of saffron as a Turkish *pilau*, with a salad (*ensalada*) of green leaves swimming in a deluge of vinegar and water, with an occasional patch of oil, no doubt borrowed from the lamp. When this sumptuous repast was at an end, we were taken to our rooms, which were already so thickly populated that we went and finished the night in the middle of the court, wrapped in a cloak, with an overturned chair for a pillow. There, at least, we were only exposed to the mosquitoes, and by putting on gloves and veiling our face with a handkerchief, we came off with no more than five or six bites. It was merely painful, and not disgusting.

Our innkeeper and his family had a somewhat hangdog expression, but we had long ceased to notice such things, accustomed as we were to more or less forbidding countenances. A fragment of their conversation which we overheard showed us that their sentiments matched their faces. Thinking that we did not understand Spanish, they asked the *escopetero* if they could not bring off a *coup* at our expense by going and lying in wait for us a few miles farther on. The former partner of José Maria replied in a tone of perfect nobility and majesty: "I cannot permit it, for these young gentlemen are in my company; besides, expecting to be robbed, they have no money with them but what is strictly necessary for the journey, and their money is in letters of exchange on Seville. Moreover, they are both of them big and strong; as for the mine-overseer, he is my *friend*, and we have four carbines in the galley." This persuasive argument convinced our host and his acolytes, who contented themselves for once with the ordinary methods of fleecing tolerated among innkeepers of all nations.

In spite of all the alarming tales about brigands related by travellers and natives of the country, our adventures went no further than this, the most dramatic incident in our long peregrinations through regions which had the worst reputation for danger in Spain, at a period which was certainly propitious to attacks of this kind; the Spanish brigand was for us a purely fictitious being, an abstraction, a mere poem. We never caught sight of so much as the shadow of a *trabuco*, and so far as robbers were concerned, we had become quite as incredulous as the young English gentleman of whom Mérimée tells the story, who, even on falling into the hands of a band who were rifling his possessions, persisted in regarding them as no more than supers in a melodrama, posted there to play him a practical joke.

We left La Carlotta at about three in the afternoon, and in the evening we halted at a wretched gypsy hut, the roof of which was formed of branches roughly cut down, and thrown on cross-poles like a sort of coarse thatch. After drinking a few glasses of water, I lay down peacefully outside the door, on the bosom of our common mother, and as I gazed at the azure abyss of the sky in which great stars appeared to dance like swarms of golden bees, their scintillating rays forming a cloud of light like that produced around their bodies by dragon-flies' wings, so rapid in their motion as to be invisible—it was not long before I fell fast asleep, as if I had been in the downiest bed in the world. Yet all I had for a pillow was a stone wrapped in my cloak, and a few good-sized pebbles were digging holes in my back. Never did a night so serene and fine enfold the earth in its blue velvet cloak. About midnight the galley started again, and when day dawned, we were no more than half a league from Cordoba.

One might imagine from the description of these stages and halts that a long distance separates Cordoba from Malaga, and that we had travelled an enormous way on this journey, which lasted no less than four and a half days. The distance we covered is no more than twenty Spanish leagues, that is, about thirty French leagues (seventy-five miles), but the cart was heavily laden, the road abominable, and there were no relays posted for changing the mules. Add to this the unbearable heat, which was enough to stifle both beast and man, if one had risked oneself out of doors during the hours when the sun is at its full strength. Yet this journey, long and trying as it was, has left us a pleasant memory; excessive rapidity of transport deprives the road of all its charm: you are carried off as by a whirlwind, with no time to see anything. If one arrives so quickly, one might as well have stayed at home. To my mind, the pleasure of travelling lies in the journey and not in the arrival.

A bridge over the Guadalquivir, which is fairly wide at this spot, forms the approach to Cordoba from the direction of Ecija. Quite near it one notices the old ruined arches of an Arab aqueduct. The bridge-head is defended by a great square crenellated tower, reinforced by casemates of more recent construction. The gates of the city were not yet open; a throng of wagons drawn by oxen, majestically crowned with tiaras of red and yellow woven grass—besides mules and white asses loaded with chopped straw, peasants in sugar-loaf hats, clad in brown woollen *capas* falling down in front and behind like a priest's cope, and put on by passing the head through a hole cut in the middle of the cloth—were awaiting the hour for opening with the customary patience and stolidity of Spaniards, who never seem to be in a hurry. Such a collection at the barriers of Paris would have raised a horrible din, indulging in abuse and insults; here there was not a sound save the tinkle of a copper bell on a mule's collar, or a silvery peal from some *colonel* (leader of a train of asses) as he changed his position, or rested his head on the neck of one of his long-eared brethren.

We took advantage of this halt to make a leisurely survey of the outward aspect of Cordoba. A fine gate like a triumphal arch, with Ionic columns, and so grand in style that one might have imagined it to be Roman, formed a stately entrance to the city of the Caliphs, though I should have preferred one of those fine Moorish arches, cut in the shape of a heart, which one sees at Granada. The mosque-cathedral rose above the walls and roofs more like a citadel than a church, with its high walls jagged with Arab crenellations, and the heavy Catholic dome crouched on its Oriental platform. It must be admitted that these walls are daubed with an abominable shade of yellow. Though not precisely one of those who love mouldering, black, leprous edifices, we have a peculiar horror of that vile pumpkin-colour which has such a charm for the priests, churchwardens and chapters of every land, that they never fail to paste it all over the marvellous cathedrals entrusted to their charge. Buildings must be, and always have been, painted, even during the purest periods; but the tone and nature of the medium should be more carefully chosen.

At last the gates were opened, and we had the preliminary pleasure of a fairly searching examination at the Customs, after which we were free to betake ourselves to the nearest *parador* accompanied by our trunks.

Cordoba has a more African appearance than any other in Andalusia; its streets, or rather alleys, have a wildly irregular pavement like a dried-up watercourse, all strewn with the chopped straw dropped from the asses' loads, and nothing about them recalls the manners and customs of Europe. One walks between interminable chalk-coloured walls, with occasional windows trellised with bars and gratings, meeting nobody but a few evil-looking beggars, pious women muffled in black veils, or *majos*, who ride past like lightning on their brown horses with white harness, striking showers of sparks from the cobble-stones. If the Moors could return, they would not have to make many changes in order to settle here again. Any idea which one may have formed in advance of Cordoba, as a city of Gothic houses, with spires like lacework, is absolutely false. The universal use of whitewashed plaster gives a uniform tone to all the buildings, filling up the lines of the architecture, effacing the decoration and preventing one from distinguishing their age. Thanks to this whitewash, a wall built a hundred years ago is indistinguishable from one built yesterday. Cordoba, once the centre of Arab civilization, is today no more than a mass of little white houses among which rise a few Indian fig-trees of a metallic green, and a few palm-trees with their leaves spread out crab-wise; they are divided into islands by narrow passages in which two mules could hardly pass each other if they met. The life seems to have ebbed away from this great body, once animated by the active circulation of Moorish blood; nothing remains of it now but a white and calcined skeleton. But Cordoba has her mosque, a building unique in the world and entirely novel, even for travellers who have already had occasion to admire the marvels of Arab architecture at Granada or Seville.

In spite of its Moorish airs, Cordoba is none the less a good Christian, under the special protection of the archangel Raphael. From the balcony of our *parador*, we could see rather a strange monument set up in honour of this celestial patron; we were curious to examine it closer. Standing on his column, sword in hand, with his outspread wings all gilt and glittering, the archangel Raphael is like a sentinel eternally watching over the city placed beneath his guard. The column is of grey granite with a Corinthian capital of gilt bronze, and stands upon a little tower, or lantern, of pink granite, the foundation of which is formed by rock-work on which are grouped a horse, a palm-tree, a lion and some most fantastical marine monsters; four allegorical statues complete the decoration. In the pedestal is sunk the coffin of Bishop Paschal, a personage celebrated for his piety and devotion to the holy archangel.

Upon a tablet one may read the following inscription:

> *Yo te juro por Jesu-Cristo cruzificado que soi Rafael angel,*
> *a quien Dios tiene puesto por guarda de esta ciudad.*
> (I swear by Jesus Christ crucified that I am the angel Raphael,
> whom God has appointed guardian of this city.)

But, you will say, how did they know that it was the archangel Raphael in particular, he and no other, who was the patron saint of the ancient city of Abderrahman? We will answer you by means of a *romance* or song printed by permission at Cordoba, by Don Raphael Garcia Rodriguez, in the Calle de la Libreria; this precious document has as a vignette at the head of it a wood-engraving representing the archangel with outspread wings and an aureole round his head, with his traveller's staff and the fish in his hand, majestically planted between two flaunting pots of hyacinths and peonies, accompanied by an inscription in the following terms: "A true narrative and curious legend of our lord St. Raphael, archangel, our advocate in time of plague, and guardian of the city of Cordoba."

In it is related how the blessed archangel appeared to Don Andres Roelas, a nobleman and priest of Cordoba, and addressed a speech to him in his room, the first phrase of which is the very one carved on the column. This address, which is preserved in the legendaries, lasted more than an hour and a half, the priest and the archangel being seated face to face, each of them on a chair. This apparition took place on May the 7th in the year of grace 1578 and it was to celebrate the memory of it that this monument was erected.

A flat space lies round this monument, enclosed within a railing, and enables it to be seen from every side. Statues shown off in this manner gain a sort of slender elegance which I like very much; it is an admirable way of breaking the bareness of a terrace, a public square or a too spacious court-yard. The statuette on a porphyry column in the court of the Palais des Beaux-Arts in Paris, gives some slight idea of the decorative advantage to which figures might be used if they were so arranged, for it gives them an imposing appearance which they would not otherwise have. This reflection had already occurred to us in the presence of the Blessed Virgin and the St. Christopher of Ecija.

The outside of the cathedral had not appealed to us much, and we dreaded lest we might meet with a cruel disenchantment. Victor Hugo's verses:

Cordoue aux maisons vieilles
A sa mosquée où l'oeil se perd dans des merveilles
(Cordoba, with her ancient houses,
has her mosque where the eye is lost in marvels),

had seemed to us too flattering before we saw it; but we were soon convinced that they did it no more than justice.

It was the Caliph Abderrahman I who laid the foundations of the mosque of Cordoba towards the end of the eighth century; the work was carried on so actively that the building was finished by the beginning of the ninth: twenty-one years were enough to bring this gigantic edifice to completion! When one considers that this wonderful piece of work, of such colossal proportions, was carried out a thousand years ago in so short a time, by a people which afterwards relapsed into the most savage barbarism, one is amazed in spirit, and refuses to believe in the so-called theories of progress which are current today; when one visits countries once occupied by vanished civilizations, one even feels tempted to espouse the contrary opinion. For my part I have always greatly regretted that the Moors did not remain masters of Spain, which has certainly done nothing but lose by their expulsion. Under their domination, if we are to believe the popular exaggerations gravely retailed by the historians, Cordoba numbered two hundred thousand houses, eighty thousand palaces and nine hundred bath-houses; twelve thousand villages served it as suburbs. Nowadays it has not forty thousand inhabitants, and seems almost deserted!

Abderrahman wished to make the Mosque of Cordoba a place of pilgrimage, a western Mecca, the principal church of Islam after that in which the body of the prophet lies. I have not yet seen the Kasbeh at Mecca, but I doubt whether it equals the Spanish mosque in size or magnificence. In it was preserved one of the originals of the Koran, and a still more precious relic, a bone of Mahomet's arm.

The lower classes even maintain that the Sultan of Constantinople still pays tribute to the King of Spain, so that mass may not be said on the spot peculiarly sacred to the prophet. This chapel is given by pious people the ironical name of the *Zancarrón*, a term of contempt which signifies the jaw-bone of an ass, or a worthless carcass.

Seven doors open into the Mosque of Cordoba, but they have nothing imposing about them, for the nature of the building is opposed to this, and excludes those stately portals imperatively demanded by the sacramental plan of Catholic cathedrals; so there is nothing in its exterior to prepare you for the wonderful spectacle which awaits you. We will pass, if you wish, through the *Patio de los Naranjos*, a vast, magnificent court planted with monstrous orange-trees dating back to the Moorish kings, surrounded with long arcaded galleries, and flagged with marble, on one side of which rises a tower in a poor style, a clumsy imitation of the Giralda, as we were able to see later at Seville. Beneath the pavement of this court lies, they say, an immense cistern. In the days of the Ommayyads, it was possible to enter the body of the mosque straight from the *Patio de los Naranjos*, for the hideous wall which blocks the view on this side was not built till later.

The truest idea which one can give of this strange edifice is to say that it is like a great terrace enclosed by walls, and planted with columns in the form of a quincunx. This space is four hundred and twenty feet broad and four hundred and forty feet long. The columns are eight hundred and sixty in number; it is only half, they say, of the original mosque.

The impression which one experiences on entering this venerable sanctuary of Islam is an indefinable one, having no resemblance to the emotions ordinarily caused by architecture: you feel that you are walking in a ceiled forest rather than a building; whichever way you turn, your eye is bewildered among the pillared glades, which intersect one another and stretch away into the distance like a vegetation of marble sprung spontaneously from the ground; the mysterious half-light which prevails in this woodland adds still further to the illusion. One can count nineteen naves breadthways and thirty-six lengthways, but the arches of the tranverse arcades are much smaller. Each nave is formed of two rows of arches one above the other, some of which intersect each other and are interlaced like ribbons, producing the most fantastic effect. The columns are all hewn in a single piece, measuring hardly more than ten to twelve feet up to the height of the capitals, and are of an Arab Corinthian type full of strength and elegance, recalling the African palm rather than the Greek acanthus. They are of rare marbles, porphyry, jasper, green and purple breccia, and other precious substances; there are even a few antique ones, brought, it is alleged, from the ruins of an ancient temple of Janus. Thus three religions have performed their rites on this spot. Of these, one has disappeared into the gulf of the past, never to return, together with the civilization which it represented; another has been cast out of Europe, where it barely maintains a foothold, into the depths of the barbarous East; the third has reached its apogee, and now, undermined by the spirit of criticism, is growing daily weaker, even in countries where it reigned as absolute sovereign; and perhaps the ancient mosque of Abderrahman may yet last long enough to see a fourth creed established beneath the shadow of its arches, celebrating with other forms and other hymns the new god, or rather the new prophet, for God is always the same.

In the days of the Caliphs, eight hundred silver lamps filled with aromatic oils lighted these long naves, awaking glittering reflections in the porphyry and polished jasper of the columns, spangling with a point of light the golden stars upon the ceiling, and revealing in the shadows mosaics of crystal and texts from the Koran entwined in arabesque and flowers. Among these lamps were to be found the bells of St. James of Compostella, carried off by the Moors; reversed and hanging from the vault by chains of silver, they lighted up the temple of Allah and his Prophet, amazed, like good Catholic bells, to find themselves transformed into Musulman lamps. Then the eye could play freely over the long colonnades, and distinguish, from within the depths of the temple, the orange-trees flowering and the fountains playing in the *patio*, beneath a torrent of light made even more dazzling by contrast with the half-light of the interior. Unluckily this magnificent prospect is nowadays obstructed by the Catholic church, an enormous heavy mass crammed into the heart of the Arab mosque. Its retables, chapels and sacristies clog and disturb the general symmetry of the whole. This parasite of a church, this monstrous fungus of stone, an architectural wart breaking out on the back of the Arab structure, was built to the designs of Hernán Ruíz, and does not lack merits of its own; anywhere else one would admire it, but it must for ever be regretted that it should occupy this place. It was erected by the chapter, in spite of the opposition of the *ayuntamiento*, by an order obtained by surprise from the Emperor Charles the Fifth, who had never seen the mosque. When he visited it a few years later, he said: "Had I known this, I would never have allowed the ancient building to be touched: you have put what can be seen anywhere in the place of what was nowhere else to be seen." These just reproaches caused the chapter to hang their heads, but the harm was done. In the choir one may admire an immense piece of carved woodwork in massive mahogany, representing subjects from the Old Testament, the work of Don Pedro Duque Cornejo, who spent ten years of his life on this prodigious piece of work, as may be seen on the poor artist's tomb, in which he lies beneath a flagstone a few steps from his work. And, talking about tombs, we noticed rather a singular one sunk in the wall; it was in the form of a chest, fastened by three padlocks. How will the dead man, thus carefully enclosed, manage to open the stone locks of his coffin on the day of the Last Judgment; and how is he to find the keys amid the general disorder?

Up to the middle of the eighteenth century the ancient ceiling of Abderrahman, in larch and cedar-wood, had been preserved with its coffering, its compartments, its lozenges and all its Oriental magnificence; it has been replaced by vaulting and half cupolas in poor taste. The ancient flagged pavement has disappeared beneath a brick floor, which has raised the level of the ground, encroached on the stems of the columns and emphasized the general defect of the building, which was already too low for its area.

All these desecrations do not prevent the Mosque of Cordoba from still remaining one of the most marvellous buildings in the world; and as if to make us feel the mutilation of the rest still more bitterly, one portion of it, called the *Mirah*, has remained scrupulously intact, as if by a miracle.

The ceiling of carved and gilt wood, with its *media-naranja* strewn with stars, the soft light filtering through the windows, cut out in patterns and furnished with gratings, the gallery with slender columns and trefoil arches, the patches of coloured-glass mosaic, the verses from the Koran in letters of gilded crystal which meander through ornaments and arabesques of the most graceful intricacy, produce a general effect of a splendour, beauty and fairy-like elegance the like of which is only met with in the *Arabian Nights*, and which has nothing to envy any other art. Never were lines better chosen, or colours better blended: the Gothic has something poor, sickly and emaciated, even in its most delicate caprices and most precious chasing, which savours of the barbarous beginnings of art. The architecture of the *Mirah*, on the other hand, reveals a civilization arrived at the height of its development, an art at its culminating period; beyond this could lie nothing but decadence. Proportion, harmony, richness and grace—nothing is lacking.

This chapel leads into a little over-ornate sanctuary, the ceiling of which is made of a single block of marble, carved like a shell and covered with excessively fine tracery. This was probably the holy of holies, the dread and holy spot in which the presence of God is felt more than elsewhere.

Another chapel, called the *Capilla de los Reyes Moros*, where the Caliphs used to pray apart from the crowd of the faithful, also displays some curious and charming details; but it has not been so fortunate as the *Mirah*, and its colour has disappeared beneath an ignoble coat of whitewash.

The sacristies are gorged with treasures; one sees nothing but monstrances glittering with jewels, silver reliquaries of incredible weight, as large as little cathedrals, candlesticks, golden crucifixes and copes embroidered with pearls: a more than royal luxury which is quite Asiatic.

As we were preparing to go out, the verger who acted as our guide led us mysteriously aside into a dark corner, and pointed out to us, as the culminating curiosity, a crucifix which they allege to have been scratched by the nail of a Christian prisoner on a porphyry column, at the foot of which he was chained up. In order to prove the authenticity of the story, he showed us a statue of the poor captive standing a few steps away. Without being unnecessarily Voltairian where legends are concerned, I could not help thinking that in olden days they had devilish hard nails, or else the porphyry was very soft. Moreover, this is not the only crucifix; there is a second one on another column, but it is much better shaped. The verger also showed us an enormous ivory tusk suspended in the middle of a cupola by iron chains, which looked like the hunting-horn of some Saracen giant, some Nimrod of a vanished world; this tusk belongs, they say, to one of the elephants used for carrying materials during the construction of the mosque. Pleased with his explanations and courtesy, we gave him a few *pesetas*, a piece of generosity which seemed greatly to annoy the former friend of José Maria, who had accompanied us, and drew from him this somewhat heretical remark: "Would it not be better to give this money to a decent bandit, instead of to a wretched sacristan?"

As we left the cathedral, we stopped for a few moments before a pretty Gothic doorway which forms the front of the Foundling Hospital. Anywhere else one would admire it, but it is crushed by these overpowering surroundings.

Having gone round the cathedral, we had nothing to keep us at Cordoba, which is not the most diverting place to stay at. The only amusement which a stranger can indulge in there is to go and bathe in the Guadalquivir or get a shave at one of the many barber-shops in the neighbourhood of the mosque, an operation which is accomplished with great dexterity, and by the aid of an enormous razor, by a little barber perched on the back of the great oaken arm-chair in which you are made to sit down.

The heat was unbearable, for it was complicated by fire. The harvest was just over, and it is the custom in Andalusia to burn the stubble as soon as the sheaves are carted away, so that the soil may be fertilized by the ashes. The country-side was aflame for three or four leagues round, and the wind, scorching its wings as it passed across this sea of flame, brought with it puffs of hot air like those which come from the mouth of a stove: we were in the position of those scorpions which children surround with a ring of lighted shavings, so that they have to break through in desperation, or commit suicide by burying their sting in themselves. We preferred the former method.

The galley by which we had come took us back by the same road as far as Ecija, where we asked for a carriage to take us to Seville. The driver, on seeing the two of us, thought us too big, brawny and heavy to drive, and raised every sort of difficulty. Our trunks, he said, were of such excessive weight that it would take four men to lift them, and they would make his carriage break down at once. We met this last objection by ourselves lifting the much maligned trunks with the greatest ease, and piling them on the back of the carriage. The fellow could raise no more difficulties, and at last made up his mind to start.

Flat or slightly rolling tracts of land, planted with olive-trees, with their grey tones made even more colourless by the dust, sandy steppes on which rounded clumps of blackish vegetation rise from place to place, like vegetable warts: such were the only objects that met our eyes for many a league.

At La Luisiana, the whole population was lying snoring in the open air before their doors. Our carriage roused to their feet whole rows of sleepers, who flattened themselves against the wall grumbling, and lavishing upon us the whole wealth of the Andalusian vocabulary. We supped in a rather evil-looking *posada*, better furnished with guns and blunderbusses than with household gear. Monstrous dogs persistently followed our every movement, and seemed to be only waiting for the signal to tear us to pieces with their teeth. The landlady appeared most surprised at the calm voracity with which we disposed of our tomato omelette. She seemed to consider this repast superfluous, and to regret this food which would do us no good. However, in spite of the sinister appearance of the place, our throats were not cut, and they were forbearing enough to allow us to go on our way.

The soil became sandier and sandier, and the wheels of the carriage sank up to the axles in the shifting earth. Then we understood why our driver had been so anxious about our specific gravity. In order to relieve the horse, we went on foot, and towards midnight, after following a road which zigzagged up the precipitous sides of a mountain, we arrived at Carmona, where we were to sleep. The kilns in which they were burning lime threw long, ruddy gleams upon the sloping rocks, producing Rembrandtesque effects of wonderful picturesqueness and power.

The room which they had given us was adorned with bad coloured lithographs representing various episodes of the July revolution, the taking of the Hôtel de Ville, etc. This pleased and almost touched us; it was like a little piece of France framed and hung on the wall. Carmona, which we had hardly time to look at before getting back into the carriage, is a little town as white as cream, to which quite a picturesque outline is given by the bell-turrets and towers of a former convent of Carmelite nuns; this is all we can say about it.

From Carmona onwards, the fleshy plants—cactuses and aloes— from which we had parted company, appeared again more bristling and savage than ever. The landscape was less bare and arid, and more broken; the heat had lost a little of its intensity. We soon reached Alcalá de los Panaderos, famous for the quality of its bread, as its name indicates, and for its fights of *novillos* (young bulls) which are attended by the *aficionados* of Seville when their bullring is closed. Alcalá de los Panaderos is very finely situated at the bottom of a little valley with a winding river; it is sheltered by a hill-side on which still rise the ruins of an ancient Moorish palace. We were approaching Seville. And, indeed, it was not long before the Giralda showed on the horizon first its pierced lantern and then its square tower; a few hours later, we were passing through the Gate of Carmona, the arch of which framed a background of dusty light in which galleys, asses, mules and ox-wagons, some going and some coming, met in a sea of golden mist. A superb aqueduct of the Roman type raised its stone arches on the left of the road; on the other side stood rows of houses; which gradually drew closer together; we were in Seville.

Cathedral of Seville

XV. Seville

THERE is an oft-quoted Spanish proverb about Seville:

"Quien no ha visto a Sevilla
No ha visto a maravilla."
(He who not seen Seville,
has missed a marvel.)

We must confess, in all humility, that this proverb would strike us as more justly applicable to Toledo or Granada than to Seville, in which we find nothing particularly marvellous, unless it is the cathedral.

Seville is situated on the bank of the Guadalquivir, in a wide plain, whence its name of Hispalis, which means, in Carthaginian, "flat land", if we are to believe Arias Montano and Samuel Bochart. It is a spacious, straggling city, quite modern, gay, smiling and animated, and must indeed seem charming to Spaniards. No greater contrast with Cordoba could be found. Cordoba is a dead city, with its houses heaped together as in a charnel-cave, an open catacomb over which is sifting the ashen dust of neglect; the few inhabitants whom one meets as one turns a corner look like apparitions which have come at the wrong time. Seville, on the other hand, has all the stir and impetuosity of life: a wild, diffused murmur floats over it at all hours of the day; it hardly takes time for a siesta. It recks little of yesterday, still less of tomorrow, but lives entirely in the present; memory and hope are the pleasures of unhappy races, and Seville is happy: she plays, while her sister Cordoba appears to brood gravely, in solitude and silence, on Abderrahman, the Great Captain, and all their vanished splendours, those beacons blazing in the night of the past, of which no more is left her now save the ashes.

To the great disappointment of travellers and antiquaries, whitewash reigns supreme in Seville; three or four times a year the houses put on a fresh coat of white, which gives them a cleanly and well-cared-for look, but conceals from investigation the remains of the Arab or Gothic sculptures which formerly adorned them. Nothing could be more monotonous than this network of streets, in which the eye can distinguish no more than two colours: the indigo of the sky and the chalk-white of the walls, on which are outlined the azure-tinged shadows of the neighbouring buildings; for shadows in hot countries are blue, not grey, so things look as if they were lighted on one side by moonlight and on the other by the sun; yet the complete absence of all sombre tones produces a general effect of life and gaiety. Through doorways closed by metal gates one catches sight of the *patios* within, adorned with columns, mosaic pavements, fountains, pots of flowers, shrubs and pictures. As for the external architecture, it has nothing remarkable about it; the height of the buildings rarely exceeds two or three stories, and it would be hard to count a dozen façades of any artistic interest. The pavement, like that of all Spanish towns, is of little pebbles, but it is striped with fairly wide bands of flat stones, forming a sort of pavement, along which file the crowds; when they meet a woman they always give way to her, with that exquisite politeness natural to Spaniards even of the lowest class. The women of Seville justify their reputation for beauty; they are almost all alike, as happens among unmixed races of a strongly marked type: their clear-cut eyes, elongated to the very temples, are fringed with long brown lashes, and produce a contrast of black and white which is unknown in France. When a woman or a young girl passes you, she deliberately lowers her eyelids, then suddenly raises them and darts at you a glance of irresistible brilliance, then she rolls her eye and once more lowers her eye-lashes. Nobody but Amany, the Eastern dancer, when she danced the Dance of Doves, can give any idea of these inflammatory glances which Spain has inherited from the Orient; we have no terms to express this play of the eye; *ojear* is a word lacking in our vocabulary. Yet the sudden, vivid flash of these glances, which almost embarrasses foreigners, has nothing particularly significant about it, and is directed impartially at whatever happens to pass by. A young woman of Andalusia will cast the same passionate glance at a passing cart, a dog running after its tail or some children playing at bullfights. The eyes of Northern races are lifeless and empty compared with these; in them the sun has never left its reflection.

Their teeth, with a brilliance like those of a Newfoundland puppy, and very pointed eye-teeth, give the smile of the women of Seville rather a wild, Arab quality which is extremely characteristic. The brow is high, full and polished; the nose slender, with an aquiline tendency; the mouth brightly coloured. Unfortunately the oval of a face which begins divinely, sometimes ends at the chin in too sudden a curve. The only imperfections which the most exacting artist could find in the Sevillanas are their rather thin shoulders and arms. The delicate extremities, the tiny hands and feet, leave nothing to be desired. Without any poetic exaggeration, one could easily find in Seville women with feet which could be contained in the hand of a child. The Andalusian women are very proud of this beauty, and wear shoes in keeping with it: from their shoes to a Chinese slipper the distance is not great.

"Con primor se calza el pié
Digno de regio tapiz."
(The foot is daintily shod
and worthy of a royal carpet.)

This is a praise as frequent in their songs as a complexion of lilies and roses is in ours.

These shoes are usually of satin, scarcely covering the toes, and seem to have no backs, for they are fitted at the heel with a little piece of ribbon of the same colour as the stocking. One of our little girls of seven or eight years old could not get on the shoe of an Andalusian girl of twenty. They are consequently never tired of jesting about the feet and shoes of northern women; out of a German dancing-shoe they made a six-oared boat for rowing on the Guadalquivir. The wooden stirrups of the *picadores* might serve as slippers for the English ladies, and a thousand other *andaluzadas* of the same sort.

I did my best to defend the feet of Parisiennes, but could find nobody to believe me. Unfortunately the Sevillanas have only remained Spanish in the head and foot, in their shoes and mantillas; coloured dresses in the French style are beginning to be in the majority. The men are dressed like fashion-drawings. Sometimes, however, they wear white drill jackets with trousers to match and the red sash and Andalusian hat; but this is rare, and, besides, this costume is not very picturesque.

On the Alameda del Duque, where people take a breath of air between the acts outside the theatre, which is quite near by, and, above all, on La Cristina, it is charming to see the pretty Sevillanas parading with little airs and graces between seven and eight o'clock, in groups of three or four, accompanied by their present or future lovers. Their movements are alert, vivacious and mettlesome, and they seem to paw the ground like a horse rather than to walk. The rapidity with which their fans open and close beneath their fingers, the flash of their eye, the assurance of their movements, the willowy lissomness of their figures, add a characteristic touch to their appearance. There may be women in England, France and Italy whose beauty is of a more perfect and regular type, but there are certainly none prettier and more piquant. They possess in a high degree what Spaniards call *la sal*. This is a thing of which it is difficult to give an idea in France: a mixture of nonchalance and vivacity, of daring retorts and childish wiles, of a grace, a piquancy and a *ragoût*, as the painters say, which may be found quite apart from beauty, and is often preferred to it. And so in Spain they say to a woman: "How *salada* (full of salt) you are!" There is no greater compliment.

La Cristina is a magnificent promenade on the banks of the Guadalquivir, having a *Salón* paved with wide flags, and surrounded by a great white marble bench with an iron back, shaded with Eastern plane-trees, and having a labyrinth, a Chinese pavilion and plantations of every kind of northern tree—ashes, cypresses, poplars and willows—which are as much admired by the Andalusians as palm-trees and aloes would be by Parisians.

Round about La Cristina there are posts with pieces of sulphured rope coiled round them, which keep a light constantly at the disposal of smokers, so that one is free from the importunities of boys carrying glowing charcoal and shouting "*fuego*", which make the Prado at

Madrid unbearable.

Pleasant though this promenade is, I prefer the actual riverbank, which offers a scene of constant and ever-changing animation. In the middle of the stream, where the water is deepest, are moored the trading-brigs and schooners, with their lofty masts and airy rigging, traced in lines of clear black on the pale background of the sky. Light craft ply in all directions upon the river. Sometimes a boat floats down, bearing a company of young men and women playing on the guitar and singing verses, whose rhymes are wafted on the light breeze, and applauded by the strollers on the banks. The view in this direction is aptly completed by the *Torre del Oro*, a sort of octagonal tower with three receding stories and Moorish crenellations, which bathes its foundations in the Guadalquivir hard by the landing-stage, and rises into the azure air from amid a forest of masts and rigging. This tower, which, as scholars maintain, was built by the Romans, was once connected with the Alcázar by walls, but these are now demolished to make room for La Cristina; in the days of the Moors it supported one end of the iron chain barring the river, the other end of which was attached to buttresses of masonry on the opposite side. The name *Torre del Oro* was given to it, they say, from the fact that the gold brought from America by the galleons was stored there.

We used to go and stroll there every evening, and watch the sun sinking behind the suburb of Triana, which lies on the other side of the river. A nobly proportioned palm-tree raised its leafy disk in the air, as if to greet the declining orb. I have always had a great love for palm-trees, and have never been able to see one without feeling myself transported into a poetic, patriarchal world, amid Oriental enchantments and Biblical magnificence.

As if to recall us to a sense of reality, as we were returning in the evening to the Calle de la Sierpa, where lived our host Don Cesar Bustamente, whose wife, born at Jerez, had the finest eyes and longest hair in the world, we were accosted by some very well-dressed fellows, of a most respectable address, with eye-glasses and watch-chains, who besought us to come and rest and take some refreshment in the house of some ladies, *muy finas, muy decentes* (very refined and respectable), who had asked them to invite us. These worthy persons seemed at first much astonished at our refusal, and, imagining that we did not understand them, entered into more explicit details; then, seeing that they were wasting their time, they confined themselves to offering us cigarettes and Murillos; for we must say that Murillo is at once the glory and the scourge of Seville. You hear nothing but his name. The most ordinary bourgeois, the most insignificant *abbé*, possesses at least three hundred Murillos of the best period: "What is this daub?" "It is a Murillo in the misty style." "And this other one?" "A Murillo in the warm style." "And the third?" "A Murillo in the cold style." Like Raphael, Murillo has three manners, which means that any sort of picture may be ascribed to him, and leaves a delightful latitude to collectors who are forming a picture-gallery. At every street-corner one knocks against the corner of a frame: it is a Murillo worth thirty francs, which some Englishman has always just bought for thirty thousand francs.—"Look, Señor Caballero, what drawing, what colour! It is the *perla*, the *perlita*."

How many pearls have been shown me which were not worth their frame and their mount! How many originals which were not even so much as copies! All of which does not prevent Murillo from being one of the most wonderful painters in Spain, and in the world. But we have strayed far from the banks of the Guadalquivir; let us return there.

A bridge of boats connects the two banks, and links the suburbs with the city. One crosses it on one's way to visit the ruins of Italica, near Santi-Ponce, the home of the poet Silius Italicus, of the Emperors Trajan, Hadrian and Theodosius; one can see there a ruined amphitheatre, the shape of which is still fairly distinct. The dens in which the wild beasts were shut up and the gladiators' dressing-rooms are perfectly recognizable, as well as the corridors and tiers of seats. It is all built of concrete, with pebbles sunk in the cement. The stone facings have probably been torn down and used for some more modern buildings, for Italica has been for long past the quarry of Seville. A few rooms have been cleared out and serve as a shelter during the fiercest heats for herds of blue pigs, which rush grunting out between the legs of visitors, and now form the sole population of the ancient Roman city. The most complete and interesting relic of all this vanished splendour is a mosaic of large dimensions, enclosed within a wall, with figures of Muses and Nereids. When it is revived with water, the colours are still very bright, though greedy hands have torn out the most precious stones. Among the ruins have also been found a few fragments of statues in a fairly good style, and no doubt carefully planned excavations would lead to important discoveries. Italica is about four miles from Seville, and it is an excursion which one can easily make by carriage in an afternoon, unless one is a rabid antiquarian, desirous of turning over, one by one, all the stones which one suspects of having inscriptions on them.

The Puerta de Triana has also some pretensions towards being Roman, and takes its name from the Emperor Trajan. Its appearance is very imposing; it is in the Doric order, with columns arranged in pairs, and is adorned with the royal arms and surmounted by pyramids. It has an alcalde of its own, and is used as a prison. The Puerta del Carbón and the Puerta del Aceite are worthy of examination. On the Puerta de Jerez can be read the following inscription:

"Hercules me edificó,
Julio Cesar me cercó
De muros y torres altas,
El rey santo me ganó
Con Garci Peréz de Vargas."
(Hercules built me;
Julius Caesar encircled me
with walls and lofty towers;
the sainted King won me,
together with Garci Peréz de Vargas.)

Seville is girt with a ring of crenellated walls, flanked at intervals with great towers, several of which have fallen into ruin, and with moats which are now almost entirely filled up. These walls, which would be no defence against modern artillery, produce quite a picturesque effect with their jagged, saw-like Arab battlements. Their foundation, in common with that of every imaginable wall or camp, is ascribed to Julius Caesar.

On an open space close by the Puerta de Triana I saw a most curious sight. It was a family of gypsies camped in the open air, composing a group which would have delighted Callot. Three pointed stakes arranged in a triangle formed a sort of rustic pot-hanger, from which, above a great fire, scattered by the wind into tongues of flame and coils of smoke, hung a great stew-pot full of queer and dubious victuals, such as Goya devised for casting into the witches' cauldrons of Barahona. Beside this improvised hearth was seated a *gitana* with her hook-nosed, tanned and bronze profile, naked to the waist, a proof that she was completely devoid of coquetry; her long black hair hung in a tangle down her lean yellow back and upon her swarthy brow. Through the untidy wisps gleamed her great Eastern eyes of pearl and jet, so dreamy and mysterious as to ennoble by their poetry the most bestial and degraded countenances. Round her sprawled three or four whimpering brats in a state of nature, as dark as mulattoes, with fat bellies and frail limbs which made them seem quadrumanous rather than bipedal in nature. I doubt whether little Hottentots are dirtier or more hideous. This state of nudity is not uncommon, and shocks nobody. One often meets beggars whose only garment is a scrap of blanket, or a most insecure fragment of drawers; at Granada and Malaga I have seen rascals of twelve and fourteen years of age roaming about the squares more unclad than Adam when he left the earthly paradise. The suburb of Triana is rich in encounters of this sort, for it contains many *gitanos,* a people with the most advanced ideas of a free-and-easy kind; the women do their frying out of doors, and the men devote themselves to smuggling, clipping mules, horse-coping, etc., when they do no worse.

La Cristina, the Guadalquivir, the Alameda del Duque, Italica and the Moorish Alcázar are undoubtedly very curious; but the real wonder of Seville is its cathedral, which is indeed an astonishing building, even after the Cathedrals of Burgos and Toledo, and the Mosque of Cordoba. The chapter which gave orders for its construction summed up its plan in the following phrase: "Let us build a monument which shall make posterity believe that we were mad." Very good; here was a comprehensive and well-conceived program; with such a free hand, the artists did wonders, and in order to hasten on the completion of the edifice the canons gave up their whole income, keeping only what was absolutely necessary to life. Thrice holy canons! Sleep sweetly beneath your gravestones, in the shade of your beloved cathedral, while your souls take their ease in Paradise in stalls which are probably not so well carved as your choir.

The wildest and most monstrously prodigious Hindu pagodas do not come up to the Cathedral of Seville. It is a hollow mountain, an inverted valley; Notre Dame de Paris could walk without bending her head down the central nave, which is of a terrific height; pillars as thick as towers, but looking so fragile that they make you tremble, spring from the ground or hang from the vaulting like the stalactites of a giant grotto. The four side naves, though less lofty, could shelter a church, steeple and all. The retable, or high altar, with its staircases, its several stages of architectural structures, its tiers of statues accumulated row above row, is a vast building in itself, which rises nearly as high as the vaulting. The paschal candle, as tall as the mast of a ship, weighs two thousand and fifty pounds. The bronze candlestick which supports it is like the column in the Place Vendôme, it is copied from the candlestick in the Temple at Jerusalem, as shown in the bas-reliefs of the Arch of Titus; everything is on this grand scale. There are twenty thousand pounds of wax burnt in the cathedral every year, and as much oil; the wine used for the consummation of the Holy Sacrifice reaches the astounding quantity of eighteen thousand seven hundred and fifty quarts. It is true that five hundred masses are said every day at the twenty-four altars! The catafalque used during Holy Week, which is known at the Monument, is nearly a hundred feet high. The organs, of gigantic proportions, look like the basalt columns of Fingal's Cave, and yet the thunder and hurricane which escape from their pipes, as thick as siege artillery, seem, beneath these colossal arches, like tuneful murmurs, or the song of birds and seraphs. One can count eighty-three stained-glass windows painted from cartoons by Michelangelo, Raphael, Dürer, Peregrino, Cambaldi and Luca Cambiaso; the oldest and most beautiful were executed by Arnold of Flanders, the celebrated glass-painter. The later ones, which date from 1819, show how far art has degenerated since the glorious sixteenth century, the grand climacteric of the world, when the plant man bore its loveliest flowers and its fruits of the finest savour. The choir, in the Gothic style, is embellished with turrets, spires, pierced niches, little figures and foliage, a vast, minute piece of work which staggers the imagination and passes the understanding of today. One is left absolutely prostrate in the presence of such work, and asks oneself anxiously whether vitality is ebbing century by century from the ageing world. This prodigy of talent, patience and genius does at least bear the name of its author, and our admiration has something to concentrate upon. On one of the panels on the Gospel side is traced this inscription: *Este coro fizo Nufro Sanchez entallador que Dios haya año de 1475.* (This choir was executed by Onufrio Sanchez, woodcarver, whom God hold in his keeping, in the year 1475.)

To attempt to describe the riches of the cathedral one after the other would be an egregious folly: it would take a whole year to examine it thoroughly, and even then one would not have seen everything; whole volumes would be insufficient merely to catalogue them. The carvings in stone, in wood and in silver by Juan de Arfe, Juan Millán, Montañes and Roldán, the paintings by Murillo, Zurbarán, Pedro Campaña, Roelas, Don Luís de Villegas, Herrera the elder and the younger, Juan Valdés and Goya, crowd the chapels, the sacristies and the chapter houses. One is crushed by the splendour, disheartened and satiated with masterpieces; one hardly knows which way to turn; the desire to see everything, and the impossibility of doing so, cause one a sort of feverish vertigo; one wants to forget nothing, but every moment one feels some name eluding one, some lineament growing blurred in one's memory or some picture effacing another. One makes desperate appeals to one's memory, one insists that one's eyes shall not waste one glance; the slightest rest, the hours given to eating and sleeping, seem to one so many thefts made from oneself, for one is borne on by sheer necessity, and soon it will be time to go; the fire is already flaming beneath the boiler of the steamboat, the water hisses and boils, the funnels vomit their white smoke; tomorrow you will leave all these marvels behind, doubtless to see them no more.

Since I cannot speak of everything, I will confine myself to mentioning Murillo's *St. Anthony of Padua*, which adorns the chapel of the Baptistery. Never has the magic of painting been carried further. The saint is kneeling in ecstasy in the middle of his cell, all the poor details of which are rendered with that vigorous realism which characterizes the Spanish school. Through the half-open door, one sees one of those long white arcaded cloisters so propitious to musing. The upper part of the picture, bathed in a golden, transparent, misty light, is occupied by groups of angels of truly ideal beauty. Drawn by the force of prayer, the infant Jesus descends from cloud to cloud and is about to place himself between the arms of the holy man, whose head is bathed in radiant emanations, and thrown back in a paroxysm of celestial ecstasy. I rank this divine picture higher than the *St. Elizabeth of Hungary* dressing a sufferer's scabs, which one sees in the Madrid Academy, higher than the *Moses*, higher than all this Master's Virgins and Infant Christs, pure and lovely though they may be. Those who have not seen the *St. Anthony of Padua* do not know the last word on the painter of Seville; like those who think they know Rubens, and have not seen the *Magdalen* of Antwerp.

All species of architecture are blended in the Cathedral of Seville. Austere Gothic, the style of the Renaissance, and what the Spaniards call *plateresco*, or Silversmiths' style, which is distinguished by an incredible riot of decoration and arabesque; rococo, Greek and Roman, nothing is missing, for each century has built its chapel or its retable, in its own special style, and the building is not even quite finished. Many of the statues representing patriarchs, apostles, saints and archangels which fill the niches over the doorways, are only in terra-cotta, and are placed there provisionally. On the same side as the court of *los Naranjos*, above the unfinished doorways, rises the iron crane, a symbol indicating that the building is not finished, and will be continued later. This gallows also appears at the summit of the church of Beauvais; but when shall the day come on which the pulley, rusty for centuries, shall creak with the weight of hewn stone slowly hoisted by the workmen into the air? Perhaps never; for the upward movement of Catholicism has been checked, and the sap which caused the earth to bloom with these cathedrals is no longer rising from the trunk to the branches. Faith, which doubts nothing, wrote the first stanzas of all these great poems in stone and granite; reason, which doubts everything, has not dared to finish them. The architects of the Middle Ages are a sort of religious Titans, piling Pelion on Ossa, not to dethrone the Thunderer, but to admire at closer quarters the sweet face of the Virgin Mother smiling upon the infant Jesus. In our days, when everything is sacrificed to some idea of gross, stupid comfort, we can no longer understand these sublime yearnings of the soul towards the infinite, which are interpreted in pinnacles, spires, turrets and pointed arches, stretching their arms of stone towards heaven, and clasping, as it were, their giant hands in prayer above the heads of the prostrate people. All this buried treasure, bringing in no interest, must make economists shrug their shoulders for pity. The people, too, are beginning to calculate how much the gold of the ciborium is worth; the people, who durst not raise their eyes of yore towards the white sun of the Host, now say to themselves that bits of glass might quite well take the place of the diamonds and jewels of the monstrance; the church is now scarcely frequented by any but travellers, beggars and horrible old women, vile duennas dressed in black, with the eyes of an owl, the smile of a death's head and the hands of a spider, who cannot move without the click of mouldy bones, medals and rosaries, and, under cover of begging for alms, whisper who knows what revolting propositions about black hair, rosy complexions, burning glances and ever-blooming smiles. Even Spain herself is no longer Catholic!

The Giralda, which serves as the bell-tower of the cathedral, and dominates all the towers in the city, is an ancient Moorish tower built by an Arab architect named Geber or Guever, the inventor of algebra, to which he gave his name. The effect is charming and most original; the rosy hue of the brick, the whiteness of the stone in which it is built, give it an air of youth and gaiety in contrast with the date of its construction, which goes back to the year 1000—a venerable age at which a tower may afford an occasional wrinkle, and dispense with a fresh complexion. The Giralda, as it is today, is no less than three hundred and fifty feet high and fifty feet wide on each front; the walls are smooth up to a certain height, at which begin tiers of Moorish windows, with balconies, trefoil-shaped arches, and miniature columns of white marble, framed in big lozenge-shaped panels of brick; the tower formerly ended in a roof of many-coloured glazed tiles crowned by an iron bar adorned with four gilt metal balls of prodigious size. This superstructure was destroyed in 1568 by the architect Francisco Ruíz, who raised the child of Guever the Moor's brain yet another hundred feet into the pure light of the sky, so that its bronze statue might look out across the Sierras and talk on a level with the passing angels. To build a tower on top of a tower was entirely in keeping with the intentions of that admirable chapter of which we have spoken, who wished to seem fools in the eyes of posterity. The work of Francisco Ruíz consists of three stories, the first of which is pierced with windows, having bells hanging in their embrasures; the cornice of the second, which is surrounded with an open balustrade, bears on each of its faces these words: *Turris fortissima nomen Domini* (The name of the Lord is a strong tower); the third is a sort of cupola or lantern on which revolves a gigantic figure of Faith, in gilt bronze, with a palm in one hand and a standard in the other, which serves as a weathercock, thus justifying the name Giralda borne by the tower. This statue is by Bartolomeo Morel, and can be seen from an enormous distance away; when it glitters in the rays of the sun through the azure air, it really seems like a seraph lingering in the sky.

One ascends to the Giralda by a series of inclined planes with no steps, so easy and gentle that two men on horseback could easily ride up side by side to the top, from which one enjoys a wonderful view. At your feet is Seville, all dazzling white, with its towers and steeples trying in vain to reach up to the wall of rosy brick encircling the Giralda. In the distance stretches the plain, across which the Guadalquivir trails like a ribbon of watered silk; one can see Santi-Ponce, Algaba and other villages. In the background appears the jagged line of the Sierra Morena, clear-cut in spite of the distance; so great is the transparency of the atmosphere in this wonderful climate. On the other side bristle the Sierras of Gibraín, Zaara and Morón, shot with the richest hues of lapis lazuli and amethyst; a marvellous panorama flooded with light, bathed in sunshine and dazzling in its magnificence.

The cathedral is surrounded by a large number of stumps of columns, cut into stone posts and connected by chains, leaving only certain spaces free for public use. Some of these columns are ancient ones, coming either from the ruins of Italica, or from the remains of the old mosque, the site of which is now occupied by the present building, and of which nothing is left but the Giralda, a few fragments of walls, and one or two arches, one of which serves as the door of the Court of the Orange-Trees. Similar posts surround the *Lonja*, or Commercial Exchange, a great square building of perfect regularity, built by the dull, heavy Herrara, the architect of tedium, who is responsible for the Escorial, the most dismal building in the world. The *Lonja* lies between the cathedral and the Alcázar, isolated on every side, and presenting four uniform fronts. It is here that are preserved the archives of the New World, the correspondence of Christopher Columbus, Pizarro and Hernán Cortés; but all these treasures are guarded by such forbidding dragons that we had to be content with the outsides of the cardboard boxes and files, arranged in mahogany presses, like bundles of haberdashery. Yet it would surely be easy to put five or six of the most precious autographs under glass, and exhibit them to the lawful curiosity of travellers.

The Alcázar, or former palace of the Moorish kings, though very fine and worthy of its reputation, has nothing to astonish one when one has already seen the Alhambra at Granada. Here are the same little columns of white marble, with gilt and painted capitals, heart-shaped arches, panels of arabesques entwined with texts from the Koran, doors of larch and cedar-wood, domes filled with stalactites and fountains encrusted with carving, which may be varied to the eye, but of which no description can express the infinity of detail and delicate minuteness; the Hall of the Ambassadors, whose magnificent doors have been preserved intact, is perhaps even richer and more beautiful than that of Granada; unfortunately somebody has had the idea of utilizing the spaces between the columns supporting the ceiling to house a series of portraits of the kings of Spain from the most ancient days of the monarchy down to the present. Nothing could be more ridiculous. The ancient kings, with their cuirasses and golden crowns, do indeed cut a tolerably good figure, but the later ones produce the most grotesque effect, with their powdered wigs and modern uniforms. I shall never forget a certain Queen with spectacles on her nose and a little dog upon her knees, who must feel very foreign there. The so-called Baths of Maria Padilla, the mistress of Don Pedro, who lived in the Alcázar, are still as they were in the days of the Arabs. The vaulting of the hot room has not undergone the slightest alteration. As in the Albambra at Granada, Charles the Fifth has left only too many traces of his visits. This mania for building one palace within another is very common and quite fatal, and the historic monuments which it has destroyed, and replaced with insignificant buildings, must for ever be regretted. The walls of the Alcázar enclose some gardens laid out in the old French style, with clipped yews of the most fantastic and distorted shapes.

Since we are in the midst of sightseeing, let us go into the tobacco-factory, a few steps away, for a minute or two. This vast building is well adapted for its purpose, and contains a large number of machines for scraping, chopping and powdering the tobacco, which make a noise like a multitude of mills and are driven by two or three hundred mules. It is here that the *polbo sevillano* is made, that pungent, impalpable, golden-yellow powder with which the marquises of the Regency loved to sprinkle their lace ruffles: this snuff is so strong and volatile that one sneezes as soon as one enters the rooms in which it is prepared. It is sold in tin boxes by the pound and the half-pound. We were taken to the work-rooms where the leaves are rolled into cigars. From five to six hundred women are employed in preparing them. As soon as we set foot in the room, we were assailed by a hurricane of noise: they were all talking, singing and quarrelling at the same time. I have never heard such an uproar. They were for the most part young, and some of them were very pretty. The extreme negligence of their dress enabled one to appreciate their charms in full liberty. Some of them had a cigar-end stuck resolutely in the corner of their mouths, with the assurance of a cavalry officer; others—O Muse, come to my aid!—chewed like old sailors, for they are allowed to take as much tobacco as they can consume on the premises. They earn from four to six reals a day. The *cigarera* of Seville is a type, like the *manola* of Madrid. You should see her on Sundays or bullfight days, with her full skirt flounced with huge frills, and her sleeves trimmed with jet buttons, inhaling the smoke of her *puro*, and passing it from time to time to her gallant.

To make an end of all this architecture, let us go and visit the famous hospital of La Caridad, founded by the famous Don Juan de Maraña, who is far from a fabulous being, as one might suppose. A hospital founded by Don Juan! Yes, indeed, upon my word. And this is how it happened. One night, as Don Juan was leaving an orgy, he met a funeral on its way to the Church of St. Isidore: masked, black-robed penitents, candles of yellow wax, something more gloomy and sinister than an ordinary burial.—"Who is the dead man? Is it a husband killed in a duel by his wife's lover, or some good father who was too slow in relinquishing his inheritance?" asked Don Juan, heated by wine.

"This dead man," answered one of the bearers, "is none other than Señor Don Juan de Maraña, and we are on our way to celebrate his funeral rites; come with us and pray for him."

Don Juan drew near, and saw by the light of the torches (for in Spain the dead are carried with uncovered faces) that the corpse had a resemblance to him, and was none other than himself. He followed his

The Giralda

own bier into the church, and recited the prayers with the mysterious monks; on the morrow he was found unconscious on the pavement of the choir. This occurrence made such an impression upon him that he renounced his wild life, assumed the habit of a monk, and founded the said hospital, where he died in the odour of sanctity. La Caridad contains some Murillos of the greatest beauty, the *Moses Striking the Rock*, the *Miracle of the Loaves*, enormous, grandly marshalled compositions, the *San Juan de Dios*, carrying a corpse and supported by an angel, a masterpiece of colour and chiaroscuro. Here is to be found the picture by Juan Valdés, known by the name of *The Two Corpses*, a fantastic and terrible picture beside which the gloomiest imaginings of Young might pass for merry jests.

The bullring was closed, to our great regret, for the bullfights at Seville are held by *aficionados* to be the most brilliant in Spain. This ring has the peculiarity of being only semicircular—so far as the boxes are concerned, that is to say, for the arena is round. They say that the whole of one side was thrown down by a violent storm, and never rebuilt. This arrangement opens up a marvellous view of the cathedral, and forms one of the finest spectacles imaginable, especially when the tiers of seats are thronged with a glittering crowd variegated with the most brilliant colours. Ferdinand VII founded an academy of bullfighting at Seville, where the pupils first practised on cardboard bulls, next on *novillos* with balls at the end of their horns, and finally on real bulls, until they were worthy to appear in public. I do not know whether the revolution has respected this royal and despotic institution. Our hopes being disappointed, there was nothing left for us but to depart; our places were taken on the steamer for Cadiz, and we set sail in the midst of the tears, screams and wails of the wives or mistresses of some soldiers moving to another garrison, who travelled with us. I do not know whether this sorrow was sincere, but never did the despair of the antique world or the woes of the Jewish women in the days of their captivity give way to such violent demonstrations.

XVI. Cadiz and the Return

AFTER travelling by mule, on horseback, by cart and in a galley, the steamboat seemed to us a thing miraculous, like a Fortunatus'-cap or a rod of Abaris. To devour the miles with the speed of an arrow, and that without trouble, fatigue or jolting, as one strolls on the deck, watching the banks unroll themselves in long bands, in spite of the caprices of wind and tide, is surely one of the finest inventions of the human mind. For the first time, perhaps, I was of opinion that civilization has its good side—I do not say its beautiful side; for all that it produces is unhappily disfigured by ugliness, thus betraying its complicated and diabolical origin. A steamship, convenient though it may be, seems hideous beside a sailing-vessel. The one is like a swan spreading its white wings to catch the breath of the breeze, the other a stove perched upon mill-wheels, and riding off as fast as its legs will carry it.

However that may be, the paddles of the wheels, aided by the current, bore us swiftly on to Cadiz. Seville was already sinking behind us; but, by a magic optical effect, in proportion as the roofs of the town appeared to shrink into the earth and melt into the horizontal lines of the distance, the cathedral grew larger, and assumed enormous proportions, like an elephant standing among a recumbent flock of sheep; it was not till then that I grasped its full immensity. The highest steeples in the city did not rise above its nave. As to the Giralda, distance lent its rosy brick hues of amethyst and aventurine which seem incompatible with architecture in our northern climates. The statue of Faith glittered on high like a golden bee at the tip of a tall blade of grass. A bend in the river soon hid Seville from our sight.

The banks of the Guadalquivir, as its approaches the sea, at least, have not the entrancing appearance ascribed to them by the descriptions of poets and travellers. I do not know where they found the forests of orange-trees and pomegranates with which their songs are fragrant. In reality one sees nothing but low-lying, sandy, ochre-coloured banks and yellow, turbid waters, whose earthy hue cannot be attributed to the rain, which is so rare in this country. I had already noticed on the Tagus this lack of limpidity in the water, perhaps caused by the great quantity of dust swept into it by the wind, and the friability of the soil through which it flows. The hard blue of the sky has also something to do with it, for its extreme intensity dulls by comparison the tone of the water, which is always less vivid. Nothing but the sea can rival such a sky in transparency and colour. The river grew broader and broader, the banks dwindled and grew flat, and the general aspect of the landscape was not unlike the look of the Scheldt between Antwerp and Ostend. This memory of Flanders in the heart of Andalusia is rather odd in connexion with the Moorish name of the Guadalquivir, but this association occurred so naturally to my mind that the resemblance must have been very real, for I swear to you that I was far from thinking either of the Scheldt or of the journey which I had made in Flanders, six or seven years before. There was, moreover, little traffic on the river, and what one could see of the country beyond it seemed uncultivated and deserted; It is true that it was in the height of the dog-days, a season at which Spain is hardly more than a vast heap of ashes without verdure or vegetation. The only living creatures were the herons and storks, with one leg folded under them, the other half-plunged into the water, waiting in such complete immobility for a fish to go by, that they might have been taken for wooden birds stuck on the end of a stick. Boats with lateen sails arranged scissorwise went up and down the river under the same wind, a phenomenon which I have never quite understood, although it has several times been explained to me. A few of these boats carried a third sail, shaped like an isosceles triangle, placed in the space created by the diverging points of the two large sails: this rigging is most picturesque.

About four or five in the evening, we were passing San Lucar, situated on the left bank of the stream. A great building in a modern style of architecture, built with that barrack- or hospital-like regularity which constitutes the charm of present-day buildings, bore on its main façade an inscription which we were unable to read, though we did not much regret it. This square thing, with its many windows, was built by Ferdinand VII. It must be a Customs House, a warehouse or some such construction. From San Lucar onwards, the Guadalquivir widens out considerably, and assumes the proportions of an arm of the sea. The banks are now no more than a gradually shrinking line between sky and sea. It is grand, but with rather a cold, monotonous grandeur, and we should have been bored if it had not been for the games, dances, castanets and tambourines of the soldiers. One of them, who had been at the performances of a couple of Italian actors, imitated the words, songs and gestures of the actors, and, above all, of the actresses, with much gaiety and animation. His companions held their sides with laughing, and seemed entirely to have forgotten the touching scenes of their departure. Perhaps, like them, their distracted Ariadnes had already wiped their eyes and were laughing with as good a will. The passengers on the steamboat joined heartily in this hilarity, and vied with each other in belying that reputation for imperturbable gravity which the Spaniards enjoy throughout the rest of Europe. The days of Philip II, of black garments, starched ruffs, a pious mien, and a cold and haughty bearing, are far more remote than is generally supposed.

Once San Lucar has been left behind by an almost imperceptible transition, one enters upon the ocean; the long waves break in regular scrolls, the water changes its colour, and so do the faces. Those foredoomed to that strange malady known as sea-sickness begin to look for solitary corners and lean sadly over the side of the ship. For my part I perched bravely on the cabin next the paddle-wheels, and made a conscious study of my sensations; for never having crossed the sea, I did not yet know whether I was doomed to these inexpressible tortures. The first rolling astonished me a little, but I soon recovered and regained my full serenity. On disemboguing from the Guadalquivir, we had turned to the left and were hugging the coast, but at such a distance that we could not make it out quite distinctly, for night was falling, and the sun was sinking majestically into the sea, down a staircase formed, as it were, of five or six steps of cloud of the richest crimson.

It was black dark when we arrived at Cadiz; the ships' lanterns, the lights of the city and the stars in heaven, strewed the rippling waves with a million spangles of gold, silver and fire; in the stiller waters the reflections of the lanterns lay along the surface with a magical effect in long pillars of flame. The vast bulk of the ramparts loomed fantastically in the density of the darkness.

In order to reach the shore, we and our belongings had to be transferred into small boats, the owners of which were snatching the travellers and their luggage from one another with an appalling clamour, rather like the drivers of the coaches for Montmorency or Vincennes in the Paris of olden days. My companion and I had all the difficulty in the world not to become separated, for we were dragged right and left with an energy which was hardly reassuring, especially when one considers that these debates were carried on in boats which the slightest movement caused to oscillate like a swing under the feet of the struggling boatmen. However, we reached the quay without accident, and after submitting to being searched at the Customs House, which was tucked away under the town gate, we went to our lodgings in the Calle de San Francisco.

As you may well imagine, we were up at dawn. To enter an unknown city at night is one of the things most stimulating to a traveller's curiosity! One makes every effort to distinguish in the darkness the lie of the streets, the outline of the buildings, and the appearance of the few passers-by. By this means, at any rate, the full impression of surprise remains still in store for one, and on the next day the effect of the whole town is suddenly revealed like a theatre scene when the curtain rises.

There are no colours on the palette either of the painter or the writer, light or luminous enough to render the vivid impression with which Cadiz burst upon us that glorious morning. Two colours, blue and white, alone assailed the eye; but a blue as vivid as turquoise, sapphire or cobalt, the utmost that the imagination can conceive in the way of blue; and a white as pure as silver, milk or snow, as marble or the finest crystallized sugar from the isles! The blue was the sky repeated in the sea; the white was the town. Nothing could be imagined more radiant and sparkling, with a light that was at once diffused and intense. What we at home call the sun is verily no more by comparison than a pale night-light expiring at a sick man's bedside.

The houses in Cadiz are much higher than in other Spanish cities, which is explained by the lie of the ground—a narrow island connected with the continent by a thin strip of land—and the desire for a sea view. Each house stands on tiptoe, peeping inquisitively over its neighbour's shoulder, and raising its head above the thick girdle of the ramparts. And since this does not always suffice, almost all the terraces have a turret or belvedere at the corner, sometimes crowned with a little dome; these aerial *miradores* enrich the outline of the city with innumerable projections, and produce the most picturesque effect. Everything is of white-washed plaster, and the whiteness of the house-fronts is still further enhanced by long lines of vermilion which divide the houses and mark the stories: the balconies project boldly and are enclosed in great glass cages, fitted with red curtains and filled with flowers. A few of the side-streets end in space and seem to lead right into the sky. These glimpses of azure give one a charming surprise. Apart from this gay, lively and luminous appearance, Cadiz has nothing remarkable in the way of architecture. Its cathedral, a vast pile dating from the sixteenth century, lacks neither nobility nor beauty, but has nothing to astonish one after the prodigies of Burgos, Toledo, Cordoba and Seville; it is something in the style of the cathedrals of Jaen, Granada and Malaga; classical architecture, with slenderer and more tenuous proportions, as it was interpreted by the artists of the Renaissance. The Corinthian capitals, based on a unit of proportion longer than that of the accepted Greek models, are most elegant. As to the pictures and decorations, there is a superabundance of bad taste, and a riot of wealth, and that is all. But I must not omit to mention a little crucified seven-year-old martyr, carved in painted wood with the perfection of sentiment and an exquisite delicacy. Ecstasy, faith and suffering are most touchingly mingled upon this charming countenance in the proportions suited to a child.

We went to see the bullring, which is a small one, and said to be one of the most dangerous in Spain. In order to reach it one goes through gardens full of giant palm-trees of different varieties. There is nothing nobler or more royal than a palm. This great leafy sun at the top of its ribbed column blazes so magnificently against the lapis lazuli of an Eastern sky! This peeling trunk, as slender as if it were drawn in by a corset, reminds one so well of a young girl's waist; it carries itself with such a majestic elegance. The palm and the oleander are my favourite trees; the sight of an oleander or palm causes me a joy and gaiety that are astonishing. I do not feel that one could be unhappy in their shade!

The bullring at Cadiz has no continuous palisades. Here and there are arranged, as it were, wooden screens behind which the *toreros* retire when they are too hotly pursued. This arrangement seems to us to make less provision for safety.

Our attention was drawn to the stalls in which the oxen are kept during the *corrida*; they are a sort of cage of great beams, closed by a door which is raised like the flood-gates of a mill or the sluice of a pond. In order to excite their fury, they are harried with goads or rubbed with nitric acid; in fact, all means are resorted to which may spoil their temper.

On account of the excessive heat, the bullfights were postponed; a French acrobat had set up his rope and trestles in the middle of the arena for the next day's performance. It was here that Lord Byron saw the bullfight of which he gives a poetical description in the first canto of *Childe Harold's Pilgrimage*, which does not, however, reflect much honour upon his knowledge of the rules.

Cadiz is enclosed by a narrow girdle of ramparts, which compress her waist like a corset of granite; a second girdle of shoals and rocks protects her from the onset of the waves; nevertheless, a few years ago, an appalling storm broke in and overthrew these formidable walls in several places, in spite of their thickness of twenty feet; and huge slices of them still lie here and there along the shore. One may walk all round the town, along the glacis of the ramparts, of which only one gate opens on the land-side, and which are dotted at intervals with sentry-boxes; and one may watch in the roads or out at sea the comings and goings and gracefully curving course of the boats, feluccas, *balancelles* and fishing-boats, as they pass each other, tack and disport themselves like albatrosses, looking, when one seems them on the horizon, like nothing so much as a dove's feather carried off into the sky by a puff of wind; many of these boats, like the Greek galleys of old, have at their prow, on each side of the cutwater, two great eyes painted in natural colours, which seem to watch over their course, and give this part of the craft a vague resemblance to a human profile; no sight could be more animated, lively and gay.

The mole, towards the gate of the Customs House, is a scene of unparalleled movement and activity. A gaily coloured crowd, in which every country in the world is represented, throngs at all hours of the day round the foot of the pillars crowned with statues which adorn the quay. From the white skin and red hair of the Englishman to the bronzed hide and black wool of the African, passing through the intermediate shades of coffee, copper and golden yellow, every variety of the human species is assembled there. In the roadstead, a little beyond, three-masted ships, frigates and brigs take their ease, hoisting the flags of their respective nations every morning at the sound of the drum. The merchantmen and steamboats, with their funnels belching forth parti-coloured steam, lie further inshore, on account of their smaller tonnage, and form the foreground of this great naval picture.

I had a letter of introduction to the Commandant of the French brig *Le Voltigeur* in the roads at Cadiz. When I presented it, M. Lebarbier de Tinan kindly invited me and two other young men to dine on board his ship, at about five o'clock on the next day. By four o'clock we were on the mole, looking for a boat and a boatman to cross from the quay to the ship, which should have taken at the outside a quarter of an hour or twenty minutes. I was most surprised when the owner asked us for a *duro* instead of a *peseta*, the usual price for the crossing. In my ignorance of nautical affairs, seeing a perfectly clear sky, and a sun sparkling as on the first day of Creation, I had innocently supposed that it was a fine day. Such was my conviction. On the contrary, it was an abominable day, and before long, when our boat tacked for the first time, I noticed as much. There was a short, choppy, difficult sea running. The wind was enough to tear the horns off an ox. We tossed up and down like a cockle-shell, and were shipping seas every moment. In a few minutes' time, we were enjoying a foot-bath which seriously threatened to become a sitz-bath. The spray from the billows got inside the collar of my coat and trickled down my back. The owner and his two attendants swore and raged, snatching the sheets and rudder out of each other's hands. One wanted this, the other wanted that, and I saw it would not be long before they came to blows. The situation became so critical that one of them began to mutter a scrap of a prayer to some saint. Luckily we were drawing near to the brig, which was lazily swinging at anchor, and seemed to look down with pitying contempt upon the convulsive evolutions of our little boat. At last we drew alongside, but it took us more than ten minutes before we could grasp the man-ropes and climb on deck.

"This is what I call having the courage of one's punctuality," said the Commandment with a smile, as he saw us coming on deck streaming with water, with our hair as dishevelled as a sea-god's beard; and he made them give us trousers, shirts, coats—in fact, a whole outfit. "This will teach you to trust the descriptions of the poets; you imagined there was never a storm without a full band of thunder, waves mingling their spray with the clouds, rain and lightning rending the dense gloom. Make no mistake, I shall probably be unable to send you on shore for two or three days."

The wind was indeed terrific, the rigging quivered like violin-strings beneath the bow of a frenzied player, the flag slapped to and fro with sharp cracks, and the bunting threatened to split and fly in tatters to the far side of the roads; the pulleys creaked, whined and hissed, and at times gave out screams which might have burst from a human throat. Two or three sailors hanging in disgrace in the shrouds, for some offence or another, had all they could do to prevent themselves from being blown away.

All this did not prevent us from making an excellent dinner, washed down by the best of wine, and seasoned with the friendliest talk, as well as by diabolical Indian spices, which would have made a man with hydrophobia drink. On the next day, it was impossible to lower the boat and fetch fresh provisions from the shore, but we made an equally delicious dinner, with this peculiarity, that all the dishes dated from some years ago. We ate green peas of 1836, fresh butter of 1835, and cream of 1834, all in a miraculously fresh state of preservation. The heavy weather lasted for two days, during which I walked on deck, never failing to admire the cleanliness, worthy of a Dutch housewife, the finish of detail and genius for arrangement of that prodigy of human intelligence which is called simply a ship. The copper of the carronades glittered like gold, the boards shone like the rosewood of some marvellously varnished piece of furniture. For every morning they proceed to make the ship's toilet, and though it may stream with rain, the deck is none the less washed, swilled, sponged and swabbed with the same scrupulous minuteness.

After two days the wind fell, and we were taken ashore in a ten-oared boat.

The only thing was that my black evening coat was so thoroughly soaked in sea-water that, even when dry, it never regained its suppleness, and remained sprinkled for good with little sparkling points like mica, and as stiff as a salt cod.

The view of Cadiz as one approaches it from the sea is charming. As one sees it so sparkling white between the azure of the sea and sky, one might think it was an immense crown of silver filigree; the dome of the cathedral, with its yellow paint, seems like a silver-gilt tiara set in the midst of it. The jars of flowers, the scrolls and turrets which give a finish to the houses lend it an infinite variety of outline.

Byron has wonderfully characterized the aspect of Cadiz in a single touch: "Fair Cadiz, rising from the dark blue sea."

In the same stanza the English poet expresses rather a free opinion, which he had no doubt good grounds for holding, upon the virtue of the ladies of Cadiz. For our part, without discussing this delicate question here, we will confine ourselves to saying that they are very lovely and of a peculiar type: their complexions have a whiteness as of polished marble, which greatly emphasizes the purity of their features. They have noses less aquiline than those of the Sevillanas, a low brow and slightly prominent cheekbones, and they closely resemble the Greek type of countenance. They also seemed to me plumper than the other Spanish women, and taller in stature. Such, at least, is the result of the observations which I was able to make while promenading in the Salón, on the Plaza de la Constitución, and at the theatre, where, in parenthesis, I saw *The Urchin of Paris* (*El Piluelo de Paris*) very nicely played by a woman dressed as a boy, and some boleros danced with great fire and spirit.

But pleasant though Cadiz may be, the idea of being shut in within a narrow space, first by the ramparts, and then by the sea, makes one long to get out of it. It seems to me that the only idea which island peoples can possibly cherish, is that of going on the Continent. This is what explains the ceaseless migrations of the English, who are to be found everywhere but in London, where there is nobody but Italians and Poles. And so the inhabitants of Cadiz are constantly engaged in crossing from Cadiz to Puerto de Santa Maria and back again. A light omnibus steamboat which runs hourly, as well as sailing-boats and rowing-boats, wait to entice loiterers. One fine morning my companion and I, reflecting that we had a letter of introduction from one of our friends in Granada to his father, a rich wine-merchant at Jerez, which ran as follows: "Open your heart, your house and your cellar to the two gentlemen herewith introduced," climbed on board the steamer, in the cabin of which was posted a notice announcing for that evening a bullfight interspersed with comic interludes, which was to take place at Puerto de Santa Maria. This filled up our day admirably. By taking a carriage, one could go from Puerto to Jerez, stay a few hours there, and come back in time for the bullfight. After a hasty lunch at the Fonda de Vista Alegre, which thoroughly deserves its name, we made a bargain with the driver, who promised to be back by five o'clock in time for the *función*; for such is the name given in Spain to every kind of show, whatever it may be. The road to Jerez leads through a hilly, seamy plain covered with humped eminences and as arid as pumice-stone. In the spring, they say, this desert is covered with a rich carpet of verdure all diapered with wild flowers. Broom, lavender and thyme perfume the air with their aromatic fragrance; but at the time of year when we were there, all traces of vegetation had disappeared. The most one sees, here and there, are a few wisps of dry, yellow, straggling grass all powdered with dust. This road, if one may believe the local accounts, is very dangerous. One often meets *rateros*, that is to say, peasants who, though not professional brigands, will take a purse by the way if it happens to turn up, and cannot resist the pleasure of rifling a solitary passer-by. These *rateros* are more to be feared than the real bandits, whose proceedings have the regularity of an organized band, subject to a leader, and who let travellers off easily, in order to subject them to further extortions on another road; besides, in the case of a brigade of twenty or twenty-five mounted men, well equipped and armed to the teeth, one attempts no resistance; whereas one struggles with two *rateros*, thereby getting killed, or at least wounded;

besides, this passing ox-herd, this labourer who greets you, this tattered, bronzed *muchacho* who sleeps, or pretends to sleep, in a narrow strip of shadow or in the cleft of a ravine—even your very coachman who is driving you straight into an ambush, may be a *ratero*. One never knows; there is danger everywhere and nowhere. From time to time the police have the more dangerous or notorious of these wretches murdered by their emissaries in a tavern brawl provoked for the purpose, and this justice, though somewhat barbarous and rudimentary, is the only feasible kind, in view of the absence of proofs and witnesses, and the difficulty of arresting the culprits in a region where it would take an army to arrest one man, and where counter-spying is carried out with such intelligence and passion, by a people whose ideas on *meum* and *tuum* are hardly in advance of those of the African Kabyles. Here, however, as everywhere else, the promised brigands did not appear, and we arrived at Jerez without difficulty.

Jerez, like all the smaller towns of Andalusia, is whitewashed from head to foot, and has nothing remarkable about it architecturally save its *bodegas,* or wine-stores, vast cellars with great tiled roofs and long white walls devoid of windows. The person to whom we had an introduction was away, but the letter produced its effect, and we were at once conducted to the cellars.

Never did a more glorious sight present itself to the eyes of a drunkard; we walked down alleys lined with barrels, stacked four or five rows high. We had to taste everything there, or at least the principal kinds, and there is an infinite number of principal kinds. We ran through the complete scale, from eighty-year-old sherry, dark and thick, with a muscat flavour, and the curious tone of the green wine of Béziers, to a dry pale-coloured sherry, with an aroma of gun-flint, somewhat resembling a Sauterne. Between these two extremes there is a whole register of intermediate wines, of the hues of gold, burnt topaz and orange-peel, and the utmost variety of flavour. Only they are all more or less mixed with brandy, especially those intended for England, where they were otherwise not considered strong enough; for to please a British throat wine must be disguised as rum.

After such a complete study of the vinous lore of Jerez, the difficulty was to regain our carriage with a sufficiently majestic uprightness to prevent us from compromising France in the eyes of Spain; it was a question of international self-respect: to fall or not to fall, that was the question—a question even more embarrassing than the one which so much exercised the Prince of Denmark. I may say, with legitimate pride, that we reached our carriage in a most satisfactorily perpendicular condition, and gloriously represented our country in this struggle with the headiest wine of the Peninsula. Thanks to the rapid evaporation provided by a heat of thirty-eight to forty degrees, on our return to Puerto we were able to discourse upon the nicest points of psychology and to give our opinion on the strokes in the bullfight. This *corrida*, in which most of the bulls were *embolados*, that is to say, had balls on the tips of their horns, and in which only two were killed, delighted us by a host of absurd incidents. The *picadores* were dressed like Turks in the carnival, with print trousers in the Mameluke style, jackets with suns on their backs and turbans like a Savoy cake, reminding one exactly of the extravagant Moorish figures sketched by Goya with three or four strokes of his etching-tool, on the plates of *La Toromaquía*. One of these fine fellows, while waiting for his turn to give the lance-thrust, blew his nose on the flap of his turban with a wonderfully stolid and philosophic air. An osier *barco de vapor* (steamboat) was driven into the middle of the arena, covered with linen and harnessed to a team of asses, decked out in red trappings and with three-cornered hats stuck anyhow on their heads. The bull charged this machine, ripping open, upsetting and tossing the wretched asses in the most comical way in the world; in this ring too I saw a picador kill the bull by a thrust of a lance in the handle of which was hidden a firework, the explosion of which was so violent that beast, horse and rider were all three thrown backwards; the first because he was dead, the two others from the shock of the recoil. The matador was an old fellow dressed in a worn-out stable-coat, with yellow stockings of too open-work a variety on his legs, looking like a peasant in musical comedy or some clown of a strolling player. He was thrown several times by the bull, and his thrusts were so unsteady that it was necessary to use the *media-luna* in order to finish the bout. The *media-luna*, as its name indicates, is a sort of half-moon with a long pole for a handle, rather like a pruning-bill for clipping tall trees. It is used to hamstring the animal, which is then finished off without any danger.

Nothing could be more hideous or more ignoble; as soon as the danger is at an end, one is seized with disgust; it is no longer a fight, it is a butchery. The poor beast, dragging himself about on the stumps of his legs, like Hyacinthe at the Variétés, when he plays the female dwarf in the sublime parade of the *Saltimbanques*, is the saddest sight one could see, and all one desires is that it should recover enough strength to disembowel its insensible tormentors by a last thrust of its horns.

This wretched fellow, turned matador for the nonce, had as his special line of business *eating*. He would absorb seven or eight dozen hard-boiled eggs, a whole sheep, a calf, etc. Seeing how thin he was, we must suppose that he was not often at work. There were a lot of people at this *corrida*; the *majos'* costumes were rich and numerous; the women, of quite a different type from those of Cadiz, wore long scarlet shawls on their heads instead of mantillas, forming a perfect frame for their beautiful olive faces, almost as dark-complexioned as those of mulatto-women, which lend peculiar brilliance to the pearly white of the eye and the ivory of the teeth. These pure lines and this tawny-golden tone would be marvellous to paint, and it is a pity that Leopold Robert, that peasant Raphael, died so young, and never travelled in Spain.

As we wandered about the streets, we came out into the market-place. It was dark. The shops and stalls were lit up with lanterns or hanging lamps, and made a charming picture, all starred and spangled with brilliant points of light. Water-melons with their green rind and rosy pulp, cactus figs, some in their prickly outer covering, the others already peeled, sacks of *garbanzos*, monstrous onions, amber-yellow grapes which would have shamed the bunch brought home from the Promised Land, strings of garlic-cloves, red peppers and other wares, were stacked in picturesque heaps. In the space left for passing between each stall came and went peasants driving their asses, and women dragging along their brats. I noticed one of rare beauty, with jet-black eyes set in a swarthy oval and hair drawn flat over the temples, shining like two loops of black satin or two raven's-wings. She walked serene and radiant, with unstockinged legs and her charming bare feet in satin slippers. This pride in the foot is general in Andalusia.

The court-yard of our inn, arranged as a patio, was beautified by a fountain surrounded with shrubs, upon which lived a tribe of chameleons. It would be difficult to imagine a more hideous animal. Picture to yourself a sort of pot-bellied lizard, measuring six or seven inches, more or less, with an inordinately wide mouth, from which darts a slimy, whitish tongue as long as his body; the enormous prominent eyes are like those of a toad when it is trodden upon; they are covered with a membrane and move quite independently of each other; one looks at the sky and the other at the earth. These squint-eyed lizards, which, the Spaniards say, live on nothing but air, but which I have seen quite clearly eating flies, have the property of changing colour according to the place in which they happen to be. They do not suddenly turn scarlet, blue or green in an instant, but by the end of an hour or two, they soak and impregnate themselves with the tone of the objects nearest them. On a tree they turn a fine green; on a blue stuff, slate-grey; on scarlet, a reddish brown. If kept in shadow they lose their colour, and turn a sort of neutral shade of yellowish white. One or two chameleons would look wonderfully well in the laboratory of an alchemist or a Doctor Faustus. In Andalusia, a rope of some length is hung from the ceiling, the end of which is placed between the animal's forefeet; it begins to climb, and goes on climbing until it comes to the ceiling, on which its claws cannot obtain a foothold. It then descends to the end of the rope again, and, revolving its eyes, measures the distance separating it from the ground; then, after careful calculations, it resumes its ascent with wonderful gravity and seriousness, and so on indefinitely. When there are two chameleons on the same rope, the sight becomes transcendent in its comicality. Melancholy personified would burst out laughing to watch the contortions and furious glances of the two ugly beasts when they meet each other. Anxious to procure myself this diverting spectacle in France, I bought a couple of these pleasing creatures, and took them away in a little cage; but they caught cold during the crossing and died of consumption on our arrival at Port-Vendres. They had wasted away, and their poor little skeletons were visible through their flabby, wrinkled skin.

A few days later, the announcement of a bullfight—the last I was to see, alas!—made me return to Jerez. The bullring is very fine and spacious, and its architecture is not lacking in character. It is built of brick, set off at the sides by stone, a mixture which produces a good effect.

There was an immense, motley and gaily coloured crowd, alive with the flutter of fans and handkerchiefs. We have already described several bullfights, and will relate only a few details of this one. In the middle of the arena was planted a post ending in a sort of little platform. On this platform was crouched a monkey rigged out as a troubadour, pulling faces and writhing its lips, and tethered to quite a long chain, which enabled it to describe a fairly wide circle, with the stake as the centre. When the bull entered the ring, the first thing which caught his eyes was the monkey on his perch. Then followed the most diverting comedy: the bull pursued the monkey, which very quickly returned to its platform. The raging animal kept striking great blows at the post with its horns, giving a violent shaking to Master Baboon, who was in a state of the deepest terror, and interpreted his agonies by irresistibly comic grimaces. Sometimes, unable to hold on to the edge of his boards firmly enough, though he clutched them with all four hands, he fell on to the bull's back, and clung to it in desperation. Then the hilarity of the crowd knew no bounds, and fifteen thousand dazzling smiles lit up all these brown faces. But comedy was followed by tragedy. A poor Negro, one of the ring-attendants, who carried a basket full of powdered earth to throw into the pools of blood, was attacked by the bull, which he imagined to be engaged elsewhere, and tossed twice into the air. He lay stretched out upon the sand immobile and lifeless. The *chulos* came up and waved their cloaks under the bull's nose and drew him off into another corner of the ring, so that they might carry out the Negro's body. He passed close to me; two *mozos* were carrying him by the head and feet. Singularly enough, from black he had become royal blue, which is apparently the Negro way of turning pale. This event in no way disturbed the *corrida*. *Nada, es un moro*, it is nothing, it is only a black man: such was the funeral oration of the poor African. But if men showed themselves unmoved by his death, such was not the case with the monkey, which wrung its arms, uttered heart-rending wails, and struggled with all its might to break its chain. The fact remains that never have I seen sorrow more intense and moving than that of the monkey mourning this Negro, and this fact is the more remarkable because he had seen *picadores* thrown from their horses, and in danger, without giving the least sign of sympathy or uneasiness. At the same moment an enormous owl settled in the middle of the ring; he came, no doubt, in his capacity as bird of night, to seek this black soul and bear it away to the ivory paradise of the Africans. Of the eight bulls fighting in this *corrida*, only four were to be killed. The others, after receiving half-a-dozen lance-thrusts and three or four pairs of *banderillas*, were led back to the *toril* by big oxen with bells round their necks. The last one, a *novillo*, was handed over to the amateurs, who tumultuously invaded the arena and finished it off; for such is the passion of the Andalusians for bullfights, that it is not enough for them to look on, they must also take part in them, or else they would go unsatisfied away.

The steamboat *L'Océan* was lying ready to sail in the roads where it had been confined for a few days by the bad weather, that glorious weather of which I have already spoken; we went on board with a feeling of inward satisfaction, for in consequence of events at Valencia, and the disturbances which had ensued upon them, Cadiz was to a certain extent in a state of siege. The newspapers came out filled with nothing but poems and feuilletons translated from the French, and at the corner of every wall were posted rather forbidding-looking little *bandos*, forbidding the assembly of more than three persons, under pain of death. Apart from these motives for desiring a prompt departure, for a long time past we had been turning our backs upon France; it was the first time for months that we had taken a step back towards our mother country. And, independent as one may be of national prejudices, it is difficult to avoid a touch of chauvinism so far from one's country. In Spain the least allusion to France roused me to excitement, and I could have hymned "glory" and "victory", "laurels" and "quarrels", with any super at the Cirque-Olympique.

Everybody was coming and going on the deck, or waving farewells to the boats returning to the shore; I, who was leaving behind on land no memory and no regrets, was ferreting about in every hole and corner of the little floating universe which was to serve me as a prison for a few days. In the course of my investigations I came across a little room filled with a large number of earthenware vessels of an intimate and suspicious shape. These hardly Etruscan vases surprised me by their number; and I said to myself: "Here is the least poetical of cargoes; O Delille, thou modest *abbé*, king of periphrasis, by what circumlocution wouldst thou have alluded, in thy stately Alexandrines, to this domestic and nocturnal pottery?"

We had hardly sailed a league, when I understood the purpose for which this crockery was used. Cries went up on every side of *me mareo!* "I am sea-sick!" "Lemons!" "Rum!" "Vinegar!" "Smelling-salts!" The deck was a lamentable sight; the women, so charming a moment ago, were turning green as corpses eight days drowned. They were lying about on mattresses, trunks and blankets, to the complete forgetfulness of all grace and modesty. A young mother who was suckling her baby was seized with sea-sickness and left her bodice unfastened, without noticing it, till we had passed Tarifa. A poor parrot was overcome in its cage, and, unable to understand the misery it was suffering, kept pouring out its repertory of words with a distressful volubility which was the most comical thing in the world. I was fortunate enough not to be ill. The two days I had spent on *Le Voltigeur* had no doubt acclimatized me. My companion, less fortunate than I, plunged down into the interior of the ship, and did not appear again till we arrived at Gibraltar. How is it that modern science, which studies the colds in the heads of rabbits with so much solicitude, and amuses itself by staining ducks' bones red, has not yet sought a serious remedy for this horrible ailment which causes more suffering than a real agony?

The sea was still a little rough, though the weather was magnificent: the air was so transparent that we could quite distinctly see the coast of Africa, Cape Spartel, and the bay within which lies Tangier, which we regretted that we were unable to visit. So that was Africa—that band of cloud-like mountains, differing from clouds only in their immobility— Africa, the land of marvels, of which the Romans used to say: *Quid novi fert Africa?* (What is the latest from Africa?), the most ancient of the continents, the cradle of Eastern civilization, the centre of Islam, the black world in which the shadow lacking in the sky is found only on the face of man; the mysterious laboratory in which nature, endeavouring to produce man, first transformed the monkey into the Negro! To see it and pass by! What a fresh refinement of the tortures of Tantalus.

At the point of Tarifa, a little village whose chalky walls rise on a precipitous cliff behind a little island of the same name, Europe and Africa draw near together, as if they would exchange a kiss of alliance. The strait is so narrow that one looks out over both continents at once. It is impossible, when one is on the spot, not to believe that the

Mediterranean was once, at no far-distant age, an enclosed sea, an inland lake, like the Caspian, the Sea of Aral and the Black Sea. The sight which offered itself to our eyes was of wondrous magnificence. On the left lay Europe, on the right Africa, with their rocky coasts, clothed by distance in hues of iris and pale lilac, like those of a silken stuff with warp and woof of different colours; before us was the boundless and ever-widening horizon; above us, a sky of turquoise; beneath us, a sapphire sea, of such limpidity that we could see the entire hull of our vessel, as well as the keel of the boats passing by us, which seemed to be flying in the air rather than floating on water. We swam in a sea of light, and the only dark tone which could have been discovered for twenty leagues round came from the long plume of thick smoke which we left behind us. The steamboat is in very truth a northern invention; its ever-glowing fires, its seething boiler, its funnels, which will end by blackening the heavens with their soot, harmonize wonderfully with the fogs and mists of the North. Among the splendours of the South, it is a blot. Nature was in a mood of gaiety; great snow-white sea-birds grazed the water with the edge of their wings. Tunnies, dorados and fish of every kind, lustrous, glossy and glittering, leapt, frolicked and sported in the waters; sail followed sail from moment to moment, white and swelling as the milky breast of some Nereid appearing above the waves. The shores were tinged with fantastic hues; their folds, clefts and crevices caught the sun's rays in such a way as to produce the most marvellous and unexpected effects, offering us an ever-changing panorama. About four o'clock we were in sight of Gibraltar, waiting for the *Sanidad* (for so the officers of the quarantine station are called) kindly to come and pick up our papers with their tongs, to see whether by any chance we were bringing with us yellow fever, blue cholera or the Black Death.

The appearance of Gibraltar absolutely staggers the imagination; one no longer knows where one can be or what one is seeing. Imagine an immense rock, or rather mountain, fifteen hundred feet high, which rises sharply and suddenly from the midst of the sea, from a shore so low and flat that one can hardly see it. There is nothing to prepare one for it, nothing to explain it, it has no connexion with any range; it is a monstrous monolith launched from heaven, the blunted fragment of a planet, fallen in some war between the stars, a relic of a shattered world. Who set it in this place? God alone and eternity can tell. What adds still more to the effect of this inexplicable rock, is its shape: one might think it was some vast, extravagantly gigantic granite sphinx, such as a sculptor-Titan might have hewn, and beside which the snub-nosed monsters of Karnak and of Gizeh are but as a mouse beside an elephant. The extended paws form what is called Europa Point; the head, slightly truncated, is turned towards Africa, at which it seems to gaze with a profound and dreaming earnestness. What can be the thoughts of this mountain with its covert, meditative look? What riddle does it propound, or else attempt to guess? The shoulders, loins and haunches stretch out towards Spain in great indolent folds and fine swelling lines like those of lions at rest. The town lies almost imperceptible at the foot, a wretched detail lost in the mass. The three-decked vessels anchored in the bay are like German toys, little miniature model ships, such as are sold in seaports; the boats, like flies drowned in milk; even the fortifications are not apparent. And yet the mountain is hollowed, mined and scooped out in every direction; it has its belly full of cannon, of artillery and mortars; it is gorged with munitions of war. It is the very luxury and coquetry of impregnability. But all this reveals nothing to the eye save some few imperceptible lines lost in the crevices of the rock, a few holes through which pieces of artillery furtively protrude their brazen nozzles. In the Middle Ages, Gibraltar would have bristled with donjons, with towers, with turrets and with crenellated ramparts; instead of lying at the foot, the fortress would have scaled the mountain and perched like an eagle's nest upon the sharpest crest. The batteries of the present day are level with the sea, which is so narrow at this point, that one may say they make its passage impossible. Gibraltar was known to the Arabs as Ghiblaltah—that is to say, the Mount of the Entrance! Never was a name better justified. Its ancient name was Calpe. Abyla, now the Apes' Hill, is on the opposite side in Africa, quite near Ceuta, a Spanish possession, the Brest and Toulon of the Peninsula, where they send the most hardened galley-slaves. We could perfectly well distinguish the shape of its precipices and its crest, muffled in clouds, in spite of the serenity of the rest of the sky.

Gibraltar, situated, like Cadiz, on a peninsula at the entry to a bay, is only attached to the continent by a narrow strip of land known as the Neutral Territory, on which the customs frontiers are established. The first Spanish possession on this side is San Roque. Algeciras, whose white houses at the edge of the sea gleam amidst the universal azure like the silver belly of a fish, is exactly opposite to Gibraltar; in the midst of this resplendent blue, Algeciras was carrying out its little revolution; one could hear a vague crackling of gunshots like grains of salt thrown into the fire. The *ayuntamiento* even took refuge upon our steam-boat, where it settled down to smoke its cigars as calmly as could be.

The *Sanidad* having decided that we were not infectious, we were hailed by the boats, and a quarter of an hour later were on land. The effect produced by the general aspect of the town is highly fantastic. One step, and you have travelled a thousand miles; a little more than the famous seven-leagued boots in the fairy-tale. A moment ago you were in Andalusia; now you are in England. From the Moorish cities of the Kingdoms of Granada and Murcia, you suddenly drop into Ramsgate; here are the brick houses with their areas, their front doors and their sash-windows, exactly as at Twickenham or Richmond. Go a little farther, and you will find cottages with painted railings and fences. The

Algiers and Gibraltar

walks and gardens are planted with ashes, birches, elms, and the green vegetation of the North, so different from those leaves cut out in varnished tin which pass for foliage in southern countries. The English have such a strong individuality that they are the same everywhere, and I really do not know why they travel, for they take all their habits with them, and carry their homes on their backs, like regular snails. In whatever place an Englishman happens to be, he lives exactly as if he were in London: he must have his tea, his rump-steak and his sherry, if he is well, and his calomel if he is ill. By means of the innumerable boxes which he drags about with him, the Englishman everywhere provides himself with the home and comfort necessary to his existence. What a number of implements these worthy islanders require in order to live! What a lot of trouble they take to be comfortable, and how greatly I prefer Spanish sobriety and bareness to all this ingenuity and complication! It was long since I had seen on women's heads those horrible pancakes, those hateful cardboard sugar-loaves covered with a scrap of stuff, which are known by the name of hats, and in the depths of which the fair sex buries its face in countries which are called civilized. I cannot describe the unpleasant sensation I experienced at the sight of the first Englishwoman I met, wearing on her head a hat with a green veil, and striding like a Grenadier of the Guards, with her large feet shod in large boots. It was not that she was ugly—on the contrary—but I had grown accustomed to the racial purity, the delicacy like that of an Arab horse, the exquisite grace of carriage, the daintiness and charm of the Andalusian women, and this face, with its straight lines, its lustreless glance, and its dead expression, accompanied by angular gestures and a methodical bearing, a savour of cant and an absence of anything natural, produced a comically sinister impression upon me. I felt as if I were suddenly brought face to face with the spectre of civilization, my mortal enemy, and as if this apparition meant that my dreams of roving liberty were at an end, and I must return to the life of the nineteenth century never to leave it again. In the presence of this Englishwoman, I felt quite ashamed of having no white gloves or eye-glass, or patent-leather shoes, and I cast an embarrassed glance down at the extravagant embroideries of my sky-blue cloak. For the first time in six months, I became aware that I was not properly dressed and did not look like a gentleman.

These long British faces, these red soldiers with movements like those of automata are out of place in the presence of this glittering sky and brilliant sea. One realizes that their presence is due to a surprise, a usurpation. They occupy their town, but do not inhabit it.

The Jews, driven out or frowned upon by the Spaniards, who, if they have no longer any religion, have still their superstition, abound in Gibraltar, which has turned heretic with the misbelieving English. They go about the streets with their hook-nosed profiles, their tight lips, their yellow shiny heads with the distinctive cap worn on the back of the head, and their threadbare, dark-hued gaberdines of a narrow cut: the Jewesses, who by some strange privilege are as beautiful as their husbands are hideous, wear black hooded mantles edged with scarlet, which are very picturesque. Meeting them makes one think vaguely of the Bible, of Rachel at the edge of the well, of primitive scenes of patriarchal life, for, like all Oriental races, they preserve in their black eyes and golden complexions the mysterious reflection of a vanished world. There are also at Gibraltar many Moroccans and Arabs from Tangier and the coast; they keep little shops full of perfumes, silk sashes, slippers, fly-whisks, cushions of patterned leather and other minor barbaric industries. As we wanted to make a few purchases of trifles and curiosities, we were taken to one of the chief of them, who lived in the upper town; we were led up streets less English than those of the lower town, and formed of flights of steps, from certain corners of which the glance might wander out over the Gulf of Algeciras, magnificently illuminated by the last gleams of the day. As we entered the Moroccan's house, we were enveloped in a cloud of Oriental aromas; the sweet, penetrating fragrance of rose-water went to our heads, and made us think of the mysteries of the harem and the marvels of the *Thousand and One Nights*. The shopkeeper's sons, fine young men of about twenty, were sitting on benches near the door enjoying the cool of the evening. They possessed that purity of features, that limpid eye, that noble nonchalance, and that air of amorous and pensive melancholy which are the attributes of pure races. The father had the ample and stately proportions of the Three Kings of the East. We felt ugly and mean beside this fine, dignified old fellow; and, hat in hand, we asked him, in our humblest tones, whether he would kindly deign to sell us a few pairs of yellow morocco slippers. He gave a sign of assent, but when we pointed out to him that the price was rather high, he answered in Spanish with a grand air: "I never overcharge: I leave that to the Christians." Thus our lack of good faith makes us an object of contempt to barbarous nations, who cannot understand how the desire to earn a few extra centimes can make a man perjure himself.

Having made our purchases, we returned to the lower town, and went for a stroll along a fine promenade planted with northern trees, interspersed with flowers, sentries and cannon, where one sees carriages and men on horseback exactly as one does in Hyde Park. Nothing is missing but the Achilles statue dedicated to Wellington. Fortunately the English have not been able to sully the sea or blacken the sky; this promenade is outside the town, towards Europa Point, in the direction of the mountain inhabited by monkeys. It is the only place on our continent where these amiable quadrumanous beasts live and multiply in a savage state. They pass from one side of the rock to the other with every change of the wind, thus serving as a barometer; one is forbidden to kill them under pain of a severe penalty. For my part, I did not see any; but the temperature of the place is sufficiently baking for the chilliest macaques and cercopitheci to live there without stoves or hot-water pipes. If we are to believe its modern name, Abyla, on the African coast, must rejoice in a similar population.

On the following day we left this park of artillery and hotbed of smuggling, and steamed off on our way to Malaga, which we already knew, but were pleased to see again, with its slender white lighthouse, its crowded port and unresting stir. Seen from the sea, the cathedral looks bigger than the town, and the ruins of the ancient Arab fortifications produce the most romantic effect on the slopes of the rocks. We returned to our inn of the *Tres Reyes*, the charming Dolores uttering a joyful exclamation when she recognized us.

On the following day, we again put out to sea, laden with a cargo of dried raisins; and as we had wasted a little time, the captain determined to sail past Almeria and go straight on to Cartagena.

We hugged the coast of Spain so close that we never lost sight of it. As the bed of the Mediterranean grew wider, the coast of Africa had long since disappeared from the horizon. So on one side we had a prospect of long ribbons of blue-tinged cliff, with fantastic bluffs and perpendicular fissures, dappled here and there with white dots indicating a little village, a watch-tower or a Customs post; while on the other side was the open sea, now broken with swirls or ripples by the currents or the breeze, now of a dull, lustreless azure, or else of a crystal clearness, now glittering with light like a dancer's skirt, now opaque, oily and grey like mercury or molten tin; an incredible range of tones and effects which would be the despair of painters and poets! A procession of red, white and golden sails, of ships of every size and flag, added gaiety to the scene and removed from it the melancholy which always fills one at the sight of infinite solitudes. A sea without a sail on it is the saddest and most heart-breaking sight that one can look upon. To think that there is not a single human thought in all that vast space, not a single heart to grasp the sublimity of the sight! An almost imperceptible point of white on this limitless, unsoundable blue, and the immensity is inhabited; it has an interest, a human drama.

Cartagena, which they call Cartagena de Levante to distinguish it from the Cartagena in South America, lies deep within a bay, a sort of funnel of rocks in which ships find perfect shelter from every wind. Its outline is not particularly picturesque; the most distinct features of it which have remained in our memory are two windmills outlined in black against a pale background of sky. We had hardly set foot in the boats to go on shore when we were assailed, not, as at Cadiz, by porters for carrying our luggage, but by some vile knaves who deafened us by vaunting the charms of a host of Balbinas, Casildas, Hilarias and Lolas.

The appearance of Cartagena is very different from that of Malaga. Malaga is as gay, smiling and animated as Cartagena is dismal and frowning, with its crown of bald and sterile mountains, as dry as the Egyptian hills from the sides of which the Pharaohs hewed out their sphinxes. Whitewash has disappeared, the walls have once more assumed a sombre hue, the windows are grated with elaborate ironwork, and the houses grow more forbidding, with that prisonlike appearance which is characteristic of the mansions of Castile. But we do not wish to fall into the error of that traveller who wrote in his note-book: "All the women in Calais are bad-tempered, red-haired and hump-backed", because the landlady at his inn united these three defects; so we are bound to say that we saw none but charming faces and angelic countenances at these heavily barred windows; it is perhaps for this reason that they are so carefully barred. While waiting for dinner, we went to look at the Marine Arsenal, an establishment planned upon a grandiose scale, but nowadays in a neglected state which is sad to see; these vast docks and basins, these idle building-yards, in which another Armada might be built, are now no use for anything. Two or three skeleton hulls, like the ribs of stranded whales, were mouldering away obscurely in a corner; millions of crickets have taken possession of these great abandoned hulks; one can hardly put down one's foot without crushing one; they make such a noise with their tiny rattles, that one can hardly hear oneself speak. In spite of my professed love for crickets—a love which I have expressed both in prose and in verse—I am bound to admit that there were rather too many of them.

From Cartagena we went as far as the city of Alicante, for which, following a verse from the *Orientales* of Victor Hugo, I had imagined a far too deeply fretted outline:

"Alicante aux clochers mêle les minarets."
(Alicante mingles spires with minarets.)

Now today, at any rate, Alicante would find it very difficult to effect this mixture, which I admit to be extremely desirable and picturesque; in the first place, because it has no minarets, and in the next place, because the only spire it possesses is nothing but a very low and inconspicuous tower. The characteristic thing about Alicante is an enormous rock rising in the middle of the town, a rock magnificent in shape and magnificent in outline, crowned with a sentry-box hanging boldly over the abyss. The town hall—or for the sake of local colour we will call it the Palace of the Constitution—is a charming and most tasteful edifice. The Alameda is paved throughout with stone flags, and shaded by two or three rows of trees, quite leafy for Spanish trees, when their roots are not bathed by a well. The houses grow higher, and once more take on a European shape. I saw two women with sulphur-yellow hats, a threatening symptom. This is all I know about Alicante, where the boat only touched long enough to take on freight and coal: a halt by which we profited to lunch on shore. As you may well imagine, we did not neglect this opportunity of making a few conscientious studies of the local wines, which I found less good than I had expected, in spite of their unquestionable genuineness; this had perhaps something to do with the taste of pitch which they had acquired from the *bota* in which they were contained. Our next stage would take us to Valencia, *Valencia del Cid*, as the Spaniards say.

Santa Maria Fountain, Alicante

From Alicante to Valencia the cliffs along the shore continue to assume fantastic shapes and unexpected aspects; our attention was drawn to a square incision in the top of a mountain which looks as if it had been made by the hand of man. Towards morning on the next day, we dropped anchor before the Grao, for this is the name given to the harbour and suburb of Valencia, which is half a league from the sea. There was quite a high sea, and we arrived at the landing-stage fairly well sprinkled. There we took a tartan in order to get to the town. The word tartan is usually interpreted in a maritime sense; the Valencian tartan is a box covered with American cloth and mounted on two wheels without a trace of a spring. Compared with the *galeras*, this vehicle seemed to us effeminately luxurious; and never was a softer carriage turned out by Clochez. We were surprised and almost embarrassed at being so comfortable. Great trees lined the road up which we drove, an attraction to which we had long grown unaccustomed.

So far as picturesqueness is concerned, Valencia hardly lives up to the idea of it which one forms from the songs and chronicles. It is a large city, flat, scattered and built on a confused plan, with none of the advantages given by their irregular construction to old towns built on hilly sites. Valencia is built in a plain called La Huerta, among gardens and cultivated fields in which a freshness very rare in Spain is maintained by irrigation. Its climate is so mild that palms and orange-trees grow in the open air side by side with the products of the North. For Valencia has a considerable trade in oranges; in order to measure them, they are passed through a ring, like bullets when one wants to gauge their calibre; those which will not go through form the choicest quality. The Guadalquivir, crossed by five fine stone bridges, passes by the side of the city, almost under its ramparts. The places in which its veins are bled for the sake of irrigation are so many that for three quarters of the year they render its five bridges a mere luxury and ornament. The Gate of the Cid, through which one passes on the way to the promenade of the Guadalquivir, is flanked with thick and rather effective crenellated towers.

The streets of Valencia are narrow, and edged with high houses of a rather gloomy appearance, on a few of which one can still decipher a few worn and mutilated escutcheons; one can make out fragments of half-obliterated carving, clawless monsters, women without noses, knights without arms. Here and there a Renaissance casement, lost and sunk in a horrible wall of modern masonry, catches the eye of the artist and wrings from him a sigh of regret; but these rare vestiges must be sought for in dark corners or hidden away in back yards, and do not impair the modern aspect of Valencia. The cathedral is in a hybrid style of architecture, and in spite of an arcaded apse with round-topped Romanesque arches, has nothing to arrest the traveller's attention after the marvels of Burgos, Toledo and Seville. A few finely carved retables, a picture by Sebastiano del Piombo, another by Lo Spagnoletto, in his softer manner, in which he tried to imitate Correggio, are all that is worthy of notice. The other churches, though rich and numerous, are built and decorated in that strange, incrusted style of ornament which we have described several times. When one sees all these extravagances, one cannot but deplore the utter waste of so much talent and ability. The *Lonja de Seda* (Silk Exchange), on the market-place, is a delightful Gothic monument; the Great Hall, the vaulting of which springs from rows of columns of the utmost lightness, with spiral ribbings, has an elegance and gaiety of appearance rare in Gothic architecture, which is in general more suited to expressing melancholy than happiness. It is in the Lonja that take place the entertainments and masked balls during carnival time. In order to finish with the antiquities, let us say a few words about the former convent of La Merced, in which have been brought together a great number of pictures, some poor and the others bad, with a few rare exceptions. What pleased me most at La Merced was a court surrounded by a cloister, and planted with palm-trees of Oriental loftiness and beauty, soaring up like an arrow into the limpidity of the air.

The real attraction of Valencia for the traveller is its population, or rather that of La Huerta, which surrounds it. The Valencian peasants wear a costume of characteristic strangeness which cannot have varied much since the Arab invasion, and differs very little from the present costume of the African Moors. This costume consists in a shirt, full drawers of coarse linen, bound close round the figure by a red girdle, and a green or blue velvet waistcoat trimmed with buttons made of silver *pesetas*; the legs are enclosed in a sort of *knemides* or leggings of white wool edged with a blue border, leaving the knee and instep uncovered.

On their feet they wear *alpargatas*, sandals of plaited rope, the sole of which is almost an inch thick, tied on with ribbons in the fashion of a Greek *cothurnos*; they keep their heads shaved in the Oriental style and almost always wrapped in a vivid-coloured handkerchief; over this kerchief is perched a little low-crowned hat with a turned-up brim, embellished with velvet, silk tufts, sequins and tinsel. A piece of striped stuff, called the *capa de muestra*, adorned with rosettes of yellow ribbon, is thrown over the shoulder to complete this costume full of nobility and character. In the corners of his cloak, which he arranges in a thousand different ways, the Valencian ties up his money, his bread, his water-melon and his *navaja*; it serves him at once as a haversack and a mantle. It goes without saying that we are here describing the full dress as worn on feast days; on ordinary working-days the Valencian keeps hardly more than the shirt and drawers: then, with his enormous black whiskers, his face scorched by the sun, his wild glance, his bronze-coloured arms and legs, he really looks like a Bedouin, especially if he loosens his kerchief and shows his shaven poll, as blue as a freshly shaved chin. In spite of Spain's pretensions to Catholicism, I shall always find it hard to believe that such fellows as these are not Musulmans. It is probably to this ferocious appearance of theirs that the Valencians owe the reputation of being bad men (*mala gente*) which they enjoy in the other provinces of Spain: I was told twenty times that in the Huerta of Valencia, if one wanted to get rid of somebody, it was not difficult to find a peasant who would undertake the job for five or six duros. This looks to me like a pure calumny: I frequently met alarming-looking fellows in the country who always saluted me politely. One evening, indeed, we had got lost and nearly had to sleep out of doors, for we found the town gates closed on our return; yet nothing unpleasant happened to us, though it had been black-dark for a long time, and Valencia and its surroundings were in a state of revolution.

By a curious contrast, the women of these European Kabyles are pale and fair, *bionde e grassotte*, like the Venetians; they have a sweet, melancholy smile on their lips, and a tender blue light in their eyes; one could not imagine a more perfect contrast. These black demons of the Paradise of La Huerta have white angels for their wives, whose lovely hair is held by a great comb with a high heading, or transfixed by long pins with their ends adorned with balls of silver or glass. In older days the Valencian women wore a delightful national costume recalling that of the Albanian women; unfortunately they have abandoned it for the horrible Anglo-French costume, for dresses with leg-of-mutton sleeves, and other such abominations. It should be remarked that the women are the first to abandon the national garments; in Spain it is now none but the lower classes who preserve the ancient costume. This lack of intelligence in matters of the toilet is surprising in a sex essentially desirous of pleasing; but our astonishment ceases when we think that women have the sense of fashion, but not of beauty. A woman will always consider the most miserable rag charming, if it is the height of fashion to wear that rag.

We had been at Valencia some ten days, waiting for another steamboat to pass by, for the weather had interfered with their departure and upset all connexions. Our curiosity was satisfied, and all we longed for now was to return to Paris and see our relatives and friends, our beloved boulevards and our beloved gutters; I believe, God forgive me, that I nourished a secret desire to be present at a vaudeville; in short, civilized life, forgotten for six months, summoned us imperatively. We desired to read the daily newspaper, to sleep in our beds and a thousand other Bœotian fancies. At last a steamboat passed by on its way from Gibraltar, picked us up and took us to Port-Vendres, by way of Barcelona, where we only stayed a few hours. The appearance of Barcelona is like that of Marseilles, and the Spanish type is hardly perceptible there; the buildings are large and regular, and if it were not for the huge blue velvet trousers and great red caps of the Catalans, one might think one was in a French town. In spite of its tree-planted Rambla and its fine straight streets, Barcelona looks a little strait and stiff, like all towns laced too tight in a corset of fortifications.

The cathedral is very fine, especially in the interior, which is gloomy, mysterious and almost frightening. The organ is of Gothic workmanship, and is enclosed in great panels covered with paintings. A Saracen's head grimaces horribly beneath the pendentive which supports them. Charming fifteenth-century lustres, with open-work chasing like reliquaries, hang from the ribbed vaulting. On leaving the church, one enters a fine cloister of the same period, full of reverie and silence, whose half-ruined arcades take on the greyish tones of the North. The Calle de la Plateria (Jewellery) dazzles the eyes with its shop-fronts and glass-cases glittering with jewels, and especially with enormous ear-rings as big as branches of grapes, rich, heavy and massive; they are rather barbarous, but quite imposing, and are bought chiefly by the well-to-do peasants.

On the next day, at ten o'clock in the morning, we entered the little bay within which blooms Port-Vendres. Shall I say it? On setting foot on the soil of my country, I felt tears in my eyes, not of joy but of regret. The vermilion towers, the silvery summits of the Sierra Nevada, the oleanders of the Generalife, the long, dewy, velvet glances, the lips like carnations in bloom, the tiny feet and tiny hands, all this came back so vividly into my mind, that though I was to find my mother there, France seemed to me a land of exile. The dream was ended.

Interlink Bestselling Travel Publications

The Traveller's History Series

The Traveller's History series is designed for travellers who want more historical background on the country they are visiting than can be found in a tour guide. Each volume offers a complete and authoritative history of the country from the earliest times up to the present day. A Gazetteer cross-referenced to the main text pinpoints the historical importance of sights and towns. Illustrated with maps and line drawings, this literate and lively series makes ideal before-you-go reading, and is just as handy tucked into suitcase or backpack.

A Traveller's History of Australia	$14.95 pb
A Traveller's History of the Caribbean	$14.95 pb
A Traveller's History of China	$14.95 pb
A Traveller's History of England	$14.95 pb
A Traveller's History of France	$14.95 pb
A Traveller's History of Greece	$14.95 pb
A Traveller's History of India	$14.95 pb
A Traveller's History of Ireland	$14.95 pb
A Traveller's History of Italy	$14.95 pb
A Traveller's History of Japan	$14.95 pb
A Traveller's History of London	$14.95 pb
A Traveller's History of Mexico	$14.95 pb
A Traveller's History of North Africa	$15.95 pb
A Traveller's History of Paris	$14.95 pb
A Traveller's History of Russia	$14.95 pb
A Traveller's History of Scotland	$14.95 pb
A Traveller's History of Spain	$14.95 pb
A Traveller's History of Turkey	$14.95 pb
A Traveller's History of the U.S.A.	$15.95 pb

The Traveller's Wine Guides

Illustrated with specially commissioned photographs (wine usually seems to be made in attractive surroundings) as well as maps, the books in this series describe the wine-producing regions of each country, recommend itineraries, list wineries, describe the local cuisines, suggest wine bars and restaurants, and provide a mass of practical information—much of which is not readily available elsewhere.

A Traveller's Wine Guide to France	$19.95 pb
A Traveller's Wine Guide to Germany	$17.95 pb
A Traveller's Wine Guide to Italy	$19.95 pb
A Traveller's Wine Guide to Spain	$17.95 pb

The Independent Walker Series

This unique series is designed for visitors who enjoy walking and getting off the beaten track. In addition to their value as general guides, each volume is peerless as a walker's guide, allowing travellers to see all of the great sites, enjoy the incomparable beauty of the countryside, and maintain a high level of physical fitness while travelling through the popular tourist destinations. Each guide includes:

• Practical information on thirty-five extraordinary short walks (all planned as day hikes and are between 2 and 9 miles), including: how to get there, where to stay, trail distance, walking time, difficulty rating, explicit trail directions and a vivid general description of the trail and local sights.

• Numerous itineraries: The Grand Tour which embraces all thirty-five walks; regional itineraries; and thematic itineraries.

• One planning map for the itineraries and thirty-five detailed trail maps.

• Trail notes broken down into an easy-to-follow checklist format.

• A "Walks-at-a-Glance" section which provides capsule summariesof all the walks.

• Black and white photographs.

• Before-you-go helpful hints.

The Independent Walker's Guide to France	$14.95 pb
The Independent Walker's Guide to Great Britain	$14.95 pb
The Independent Walker's Guide to Italy	$14.95 pb
The Independent Walker's Guide to Ireland	$14.95 pb

Wild Guides

An unrivalled series of illustrated guidebooks to the wild places far from home and work: the long walks, mountain hideaways, woods, moors, sea coasts and remote islands where travellers can still find a refuge from the modern world.

"The Wild Guides will be enjoyed by everyone who hopes to find unspoiled places."
—The Times (London)

Wild Britain	$19.95 pb
Wild France	$19.95 pb
Wild Ireland	$19.95 pb
Wild Italy	$19.95 pb
Wild Spain	$19.95 pb

Cities of the Imagination

A new and innovative series offering in-depth cultural, historical and literary guides to the great cities of the world. More than ordinary guidebooks, they introduce the visitor or armchair traveller to each city's unique present-day identity and its links with the past.

Buenos Aires: A Cultural and Literary Companion	$15.00 pb
Edinburgh: A Cultural and Literary Companion	$15.00 pb
Havana: A Cultural and Literary Companion	$15.00 pb
Kingston: A Cultural and Literary Companion	$15.00 pb

Lisbon: A Cultural and Literary Companion	$15.00 pb
Madrid: A Cultural and Literary Companion	$15.00 pb
Mexico City: A Cultural and Literary Companion	$15.00 pb
Oxford: A Cultural and Literary Companion	$15.00 pb
Rome: A Cultural and Literary Companion	$15.00 pb
Venice: A Cultural and Literary Companion	$15.00 pb

The Spectrum Guides

Each title in the series includes over 200 full-color photographs and provides a comprehensive and detailed description of the country together with all the essential data that tourists, business visitors or students are likely to require.

Spectrum Guide to Ethiopia	$22.95 pb
Spectrum Guide to India	$22.95 pb
Spectrum Guide to Jordan	$22.95 pb
Spectrum Guide to Malawi	$23.95 pb
Spectrum Guide to Maldives	$22.95 pb
Spectrum Guide to Mauritius	$19.95 pb
Spectrum Guide to Nepal	$22.95 pb
Spectrum Guide to Pakistan	$22.95 pb
Spectrum Guide to Tanzania	$22.95 pb
Spectrum Guide to Uganda	$19.95 pb
Spectrum Guide to the United Arab Emirates	$23.95 pb
Spectrum Guide to the Zimbabwe	$23.95 pb

The In Focus Guides

This new series of country guides is designed for travellers and students who want to understand the wider picture and build up an overall knowledge of a country. Each In Focus guide is a lively and thought-provoking introduction to the country's people, politics and culture.

Belize in Focus	$12.95 pb
Bolivia in Focus	$12.95 pb
Brazil in Focus	$12.95 pb
Chile in Focus	$12.95 pb
Costa Rica in Focus	$12.95 pb
Cuba in Focus	$12.95 pb
The Dominican Republic in Focus	$12.95 pb
Eastern Caribbean in Focus	$12.95 pb
Ecuador in Focus	$12.95 pb
Guatemala in Focus	$12.95 pb
Haiti in Focus	$12.95 pb
Jamaica in Focus	$12.95 pb
Mexico in Focus	$12.95 pb
Nicaragua in Focus	$12.95 pb
Peru in Focus	$12.95 pb

We encourage you to support your local independent bookseller

To request our complete 48-page full-color catalog,
please call us toll free at **1-800-238-LINK,** visit our
website at **www.interlinkbooks.com**, or write to
Interlink Publishing
46 Crosby Street, Northampton, MA 01060
e-mail: sales@interlinkbooks.com